Modern Health Care Marketing

Modern Health Care Marketing

Gamini Gunawardane
California State University at Fullerton, USA &
California State University at Los Angeles, USA

World Scientific

NEW JERSEY · LONDON · SINGAPORE · BEIJING · SHANGHAI · HONG KONG · TAIPEI · CHENNAI · TOKYO

Published by

World Scientific Publishing Co. Pte. Ltd.
5 Toh Tuck Link, Singapore 596224
USA office: 27 Warren Street, Suite 401-402, Hackensack, NJ 07601
UK office: 57 Shelton Street, Covent Garden, London WC2H 9HE

Library of Congress Cataloging-in-Publication Data
Names: Gunawardane, Gamini, author.
Title: Modern health care marketing / Gamini Gunawardane.
Description: Hackensack : World Scientific, [2020] | Includes bibliographical references and index.
Identifiers: LCCN 2020014381 | ISBN 9789813279513 (hardcover) |
 ISBN 9789813279520 (ebook) | ISBN 9789813279537 (ebook other)
Subjects: MESH: Marketing of Health Services--methods | Health Care Sector | Internationality
Classification: LCC RA410.56 | NLM W 74.1 | DDC 362.1068/8--dc23
LC record available at https://lccn.loc.gov/2020014381

British Library Cataloguing-in-Publication Data
A catalogue record for this book is available from the British Library.

Copyright © 2020 by World Scientific Publishing Co. Pte. Ltd.

All rights reserved. This book, or parts thereof, may not be reproduced in any form or by any means, electronic or mechanical, including photocopying, recording or any information storage and retrieval system now known or to be invented, without written permission from the publisher.

For photocopying of material in this volume, please pay a copying fee through the Copyright Clearance Center, Inc., 222 Rosewood Drive, Danvers, MA 01923, USA. In this case permission to photocopy is not required from the publisher.

For any available supplementary material, please visit
https://www.worldscientific.com/worldscibooks/10.1142/11250#t=suppl

Desk Editor: Yulin Jiang

Typeset by Stallion Press
Email: enquiries@stallionpress.com

Introduction

This book, as its title suggests, aims to address modern concerns and issues facing health care marketing. In that sense, it deviates from many other books that do not sufficiently acknowledge trends in health care marketing recognized by industry experts and practitioners, and only attempt to apply general theories of management and marketing, usually taught in MBA type courses, to health care settings. They also do not seem to recognize and apply vast developments in the fields of service management and services marketing, for example, the vital concept of customer/patient experience and the inadequacy of the traditional and archaic 4P view of a marketing mix for health care marketing.

This book will carry throughout, and devote dedicated chapters to, eight key concepts affecting today's health care marketing. These are:

1. *The need to focus health care management and marketing on enhancing customer/patient experience.*

Price Waterhouse Cooper (2017) in their report, *Top Health Industry Issues of 2018*, emphasizes that "Patient experience as a priority and not just a portal" and that 49% of provider executives said revamping the patient experience is one of their organization's top three priorities over the next five years. Franklin Street (2019) in their 2019 *Healthcare Marketing Trends Report* states, "Align your entire organization around desired consumer experiences. Audit your consumer-patient journeys, from initial perceptions through post-care, to identify quick wins and needed strategic initiatives for improved consumer experiences…In what ways does your strategic plan account for changing patient expectations…In what ways could you modify services to meet these evolving patient expectations?"

2. *The need to recognize that a "one shoe fits all" marketing strategy would not work for today's wide array of diverse health care services and products.*

Medicare Advantage expanded vastly during 2018 and is expected to grow further over 2019 and beyond as more baby boomers reach age 65. Competition among Medicare Advantage provider health plans is intense and marketing Medicare Advantage plans is entirely different from marketing other health care services in terms of promotion, communications, and regulatory compliance. This book will provide substantial coverage to marketing such diverse products as physician services, hospital services, managed care products, pharmaceuticals, and public health.

3. *The need to focus modern health care marketing on consumers and patients living in this digital world.*

This book will discuss how health care marketing should handle increased use of modern technology-based digital marketing, use of internet, social media, mobile devices, blogs, websites, email marketing, health apps, and artificial intelligence, as well as smart use of these modern technologies involving search engine optimization (SEO) for the organization's website, creating smart content (Content Marketing), health explanatory videos, and experiential marketing. This book will also address modern consumers' affinity to targeted, personalized, and interactive video communications and the growing acceptance of video as a tool to both collect and share information, particularly to create personalized connections (Franklin Street, 2019).

4. *The need for modern health care marketing to depend on sophisticated data analysis.*

Increased use of analytics with big data (data from clinical records, billing records, claims data, call center transcripts, social network data, and market intelligence) within legal and ethical limitations is essential. "Using sophisticated analytics, healthcare marketing teams can understand their patients, pinpoint their target audiences, develop effective education and wellness programs and build successful marketing campaigns" (Evariant, 2017). This book will devote a dedicated chapter on Integrating Digital Technology into

Modern Health Care Marketing covering impact of digital technology on modern health care marketing, impact of social media, online sources available for health care marketing, and digital health care marketing tools.

5. *The need to recognize that modern health care marketing is not simply advertising and promoting products and services provided by the health care organization (e.g. hospital or health plan), but the active involvement with the top management, in customer/patient services and health care delivery operations in new service development, improving service operations, and enhancing customer service and customer experience.*

See, for example, Weiss (2013). "Increased interactions with operations and customer service functions of the organization to resolve and improve customer/patient and health care provider concerns and experience. The organization's 'marketing team' concept."

6. *The need to recognize the vital role of employee engagement, internal marketing, and physician engagement in creating a brand image that health care marketing could effectively exploit.*

As we recognize the importance of customer/patient experience, the role of first line employees and physician and nursing staff becomes evident. Gambie (2013), citing from a survey from Catalyst Healthcare Research and the Beryl Institute based on more than 1,000 hospitals or hospital systems representing 672 unique organizations, highlights that 70% of the respondents ranked patient satisfaction and experience, and 22% ranked employee engagement and satisfaction, as their top priorities for the next three years.

7. *The need to recognize the increased emphasis on, and oversight of, legal and ethical health care marketing practices.*

Federal and state government agencies perform stringent scrutiny of health care marketing through Medicare and Medicaid marketing regulations and Health Insurance Portability and Accountability Act of 1996 (HIPAA) regulations.

For hospitals, the Joint Commission now requires hospitals to follow ethical practices for marketing and billing, and marketing materials to accurately represent the hospital and address the care, treatment, and services that the hospital provides either directly or by contractual arrangement.

This book will devote a dedicated chapter on legal and ethical considerations in health care marketing.

8. *Need to recognize the modern status of globalization of health care and health care marketing.*

The global medical tourism market was valued at US$61,172 million in 2016 and is estimated to reach at US$165,345 million by 2023 (Sumant and Sheikh, 2017). Patients Beyond Borders (2017) estimates that some 1.9 million Americans will travel outside the US for medical care in 2019. At the same time, a 2008 report of McKinsey and Co. estimates that between 60,000 and 85,000 medical tourists would be traveling to the United States for the purpose of receiving inpatient medical care (Van Dusen, 2008). This book will address marketing issues in this huge market such as identifying potential outbound and inbound medical tourists, and strategies for marketing to these potential medical tourists.

Covering such a large variety of issues impacting modern health care marketing is not an easy task. Therefore, we have elected to present many issues and guidelines in easy-to-read point form rather than the traditional long essay and paragraph format of text books. We have, of course, backed up these presentations with citations and references. Instructors using this book for university courses and company training are advised to refer to these references and other materials to expand on the point form presentations and add further details for the benefit of the students.

I wish to acknowledge support extended to me by Professors Angela Young, Andre Avramchuck and Kwok Kwong at California State University at Los Angeles, who provided me the opportunity to teach in, and be associated with, their Health Care Management Program. I owe my inspiration and motivation to write this book, and work on research projects in customer and patient experience, to my association with that program.

I must also thank health care management, marketing, and contracting executives I have been associated with at Care1st Health Plan/Blue Shield of California, especially Anna Tran, Janet Jan, Jorge Weingarten, M.D., Brian Barry, Brad Wolff, Roger Mullendore, Peter Goll, Steven Chin and Dolores Olague-Swanson from whom I learnt a lot about health care management, marketing, contracting, and provider relations.

My thanks also to World Scientific Publishing Company editors David Sharp and Yulin Jiang who assisted me in many ways to bring this project to a successful conclusion.

I also want to record my appreciation to my wife Shirani who sacrificed much time while I was involved in research and writing of this book.

Gamini Gunawardane, MBA, Ph.D., JD
Professor of Management Emeritus,
California State University at Fullerton
Adjunct Professor in the Health Care Management
Program at California State University at Los Angeles
Former Associate Vice President, Care First Health Plan/Blue Shield
of California
California, USA
March 28, 2019

References

Evariant (2017). Big Data and Healthcare Analytics. Evariant white paper.
Franklin Street (2019). "2019 Healthcare Marketing Trends Report", https://cdn2.hubspot.net/hubfs/4267451/Resources/2019%20Trends%20Report.pdf.
Gambie, M. (2013). "28 Statistics on Hospitals' Patient Experience Strategies", Becker's Hospital Review, https://www.beckershospitalreview.com/hospital-management-administration/28-statistics-on-hospitals-patient-experience-strategies.html.
Price Waterhouse Cooper (2017). *Top Health Industry Issues of 2018*, https://www.pwc.com/us/en/health-industries/assets/pwc-health-research-institute-top-health-industry-issues-of-2018-report.pdf.
Patients Beyond Borders (2017). "Medical Tourism Statistics & Facts", https://patientsbeyondborders.com/medical-tourism-statistics-facts.
Sumant, O. and Shaikh, S. (2017). "Medical Tourism Market by Treatment Type (Cardiovascular Treatment, Orthopedic Treatment, Neurological Treatment, Cancer Treatment, Fertility Treatment, and Others) — Global Opportunity Analysis and Industry Forecast, 2017–2023", https://www.alliedmarketresearch.com/medical-tourism-market.
Van Dusen, A. (2008). U.S. Hospitals Worth the Trip. Forbes, May 29, 2008. https://www.forbes.com/2008/05/25/health-hospitals-care-forbeslife-cx_avd_outsourcing08_0529healthoutsourcing.html#1e131e9152e1.
Weiss, R. (2013). "Modern Marketing Defined: Health Care Marketing's Organizational Impact Cannot be Easily Labelled", *Marketing Health Services*, Winter.

Contents

Introduction   v

Part 1 Health Care Marketing: Evolution and Modern Trends   1

Chapter 1   Introduction to Health Care Marketing   3

  1.1. Introduction and Plan of the Book   3
  1.2. Health Care as a Key Component of the Service Sector   6
  1.3. Types of Health Care Services Usually Marketed   8
  1.4. Who are the "Customers" in Health Care Marketing?   9
  1.5. Special Characteristics of Health Care Services Affecting
      Health Care Marketing   11
  1.6. Plan of the Book   15
  References   17
  Suggested Additional Readings   19

Chapter 2   Health Care Marketing: Evolution and Modern Trends   21

  2.1. Health Care Marketing as a Specialized Subfield of
      Services Marketing   21
  2.2. Recent Developments in Marketing Thought   22
  2.3. Evolution and Definition of Services Marketing   25
  2.4. Evolution and Definition of Health Care Marketing   26
  2.5. Modern Trends and Practices in Health Care Marketing   30
  References   37
  Suggested Additional Readings   40

Part 2 Health Care Marketing Strategy Formulation and Implementation Process — 41

Chapter 3 Health Care Marketing Strategy Formulation Process — 43

3.1. What is Health Care Marketing Strategy? — 43
3.2. What are the Strategies at Each Level of the Health Care Organization? — 44
3.3. Strategic Planning Process in the Health Care Organization I: Vision, Mission and Values — 49
3.4. Strategic Planning Process in the Health Care Organization II: Complete Process — 53
3.5. Information Needed for Strategic Planning — 58
3.6. From Formulating Health Care Marketing Strategy to Implementation — 58
References — 59
Suggested Additional Readings — 60

Chapter 4 Health Care Market and Marketing Research — 63

4.1. Market Research vs. Marketing Research in Health Care — 63
4.2. Market Research: Overview of Steps — 66
4.3. Use of Secondary Data Sources for Health Care Market/Marketing Research — 71
4.4. Primary Data Collection in Market/Marketing Research — 74
4.5. Guidelines for Managing Market/Marketing Research — 76
References — 77
Suggested Additional Readings: Readings in Statistical Methods for Quantitative Market Research — 79

Chapter 5 Understanding the Health Care Organization's Competition — 81

5.1. Why Study Competition in the Health Care Industry? — 81
5.2. Competition in the Health Care Industry — 82
5.3. Measuring Competition for Health Care Management and Marketing — 91
5.4. Porter's Five Forces Competition Analysis Applied to Health Care Organizations — 93
5.5. Porter's New Thinking on Competitive Analysis as Applied to Health Care Organizations — 95

5.6. Sources of Information for Market Research of Competition in Health Care	95
References	98
Suggested Additional Readings	100

Chapter 6 Understanding Customer/Patient Characteristics and Behavior Affecting Health Care Marketing — 103

6.1. Who are the Customers in Health Care?	104
6.2. Why Study Health Care Customer/Patient Characteristics and Behavior?	105
6.3. Role of Demographics in Planning Health Care Marketing	108
6.4. Understanding the Health Care Consumer/Patient Decision-Making Process	117
6.5. Factors Influencing Provider Selection and Retention Decisions of Health Care Consumers/Patients	123
6.6. Recent Trends in Health Care Consumer/Patient Behavior Affecting Health Care Marketing	129
6.7. Sources of Information on Customer Characteristics and Behavior: Primary Data	137
6.8. Sources of Information on Customer Characteristics and Behavior: Secondary Data	137
References	139
Suggested Additional Readings	147

Chapter 7 Customer/Patient Experience: Key Driver of Modern Health Care Marketing — 149

7.1. Introduction to Customer Experience (CX) and Patient Experience (PX)	149
7.2. Significance of CX/PX in Modern Health Care Marketing	154
7.3. Basic Principles of CX/PX	161
7.4. Factors Influencing Customer/Patient Experience	165
7.5. Marketing's Role in Improving CX/PX	167
7.6. Customer Experience Management (CXM) and Customer Relationship Management (CRM)	170
7.7. Current Status of Customer/Patient Experience Management (CXM/PXM) in Health Care Organizations	172
7.8. Customer/Patient Journey Mapping (CJM); Touchpoints; Moments of Truth	173
7.9. Measuring CX/PX	175

xiv Modern Health Care Marketing

7.10. Guidelines for Effective Customer/Patient Experience Management	186
Reerences	190
Suggested Additional Readings	196

Chapter 8 Market Segmentation in Health Care Marketing — 197

8.1. Market Segmentation — Definition and Overview	197
8.2. Need for Market Segmentation in Health Care Marketing	201
8.3. Characteristics of a Segment to be Useful in Formulating Health Care Marketing Strategy	204
8.4. Generic Market Segmentation Methods	206
8.5. Types of Market Segmentation Commonly Used in Health Care Marketing	208
8.6. Customer-Centric Segmentation	215
8.7. Analytical Techniques for Segmenting a Health Care Market	219
8.8. Using Segmentation Results	222
References	222
Suggested Additional Readings	225
Specialized Texts on Statistical Techniques for Market Research and Market Segmentation	225

Chapter 9 Health Care Marketing Mix: Planning Health Care Marketing Strategy for Each Segment/Niche — 227

9.1. The Concept of Marketing Mix	227
9.2. Traditional 4P Marketing Mix: Application in Health Care Marketing	229
9.3. Inadequacy of Traditional 4P Marketing Mix for Services Marketing (Including Health Care Marketing)	231
9.4. Modern 7P Health Care Marketing Mix	233
9.5. "Product" in Health Care Marketing	236
9.6. "Place" in Health Care Marketing Mix Means "Access", i.e., Enhancing Access to Health Care Services	238
9.7. "Price" in the Health Care Marketing Mix Means "Value"	240
9.8. "Promotion" in Health Care Marketing is "Communication and Education" of Health Care Customers	243
9.9. "People" in Health Care Marketing are Health Care Service Staff, Employees, and Physicians	248
9.10. "Process" in Health Care Marketing is the Entire Customer/Patient Journey	248

9.11.	Physical Evidence/Servicescape	250
9.12.	Relationship Marketing in Health Care	250
References		254
Suggested Additional Readings		258

Part 3 Health Care Marketing Program Implementation — 259

Chapter 10 Integrating Digital Technology into Modern Health Care Marketing — 261

10.1.	Digital Technology in Health Care	261
10.2.	Impact of Modern Digital Technology on Health Care Marketing	265
10.3.	Impact of Social Media on Health Care Industry and Marketing	272
10.4.	Online Sources for Health Care Marketing	277
10.5.	Digital Health Care Marketing Tools	281
10.6.	Social Media Marketing in Health Care	285
10.7.	Content Marketing	291
10.8.	Additional Implementation Issues	296
References		304
Suggested Additional Readings		309

Chapter 11 Employee Engagement and Internal Marketing in Health Care Marketing — 311

11.1.	What is Employee Engagement?	311
11.2.	Importance of Employee Engagement in Health Care Marketing	315
11.3.	Management Practices to Promote Employee Engagement I: Selection, Development, and Retention of Customer-Oriented Service Employees	317
11.4.	Management Practices to Promote Employee Engagement II: Internal Marketing	321
11.5.	Management Practices to Promote Employee Engagement III: Health Care Employee Engagement Measurement	325
11.6.	Role of Health Care Marketing in Employee Engagement and Internal Marketing	326
11.7.	Concept of Employee Experience	329
References		333
Suggested Additional Readings		337

Chapter 12 Marketing to Physicians: Physician Engagement and Physician Relations Management in Health Care Marketing — 339

12.1. Relevance of Physician Engagement in Health Care Marketing — 339
12.2. Physician Characteristics that Affect Marketing to Physicians — 342
12.3. Hospital Marketing to Physicians — 346
12.4. Marketing Pharmaceutical Products/Medical Devices to Physicians — 348
12.5. Physician Relations Management — 351
References — 354
Suggested Additional Readings — 357

Chapter 13 Legal and Ethical Issues Affecting Health Care Marketing — 359

13.1. Evolution of Legal and Ethical Environment in Health Care Marketing — 359
13.2. Medicare and Medicaid Marketing Regulations — 370
13.3. Health Care Marketing and Anti-Kickback Statutes — 377
13.4. Truth-in-Advertising Laws Applicable to Health Care Marketing — 379
13.5. HIPAA Laws Affecting Health Care Marketing — 383
13.6. Regulations Applicable to Digital Health Care Marketing — 386
13.7. Health Care Marketing Ethics — 390
13.8. Principles and Tools for Analyzing Ethical Dilemmas in Health Care Marketing — 398
13.9. Contracting in Health Care Marketing — 400
References — 404
Suggested Additional Readings — 406

Part 4 Health Care Marketing in Special Sectors — 409

Chapter 14 Direct Health Care Marketing in Special Sectors: Physician Services, Hospital Services, Managed Care Products (HMOs and ACOs), Pharmaceuticals, and Public Health — 411

14.1. What is Direct Marketing in Health Care? — 411

14.2.	Direct Marketing of Physician Services	414
14.3.	Marketing Hospital Services	422
14.4.	Marketing Managed Care Plans/Services	430
14.5.	Direct Marketing by Pharmaceutical Companies	443
14.6.	Public Health Marketing	447
References		456
Suggested Additional Readings		461

Chapter 15 Marketing Health Care Globally — 463

15.1.	The Modern Global Health Care Market	463
15.2.	Outbound Medical Travel Customer/Patient Characteristics	469
15.3.	Medical Tourism Destinations and Treatment Sought	472
15.4.	Sources of Information Used for Researching Outbound Medical Travel	475
15.5.	Inbound Medical Travel Marketing	477
15.6.	Inbound Medical Customer/Patient Characteristics	478
15.7.	Guidelines for Global Health Care Marketing	480
References		483
Suggested Additional Readings		485

Index — 489

Part 1

Health Care Marketing: Evolution and Modern Trends

Chapter 1

Introduction to Health Care Marketing

1.1. Introduction and Plan of the Book

1.1.1. Health marketing vs. health care marketing

At the very beginning of this book, it will be prudent to clarify and distinguish certain concepts and terms used in the health care marketing and allied fields.

One of these terms is *health marketing*. Centers for Disease Control and Prevention (2011) defines health marketing as, "a multidisciplinary area of public health practice" and further explains that health marketing draws from fields like marketing, communication, and public health promotion to develop theories, strategies, and techniques for public health improvement. Therefore, health marketing is mainly about improving public health and it uses marketing research to develop effective methods to inform, educate, and motivate the public.

The term *health care marketing*, on the other hand, is used to address efforts by private health care product and service organizations to market their health care products and services. Examples are physicians who desire to increase their patient population, hospitals promoting potential patients to select their hospital over other hospitals in the area for inpatient and outpatient services, and pharmaceutical companies who desire acceptance of one of their prescription drugs by physicians and patients over competing drugs. Thus, the term health care marketing is used really to mean marketing health care services. In this sense, some educators and writers advocate the use of the term *health care services marketing*.

Health care marketing encompasses promoting public health. As such, health marketing can be said to be the more general term. This book is about health care marketing. It has a section on effective marketing of public health. This book can also be classified as a book in health care service marketing. However, to be consistent, we will use the term health care marketing in the title of this book and subsequent discussions.

A brief clarification on the use of the term "modern" in the title of this book may also be proper. Traditionally, health care marketing had been equated to advertising and promotion of health care services by large health care product and service organizations such as hospitals and pharmaceutical companies, and to a lesser extent by physicians. For example, a definition in the Farlex Financial Dictionary (2012) is

> "Health Care Marketing: The process of advertising hospitals, medical offices, pharmaceuticals and so forth."

However, health care marketing has undergone major changes since its origin in the 1970s and especially during the last two decades to meet significant changes that have occurred in the health care industry during this period. This is indicated by the following more recent definition by Evariant (2017).

> "Health care marketing integrates multi-channel, highly-segmented and targeted online and offline tactics that are designed to find and acquire the right patients, engage with them through strategic outreach, and nurture them to form lasting relationships throughout the entire patient journey."

Implicit in this view is that modern health care marketing is no longer limited to billboards, radio and TV advertisements, and direct mail. While Chapter 2 provides a comprehensive summary of modern trends in health care marketing, the following is a brief introductory note on three of the most significant of these changes:

- Modern health care consumer is more informed.
  - According to Gallagher (2017), in an article, "How Has Healthcare Marketing Changed in the Last Decade?",

    "The patients have become more informed. When you have an informed patient, it's very difficult to market the same way that you (did) in the past."

  - Also, "When you have an informed patient, it's very difficult to market the same way that you were in the past" (Whitler, 2015).

- Furthermore, in today's digital world, consumers are no longer reliant on traditional methods of communication to get their information, e.g., billboards, direct mail, radio ads, etc. Mobile technology and the rise of smartphones have made health care information easily accessible. Health apps on smartphones are one of the most highly used apps as nearly 30% of US adults use health apps (Kratzke and Cox, 2012).

  One in 20 Google searches are for health-related information (Google, 2015). One in three American adults have gone online to figure out a medical condition. About 72% of internet users say they looked online for health information within the past year. Around 47% of internet users search for information about doctors or other health professionals. Additionally, 38% of internet users search for information about hospitals and other medical facilities (Fox and Duggan, 2013). Modern health care marketing focuses on consumers and patients living in this digital world.

- For health care consumers, personal experience is the number one reason for choosing a doctor or hospital. The need for health care marketing to recognize this health care consumer behavior is emphasized by many contemporary experts. For example, such emphasis is in "Patient Experience: The Forgotten 'P' in Your Medical Marketing Plan" (Gandolf, 2012) and "2018 Healthcare Marketing Trend #1: Customer Experience" (Kernan, 2017).

  Modern health care marketing acknowledges the significance of consumer/patient personal experience and their emotional ties with health care providers such as physicians and hospitals. Connolly (2017), in an article titled "Why Authenticity is the Prescription for Modern Healthcare Marketing" describes this well: "Healthcare marketing of the past focused on what a person felt internally during a physical ailment. (Now) smart healthcare marketers are recognizing a commonality between their patients/consumers that can be used to connect with them emotionally."

> Modern health care marketing recognizes that the present health care consumer lives in a digital and experience economy that significantly affects his/her consumer behavior toward health and health care services.

1.1.2. Focus and scope of this book

This book is on health care marketing, which will also discuss health marketing, i.e., marketing of public health services. In other words, this book will address marketing health care products and services provided by key providers such as physicians, hospitals, pharmaceutical companies, managed care organizations (such as Health Maintenance Organization or HMOs and Accountable Care Organizations or ACOs), and governmental public health promotion agencies.

This book will trace recent changes in the health care industry and health care consumer behavior. For example, the modern health care consumer is known to be engaged in social media and explore the internet for information on health issues and health care services, and thus, he/she is more informed (Gallagher, 2017). Advances in technology have made a great impact on modes of communication between health care providers and consumers. Due to the aforementioned reasons and many other changes in the health care industry and consumer behavior, changes are required while marketing health services. For example, "when you have an informed patient, it's very difficult to market the same way that you were in the past" (Gallagher, 2017). Over the last six years, more than US$18 billion has been invested in health care technology ventures with 2017 going down in history as the largest year ever for digital health funding (Resnick, 2017). More than 65% of chief health care marketing officers say they use social media to drive business and build their digital brand (Resnick, 2017).

This book will address these and many other recent changes in the health care industry and resulting changes in health care marketing strategies and practices.

1.2. Health Care as a Key Component of the Service Sector

Health care is a key subsector of the service sector of an economy, other subsectors of the service sector of an economy being public services (including social services, judicial services, military, fire and police services, waste disposal services, etc.); educational services; banking, insurance and financial services; entertainment services; transportation and distribution services; legal services; information and information technology (IT) services; construction and repair services; communication services including library and mass media; tourism, leisure, restaurant, and hospitality services; retail sales services; real estate services; and professional and consulting services.

Services account for a significant portion of an economy and health care services make up a substantial portion within the service sector of many economies.

- In 2015, service sector's share of nominal US gross domestic product (GDP) was 79.7% (Central Intelligence Agency, 2016: "The World Fact Book" cited in Index Mundi, 2016). The estimate for 2017 is 80.2%. In 2016, 80.3% of US employment was in the service sector (Bureau of Labor Statistics, 2017). The projection for 2026 is 81%.
- Globally, service sector's share of the GDP in the world in 2015 was 63.6%. Economic data from countries across the world show similar patterns of large contribution by the service sector to the economy of these countries. For example, the percentage of value added to GDP in 2014 by the services sector in India, Singapore, UK, Australia, and Hong Kong was 52.1%, 75.0%, 78.4%, 70.5%, and 92.7%, respectively (World Bank, 2016).
- Health care services are a significant subsector within the service sector of many economies. For example, global health care spending is projected to increase at an annual rate of 4.1% in 2017–2021 (Deloitte Global Health Care Sector Outlook, 2015).
- In 2016, health care and social assistance accounted for 10.2% of US employment (Bureau of Labor Statistics, 2017). The projection for 2026 is 13.8%.
- By 2016, 56.8 million individuals were enrolled in the US Medicare program (National Committee to Preserve Social Security and Medicare, 2017). Managed care for the elderly under Medicare Advantage Programs was projected to cover nearly 21 million people in 2018, a 5% increase over 2017 (Price Waterhouse Cooper, 2017).

From these statistics, we can conclude that both the service sector and the health care services sector are key components of the US economy. Predictions are that the share of these sectors will continue to grow. Growth in the health care services sector is led mainly by the increasing elderly population and health care reforms creating new health care programs, e.g., Medicaid expansion and state programs that add health care benefits to certain immigrant groups.

1.3. Types of Health Care Services Usually Marketed

There are many health care services, and health care-related products such as durable medical equipment and pharmaceuticals, that are marketed on a continuing basis in the US.

We will first compile a comprehensive list of these products and services. Later chapters in this book will address variations in marketing strategy and practices among these products and services.

Health care products and services regularly marketed include the following:

- *Physician services by individual practitioners and medical groups/IPAs*: "IPAs (Independent Practice Associations)" are medical corporations formed by physicians that cover primary and specialist care by physician owners or contracted physicians. A "medical group" serves the same purpose, but medical groups are usually physician partnerships whereas an IPA is a more formal legal entity with enhanced financial strength and management structures that enables contracting with health plans.
- *Hospital services*: Inpatient, outpatient, and emergency care.
- *Comprehensive health care services*: These are arranged by managed care health plans (also called Health Maintenance Organization or HMOs), independent practice associations under contracts with HMOs, and Accountable Care Organizations (ACOs). Organizations arranging comprehensive health care services are also called Managed Care Organizations (MCOs). These entities provide or arrange the provision of the following:
    o Medicare/Medicaid managed care products;
    o Medicare supplement products (also called "Medigap" products);

> The term *health plan* is used in this book to denote an entity that provides or arranges for coverage of health care services needed by persons enrolled in the health plan (called "plan members"). Health plans receive a monthly premium (called "capitation") for each plan member from the ultimate payers such as federal government, state governments, employers, and individuals desirous of purchasing health insurance. In this sense, health plans fulfill the role of an insurer. Health plans could be full-service health plans or specialized health plans. Examples of the latter are health plans that offer dental services only.

- Medicare part D prescription plans; and
  - Private insurance products primarily marketed B2B to employers. These include Consumer Directed Health Care (CDHC) programs — Health Reimbursement Arrangements (HRA), Health Savings Accounts (HSA), and Flexible Savings Accounts (FSA) involving B2B marketing.
- Pharmaceuticals and medical devices (including durable medical goods).
- Urgent care services/centers.
- Physical therapy and rehabilitative care.
- Long-term care: Home health care, assisted living care, and skilled nursing facility (SNF) care.
- Mental health care.
- Ancillary health services (e.g., audiology, speech therapy, and podiatry).
- Diagnostic services (laboratories and imaging centers).
- Outpatient surgery services/centers.
- Long-term services and support (LTSS).
- Dental care services.
- Optometric services.
- Public health services: As discussed earlier, the term "health marketing" is used to address public health marketing.

1.4. Who are the "Customers" in Health Care Marketing?

Ordinarily, marketing of health care products and services would appear to be directed at consumers with the intention of influencing their decision to select a health care product, service, or service provider. However, health care marketing (as the book will emphasize later) is not only about mass advertising and promotion of health care products and services directly to consumers. It is also about communicating the advantages of a health care product or service. Sometimes this is more effectively possible by directing the message via other parties and stakeholders that influence the ultimate customer or user.

A comprehensive classification of "customer" in health care marketing should include the following:

- **End user customer: The patient**
It is the patient that will eventually visit the physician, get inpatient services from the hospital, or use a prescription drug. However, the patient is not always the person making the selection of physician, the hospital, or the

drug. Patient's selection of a physician may be influenced by family and the selection of a hospital is highly influenced by the referring physician. Therefore, we will extend our list of customers to include these other influencing parties.

- **A patient's family**

Often health care decisions of a patient are influenced by the family. Miliard (2014) cites an article by Urmila Sarkar, MD and David W. Bates, MD, from University of California, San Francisco (UCSF) and Brigham and Women's, respectively, in the *Journal of the American Medical Association*, that states that each year, more than 65 million people in the US (29–39% of the population) provide care for a chronically ill, disabled, or elderly family member or friend. "Provide care" here means that they are involved in the decision-making relating to care. This feature is most common in the independent and assisted living provider community. Smart providers of independent care, assisted care, and skilled nursing care welcome the involvement of children in selecting retirement homes and communities for their parents and focus their marketing efforts toward these children.

- **The well person: The consumer**

Health plans call individuals enrolled in their plan "members" or "enrollees". The decision of which health plan to select and which physician in the health plan's network of providers to select for services is made by the enrollee way before he or she falls sick. Therefore, the consumer in general is a customer in health care. Remember that, an ordinary person, other than a person with chronic illnesses, disabled, or terminally ill person, is well, most of the time.

> Two-thirds of an individual's interaction with a health care provider is as a customer pre- and post-treatment. Only one-third of their encounter is as a patient during treatment (Krivich, 2011).

- **Physicians**

Hospitals and pharmaceutical companies direct a major portion of their marketing efforts and budgets toward physicians. The primary care physician is the primary source of information and advice for the patient on treatment options, medication, specialist physicians to consult, and hospitals.

- **Pharmacists**

Pharmacists play a major role in providing consumers information on generic drugs and non-prescription over-the-counter medications. For this reason, pharmacists are valuable customers to pharmaceutical companies. Myers (2018) identifies special groups of health care consumers who depend on pharmacies and pharmacists for health care-related information. These include consumers who have no insurance, consumers who think that they are not sick enough to visit a physician, and rural consumers.

- **Care coordinators**

Patient-centered coordinated care is highly emphasized in modern health care. In this sense, patient care coordinators play a significant role in educating patients and their families, initiating and monitoring the care plan and coordinating the care plan with direct care providers. In this sense, care coordinators are valuable "customers" for health care marketers who should recognize them as key targets for their marketing communications.

- **Communities and consumers**

Communities and consumers are the customers for public health marketing. Federal and State health departments and agencies (e.g., CDC) spend large amounts of their budgets to promote healthy behavior like smoking and substance use cessation.

- **Internal customers: The staff of the health care organization**

Customer satisfaction and customer/patient experience enhancement efforts should be first preceded by improvements in internal customer (i.e., employee) relationships. Improvements in employee relationships come about via an organizational implementation of internal marketing. By focusing on internal marketing, health care managers will gain a motivated staff composed of knowledgeable and prepared employees. In modern health care marketing, internal marketing is considered an integrative effort that includes participation of the health care marketing function of the organization. Employee engagement and internal marketing are discussed in Chapter 11.

1.5. Special Characteristics of Health Care Services Affecting Health Care Marketing

In Section 1.2, we highlighted that health care is a key subsector of the service sector of an economy. Therefore, special features in services (as opposed to tangible products) are inherent in health care services.

> First, we will briefly review special characteristics of services in general. Next, we will review certain special characteristics of health care services that affect the marketing of health care services.

Special characteristics of services include the following:

- *Contact between customer and service staff*: Degree of customer contact with organization's staff is much higher in services compared to manufacturing. Some services such as medical encounters are classified as "high contact" as opposed to phone or online ordering which can be classified as "low contact". High contact usually brings about behavioral and personality-related issues and problems.
- *Variability in input*: Customers seek from service providers solutions to non-uniform (varying) needs. In products, all customers will be buying the same product with some variations in price, performance, and size. For example, a computer store may have three or four types of computers varying in price, size, and capability. In the case of services, customers' needs have greater variability. Each patient needs a different diagnosis and each car repair needs a different treatment.
- *Variability in output*: Service provided by different employees of the same service organization, e.g., a bank, may be different in terms of time taken and quality (such as percentage of errors). Service employees differ in experience and personality. Products purchased by customers, say from a store, are all the same with perhaps minor variations like color.
- *Services usually have a greater labor content*: Manufacturing operations are usually capital intensive whereas service operations are labor intensive. Coupled with the variability of customer needs, service employees will be expected to have broader and flexible skills.
- *Services are intangible*: Services cannot be stored in an inventory like products since they are intangible. When the customer needs the service, it must be provided. Another factor related to intangibility is the difficulty to explain to the customer the quality of the service. In products, we have something tangible to show. In services, we do not have a tangible product or a model to show the customer.
- *Greater subjectivity in customer's evaluation of the quality of a service*: In evaluating the quality of a product, a customer can be presented with an objective performance, facts, and results. Evaluation of the goodness of a

service is made by the customer using many subjective measures, such as fair treatment, courtesy, and friendliness, in addition to the service outcome.

- *Services are provided simultaneously as customer goes through the service process*: With products, a customer has the pre-purchase opportunity to test the product. The customer also gets to take the product home and use and observe its performance. In services, the customer receives the services while going through the service. For example, in a medical clinic, the patient receives treatment (e.g., an injection) while being in the clinic. Once done, the service is over. The process cannot generally be reversed.
- *Customer participation in the service*: In services, the customer participates in the process. Products are made in a factory and the customer would test and purchase the product. In a service, the customer is physically present while receiving the service. Therefore, the customer is impacted not only by the outcome but also by the process itself. Rudeness of one service employee may lead to customer dissatisfaction with the service provider although the outcome (e.g., a repair or a medical diagnosis) may have been mostly positive.

1.5.1. Additional special characteristics of health care services

While all the above special characteristics of services in general are inherent in health care services, there are additional characteristics of health care services that affect health care marketing. These are as follows:

- Consumer/patient behavior, expectations, and perceptions in health care services are different from behavior, expectations, and perceptions applicable to other services (such as hospitality and travel). Notable features in health care services that affect consumer/patient behavior include the following:
    - High uncertainty, anxiety, and emotions associated with health care encounters and outcomes.
    - Lack of full information about illnesses and treatments.
    - Both outcome and process components are extremely important to the health care customer/patient.
    - Health care services involve handling functional as well as emotional outcomes of customers/patients.

- Trust is a key dimension in consumer/patient satisfaction (for example, see, Ameryoun et al., 2017, "Trust in services has the strongest influence on perceived hospital service quality").
- Customer/patient experience has become the leading driver of health care management and marketing. Some expert opinions related to significance of customer/patient experience in health care are as follows:
    - Kernan (2017): "2018 Healthcare Marketing Trend #1: Customer Experience".
    - Gallagher (2017): "Nowadays I think they have to put customer experience at the very top (of priorities)".
    - Gandolf (2012): "For healthcare consumers, personal experience is the number one reason for choosing a doctor or hospital" in "Patient Experience: The Forgotten 'P' in Your Medical Marketing Plan".
- Multidimensional nature of customer expectations in health care: Competence, trust/assurance, empathy and concern, courtesy, access/waiting times, cost/value, information and communication, responsiveness, fairness, physical facilities/tangible factors, and social interactions with other customers/patients.

- Increased use of internet and social media by health care consumers/patients for information. This requires health care marketers to adopt modern forms of digital marketing.
- Heavy dependence of health care consumers/patients on family, friends, and physicians in selecting health care products/services. Therefore, there is a need to market health care services to intermediate parties rather than the end user, e.g., marketing to physicians to encourage referral of consumers/patients to a managed care health plan or hospital.
- Intense regulation of health care delivery and marketing via federal and state laws and regulations. Health care services is one of the most regulated services. Marketing Medicaid and Medicare products are highly regulated and monitored by federal and state agencies.
- Health care services and health care marketing are subject to some of the most stringent and monitored ethical standards.
- Variations in health care services that make it impossible to adopt "one shoe fits all" marketing strategies and practices. For example,

- - Marketing Medicare advantage plans is completely different from B2B marketing of private insurance plans.
  - Marketing hospital services to physicians and consumers is completely different from marketing physician services to consumers.
- Modern patient care is highly patient centered. This requires health care marketing to move from segmenting customers/patients into large segments to niche segments and customer-centric marketing.
- Inherent intangibility of health care services requires "tangibilization" using techniques such as content marketing (to be addressed later in the book).
- Health care services are very high contact. This makes employee customer orientation, employee engagement, and internal marketing extremely important.
- Health care services are significantly affected by cultural and ethnic backgrounds of patients. While this is true for health care services in the US, it is more applicable in medical tourism where patients cross borders and go to foreign countries to receive medical treatment.
- Need for integration with other functions. The patient/customer experience depends on health care operations (including service recovery), health care informatics (IT), and customer service. This requires health care marketing to work closely with these other functions.

> Summarizing, health care service delivery and health care marketing are significantly affected by the huge array of special characteristics relevant to health care services. Therefore, general principles and practices of marketing advocated in business school marketing texts and courses cannot be applied for health care services marketing. This book will address special circumstances relevant to health care service management and marketing.

1.6. Plan of the Book

This book is organized in four parts.

Part 1: Health Care Marketing: Evolution and Modern Trends

In this part, we will clarify key terms such as health care marketing and health marketing, and discuss role of health care services in the overall service sector, types of health care services typically marketed, and special characteristics of health care services that affect marketing such services (Chapter 1).

This part will also trace (Chapter 2) evolution of the fields of marketing, services marketing and health care marketing, and adoption of developments in services marketing to health care marketing. Finally, this part will discuss modern trends in health care marketing.

Part 2: Health Care Marketing Strategy Formulation and Implementation Process

This part will discuss how health care marketing in a health care organization starts with formulating the health care marketing strategy, discussing in detail the process of formulating strategy at the organizational level and market segment and niche level (Chapter 3).

This part will also discuss the role of market and marketing research in the health care organization (Chapter 4) and use of primary and secondary data to study competition (Chapter 5), consumer behavior (Chapter 6), and factors affecting consumer/patient experience (Chapter 7). This will be followed up by a discussion on how to segment the market and identify niches (Chapter 8).

Finally, this part will explain how the ground-level marketing mix is developed for each market segment and niche identified (Chapter 9).

Part 3: Health Care Marketing Program Implementation

This part picks up from health care marketing strategy formulation and moves on to implementing strategy and the marketing mix.

It will discuss in detail about integrating digital technology into health care marketing, social media marketing, and content marketing (Chapter 10).

Also discussed is the concept of internal marketing, which deals with how to engage employees of the organization in delivering a memorable experience to the customer/patient (Chapter 11), and how to engage physicians who are the key source of information and referral for potential customers of health plans, hospitals, and pharmaceutical companies (Chapter 12).

Finally, this part will address an important issue in implementing health care marketing, namely compliance with applicable laws and regulations, and adhering to high ethical standards and practices. Included in this discussion are guidelines for executing legal contracts between parties such as health plans and hospitals, and health plans and physicians that ensure compliance with applicable laws and regulations and consumer/patient protection (Chapter 13).

Part 4: Health Care Marketing in Special Sectors

This part will address health care marketing in special sectors of the health care industry such as direct health care marketing of physician services, hospital services, managed care plans/services, pharmaceuticals, and public health (Chapter 14).

Also discussed is health care marketing globally covering outbound medical travel consumer/patients (called medical tourism) and in-bound medical travel customers/patients (Chapter 15).

References

Ameryoun, A., Najafi, S., Nejati-Zarnaqi, B., Khalilifar, S. O., Ajam, M. and Ansarimoghadam, A. (2017). "Factor Selection for Service Quality Evaluation: A Hospital Case Study", *International Journal of Health Care Quality Assurance*, 30 (1), 58–66.

Bureau of Labor Statistics (2017). "Employment by Major Industry Sector", https://www.bls.gov/emp/tables/employment-by-major-industry-sector.htm. Accessed September 25, 2018.

Centers for Disease Control and Prevention (2011). "What is Health Marketing?", https://www.cdc.gov/healthcommunication/toolstemplates/whatishm.html. Accessed September 18, 2018.

Connolly, B. (2017). "Why Authenticity is the Prescription for Modern Healthcare Marketing", http://www.olapic.com/resources/authenticity-prescription-modern-healthcare-marketing_blog-p1aw-g1lo-v1hc/. Accessed September 23, 2018.

Deloitte Global Health Care Sector Outlook (2015). https://www.slideshare.net/deloitte14/deloitte-global-health-care-sector-outlook-2015-46256856. Accessed July 4, 2018.

Evariant (2017). "What is Health Care Marketing?", https://www.evariant.com/faq/what-is-healthcare-marketing. Accessed September 22, 2018.

Farlex Financial Dictionary (2012). "Definition of Health Care Marketing", https://financial-dictionary.thefreedictionary.com/Healthcare+Marketing. Accessed September 25, 2018.

Fox, S. and Duggan, M. (2013). "Health Online 2013", Pew Research Center, http://www.pewinternet.org/2013/01/15/health-online-2013/. Accessed June 23, 2018.

Gallagher, B. (2017). "How Has Healthcare Marketing Changed in the Last Decade?", https://www.sharecare.com/video/healthmakers/brendan-gallagher/what-is-the-future-of-healthcare-marketing. Accessed June 1, 2018.

Gandolf, S. (2012). "PwC Finds Patient Experience is the Number One Factor for Choosing a Doctor or Hospital", *Culture, Doctor Interactions, Doctors, Health Plans, Hospitals, Leadership, Medical Practices*, September 12, http://patientexperience.com/pwcstudy1/. Accessed September 28, 2018.

Google (2015). "A Remedy for Your Health-Related Questions: Health Info in the Knowledge", February 10, https://googleblog.blogspot.com/2015/02/health-info-knowledge-graph.html. Accessed September 30, 2018.

Index Mundi (2016). "United States GDP — Composition by Sector", https://www.indexmundi.com/united_states/gdp_composition_by_sector.html. Accessed September 25, 2018.

Kernan, J. (2017). "2018 Healthcare Marketing Trend #1: Customer Experience", *Smith & Jones*, https://smithandjones.com/resources/blog/2018-healthcare-marketing-trends-customer-experience. Accessed September 27, 2018.

Kratzke, C. and Cox, C. (2012). "Smartphone Technology and Apps: Rapidly Changing Health Promotion", *International Electronic Journal of Health Education*, 15, 72–82.

Krivich, M. (2011). "Customer Experience Management Applied to Healthcare", *Healthcare Marketing Matters*, January 5, http://healthcaremarketingmatters.blogspot.com/2011/01/customer-experience-management-applied.html. Accessed September 24, 2018.

Miliard, M. (2014). "A Family Affair — New ICU-Based Programs Look for Ways to Better Use the 'Untapped' Resource of Patients' Loved Ones", *Healthcare IT News*, February 15, https://www.healthcareitnews.com/news/family-affair. Accessed August 12, 2018.

Myers, S. (2018). "Why Healthcare Marketers Should Focus on the Pharmacy as a Customer Touchpoint", https://www.targetmarketingmag.com/article/healthcare-marketers-focus-pharmacy-customer-touchpoint/. Accessed October 1, 2018.

National Committee to Preserve Social Security and Medicare (2017). "Medicare Fast Facts", http://www.ncpssm.org/our-issues/medicare/medicare-fast-facts/. Accessed September 25, 2018.

Price Waterhouse Cooper (2017). "The 2017 Annual Report of the Boards of Trustees of the Federal Hospital Insurance and Federal Supplementary Medical Insurance Trust Funds", The Board of Trustees, Federal Hospital Insurance and Federal Supplementary Medical Insurance Trust Funds, July 13.

Resnick, L. R. (2017). "Six Healthcare Marketing Trends for 2018", *Managed Healthcare Executive*, November 30, http://www.managedhealthcareexecutive.com/healthcare-executive/six-healthcare-marketing-trends-2018. Accessed July 1, 2018.

Whitler, K. A. (2015). "The New World of Healthcare Marketing: A Framework for Adaptation", *Forbes CMO Network*, https://www.forbes.com/sites/kimberlywhitler/2015/09/06/the-new-world-of-healthcare-marketing-a-framework-for-adaptation/#4d43116a1c10. Accessed July 1, 2018.

World Bank (2016). "World Bank Group Reports 2016", http://data.worldbank.org/indicator. Accessed July 1, 2018.

Suggested Additional Readings

Agrawal, A. J. (2016). "7 Content Marketing Tips for Healthcare Companies", *Forbes CMO Network*, https://www.forbes.com/sites/ajagrawal/2016/01/17/7-content-marketing-tips-for-healthcare-companies/#59bfcab63c44. Accessed June 25, 2018.

Batt, R. (2007). "Service Strategies: Marketing, Operations, and Human Resource", http://digitalcommons.ilr.cornell.edu/articles/943. Accessed June 15, 2018.

Beckham, D. (2001). "20 Years of Health Care Marketing", *Health Forum Journal*, 44 (4), 37–40.

Center for Medicare & Medicaid Services (CMS) (2016). "Medicare Marketing Guidelines", https://www.cms.gov/Medicare/Health-Plans/ManagedCareMarketing/FinalPartCMarketingGuidelines. Accessed June 20, 2018.

Haefner, M. (2017). "8 Healthcare Marketing Trends for 2018", *Becker's Hospital Review*, October 18, https://www.beckershospitalreview.com/hospital-management-administration/8-healthcare-marketing-trends-for-2018.html. Accessed July 25, 2018.

Hixon, T. (2015). "Are We Patients, Consumers, or Customers?", October 22, https://www.forbes.com/sites/toddhixon/2015/10/22/are-we-patients-consumers-or-customers/#708cfc801434. Accessed September 29, 2018.

Joint Commission Governance Institute (2009). "Leadership in Healthcare Organizations: A Guide to Joint Commission Leadership Standards", https://www.jointcommission.org/assets/1/18/WP_Leadership_Standards.pdf. Accessed October 1, 2018.

Leone, R., Walker, C., Curry, L. and Agee, E. (2012). "Application of a Marketing Concept to Patient-Centered Care: Co-Producing Health with Heart Failure Patients", *The Online Journal of Issues in Nursing*, 17 (2), 7.

Medical Tourism Association (2015). "Facts and Statistics", http://medicaltourism.com/Forms/facts-statistics.aspx. Accessed July 2, 2018.

OECD (2016). "Medical Tourism: Treatments, Markets and Health System Implications: A Scoping Review", http://www.oecd.org/els/health-systems/48723982.pdf. Accessed October 2, 2018.

Weiss, R. (2013). "Modern Marketing Defined: Health Care Marketing's Organizational Impact Cannot be Easily Labelled", *Marketing Health Services*, 33 (1), 12–13.

Whitler, K. A. (2017). "The New World of Healthcare Marketing: Lessons from Across the World", *Forbes*, https://www.forbes.com/sites/kimberlywhitler/2017/07/22/the-new-world-of-healthcare-marketing-lessons-from-across-the-world/#109f90546084. Accessed June 30, 2018.

WHO (2015). "Evidence on Global Medical Travel", http//www.who.int/bulletin/volumes/93/11/14-146027/en/. Accessed October 2, 2018.

Chapter 2

Health Care Marketing: Evolution and Modern Trends

2.1. Health Care Marketing as a Specialized Subfield of Services Marketing

Health care marketing is a specialized subfield of *services marketing*, which in turn is a specialized subfield of *marketing*. This hierarchy of marketing activities is shown in Figure 2.1.

Marketing is a major functional area in any organization whether it is a private or public organization, or whether it is a manufacturing or service organization. Traditionally, marketing has been associated with advertising and selling.

One definition of traditional marketing is that it incorporates many forms of advertising and marketing using strategies, such as print, broadcast, direct mail, and telephone (Marketing-Schools, 2012). However, marketing thought has significantly changed over time to meet the challenges of the modern digital and experience economy. These will be discussed later in this chapter.

Similarly, services marketing thought has also changed significantly over the past 40 years from merely distinguishing itself from product marketing to integrating it with product marketing in what is now known as a service-dominant logic (SDL). In the mid-2000s, the view of marketing itself changed significantly with the practitioners and academics starting to realize that marketing should be based on a service-dominant logic (SD Logic) rather than a goods-dominant logic (GD Logic). The turning point was the work of Vargo and Lusch (2004, 2008) who boldly claim the following:

- All economies are service economies.
- Goods are a distribution mechanism for service provision.

22 Modern Health Care Marketing

Figure 2.1. Hierarchy of marketing activities.

- Goods derive their value through use, i.e., the service they provide.
- Consumers do not buy goods or services. They buy offerings which render services which create value.
- Focus is shifting from tangibles toward intangibles, such as skills, information and knowledge, and toward interactivity, connectivity, and ongoing relationships.
- The traditional goods-centered marketing logic (GDL) must be replaced by service-centered dominant marketing logic (SDL).

> Therefore, to understand the evolution of, and modern thinking in, health care marketing, it would be prudent to first understand the evolution of the two fields: marketing and services marketing.

We also believe that this approach will benefit students and practitioners who have not had an exposure to a formal marketing education.

2.2. Recent Developments in Marketing Thought

The term "marketing" is believed to have first appeared in dictionaries in the 16th century where it referred to the process of buying and selling at a market (Etymology Dictionary Online, 2000).

In a 1991 treatise (Kotler, 1991), the internationally recognized marketing expert, Phillip Kotler defines marketing as follows:

- The process by which an organization relates creatively, productively, and profitably to the marketplace.
- The art of creating and satisfying customers at a profit.
- Getting the right goods and services to the right people at the right places at the right time at the right price with the right communications and promotion.

Many would recognize this last definition as the one based on the well-known traditional 4P Marketing Mix (Product, Price, Place and Promotion).

After many years of adhering to the understanding of marketing as mainly a process of selling goods and services based on the well-known 4Ps, in the mid-2000s, the view of marketing itself changed significantly with practitioners and academics starting to realize that marketing should be based on an SD Logic rather than a GD Logic. This change in thinking following the work of Vargo and Lusch (2004, 2008) is discussed in Section 2.1.

The American Marketing Association (AMA) has since then changed its definition of marketing as follows:

> "Marketing is the activity, conducted by organizations and individuals that operates through institutions and processes for creating, delivering, and exchanging market offerings that have value for customers, clients, marketers, and society at large." (AMA, 2007)

This was a change from the former 2004 version which stated the following:

> "Marketing is an organizational function and a set of processes for creating, communicating and delivering value to customers and for managing customer relationships in ways that benefit the organization and its stakeholders."

AMA's rationale for the change was as follows:

- Marketing is not limited to one department. Hence, the term "organizational function" has been dropped.
- Marketing is an action word. It is what organizations and individuals (entrepreneurs and consumers) engage in or do. The new definition points out who (i.e., organizations and individuals) conducts (i.e., guides or directs) the activity called "marketing".
- The previous phrase "a set of processes", does not clearly say who is engaged in the processes. The new definition says, "A set of institutions and processes," which acknowledges that institutions, such as manufacturers, wholesalers, retailers, and marketing research firms are an important part of marketing. The phrase "institutions and processes" implies that marketing systems, such as channels of distribution are a part of marketing as are social processes (e.g., regulations and norms).
- The previous definition included "creating, communicating, and delivering", but not "exchanging". The new definition reads "creating,

communicating, delivering, and exchanging". It acknowledges that exchange of information — both ways, between customer and the organization — continues to be an important part of marketing.
- The previous definition included "value" but left the concept ambiguous. The new definition focuses on market offerings (i.e., "ideas, goods, and services") that have value to someone. In other words, what is created is *market offerings*. Note the recognition of services here.
- The previous definition indicated that organizations create "value to customers and for managing customer relationships in ways that benefit the organization and its stakeholders". However, marketing creates market offerings that have value also to those who are not "customers". Also, marketing is more than managing customer relationships. Mixing up marketing and customer relationship management is not appropriate.
- The new definition adds "clients, marketers, and society at large" and states that market offerings have value for "customers, clients, marketers, and society at large". Adding "clients" acknowledges that non-profit institutions and government/public services also should engage in marketing. Such organizations normally do not see themselves as having "customers". Rather, they have clients.
- Adding "marketers" acknowledges that those organizations and individuals that do the marketing benefit from the created, communicated, delivered, and exchanged market offerings.
- Adding "society at large" acknowledges the aggregated nature of marketing across competing organizations that impels innovations, improvements, and price competition. Creating market offerings that have value benefits society, as do communications about, and the delivery of, marketing offerings. In short, the practice and activity of marketing benefits society.

In summary,

> Modern marketing of products or services is no longer personal selling using aggressive sales pitches and advertising by the marketing department of the organization. It is a comprehensive activity undertaken by the organization to communicate the value of the service (or product) to present customers, potential customers in the marketplace, society in general, clients, suppliers and employees, in an exchange of information.

2.3. Evolution and Definition of Services Marketing

Services marketing is believed to have emerged as a distinct subfield of marketing discipline in the late 1970s (Kunz and Hogreve, 2011).

Baker and Magnani (2016) trace the evolution of services marketing and claim that the development of service-oriented concepts and models began with Shostack's (1977) seminal article promoting service marketing as an acceptable field of research that separated it from product-based marketing. Recognition was made of people (employees, customers), physical evidence (facility, uniforms, equipment), and process (flow of activities, level of customer involvement), which were said to differentiate products from services marketing, and the special characteristics of services, such as intangibility, heterogeneity, inseparability, and perishability. Baker and Magnani (2016) also recognize the seminal articles "Building a New Academic Field: The Case of Services Marketing" (Berry and Parasuraman, 1993) and "Tracking the Evolution of the Services Marketing Literature" (Fisk *et al.*, 1993) as some of the first to officially recognize "services marketing" as a discipline.

In the services marketing arena, practitioners and writers soon recognized that the traditional 4P marketing mix was not suitable or adequate. This led to the traditional 4Ps of marketing being expanded to include three more factors: People (service staff), Process and Physical Evidence making up a 7P marketing mix (Bitner, 1990; Booms and Bitner, 1981). This new 7P marketing mix will be fully discussed in Chapter 9.

2.3.1. Definition of services marketing

Let us first review a few traditional definitions of services marketing. These include the following:

- The active marketing of something that is intangible and which is usually consumed at the point of delivery (Doyle, 2016).
- Service marketing is the promotion of economic activities offered by a business to its clients. Service marketing includes building public relations, advancing customer loyalty, developing quality of services, handling relationships, and complaints management (Agrawal, 2016).
- The promotion of economic activities offered by a business to its clients. Service marketing might include the process of selling telecommunications, health treatment, financial, hospitality, car rental, air travel, and professional services (Business Dictionary, 2018).

- Service marketing is defined as the integrated system of business activities designed to plan, price, promote, and distribute appropriate services for the benefit of existing and potential consumers to achieve organizational objectives (Jha, 2000).

It would be seen that these traditional views of services marketing did recognize the special characteristics of services, such as intangibility, heterogeneity, inseparability, and perishability, to distinguish it from marketing tangible products *but lacked the broad view of modern marketing that, as discussed before, had evolved.*

2.3.2. A modern definition of services marketing

Based on our understanding of modern views of marketing and services marketing developed earlier in this chapter, we can adopt the following modern definition of services marketing (Gunawardane, 2017):

> "The exchange of information between the service organization and its customers, potential customers (market), society at large, suppliers, government regulators and employees, to convey the value of the services or services offered, taking into account the special differences of a service from tangible products, such as, intangibility, inseparability of production and consumption, heterogeneity (non-standard nature), and perishability."

It is important to note the keywords/concepts in this definition. These are as follows:

- Exchange of information with customers and potential customers;
- Inclusion of community at large (including community-based organizations and health care services advocates);
- Inclusion of employees in the marketing process; and
- Focus on overcoming inherent characteristics of services, such as intangibility and co-creation of the service by the customer and service organization.

2.4. Evolution and Definition of Health Care Marketing

Marketing of health care services was historically considered unethical and a violation of professional code of conduct.

In the following, a brief review of the key milestones in the history and evolution of health care marketing is presented:

- **1950s:** Hospitals and physicians considered marketing unethical.
- **1970s:** Health care providers benefitted from efforts by the legal profession. Following a US Supreme Court decision (Bates v. State Bar of Arizona, 1977), state bar associations could no longer universally prohibit attorney advertising.
- Hospital marketing event by Evanston Hospital and North Western University (Beckham, 2001).
- **1977:** Society for Healthcare Planning and Marketing founded.

Today, there are several regional organizations (e.g., Michigan and New Jersey) under this name that are affiliated with The Society for Healthcare Strategy & Market Development (SHSMD), a professional membership group of the American Hospital Association.

- **1980s:** Goldsmith (1980): "Health care must borrow proven marketing techniques from business to survive in an environment of scarce resources, tough competition, government regulation, and cost containment."

Parrington and Stone (1991): By the mid-1980s, the marketing concept was being applied. The 4Ps were generally accepted as a paradigm, but the headline-grabbers were the promotional and product strategies. In the promotion category, many hospitals launched image campaigns to create preference for their services. The era of "smiling faces" and value-added amenities was ushered in and guest relations programs were developed as a strategy to ensure satisfied and loyal patients (Goldsmith and Leebov, 1986).

Attention was devoted to identifying and capitalizing on market niches and product-market segments. With the advent of "marketing warfare", or marketing as a competitive response (Malhotra, 1988), focus turned from consumer markets to physicians and third-party payers, including the employer contracting market (Hill, 1988; Wright and Stodghill, 1988). Pricing was discovered as a tool in the marketing arsenal (Leven, 1984; Nimer, 1985).

- **1987:** Medicare and Medicaid Patient Protection Act of 1987.

This legislation, referred to as the Anti-Kickback Statute, affects marketing to, and via, physicians, and provides criminal penalties for certain acts impacting Medicare and Medicaid reimbursable services.

28 *Modern Health Care Marketing*

- **1990s:**
    - Emergence of large health systems due to the consolidation of hospitals, advent of HMOs, and managed care.
    - Focus on customer/patient segmentation, ethnic markets.
    - Focus on customer/patient satisfaction.
    - Direct marketing to consumers by pharmaceutical companies.
    - Hospitals and HMOs established marketing departments managed by marketing specialists.

- **1996:** Society for Healthcare Strategy and Market Development (SHSMD), a professional membership group of the American Hospital Association, formed. SHSMD claims to serve more than 4,000 members — professionals who work in all sectors of health care, including hospitals and health systems, physician groups, consulting firms, advertising and public relations agencies, and service providers. Aims to be a voice for health care strategists in planning, marketing, communications, public relations, business development, and physician strategy (*Source*: SHSMD website, http://www.shsmd.org/).

- **2000s:**
    - Marketing laws created to protect vulnerable populations, such as Medicare and Medicaid populations.
    - CMS: Medicare Marketing Regulations (CMS, 2016).
    - CMS: Medicaid Managed Care Final Rule, 2016; state laws and regulations on Medicaid managed care marketing.
    - Non-discrimination in marketing Medicare and Medicaid products.
    - Broker commission limits in Medicare product marketing.
    - Marketing material language requirements in Medicare and Medicaid.

    These laws and regulations will be discussed in detail in Chapter 13.

- **2010:** Affordable Care Act (ACA or Obamacare) brought in several provisions affecting health care marketing practices.

This expanded the liability of the False Claims Act to definitively include Anti-Kickback claims as grounds for violation. Else, as exchanges created under ACA are not federal health care programs, The Federal Anti-Kickback law, 42 U.S.C. § 1320a-7b(b) would not have applied to these exchanges.

Presently, studies indicate that individual physicians and dentists are still conservative about marketing, and that younger physicians are more receptive to marketing than older physicians. The average physician or dentist appears not to believe in the success of direct marketing to expand the patient base. They also seem to be cautious about the risks of violating privacy laws and potential claims of deceptive advertising. We will discuss direct marketing of physician services in Chapter 14.

It is interesting to note that even in modern times, health care organizations, physicians in particular, express skepticism about health care marketing. Health Care Success (2019) reports (in an article, "Myths of Health Care Marketing") some of the common misconceptions of physicians. These include, "I don't need marketing. I have enough patients," "Health care marketing is unethical," and "People in the community already know about us."

2.4.1. Definition of health care marketing

We will first examine a few traditional definitions of health care marketing, as follows:

- Health care marketing is the process of advertising hospitals, medical offices, pharmaceuticals, and so forth (Farlex Financial Dictionary, 2012).
- Health care marketing involves activities that relate to the development, packaging, pricing, and distribution of health care products and to any mechanisms used for promoting these products (Thomas, 2008).

In the light of modern understanding of "marketing" and "services marketing" noted in the previous sections of this chapter, the above traditional definitions and understanding of health care marketing have several shortcomings that affect a proper understanding of health care marketing in the modern digital and experience era. These are as follows:

- Emphasis on the traditional 4P marketing mix. We discussed earlier how modern services marketing is based on a 7P marketing mix. As such, modern health care marketing should adopt the same expanded marketing mix.
- Missing the concept of "exchanging" information in two-way communication (with customers/patients/other stakeholders).
- Lack of focus on customer/patient lifetime engagement and experience.
- Lack of recognition of modern service customers' dependence on digital communications and, therefore, the need to focus on modern technologies in health care marketing.

These shortcomings are, to a limited extent, addressed by the following more recent definition (Evariant, Inc., 2017):

> "Healthcare marketing integrates highly segmented and targeted online and offline tactics that are designed to communicate, nurture, and encourage interaction with patients and consumers over the patient's lifecycle."

Having seen the evolutions in marketing thought in marketing in general, in services marketing, and finally in health care marketing, we are now able to formulate a more comprehensive definition of health care marketing consistent with the modern definitions of marketing and service marketing.

Health Care Marketing

The exchange of information between the health care organization and its customers/patients, potential customers (market), society at large, health care providers and suppliers, government regulators and employees, to

- convey the value of the service or services offered,
- taking into account the special differences of a service from tangible products, such as, intangibility, inseparability of production and consumption (co-creation), and heterogeneity (non-standard nature),
- using conventional and modern advanced technological–digital methods of communication,
- with the primary focus on customer/patient lifetime engagement and enhancing customer/patient lifetime experience.

Presentations of concepts, principles, and applications of health care marketing in this book will be based on this understanding of the role of health care marketing.

2.5. Modern Trends and Practices in Health Care Marketing

Our review of modern trends and practices in health care marketing will be based on the following:

- Topics discussed by health care management and marketing professionals at recent professional meetings;

- Practitioner and consulting firm exchanges over the internet using articles and blogs; and
- Recent conceptual and empirical-based papers in academic journals (such as *Journal of Healthcare Marketing, International Journal of Pharmaceutical and Healthcare Marketing, Journal of Healthcare Communications*, and *Journal of Patient Experience*).

Following is a list of topics/issues addressed at recent health care marketing conferences:

- **American Marketing Association (AMA): Health Care Marketing Conference, March 2018, San Francisco**
  Learning Objectives:
    - Effect on HCM by health care reform, quality/patient-centered care movements.
    - Handling health-conscious consumers.
    - Use of social media.
    - Targeting by age, culture, ethnicity, and health status.
    - Explore techniques to engage physicians.
    - Employee engagement.
    - Use of multitudes of mediums across many platforms to maximize their messages.
    - Branding, creative content, and content marketing.

- **23rd Annual Health Care Marketing & Physician Strategies Summit on April 30–May 2, 2018, in Salt Lake City**
    - Interactive and digital strategies; aligning digital strategy with technology tools.
    - Content marketing; getting your content ready for voice activated search.
    - Marketing's role in behavior change.
    - A new era of employee engagement.
    - Customer communication and engagement.
    - The science of audience journey mapping.
    - Value of physician relations; physician communication and strategies; fostering physician loyalty.

- **The 21st Annual Health Care Internet Conference 2017**
    - Consumer engagement.
    - Mapping the ideal patient experience in the digital age.

- How to own your digital health care experience.
- Digital marketing and advertising.
- Multichannel marketing.
- Customer relations management (CRM) and Big Data; how to define CRM requirements: demystifying the path to digital marketing.
- Using emerging technologies to grow physician referrals.
- The journey to transform into a consumer-focused organization.
- Website design; patient-centered approach for system-wide website redesign.
- Overcoming challenges to improve patient experience.
- Consumer content marketing in health care.
- Engaging employees to boost operational performance: the nexus between patient and employee engagement.

Following is a list of topics frequently addressed in academic journals in health care management and marketing during the period 2014–2018:

- Integrated nature of health care marketing, operations management, and human resource management (Batt, 2007).
- Increased interactions with operations and customer service functions of the organization to resolve and improve customer/patient and health care provider concerns and experience; the organization's "marketing team" concept (Weiss, 2013).
- Digital health care marketing.
- Customer/patient segmentation/targeting.
- Physician engagement; influencer (physicians, family, and community) marketing.
- Internal marketing: Why employee recognition matters.
- Increased use of social media; effectively outsourcing social media.
- Website redesign: "Not just a patient portal to meet CMS requirements."
- Big Data use; Predictive analysis.
- Reaching out to minorities/ethnic groups, e.g., Latinos, Asians?
- Customer/patient experience: "Redesign emergency rooms to experience rooms"; patient journey mapping.
- Customer engagement: Customer/patient satisfaction, loyalty.
- Content marketing: "Improving company's on-line reputation." On line videos scripts.
- Developing customer trust.
- Educating customers/patients: "demystify Medicare."
- Globalization of health care and health care marketing.

- Greater emphasis on ethical health care marketing practices.
- Transforming Big Data into actionable insights.
- Leverage new/emerging technologies like artificial intelligence (AI) to transform Big Data into actionable insights.

Now, we can make a summary list of these modern concepts and practices in health care marketing:

- Increased use of modern technology-based digital marketing.
    - Use of internet, social media, mobile devices, blogs, websites, email marketing, health apps, and (the new and growing interest in using) AI.
    - Smart use of these modern technologies. For example, search engine optimization (SEO) for the organization's website, creating smart content (content marketing), health explanatory videos, and experiential marketing.
- Increased use of analytics with Big Data (data from clinical records, billing records, claims data, call center transcripts, social network data, and market intelligence) within legal and ethical limitations.
    - "Using sophisticated analytics, health care marketing teams can understand their patients, pinpoint their target audiences, develop effective education and wellness programs and build successful marketing campaigns." (Evariant, Inc., 2017)
- Greater emphasis on customer engagement and customer/patient experience.
    - Focus on customer experience (and therefore, long-term customer relationship management or CRM) rather than simple customer satisfaction by encounter. Increased efforts to understand what consumers want (Greene, 2015).
    - Health marketing calls for an integrative perspective because the health care system is an integrated whole, uniting all actors within a number of convergences: patient-centered approach, payer influence, constraints on marketing mixes (Crié and Chebat, 2013).
    - "Engaging with consumers and improving patient experience" is among the top five issues in health care in 2018 (Deloitte, 2018).

- Increased emphasis on compliance with changes in public policy, laws, and regulations affecting health care delivery in USA, such as the ACA or Obamacare and HIPAA laws.
- Expanding into specialized health care markets (such as Medicare, Medicaid, dual eligible, mental health, ACA, or Obamacare exchange products, and Part D prescription drug plans.
  - Medicare advantage and Medicaid managed care will swell.
  - Growth of Consumer Directed Health Care (CDHC) programs — Health Reimbursement Arrangements (HRA), Health Savings Accounts (HSA), and Flexible Savings Accounts (FSA).
- Value-based care is here to stay imposing new challenges to health care marketers (Resnick, 2017).
  - New health care management systems: pay-for-performance reimbursement — from basic risk sharing to accountable care organizations to bundled payments — are rapidly moving health care toward outcomes-based financing system.
  - Incentives and disincentives based on quality of care and patient clinical results are the new normal.
  - Challenge to health care marketers:
    - Bringing key stakeholders together.
    - Using successes to demonstrate the value in value-based care and using any failures as lessons learned.
- Recognition of health care marketing as an integral part (not just a separate department) of the organization's strategic planning, and the need for input by marketing for influencing organizational culture to be consumer/patient experience-oriented.
  - Tie health care marketing more closely to business/financial planning and metrics (Affect Report, 2017).
- Integrated nature of health care operations management, marketing, information technology (IT), and human resource management.
  - Many companies have, indeed, created integrated systems of service delivery by targeting distinct customer segments and organizing their marketing, operations, and human resource systems around these targets (Batt, 2007).

- Recognition of family, caregivers and involved providers, and the community (community resources, community-based organizations) as resources for consumer/patient decision-making.
- Recognition of the impact of modern patient-centered care management on health care marketing.
  - Experts in marketing and health care have witnessed an emergence of consumers who examine market offerings and create a customized consumption experience for themselves (Leone *et al.*, 2012; Payne and Frow, 2005). Health care marketing should focus on educational marketing that will engage patient populations.
  - Better segmentation into niches and customer-centric segmentation (Resnick, 2017).
- Consumer/patient education will be a key task of health care marketing.
  - Consumers are drawn to more educational than promotional ads (Affect Report, 2017; Haefner, 2017).
  - Wellness initiatives will be on the rise (Haefner, 2017).
  - Consumers/patients need information to understand the complex health care insurance environment. Health care marketers need to create reliable, understandable information and decision-support tools to help consumers navigate health care's massive maze of bureaucracy with confidence (Resnick, 2017).
  - Consumers/patients will continue to seek price transparency.
- Content marketing.
  - Interview with senior marketers from health care and life sciences organizations including Pfizer, Phoenix Children's Hospital, Illumina, MDxHealth, and others. "What are your top marketing & PR priorities this year and heading into 2018?" (Affect Report, 2017).
    - Creating more customized content for target audiences.
    - Educating customers/patients/influencers through content is top priority.
    - Increased focus on consumer engagement and content marketing through social channels.
  - "Social engagement is king, and content is queen" (Resnick, 2017).
- Marketing mix will have to be restructured.

- The marketing mix is shifting to digital (Affect Report, 2017).
  - Adoption of modern 7P services marketing mix to health care marketing in place of the archaic 4P marketing mix (White and Abrams, 2017; Zeithaml et al., 2018).
  - More social media (and advanced social media) is included in the mix.
- Increased partnerships with physicians and other providers for referral of new enrollees/subscribers and hence, emphasis on "physician engagement" and "provider relations".
- Increased emphasis and oversight on legal and ethical health care marketing practices (CMS, 2016; Greene, 2015).
  - Hospital Marketing: See, for example Joint Commission Governance Institute (2009).
    - The hospital follows ethical practices for marketing and billing.
    - Marketing materials accurately represent the hospital and address the care, treatment, and services that the hospital provides either directly or by contractual arrangement.
- Globalization of health care and health care marketing.

According to recent studies (Medical Tourism Association, 2015; OECD, 2016; WHO, 2015), inbound and outbound medical tourism is on the increase. According to WHO, in 2015, medical tourism generated between US$60 billion and US$70 billion. Within five years, it is very likely that health tourism will generate at least twice these revenues. The number of medical tourists from the United States had increased from about half a million in 2007 to an expected estimate of 1.25 million Americans who would travel abroad for medical treatment in 2014. Beyond the US estimate, there are up to 50 million medical tourists worldwide annually. The industry is expected to grow approximately 20% per year.

These developments have brought about increased interest and activity among health care organizations and marketers in global health care markets.

> The aim of this book is to address these issues, concepts, and practices, which we hope, would provide a good understanding of health care marketing in the modern digital and experience era.

References

Affect Report (2017). "Healthcare Marketing 2018: Guide to Meeting New Priorities in a Shifting Environment", http://www.affect.com/wp-content/uploads/2017/11/Affect_Healthcare_White_Paper.pdf. Accessed October 15, 2018.

Agrawal, A. J. (2016). "7 Content Marketing Tips for Healthcare Companies", Forbes CMO Network, https://www.forbes.com/sites/ajagrawal/2016/01/17/7-content-marketing-tips-for-healthcare-companies/#59bfcab63c44. Accessed June 25, 2018.

American Marketing Association (AMA) (2007). "About AMA: Definition of Marketing", www.marketingpower.com/AboutAMA/Pages/DefinitionofMarketing.aspx. Accessed July 5, 2018.

Baker, M. A. and Magnani, V. A. (2016). "The Evolution of Services Marketing, Hospitality Marketing and Building the Constituency Mode for Hospitality Marketing", *International Journal of Contemporary Hospitality Management*, 28 (8), 1510–1534.

Batt, R. (2007). "Service Strategies: Marketing, Operations, and Human Resource", http://digitalcommons.ilr.cornell.edu/articles/943. Accessed July 5, 2018.

Beckham, D. (2001). "20 Years of Health Care Marketing", *Health Forum Journal*, 37–40.

Berry, L. L. and Parasuraman, A. (1993). "Building a New Academic Field — The Case of Services Marketing", *Journal of Retailing*, 69 (1), 13–60.

Bitner, M. (1990). "Evaluating Service Encounters: The Effects of Physical Surroundings and Employee Responses", *Journal of Marketing*, 54(2), 69–82.

Booms, B. H. and Bitner, M. J. (1981). "Marketing Strategies and Organizational Structures for Service Firms", in Donnelly, J. H. and George, W. R. (Eds.), *Marketing of Services*, American Marketing Association, Chicago, IL, 47–51.

Business Dictionary (2018). "Services Marketing", www.businessdictionary.com/definition/servicesnarketing.html. Accessed October 24, 2018.

CMS (2016). *Medicare Marketing Manual*.

Crié, D. and Chebat, J. (2013). "Health Marketing: Toward an Integrative Perspective", *Journal of Business Research*, 66 (1), 123–126.

Deloitte (2018). "2018 Global Health Care Outlook. The Evolution of Smart Health Care", https://www2.deloitte.com/content/dam/Deloitte/global/Documents/Life-Sciences-Health-Care/gx-lshc-hc-outlook-2018.pdf. Accessed November 30, 2018.

Doyle, C. (2016). *A Dictionary of Marketing, 4th ed.*, Oxford University Press.

Etymology Dictionary Online (2000). http://www.etymonline.com/index.php?term=marketing. Accessed September 30, 2018.

Evariant, Inc. (2017). "What is Health Care Marketing?", https://www.evariant.com/faq/what-is-healthcare-marketing. Accessed September 22, 2018.

Farlex Financial Dictionary (2012). https://financial-dictionary.thefreedictionary.com/Healthcare+Marketing. Accessed October 2, 2018.

Fisk, R. P., Brown, S. W. and Bitner, M. J. (1993). "Tracking the Evolution of the Services Marketing Literature", *Journal of Retailing*, 69 (1), 61–103.

Goldsmith, J. (1980). "The Health Care Market: Can Hospitals Survive?", *Harvard Business Review*, 58, 100–12.

Goldsmith, M. and Leebov, W. (1986). "Strengthening the Hospital's Marketing Position Through Training", *Health Care Management Review*, 11, 83–93.

Greene, J. (2015). "Health Care Marketers Reshape Ad Strategies", *Modern Healthcare*, October 30.

Gunawardane, G. (2017). *Service Management: Concepts, Principles and Applications for Sri Lanka*, Dayawansa Jayakody & Company, Colombo, Sri Lanka.

Haefner, M. (2017). "8 Healthcare Marketing Trends For 2018", *Becker's Hospital Review*, October 18, https://www.beckershospitalreview.com/hospital-management-administration/8-healthcare-marketing-trends-for-2018.html. Accessed November 17, 2018.

Health Care Success (2019). "10 Biggest Myths of Healthcare Marketing: Don't Sabotage Your Organization!", https://www.healthcaresuccess.com/blog/healthcare-marketing/healthcare-marketing-myths.html?utm_campaign=HSS%20Newsletter&utm_source=hs_email&utm_medium=email&utm_content=64843411&_hsenc=p2ANqtz--fE_VfdnmL0c1rgj8sa5AZCicbxsIM7gwcGEOncpRTx0lPFKx8eshaFfmqlgEf2MAH49t607lrtMH7e4cmwMOmYYfA4w&_hsmi=64843878. Accessed January 31, 2019.

Hill, R. C. (1988). "A New 'P' for Hospital Marketing?", *Journal of Hospital Marketing*, 2 (2), 5–18.

Jha, S. M. (2000). *Services Marketing*, Himalaya Publishing House, Mumbai, India.

Joint Commission Governance Institute (2009). "Leadership in Healthcare Organizations. A Guide to Joint Commission Leadership Standards", https://www.jointcommission.org/assets/1/18/WP_Leadership_Standards.pdf. Accessed October 1, 2018.

Kotler, P. (1991). *Marketing Management: Analysis, Planning, Implementation, and Control*, 7th ed., Prentice Hall, Upper Saddle River, NJ.

Kunz, W. H. and Hogreve, J. (2011). "Toward a Deeper Understanding of Service Marketing: The Past, Present and the Future", *International Journal of Research in Marketing*, 28, 231–247.

Leone, R., Walker, C., Curry, L., Agee, E. (2012). "Application of a Marketing Concept to Patient-Centered Care: Co-Producing Health with Heart Failure Patients", *OJIN: The Online Journal of Issues in Nursing*, 17 (2), 7.

Leven, E. L. (1984). "Price — A Primer on the 2nd 'P' for Hospital Marketers", *Health Marketing Quarterly*, 2, 33–42.

Malhotra, N. K. (1988). "Health Care Marketing Warfare", *Journal of Health Care Marketing*, 8, 17–29.

Marketing-Schools (2012). "Traditional Marketing Guide", http://www.marketing-schools.org/types-of-marketing/traditional-marketing.html#link1. Accessed October 30, 2018.

Medical Tourism Association (2015). "Facts and Statistics", http://medicaltourism.com/Forms/facts-statistics.aspx. Accessed July 2, 2018.

Nimer, D. A. (1985). "Is Pricing Health Care Services a Marketing Decision?", *Hospital Forum*, 29, 57–58.

OECD (2016). "Medical Tourism: Treatments, Markets and Health System Implications: A Scoping Review", http://www.oecd.org/els/health-systems/48723982.pdf. Accessed October 2, 2018.

Parrington, M. and Stone, B. C. (1991). "The Marketing Decade: A Desktop View", *Journal of Health Care Marketing*, 11 (1), 45–50.

Payne, A. and Frow, P. (2005). "A Strategic Framework for Customer Relationship Management", *Journal of Marketing*, 69 (4), 167–176.

Resnick, L. R. (2017). "Six Healthcare Marketing Trends for 2018", *Managed Healthcare Executive*, November 30, http://www.managedhealthcareexecutive.com/healthcare-executive/six-healthcare-marketing-trends-2018. Accessed July 1, 2018.

Shostack, G. L. (1977), "Breaking Free from Product Marketing", *Journal of Marketing*, 41, 73–80.

Thomas, R. (2008). *Health Services Marketing, A Practitioner's Guide*, Springer-Verlag, New York.

Vargo, S. L. and Lusch, R. F. (2004). "Evolving to a New Dominant Logic for Marketing", *Journal of Marketing*, 68, 1–17.

Vargo, S. L. and Lusch, R. F. (2008). "Service — Dominant Logic: Continuing the Evolution", *Journal of the Academy of Marketing Science*, 36, 1–10.

Weiss, R. (2013). "Modern Marketing Defined: Health Care Marketing's Organizational Impact Cannot be Easily Labelled", *Marketing Health Services*, 33 (1), 12–13.

White, K. and Abrams, M. (2017). "Leveraging the 7P's of Marketing in Healthcare", *Becker's Hospital Review*, March 23, https://www.beckershospitalreview.com/hospital-transactions-and-valuation/leveraging-the-7p-s-of-marketing-in-healthcare.html. Accessed July 7, 2018.

WHO (2015). "Evidence on Global Medical Travel", http://www.who.int/bulletin/volumes/93/11/14-146027/en/. Accessed October 2, 2018.

Wright, R. A. and Stodghill, A. S. (1988). "Physician Marketing Comes of Age", *Journal of Health Care Marketing*, 8, 3.

Zeithaml, V., Bitner, M. J. and Gremler, D. (2018). *Services Marketing*, 7th edn., McGraw-Hill.

Suggested Additional Readings

Altringer, B. (2010). "The Emotional Experience of Patient Care: A Case for Innovation in Health Care Design", *Journal of Health Services Research & Policy*, 15 (3), 174–177.

Bryan, G. O. and Gauff Jr., J. F. (1986). "Marketing 'Health Care Marketing'", *Health Marketing Quarterly*, 3 (4), 11–23.

Cebrzynski, G. (1985). "Marketing, Tradition Clash in Health Care", *Marketing News*, 19 (23), 1–30.

Cellucci, L. W., Wiggins, C. and Farnsworth, E. (2013). *Healthcare Marketing: A Case Study Approach*, 1st edn., Health Administration Press.

Centers for Disease Control and Prevention (CDC) (1995). "Trends in Length of Stay for Hospital Deliveries — United States, 1970–1992", *MMWR Weekly*, 44 (17), 335–337.

Clarke, R. N. (1978). "Marketing Health Care: Problems in Implementation", *Health Care Management Review*, 3 (1), 21–27.

Conick, H. (2017). "Technology No. 1 Concern of Health Care Marketing in 2018", https://www.ama.org/publications/eNewsletters/Marketing-News-Weekly/Pages/technology-top-concern-healthcare-marketing--2018.aspx. Accessed August 3, 2018.

Dodson, D. C. (1985). "Health Care Marketing: Advancements but No Cigar", *Health Marketing Quarterly*, 2 (4), 13–23.

Fredricks, D. (2011). "The Decline of Traditional Health Care Marketing", *Marketing Health Services*, 31 (3), 3–5.

Friedman, A. (2017). "How Digital Marketing Will Change the Health Care Industry", https://www.inc.com/adam-fridman/how-digital-marketing-will-change-the-healthcare-industry.html. Accessed August 5, 2018.

Healthcare Marketing Matters (2012). "Advancing the Vision, Strategy and Leadership of Healthcare Marketing Around the World", March 18, http://healthcaremarketingmatters.blogspot.com/2012/03/has-role-of-healthcare-marketing.html. Accessed October 4, 2018.

MacStravic, R. E. (1990). "The End of Health Care Marketing?", *Health Marketing Quarterly*, 7 (1-2), 3–7.

Mangrolia, A. (2017). "Top 10 Healthcare Marketing Trends for 2018", *Practice Builders*, https://www.practicebuilders.com/blog/top-10-healthcare-marketing-trends-for-2018/. Accessed July 7, 2018.

Prasad, A. (2017). "6 Healthcare Marketing Trends in 2018: How to Leverage Them", November 29, http:// blog.gmrwebteam.com/2018-healthcare-marketing-trends-how-to-leverage-them/. Accessed July 8, 2018.

Trombetta, W. (2011). "Review of The Current Health Care Marketing Literature", *Health Marketing Quarterly*, 19, 1.

Part 2

Health Care Marketing Strategy Formulation and Implementation Process

Chapter 3

Health Care Marketing Strategy Formulation Process

3.1. What is Health Care Marketing Strategy?

Marketing is only one functional area in any business organization. This is true for health care organizations too. In a health care organization such as a hospital, health plan, or a physician group, there are several functional areas, often called "departments". These are finance, human resources, service operations, marketing, management information systems/information technology (MIS/IT), legal, compliance, quality management, claims payment, and customer services/member services.

Each of these functional areas formulate and implement long-term plans and short-term action programs. These long-term plans are called "functional strategies". Marketing strategy of the organization, thus, is a functional strategy just like its finance strategy. The following are examples of marketing strategies and programs:

- The marketing department of a hospital decides to focus on referring physicians to expand its inpatient business. This is a long-term plan and hence a *marketing strategy*. It does not say exactly how the physicians are approached and convinced.
- The marketing department then decides to have six promotional meetings, one in each local city, for area physicians (usually in appealing environments like restaurants). This is an action plan to implement the strategy in the earlier paragraph. This is a *marketing program* (or a marketing campaign).

Does the marketing department of the hospital come up with such strategies and programs arbitrarily on their own? Obviously not. These strategies and programs have to be derived from overall strategies formulated at higher levels (corporate level and business line level).

This chapter will describe this hierarchy of strategic planning, but we need to first clarify the basic concepts and processes.

Therefore, the plan of this chapter is as follows:

- Understand what strategies are;
- Understand that there are strategies applicable to the whole health care organization (e.g., expansion) and strategies applicable to specific product/service lines (e.g., inpatient services);
- Understand that there is a hierarchy in the strategy formulation process: Corporate level, business or product/service line level, and finally, function level (e.g., health care marketing function level);
- Understand how strategies are formulated at each of the three levels and what choices are available at each level ("Strategic Management Process" or "Strategy Planning Process"); and
- Understand what information is needed in this process.

3.2. What are the Strategies at Each Level of the Health Care Organization?

The term "strategy" has many interpretations and usage in business management. Some equate business strategy to a business plan. Others equate business strategy to activities like advertising.

For example, consider a case where the health care marketing department decides to place advertisements at bus stops promoting their dental plan. Is this a "strategy" or is it a marketing activity aimed at achieving the larger objective of expanding the dental patient base within a target geographical area? Also, this decision to place advertisement at bus stops, a decision that would be taken by the marketing department on its own, or is it based on decisions (strategies) formulated by higher level top and middle management?

When a group of physicians formulate a marketing plan to attract more patients to their practice, can we call the business plan their business strategy? Is there a difference between a "business strategy" and "a business plan"?

With such ambiguities, it would be prudent to start by clarifying what "strategy" is in a business context.

In a seminal article "What is Strategy" published in the *Harvard Business Review*, Porter (1996), who is considered the foremost authority on business strategy, describes strategy as follows:

- The essence of strategy is choosing a unique and valuable position rooted in systems of activities that are much more difficult to match.
- Operational effectiveness is necessary but that alone is not sufficient for the long-term survival and growth of an organization.
- A company can outperform its competitors only if it can establish a difference it can preserve for a decade or longer, not for a single planning cycle.

What is evident is that strategies have the following characteristics:

- Aim to achieve a sustainable competitive strength;
- Aim to achieve a difference than what the competitors offer;
- Are long-term directions and not short-term actions like hiring a few more marketers or advertising in newspapers;
- Are usually taken by top management and senior managers of functional areas (marketing, human resource management, finance, operations, and IT);
- Are rare and few in the organization;
- Are major decisions like expansion, downsizing, diversification, mergers, strategic partnerships; and
- Affect all downstream decisions in all functional areas.

An Example of a Strategic Decision in Health Care

A health plan currently engaged only in commercial insurance markets decides to enter the Medicare market. This is a major diversification decision. This is not something the health plan can achieve in a short time; in fact, it will likely take a few years. The health plan will have to offer a product that is different from what competing health plans are offering. The difference can be in terms of lower premiums, additional services, or conveniences like transportation. These form the health care organization's strategy at corporate and business line levels (Medicare, in this case).

Note that marketing activities aimed at the target senior market, such as promotional channels and message content will be decided only after the above strategic decisions are made.

3.2.1. Levels of strategy in the health care organization

The confusion between "strategy", "plans", "action programs", and "policies" stems from the fact that strategies are formulated at different levels of the organization. For example,

- When the Chief Executive Officer (CEO) of a health care organization such as a hospital says that they are entering into a new line of business, e.g., urgent care, and calls it their latest "strategy", that is a correct statement.
- When the Director in charge of this new line of business says that their "strategy" is to offer lower prices, that too is correct.
- Finally, when the marketing department of the hospitals decides to embark on advertising this new service in local newspapers, and calls it their "strategy", that too is correct.

What is happening is that top (corporate), middle (business), and functional (marketing) levels of the hospital are all formulating strategies, that is long-term directions. They, like any medium to large corporation, will formulate and operate under three levels of strategy: corporate-level strategy, business-level strategy, and functional-level strategy.

> Although we are yet to fully discuss health care marketing strategy, we can see from the existence of aforementioned three levels of strategy in a business organization that marketing strategies, e.g., health care marketing strategies, fall under this third category. As such, health care marketing strategy cannot be made in isolation. They are derived from business-level strategies, which are derived, in turn, from corporate-level strategies.

- *Corporate-level strategy*: Corporate strategy refers to the overall strategy of the firm. A corporate strategy answers questions such as "in which businesses should we compete?" and "how does being in these businesses create or add to the competitive advantage of the corporation as a whole?" For example, corporate-level strategy of a hospital may include expanding its emergency services.

- *Business-level strategy*: Business strategy refers to the key strategy of a single line of business of the firm or a given product/service in a multi-product/service organization.

  For example, a health plan having made the corporate-level strategic decision to go into Medicare Advantage program business will now have to decide what strategies would enable the organization to successfully compete with other health plans in the area engaged in the Medicare Advantage program business. This is what we referred earlier as, "aim to achieve a difference than what the competitors offer".

  According to Michael Porter, a firm has the following choices in formulating business-level (product/service line) strategy:

  o *Cost leadership*: Cost leadership is defined as being able to provide a cost–benefit advantage to the consumer/patient or health care providers that the health plan desires to have in its network of providers. Cost leadership is basically providing the lowest cost service in the industry. The service will not have the highest quality or variety, but the quality will be comparable to the competing services that also have low costs.
  o *Differentiation*: Differentiation is defined as providing something different, if unique, in terms of value, to consumer/patient or health care providers. These could include enhanced access (e.g., a larger network of physicians and hospitals, or online access to medical records and appointment scheduling), enhanced quality of service, a larger array of services or benefits, or improved customer services and enhanced customer/patient experience. Improving the service process to provide a better service experience is a key modern day differentiation strategy. In other words, the output of the service (e.g., a medical encounter where the patient is correctly diagnosed and treated) is the same as before; the process the patient goes through has the same sequence; however, the overall patient experience can be improved by providing better facilities and waiting areas, useful information, fairness in scheduling, etc.
  o *Focus*: This is the decision on what segment/niche of customers/patients to focus on, i.e., what segment/niche would likely be attracted by a cost leadership or a specific differentiation strategy?

Note that selecting a focused group of customers will be complete only if the organization is clear on what would be provided to this selected group, i.e., low cost or some form of differentiation.

> The correct way to understand business-level strategy is to realize that the two options are as follows:
>
> (1) Cost leadership for a focused segment of consumers/patients, and
> (2) Differentiation and the type of differentiation (quality, variety, access, flexibility, or customer experience) for a focused segment of consumers/patients.

- *Functional-level strategy*: Functional level in a health care organization consists of what are usually called departments such as quality management, utilization review, human resources, finance, *marketing*, customer service, and MIS/IT. As such, our activity of interest in this book, namely health care marketing, is usually conducted by a department, namely the marketing department, at the functional level in the health care organization's structure. These departments will be formulating strategies for their departments such as marketing strategies, new product development strategies, human resource strategies, financial strategies, legal strategies, supply-chain strategies, and information technology management strategies. The emphasis is on short- and medium-term plans and is limited to the domain of each department's functional responsibility. Each functional department, like our health care marketing department, will do its part in meeting overall corporate objectives and the selected business-level (product line level) strategy.

Thus, health care marketing strategy is a functional-level strategy. There will be a marketing strategy for each product line, e.g.,

- *In a health plan*: Medicare products, Medicaid products, and Commercial insurance products.
- *In a hospital*: Outpatient services, inpatient services, and emergency services.
- *In a retirement home*: Independent living services, assisted living services, and skilled nursing services.
- *In a pharmaceutical company*: Over-the-counter drugs, prescription drugs, and specialty drugs.
- *In a physician group*: Primary care services or selected specialist services.

For each product line, a marketing plan will be formulated according to the selected business-level strategy:

- Cost leadership for a focused segment of consumers/patients, or
- Differentiation and the type of differentiation (quality, variety, access, flexibility, or customer experience) for a focused segment of consumers/patients.

The marketing plan will define the marketing mix (discussed in Chapter 9). Marketing mix will define the particular service marketed (e.g., inpatient services in a hospital), whom marketing will be focused on (e.g., referring physicians), what unique values of this hospital's inpatient services should be highlighted, cost–benefits of this hospital's inpatient services over competing hospitals, and metrics to measure success of marketing activities.

Example: Corporate Strategy to Business Strategy, then to Functional Strategies

A private hospital is adding a new service for children. This is a corporate-level strategy of diversification. At business-level strategy making, the hospital has decided that the services will be limited to primary and secondary care services (i.e., no tertiary-level advanced services and surgeries). This, therefore, is a cost leadership strategy. Hospital will set up only basic equipment for limited scope of diagnosis and treatment. It will not need to hire nursing staff with long experience in tertiary-level hospitals. It will establish a referral network of facilities for service beyond the limited scope of children's services at this hospital. These are all functional strategies. Note that the functional-level strategies are consistent with business-level strategies, and the latter are consistent with the corporate-level strategies.

3.3. Strategic Planning Process in the Health Care Organization I: Vision, Mission and Values

Strategies at all three levels are not formulated arbitrarily. There is a formal process for doing so.

Strategies are based on the health care organization's *Vision, Mission and Values*.

3.3.1. Mission statements vs. vision statements

Although they are often thought of as equivalent and are almost always used together, mission and vision statements serve different purposes. A mission statement is what a business defines as its purpose today. Vision statements are what the organization wishes to be in the future. Vision statements indicate the larger scenario the health care wishes to be, and consumers and society will see the organization as, in the future, e.g., leading high-technology hospitals in USA. The following examples will illustrate these concepts:

- *A vision statement* of the health care organization outlines what the organization wants to be in the future.
- *A mission statement* describes what the organization wants to do now. It is there for all levels of management and staff to know what services the organization is limited to (and what services the organization is not in), the markets focused, and the service delivery strategy (such as a variety of services with many options for the customer or a standard, low-cost, and reasonable quality service).
- *Values* represent core priorities in the organization's culture. Values often emphasized by health care organizations include honesty and integrity, customer care, equal treatment of all customers, and preservation of environment.

Example 1: Mayo Clinic (https://mayoclinichealthsystem.org/locations/eau-claire/about-us/mission-vision-and-value-statements).

Mission: To inspire hope and contribute to health and well-being by providing the best care to every patient through integrated clinical practice, education, and research.

Vision: Mayo Clinic will provide an unparalleled experience as the most trusted partner for health care.

Values: The needs of the patient come first.

Example 2: Cedars-Sinai Medical Center, a non-profit, independent health care organization based in Los Angeles, California, USA (https://www.cedars-sinai.org/about/mission.html).

Mission Statement: Leadership and excellence in delivering quality healthcare services; Expanding the horizons of medical knowledge through biomedical research; Educating and training physicians and other healthcare professionals; Strive to improve the health status of the community; Quality patient care is our priority. Providing excellent clinical and service quality, offering compassionate care, and supporting research and medical education are essential to our mission. This mission is founded in the ethical and cultural precepts of the Judaic tradition, which inspire devotion to the art and science of healing and to the care we give our patients and staff.

Strategic Vision: Cedars-Sinai will continue as the leading healthcare organization in Los Angeles, while enhancing its position as a recognized leader among the nation's most respected, admired, and trusted healthcare organizations. In fulfilling this role, Cedars-Sinai will:

- Demonstrate national leadership in providing high value healthcare and delivering excellent clinical quality, patient safety, and service.
- Drive transformation and innovation in care delivery, and more fully engage our patients in their wellness and care.
- Advance the frontiers of medicine and science through a major ongoing commitment to biomedical research and medical education.
- Expand and strengthen its regional, national, and international position as a model health system that delivers high value services at all sites of care, including physical interactions in physician offices and clinics, ambulatory and outpatient centers, and inpatient facilities, as well as through electronic and other remote linkages.

To achieve this, Cedars-Sinai will:

- Attract and enhance relationships with the best and most respected physicians, scientists, nurses, other healthcare professionals and staff, sharing institutional commitments to leadership, quality, and value.
- Reach out to a broader and more diverse Los Angeles community, serving as a model for other healthcare organizations in providing a wide range of community benefit and community service programs.
- Provide superior facilities, as well as leading edge medical and information technology.
- Maintain a secure financial base including a growing endowment, enhancing Cedars-Sinai's long-term ability to achieve its Mission and Vision.
- Consider partnerships and affiliations with other leading high quality healthcare organizations and other industry participants.

Our Values: In the pursuit of this vision, the actions of leadership, staff and other physicians will be guided by the following values:

- Integrity
- Excellence
- Teamwork and collaboration
- Respect
- Compassion
- Innovation
- Stewardship
- Efficiency
- Diversity.

3.3.2. Importance of developing detailed vision, mission, and value statements in the health care organization

- *Mission statements* are for the organization itself, to clarify to management and employees of the organization the purpose and objectives of the organization. A mission statement will keep management and employees focused on the key purpose and objectives of the health care organization and prevents them from deviating and wasting scarce resources aiming at other purposes. The mission statement attracts and retains employees who like the mission.

  For example, Grace Health serving over 30,000 patients in Calhoun County, Florida has a simple mission statement: "To provide patient-centered healthcare with excellence in quality, service, and access." This gets management and employees to focus on the patient-centered care concept in modern health care. With effective training and orientation, management and employees can be taught the elements of patient-centered care such as caring for patients (and their families) in ways that are meaningful and valuable to the individual patient, and that would require listening to, communicating important information to, and continuous engagement of patients and families.

- *Vision statements*, unlike mission statements, do not provide detailed directions to plan and execute action plans of the health care organization. Nevertheless, it is essential for strategic planning. It attracts investors and top management who share the same long-term vision.

  Becker's Hospital Review (2012) describes how a hospital in Georgia that was losing millions of dollars had a low market share and losing employees set

a new vision to be one of the *Fortune* magazine's 100 best companies to work for and become one of the top 100 hospitals in the country. In five years, the hospital reached both these goals and started making profit. The article makes the important point that this was possible because, "Strategic planning framework was strong, and vision were clear, bold, inspiring and time bound."
- *Value statements* define the health care organization's basic philosophy, principles, and ideals. They describe the organization's emphasis on ethical practices in health care delivery, management, and marketing. As described earlier in this book, and discussed in detail in Chapter 13, ethical considerations play a major role in modern health care marketing. As such, the organization and its management clearly declaring its values is important.

> Although vision, mission, and values statements form an essential foundation for formulating strategy of the health care organization, simply writing them out will not be sufficient. Strategic planning must be conducted following a systematic process involving careful study of external and internal factors. This process is discussed in Section 3.4.

3.4. Strategic Planning Process in the Health Care Organization II: Complete Process

The strategy planning process in the health care organization follows the following steps:

Step 1: An Examination of the Organization's External Environment

The external environment of a health care organization consists of the economic environment, legal and political environment, competition, health care providers (physicians, diagnostic services, and ancillary providers), and suppliers/subcontractors needed to provide health care services, trends in consumer/patient behavior and decision-making, trends in societal needs, trends in technology affecting the industry, and trends in global health care services and marketing. Forecasting the future trends in these factors and identifying opportunities and potential threats must be done.

A key element in the external environment of a health care organization is its competition, unless, of course, the organization is a public health organization which is federal and state run. Studying the competition of any organization is a huge task. The best-known method for analyzing industry competition is the "Five Factor Model" developed by Porter. This model is discussed in Chapter 5.

Step 2: An Examination of the Organization's Internal Environment

Internal environment of an organization consists of its vision and mission, and strengths and weaknesses in functional areas (finance, marketing, human resources, operations, and information technology), organization structure, and the corporate culture.

Steps 1 and 2 are called "Environmental Analysis".

Step 3: Matching Opportunities and Threats of the External Environment with Strengths and Weaknesses of the Organization (Internal Environment)

This is usually referred to as the SWOT analysis. The term SWOT is derived from internal environment strengths (S) and weaknesses (W) and external environment opportunities (O) and threats (T). For details, see Wheelen *et al.* (2015). An example of SWOT analysis in a health care organization is shown in Figure 3.1.

The SWOT enables the health care organization to focus on organizational and product line-level strategies (directions) in the next few years to come. For example,

- A health plan might realize that the competition in commercial health insurance is fierce and that it does not have the resources and know-how to battle competitors. The health plan might decide to give up commercial insurance line of business and rethink its vision/mission and reallocate its resources toward, say, government-sponsored health products such as Medicare and Medicaid.
- A health plan might realize that there are supplementary funds available for emergency care for consumers without health insurance, and thus expand its emergency services unit and staff.

> Following a SWOT analysis, the health care organization's vision and mission may be revised. The organization may realize that its vision and mission are too ambitious and may want to lower its objectives. For example, eliminating certain product lines or operating regions.

Health Care Marketing Strategy Formulation Process 55

Figure 3.1. SWOT analysis for a health care organization.
Source: Reprinted with permission from Healthcare Success (2019).

Step 4: Formulating Corporate (High) Level Strategies

This involves formulating the health care organization's revised mission and long-term objectives followed by formulating corporate (high) level strategies such as

- *Expansion*: Introducing new services, expanding current services, and opening new facilities.
- *Downsizing*: Eliminating certain services or reallocating services at given facilities.
- *Diversification*: Changing the product/service mix and adding new services.
- *Vertical integration*: Expanding into activities in the service supply chain or outsourcing certain current activities. For example, a health plan sub-contracting its enrollment function to a licensed marketing organization, or a physician group delegating certain management functions to a Management Service Organization (MSO).
- *Mergers and acquisitions*: Forming mergers and strategic partnerships with competitors, suppliers, and customer segments.

Step 5: Selecting Competitive Strategies for Each Health Care Service/Line of Business

For example, on what strengths are we going to compete in the market for our Medicare Advantage products or our assisted living programs?

Should we compete on low cost or differentiation (providing a service with a difference)? These were discussed in Section 3.1 as cost leadership and differentiation. These are also called business-level strategies or service market strategies.

> Formulating good corporate-level strategies and good business line-level competitive strategies requires a thorough analysis of the competition. The "Five Factor Model" developed by Porter for analyzing the competition is discussed in Chapter 5.

Step 6: Decisions on Long-Term Needs of Each Functional Area (Marketing, Finance, Operations, Human Resources, and IT)

Each functional area must be prepared to support the chosen corporate- and business-level strategies. This step called formulation of functional strategies was also discussed previously in Section 3.1. Note that this is where health care marketing strategies are formulated.

Corporate-level, competitive/business-level, and functional-level strategies together form the service organization's strategy package, i.e., the organization's long-term directions.

Step 7: Defining the Service Concept, Formulating Policies, Short-Term Programs, and Budgets to Fit the Chosen Strategies

In this final step, the *health care service concept* is defined, that is how the health care service should be designed in line with the business-level strategy (cost leadership or differentiation) decided upon in Step 5.

Sasser *et al.* (1978) describe the "service concept" as a bundle of elements packaged to be sold to the customer. The service concept has been conceptualized as the way in which the "organization would like to have its services perceived by its customers, employees, shareholders and lenders" (Heskett, 1986) and "a bundle of goods and services" (Anderson *et al.*, 2008, p. 365), defining the "how" and the "what" of service design, helping the mediation between customer needs and the organization's strategic intent. The service concept is used to develop new services, being "the central component in designing services" (Goldstein *et al.*, 2002). For a detailed description of the evolution of the service concept, see Paulišić *et al.* (2016).

According to Johnston *et al.* (2012), the service concept is an attempt to create a clear, agreed, shared, and articulated definition of the nature of the service provided and received, in order to ensure that the essence of the service is delivered. In this way, the service concept is a shared view and is articulated in detail so operations could know how the health care service should be delivered and the marketers would know to present the value of the service to market participants (Paulišić *et al.*, 2016).

Health care service delivery is designed according to the health care service concept. Elements of health care service design are as follows:

- Core attributes of the health care service, e.g., patient care, patient–physician encounter, patient–nursing and other staff encounters.
- Peripheral attributes: Supporting services, such as appointment scheduling, customer service, medical record maintenance, billing, and physical attributes, such as facilities and goods used in the service (e.g., forms).
- Information systems.
- Customer participation level, level of automation including customer self-service, if any.
- Facility design: Front and back office design, capacity planning, waiting areas, and waiting time management.
- Providing multilanguage and multicultural assistance.
- Interactional and emotional attributes such as customer/patient satisfaction and customer experience.

In summary, service design should not be done arbitrarily. Service design should follow the service concept which is derived from service strategy. Service design should address multiple factors and issues discussed above.

Development of the health care service concept will be followed by:

- Establishing policies and procedures of the health care organization;
- Designing action plans, such as the marketing plan; and
- Budgets for implementing programs and plans.

Thus, the strategy formulation and implementation process of the health care organization can be summarized as follows:

- o Environmental scanning
- o SWOT analysis
- o Revised mission statement
- o Strategies: Corporate, business line, and functional strategy including *marketing strategy*
- o Health care service concept for each service line
- o Health care service and marketing design
- o Policies
- o Programs/Actions (for service delivery and marketing), and
- o Budgets

3.5. Information Needed for Strategic Planning

A variety of information is needed in the health care organization's strategy planning process. These will be discussed in later chapters of the book.

Much of the information needed in this process arises during the analysis of the external environment of the organization. These are as follows:

- Market and marketing research. Chapter 4 is devoted for this subject.
- Understanding the competition, overall and in each market segment. This is discussed in Chapter 5.
- Understanding consumer/patient characteristics and behavior. This is addressed in Chapter 6.
- Understanding customer/patient experience in health care. This subject is addressed in Chapter 7.
- Trends and advances in technology, especially digital technology that provides a framework for selecting strategies. Chapter 10 covers issues relating to integrating digital technology into health care marketing.
- Legal and ethical issues governing strategic choices and implementing strategy including marketing strategies and programs. These are discussed in Chapter 13.

3.6. From Formulating Health Care Marketing Strategy to Implementation

Previously in this chapter, we saw that health care marketing strategy is a functional-level strategy of the health care organization. There will be a marketing strategy for each product line such as Medicare Advantage products, Medicaid products, senior living products, various pharmaceutical products, and different physician specialties.

The strategic planning and implementation processes we saw previously were (1) Environmental scanning; (2) SWOT analysis; (3) Revised mission statement; (4) Strategies: Corporate, business line, and functional strategy including *marketing strategy*; (5) Health care service concept for each service line; (6) Health care service and marketing design; (7) Policies; (8) Programs/Actions (for service delivery and marketing); and (9) Budgets.

The steps highlighted above come within health care marketing.

Health care marketing would pick up from the health care service concept for each service line and market segment and formulate a marketing plan for each product/service line and each market segment/niche. Market segmentation is discussed in Chapter 8.

The first step in formulating a marketing plan is defining the *marketing mix* for each product/service line within each market segment. The *health care marketing mix* consists of product, price, place, promotion, people (employees of the service organization, especially contact staff), process, and physical evidence (tangibles such as facilities, equipment, and supporting material) (White and Abrams, 2017; Zeithaml *et al.*, 2018).

Health care marketing mix is discussed in Chapter 9.

References

Anderson, S., Pearo, L. K. and Widener, S. K. (2008). "Drivers of Service Satisfaction Linking Customer Satisfaction to the Service Concept and Customer Characteristics", *Journal of Service Research*, 10 (4), 365–381.

Becker's Hospital Review (2012). "Strategic Planning Framework: The Importance of Vision", October 12, https://www.beckershospitalreview.com/strategic-planning/strategic-planning-framework-the-importance-of-vision.html. Accessed February 9, 2019.

Goldstein, S. M., Johnston, R., Duffy, J. and Rao, J. (2002). "The Service Concept: The Missing Link in Service Design Research?", *Journal of Operations Management*, 20 (2), 121–134.

Healthcare Success (2019). "SWOT: The High-Level Self-Exam that Boosts Your Bottom Line", https://www.healthcaresuccess.com/blog/medical-advertising-agency/swot.html. Accessed February 10, 2019.

Heskett, J. L. (1986). *Managing in the Service Economy*, Boston, MA: Harvard Business School Press.
Johnston, R., Clark, G. and Shulver, M. (2012) *Service Operations Management: Improving Service Delivery*, 4th ed., Pearson.
Mayo Clinic (2019). "Vision, Mission and Value", https://mayoclinichealthsystem.org/locations/eau-claire/about-us/mission-vision-and-value-statements. Accessed February 9, 2019.
Paulišić, M., Tanković, A. C. and Hrvatin, M. (2016). "Managing the Service Concept in Creating an Innovative Tourism Product", *Tourism & Hospitality Industry Congress Proceedings*, 232–249.
Porter, M. E. (1996). "What is Strategy?", *Harvard Business Review*, 74 (6), 61.
Sasser, W. E., Olsen, R. P. and Wyckoff, D. D. (1978). *Management of Service Operations: Text, Cases, and Readings*, Allyn & Bacon.
Wheelen, T. L., Hunger, D., Hoffman, A. N. and Bamford, C. E. (2015). *Strategic Management and Business Policy: Globalization, Innovation and Sustainability*, 14th edn., Pearson.
White, K. and Abrams, M. (2017). "Leveraging the 7P's of Marketing in Healthcare", March 23, *Becker's Hospital Review*, https://www.beckershospitalreview.com/hospital-transactions-and-valuation/leveraging-the-7p-s-of-marketing-in-healthcare.html. Accessed February 3, 2019.
Zeithaml, V., Bitner, M. J. and Gremler, D. (2018). *Services Marketing*, 7th edn., McGraw-Hill.

Suggested Additional Readings

Khanna, R. (2013). "Segmentation of the Healthcare Customer Base", March 7, http://www.pmlive.com/pharma_news/segmentation_of_the_healthcare_customer_base_466335.
Kotler, P., Shalowitz, J. and Stevens, R. J. (2008). *Strategic Marketing for Health Care Organizations: Building a Customer-Driven Health System*. John Wiley & Sons.
Nasution, R. A., Sembada, A. Y., Miliani, L., Resti, N. D. and Prawono, D. A. (2014). "The Customer Experience Framework as Baseline for Strategy and Implementation in Services Marketing", *Procedia — Social and Behavioral Sciences*, 148, 254–261.
Porter, M. E. (1980). *Competitive Strategy*, New York, NY: Free Press.
Porter, M. E. (2008). "The Five Competitive Forces That Shape Strategy", *Harvard Business Review*, 86 (1), 78–93.
Porter, M. E. and Teisberg, E. O. (2004). "Redefining Competition in Health Care", *Harvard Business Review*, 82 (6), 64–76.

Smith, W. R. (1956). "Product Differentiation and Market Segmentation as Alternative Marketing Strategies", *Journal of Marketing*, 21 (1), 3–8.
Tracy, B. (2014). "The 7 Ps of Marketing", *Healthcare Success*, https://www.healthcaresuccess.com/blog/medical-advertising-agency/the-7-ps-of-marketing.html.

Chapter 4

Health Care Market and Marketing Research

4.1. Market Research vs. Marketing Research in Health Care

As discussed in the previous chapter, environmental analysis is the first step in a health care organization's strategic planning. Environment analysis has two components: the external environment and the internal environment. The external environment consists of the external factors that have an impact on the future of the health care industry and the future of the health care organization's lines of business.

The factors in the external environment of the health care industry are the economy, laws and regulations, competition, consumer behavior, social values, technological developments, suppliers, and global economic and health care market trends. Of these external environment factors, comparatively more important for health care marketing are competition, customer/consumer behavior, technology, laws and regulations, suppliers, and global trends. This book will devote a chapter on each of these six factors.

To study the opportunities and threats in these factors, the health care organization needs reliable information relevant to each factor. This chapter is about gathering such information.

We will first clarify two concepts related to research undertaken to gather this information. These concepts are *market research* and *marketing research*.

Market research focuses on all external environment factors of the health care organization discussed earlier in Chapter 3, i.e., competition, consumers, technology, laws and regulations, suppliers/partners, and economic/political/

legal/social/global trends. *This is the "market" for the health care organization.*

- According to the Entrepreneur's Small Business Encyclopedia (Conner, 2016), market research is: "The process of gathering, analyzing and interpreting information about a market, about a product or service to be offered for sale in that market, and about the past, present and potential customers for the product or service; research into the characteristics, spending habits, location and needs of your business's target market, the industry as a whole, and the particular competitors you face."
- Market research is performed at the initial strategic planning levels of the organization. Greater interest is usually paid to the key factors: competition, customers, technology and suppliers/partners (called the task environment, Wheelan *et al.*, 2015).
- Findings from market research are then combined with strengths and weaknesses of the internal environment of the organization to perform *SWOT analysis* leading to formulation of corporate strategy, business (product/service line-level) strategy and finally functional strategy (which includes marketing strategy).
- Market segmentation, discussed in Chapter 8, is an outcome of the corporate/business-level strategy formulation phase. *Information needed for market segmentation, thus, comes from market research.*

Marketing research involves research related to marketing.

- *American Marketing Association (AMA) definition of marketing research*: "The systematic and objective identification, collection, analysis and dissemination of information for the purpose of improving decision making related to the identification and solution of problems and opportunities in marketing." (AMA, 2017)
- Starting from marketing strategy, marketing research studies how best to plan and implement the 7P marketing mix relating to the particular service (market segment). The 7P marketing mix is discussed in Chapter 9.

> In summary, market research is gathering information and data about external environment factors and marketing research is research performed to identify the most effective marketing strategies and methods.

For example, say, a retirement homes/assisted living service provider is interested in knowing the best strategies and methods to promote their retirement homes. The first step this service provider might take is gathering information on older health care consumers' behavior, especially the sources of information they rely on to make health care-related decisions. The service provider might conduct their own surveys or research the internet for secondary sources of information on these aspects of senior consumer behavior. The provider will also study the competition in the relevant geographical area and several other relevant factors in the external environment. This is market research.

Let us assume that this service provider finds out that the percentage of seniors using the internet for health-related information is low and that they depend more on opinions and advice of their physician and family members. Therefore, the service provider might study surveys conducted regularly by the industry to determine the sources of information physicians and consumers depend on to select or advise others on selection of retirement homes. A retirement home company would access such sources on the internet or conduct their own surveys. This step is a part of marketing research.

Market research and marketing research often involve same information. Therefore, research, data collection, and data analysis are typically conducted simultaneously and in an integrated fashion. For example, a survey of hospital patients may be conducted from which a demographic pattern of the patients (an element of market research) as well as communication methods preferred by the patients may be determined (an element of marketing research).

Conner (2016) explains this by stating, "The terms overlap, but it's safe to conclude that market research is a subset of marketing research." Surbhi (2015) explains this further by saying that market research is a study undertaken to collect information about the market statistics whereas marketing research is the systematic and objective study, analysis, and interpretation of problem related to marketing activities.

The two concepts — market research and marketing research — overlap. And the two activities are conducted simultaneously. Some writers prefer to use market research as the core activity and marketing research as the subactivity, and others follow the opposite. In this book, we will use the two terms as synonyms.

> The purpose of the marketing/market research activity of the health care organization (e.g., a hospital, a health plan, a physician group, or a pharmaceutical company) is to gather information about the organizations' relevant market or markets and perform market segmentation in order to focus on target marketing.

4.2. Market Research: Overview of Steps

Market/Marketing research must be conducted in a systematic way. The typical steps in this process can be summarized as follows (DeVault, 2017; Kotler, 2003):

- Problem statement and setting objectives of the study;
- Developing the overall research plan;
- Data and information collection;
- Data and information analysis;
- Presenting and disseminating the findings; and
- Using the findings to make decisions on market segmentation, service concepts, and marketing mix(es).

4.2.1. Problem statement and setting objectives of the study

This is probably the most important step in the process. Often health care organizations define the scope of a market research project too broadly or two narrowly. Questions to address are as follows:

- Are we studying the entire health care industry or a segment of the industry such as the senior health care consumer market?
- Are we interested in a specific geographic area such as a specific state or county?
- Are we studying a specific product such as commercial insurance products in each selected county?

The problem statement can be generated by open discussions among top management, functional area management, and in particular, the marketing staff of the health care organization. These could take place by:

- Asking broad questions such as "How large is the expected market in senior care in California?" or
- Formulating hypothesis such as, "Social media promotion is more effective than traditional promotional methods such as TV and newspapers for marketing ACA/Obamacare exchange plans."

4.2.2. Developing the overall research plan

The scope and scale of the research plan must fit the information already available within the organization, additional information that is essential to formulate marketing strategies and plans, and the budget available for the marketing research exercise. Often, health care organizations get carried away by outside consultants who sell the organization large-scale market research projects beyond the basic needs of the organization.

Following are questions that must be addressed by the management of the health care organization:

- What information and data should be gathered? And how?
- What information and data do we already have on hand from previous studies and our recent activities? A good example is a health plan that has large amounts of grievance/complaint data from their enrollees.
- What other secondary data are readily available from government, research organizations, and industry sources?
- Online data collection, and surveys and polls available on the Web. Forums and chat rooms sponsored by the organization.
- Are there useful secondary information and data that can be purchased? There are several such sources to purchase secondary data from. Some of these are listed later in the chapter.

> A notable development affecting health care market/marketing research is the advent of *Big Data*. Basically, the concept of Big Data highlights that there is, nowadays, an abundance of data (see Kaden *et al.*, 2012, "Data has moved from being a scarce commodity to a burdensome surplus"), and that this makes it more difficult for health care data analysts and managers to decide which data provide a more valid representation of the issue being studied as all data from various sources may not be consistent. See Chapter 10 for a discussion on managing big data in health care marketing.

- Do we really have to conduct our own surveys and collect primary data? This is usually an expensive, time consuming, and complex exercise which should not be undertaken by smaller health care providers and organizations. Outside research agencies are, of course, available for such surveys and analysis but they are not inexpensive.

If primary data collection is selected as part of the project, consider various methods to do this. Primary data collection methods include inexpensive methods such as the Delphi Method which is a survey of knowledgeable persons both in and outside the organization, use of questionnaires and comment cards given to customers and patients, personal interviews, telephone interviews, and focus groups. Primary data can also be collected using formal scientific surveys which are quite expensive. See Section 4.2.3 for a detailed discussion on primary and secondary data collection.

- Evaluate the legal and ethical issues in collecting and using data as determined in the research plan. Some secondary data may be owned by third parties. Privacy of information acts (such as the Health Insurance Portability and Accountability Act of 1996, also called HIPAA) prohibit the use of individually identifiable information of members and patients.
- Evaluate the cost of the research plan. Add all the aforementioned items and evaluate the cost and benefit of alternative choices. Remember that in many health care marketing situations, inexpensive informal research methods yield enough information the organization's management and marketing staff can absorb. Formal expensive methods are often too complex for management and marketers to understand and use.

4.2.3. Data/Information collection

Data and information collected in marketing research as well as other health care-related studies fall into the following two categories (Rural Health Information Hub, 2018):

- *Qualitative data* is descriptive data that is often used to capture the context around the outcomes of the program. Qualitative data collection strategies that may be used include interviews, focus groups, and qualitative program reviews.
- *Quantitative data* is numeric data that can be counted to show how much change has occurred as a result of the program. Quantitative data can be collected from surveys, questionnaires, or program tracking materials.

Qualitative data and the associated analysis are intuitive and easy for health care managers to understand as opposed to quantitative data and accompanying analysis which normally use mathematical and statistical methods. Methods used in collecting qualitative data are quite familiar to health care managers and are readily acceptable to them than formal surveys designed by outside experts. These methods are (outlined in a publication by Substance Abuse and Mental Health Services Administration, 2008) as follows:

- Observation, e.g., consumers and patient behavior;
- Discussions at management meetings;
- Focus groups;
- Interviews; and
- Consulting industry managers and experts.

> Therefore, qualitative data analysis is often preferred in practical health care management and marketing studies. Al-Busaidi (2008) confirms this and states that recently, there has been a greater acceptance of the qualitative approach, even as a stand-alone method, in health care research. He also points out that more qualitative research articles are published in health-related journals, in addition to a new qualitative research journal, called *Qualitative Health Research*.

- Gathering data/information available within the organization. Data and information collection in health care marketing research should always start within the organization. Health care organizations such as hospitals, health plans, and physician groups have an abundance of clinical data, utilization data, quality management data, and complaints and grievances data. Extreme care must be exercised to use only aggregate data and not personal individually identifiable data of customers, patients, or health plan members.
- Gathering secondary data as determined by the research plan (see Section 4.3).
- Primary data collection as determined by aforementioned steps of the research plan if this is part of the overall research plan (see Section 4.4).

4.2.4. Data/Information analysis

The first step here would be a review of collected data for completeness and validity. Many surveys yield incomplete and ambiguous responses. Though these are more than often due to improper survey designs, the responses, nevertheless, should be examined and cleaned up.

Data analysis methods include the following:

- *Qualitative data analysis*: This is the most common method undertaken by small to medium size health care providers and organizations. It basically avoids sophisticated statistical analysis and uses simpler methods like averages, extrapolations, and subjective discussion and analysis by managers. See Kawaulich (2004) for a comprehensive list of methods used in qualitative analysis of data where she also states, "Analyzing qualitative data typically involves immersing oneself in the data to become familiar with it, then looking for patterns and themes, searching for various relationships between data ..."
- *Quantitative data analysis*: Quantitative data analysis uses statistical methods to analyze data. These include means, standard deviations, simple and multiple regression, discriminant analysis, factor analysis, cluster analysis, and conjoint analysis.

4.2.4.1. Which type of data analysis is more suited for health care marketing research?

Moffatt *et al.* (2006) conducted a mixed methods study to examine whether there are discrepancies between qualitative and quantitative research data. This study evaluated whether welfare rights advice has an impact on health and social outcomes among a population aged 60 and over. They collected quantitative and qualitative data contemporaneously. Quantitative data were collected from 126 men and women aged over 60 within a randomized controlled trial. Participants received a full welfare benefits assessment which successfully identified additional financial and non-financial resources for 60% of them. A range of demographic, health, and social outcome measures were assessed at baseline, 6, 12, and 24 months follow-up. Qualitative data were collected from a subsample of 25 participants purposively selected to take part in individual interviews to examine the perceived impact of welfare rights advice.

Separate analysis of the quantitative and qualitative data revealed discrepant findings.

- The quantitative data showed little evidence of significant differences of a size that would be of practical or clinical interest, suggesting that the intervention had no impact on these outcome measures.
- The qualitative data suggested wide-ranging impacts, indicating that the intervention had a positive effect.

4.2.4.2. Conclusion

The study demonstrated how using mixed methods can lead to different and sometimes conflicting accounts. The authors saw a positive effect in these conflicting viewpoints in that it led to multiple and useful insights. Not only does this enhance the robustness of the study, it may lead to different conclusions from those that would have been drawn through relying on one method alone and demonstrated the value of collecting both types of data within a single study. More widespread use of mixed methods in trials of complex interventions is likely to enhance the overall quality of the evidence base.

> Use of mixed methods that rely on qualitative data and quantitative data, and subsequent data analysis using qualitative as well as quantitative techniques seem to be more useful in health care market/marketing research.

- *Presenting or disseminating the findings*: Use the findings to make decisions on market segmentation, service concepts, and marketing mix(es).

4.3. Use of Secondary Data Sources for Health Care Market/Marketing Research

4.3.1. Definition of secondary data

Secondary data are information that have been collected for a purpose other than one's current research project but have some relevance and utility for the research project.

4.3.2. Sources of secondary data

You can break the sources of secondary data into internal sources and external sources. Internal sources include data that exist and are stored inside your organization. External data are data that are collected by other people or organizations from your organization's external environment.

Let us dig a little deeper into each of these general categories.

Examples of internal sources of data include, but are certainly not limited to, the following:

- Profit and loss statements;
- Balance sheets;
- Sales figures;
- Inventory records; and
- Previous market and marketing research studies.

4.3.3. External sources of data for health care market/ marketing research

If the secondary data collected from internal sources are not sufficient, one can turn to external sources of data. Some external sources include the following:

- Government sources, such as the US Census Bureau;
- Corporate filings, such as annual reports to the US Securities and Exchange Commission (SEC);
- Trade, business, and professional associations;
- Media, including broadcast, print, and internet;
- Universities;
- Foundations; and
- Think tanks, such as the Rand Corporation or Brookings Institute;
- Commercial data services, which are businesses that find the data for a fee.

4.3.4. Useful secondary data sources for health care marketing research

Table 4.1 lists the useful secondary data sources for health care marketing research, including a small sample of health and population statistics.

Table 4.1. Useful Secondary Sources for Health Care Marketing Research

Sources	Remarks
The Agency for Healthcare Research and Quality (AHRQ). See https://www.ahrq.gov/research/data/dataresources/index.html.	Online, searchable databases. Data on topics such as the use of health care, the costs of care, health care systems, trends in hospital care, health insurance coverage, out-of-pocket spending, patient satisfaction, accessibility of care, ambulatory surgeries, emergency department visits, health care disparities, health care quality, health care spending, hospitalizations, and state-specific health care information.
National Information Center on Health Services Research and Health Care Technology (NICHSR). See https://www.nlm.nih.gov/nichsr/usestats/sources.html.	—
Centers for Medicare & Medicaid Services (CMS) Program Statistics — CMS, HHS	—
CMS Research, Statistics, Data & Systems — CMS, HHS	
Medicare Enrollment Dashboard — CMS, HHS	
Adult Obesity Facts — Centers for Disease Control and Prevention (CDC), HHS	—
AgingStats.gov — National Center for Health Statistics (NCHS), CDC, National Institute on Aging (NIA), NIH	—
Ambulatory Health Care Data — NCHS, CDC	—
Behavioral Health Barometers — Substance Abuse & Mental Health Services Administration (SAMHSA), HHS	—
Blue Cross Blue Shield Health Index — Blue Cross Blue Shield Association (BCBSA) USA	The BCBS Health Index measures the impact of more than 200 common diseases and conditions on overall health and wellness by assigning each county in the United States a health metric.

(Continued)

Table 4.1. (*Continued*)

Sources	Remarks
Bureau of Justice Statistics — US Department of Justice (DOJ) USA	Statistical data on crime and violence is available.
Bureau of Labor Statistics — US Department of Labor (DOL)	—
County Health Rankings & Roadmaps — Robert Wood Johnson Foundation (RWJF), University of Wisconsin	—
Emergency Department Visits — NCHS, CDC	—
Global Health Atlas — World Health Organization (WHO)	—
Health Insurance Data — US Census Bureau, ESA	—
Health, United States — NCHS, CDC	An annual report of United States health statistics
Kaiser State Health Facts — Kaiser Family Foundation (KFF) USA	Provides health data on more than 700 health topics including demographics, health insurance coverage, health costs, minority health, and women's health for all 50 states.
Multinational Comparisons of Health Systems Data, 2014 — Commonwealth Fund	—

4.4. Primary Data Collection in Market/Marketing Research

Primary data are information collected specifically for the purpose of a particular market/marketing research project.

Besides these, health care organizations also:

- Collect primary data mandated by federal/state/accreditation (e.g., National Committee for Quality Assurance (NCQA)) agencies on race, ethnicity, and primary language, and
- Have access to encounter, claims, utilization review, and grievances data that can be used in aggregate form.

> In using internal data for market research, extreme care must be exercised to protect privacy of individual health information as required by the Health Insurance Portability and Accountability Act of 1996 (HIPAA) and applicable state laws. Use only aggregate data and not any individually identifiable data.

4.4.1. Primary data collection: Qualitative data vs. quantitative data

Both qualitative and quantitative data are used in health care market research (Brandenburg, 2013).

Typical qualitative market research methods in health care include the following:

- Focus groups;
- Group discussions;
- Depth interviewing, usually one-on-one; and
- Observation.

See, Al-Busaidi (2008) for a comprehensive discussion on the importance of qualitative research in health care management. He summarizes,

> "Qualitative research methods are receiving an increasing recognition in health care related research. The use of qualitative research in health care enables researchers to answer questions that may not be easily answered by quantitative methods. Moreover, it seeks to understand the phenomenon under study in the context of the culture or the setting in which it has been studied, therefore, aiding in the development of new research instruments, such as questionnaires that are more culturally acceptable."

Commonly used quantitative market research methods in health care include the following:

- Mail questionnaires;
- Face-to-face interviews;
- Telephone surveys;
- Email surveys; and
- Online survey techniques.

Key issues in quantitative market research involve sample size determination, questionnaire design, and data analysis. We discuss some of these briefly in the following section but refer the reader, with guidance from instructors, to learn these advanced topics involving statistical methods from references provided at the end of the chapter under "Readings in Statistical Methods for Quantitative Market Research".

4.5. Guidelines for Managing Market/Marketing Research

- Use traditional survey tools with reservation.
  - The traditional surveys are known to have several deficiencies. These include low participation rates, respondents' lack of attention, data quality issues, and questionable validity for prediction (Kaden *et al.*, 2012).
- Use focus groups carefully.
  - A focus group will only succeed if it is based on a well-structured guide and conducted by a skilled moderator flexible enough to work both through and around the structure (Sofaer, 2002).
  - Include influencers of health care decisions, e.g., family members and friends, especially for older consumers such as Medicare beneficiaries.
  - Ensure inclusion of key demographic groups: age, gender, income, and educational level.
  - Use linguistically and culturally appropriate survey instruments and techniques.
- Adopt your marketing research to the information age.
  - Use social media, online surveys, mobile technology, and web-use tracking.
  - Use "communities insight" sources. An insight community is composed of the most trusted stakeholders — customers, partners, employees, fans, donors, or alumni. As insight community members, they give rapid and ongoing feedback — actionable intelligence used to make confident business decisions. Insight communities allow companies to engage with customers in an ongoing, two-way dialogue that respects their individuality and their humanity, and

which complements other data sources, like Big Data, Customer Relationship Management (CRM), and social media analytics (Vision Critical, 2018).

- Qualitative research is sometimes more revealing (Al-Busaidi, 2008).
- Use conjoint analysis (Steblea *et al.*, 2018).

Conjoint analysis is a survey-based statistical technique used in market research that helps determine how people value different attributes (feature, function, benefits) that make up an individual product or service. Conjoint analysis methods ask customer/patient on what they would be willing to sacrifice in the real world and trade off, what they are likely to weigh. For example, weights assigned when selecting a hospital to factors such as location, physicians, technology, personal care, and hospital reputation.

Advantages of using conjoint analysis include the ability to measure preferences at the individual level, ability to draw out a comprehensive array of factors important to consumers/patients, ability to draw conclusions that can be used in need-based market segmentation, e.g., patients for whom hospital reputation is by far the most important factor.

Disadvantages include the complexity of designing conjoint studies, difficulties encountered by consumers in understanding the objective of the study thereby resorting to easy responses, difficulty of aggregating individual response weights into workable market segment preferences, and tendency for respondents to give higher weight to emotional factors.

There are many well developed software for conjoint analysis. Some of them are Survey Analytics, XLSTAT, and Conjoint.ly. Cost of these software by Conjoint.ly range from US$3,000 to US$12,000.

References

Al-Busaidi, Z. Q. (2008). "Qualitative Research and Its Uses in Health Care", *Sultan Qaboos University Medical Journal*, 8(1), 11–19.

American Marketing Association (AMA) (2007). "About AMA: Definition of Marketing", www.marketingpower.com/AboutAMA/Pages/DefinitionofMarketing.aspx. Accessed October 3, 2018.

Brandenburg, E. (2013). "Quantitative Market Research vs Qualitative Market Research", June 14, https://www.business2community.com/marketing/quantitative-market-research-vs-qualitative-market-research-C523710. Accessed November 25, 2018.

Conner, M. (2016). "Marketing Research vs Market Research the Great Debate", https://www.business2community.com/marketing/market-research-vs-marketing-research-great-debate-01434066. Accessed October 5, 2018.

DeVault, G. (2017). "Market Research Problems, Alternatives, and Questions", https://www.thebalance.com/market-research-101-problems-alternatives-and-questions-2296950. Accessed October 11, 2018.

Kaden, R. J., Linda, G. and Prince, M. (Eds.) (2012). *Leading Edge Marketing Research: 21st Century Tools and Practices*, Sage Publications.

Kawaulich, B. (2004). "Qualitative Data Analysis Techniques", *Sixth International Conference on Social Science Methodology (RC33) (ISA)*, Amsterdam, The Netherlands, https://www.researchgate.net/publication/258110388_Qualitative_Data_Analysis_Techniques. Accessed February 10, 2019.

Kotler, P. (2003). *Marketing Management*, 11th edn., Upper Saddle River, NJ: Pearson Education, Inc., Prentice Hall.

Moffatt, S., White, M., Mackintosh, J. and Howel, D. (2006). "Research Using Quantitative and Qualitative Data in Health Services Research — What Happens When Mixed Method Findings Conflict?", *BMC Health Services Research*, 6, 28.

Rural Health Information Hub (RHIB) (2018). "Collect and Analyze Quantitative and Qualitative Data", https://www.ruralhealthinfo.org/toolkits/rural-toolkit/4/quantitative-qualitative. Accessed October 14, 2018.

Sofaer, S. (2002). "Qualitative Research Methods", *International Journal for Quality in Health Care*, 14 (4), 329–336.

Steblea, I., Steblea, J. and Pokela, J. (2018). "The Best-Kept Secret in Health Care Marketing Research: Why the Most Valuable Tool in Your Research Toolkit is the One You Might Not Be Using", Market Street Research, Inc., http://www.marketstreetresearch.com/images/The%20Best%20Kept%20Secret%20in%20Healthcare%20Marketing%20Research.pdf. Accessed February 10, 2019.

Substance Abuse and Mental Health Services Administration (2008). "Qualitative and Quantitative Assessment Methods", https://www.samhsa.gov/workplace/toolkit/assess-workplace/methods. Accessed October 14, 2008.

Surbhi, S. (2015). "Difference between Market Research and Marketing Research", December 28, https://keydifferences.com/difference-between-market-research-and-marketing-research.html. Accessed October 11, 2018.

Vision Critical (2018). "What is an Insight Community?", https://www.visioncritical.com/what-is-an-insight-community/. Accessed February 10, 2019.

Wheelan, T. L., Hunger, J. D., Hoffman, A. N. and Bamford, C. E. (2015). *Strategic Management and Business Policy: Globalization, Innovation and Sustainability*, 14th edn., Pearson.

Suggested Additional Readings: Readings in Statistical Methods for Quantitative Market Research

Belk, R., Fischer, E. and Kozinets, R. V. (2013). *Qualitative Consumer & Marketing Research*, Sage Publications.

Creswell, J. W. and Creswell, J. D. (2018). *Research Design: Qualitative, Quantitative, and Mixed Methods Approaches*, 5th edn., Sage Publications.

Green, P. and Srinivasan, V. (1978). "Conjoint Analysis in Consumer Research: Issues and Outlook", *Journal of Consumer Research*, 5, 103–123.

Green, P. E. and Srinivasan V. (1990). "Conjoint Analysis in Marketing: New Developments with Implications for Research and Practice", *Journal of Marketing*, 54, 3–19.

Lewis, J. B., McGrath, R. J. and Seidel, L. F. (2011). *Essentials of Applied Quantitative Methods for Health Services*, Jones & Bartlett.

Chapter 5

Understanding the Health Care Organization's Competition

5.1. Why Study Competition in the Health Care Industry?

As we discussed in Chapter 3, health care marketing strategy is not formulated by the marketing department alone. Marketing strategies and programs of the health care organization are derived from corporate and business line strategies. The first step in formulating corporate strategies is an environmental analysis, i.e., studying the external and internal environments.

> A major factor in the external environment of any organization is its competition.

No organization can formulate effective strategies without a full understanding of the competition. This is sometimes called *Industry and Competitive Analysis* (Thompson and Strickland, 2003). This is not surprising because the objective of strategic management is to formulate strategies and programs to achieve a competitive advantage. This is done by:

- Understanding the industry and competition well;
- An examination of the organization's position with respect to industry trends and competitor strategies; and
- Deciding either to continue to follow the organization's current strategies or to modify them.

Berry (2005) confirms this by highlighting how every business plan needs to include information on competitive analysis. A competitive analysis is the organization's opportunity to look closely at its market and its competition, to learn what the others are doing and why. Companies that annually update their plans should always include a competitive analysis to catch changes in the marketplace and in their competition; startups need to know the landscape before they begin.

The approach in the health care industry should be no different. Some analysts argue that health care is inherently different from other competitive industries and is therefore incapable of functioning in a similar manner (Arrow, 1963). However, others argue that the evolution of the health care industry, coupled with recent academic literature, suggests that health care can and should operate like many other industries. In fact, the academic literature suggests that proper reforms to move health care in this direction would significantly increase quality of care at lower cost (Dayaratna, 2012, 2013; Gaynor and Town, 2012).

It must also be pointed out that competition in the health care industry is beneficial to the health care consumer and patient. Federal Trade Commission makes this argument by stating, "Competition in health care markets benefits consumers because it helps contain costs, improve quality, and encourage innovation" (Federal Trade Commission, 2018).

5.2. Competition in the Health Care Industry

The health care industry in the United States is highly competitive. The most competitive subsectors are hospital services, health plan services (such as managed care services), pharmaceuticals, and home health and retirement home services. This last subsector is one that has expanded in recent times due to the large increase in baby boomers turning 65 years of age which some estimates place at 10,000 every day (Heimlich, 2010).

5.2.1. Recent trends affecting competition in the health care industry

Competition in the health care industry over the last 20 years has continuously changed due to several factors. These are as follows:

- **Advent of the Managed Care Model**
Ginsburg (2005) cites a KPMG Peat Marwick's 1996 survey of employers in which 73% of those obtaining coverage through employment were in

managed care plans, compared with 27%, eight years earlier. Health maintenance organizations (HMOs) were the most popular plan type, accounting for 31% of the market.

Ginsburg adds,

> "Managed care transformed the health insurance industry. Companies that were most successful in offering managed care products, especially HMOs, were those that had started up as local or regional HMOs. UnitedHealthcare, which started as an HMO company, later acquired a large traditional insurer to expand its reach. Blue Cross and Blue Shield (BCBS) plans lost market share to other insurers, although they continued to be the dominant insurers in many markets."

- **Hospital Consolidation as a Reaction to the Managed Care Way of Doing Business**

Many hospitals acquired primary care practices creating physician–hospital organizations (PHOs). PHOs would negotiate with health plans on behalf of hospitals and physicians together. Hospitals also formed management service organizations (MSOs) that provided management services to physician practices.

- **Advent of Accountable Care Organizations (ACO)**

The Affordable Care Act (ACA) encouraged forming entities where provider groups care for a population of patients while meeting cost and quality benchmarks established by payers, e.g., Medicare program. If the ACO manages to meet all the quality benchmarks and the population's cost of care is below the established threshold, the ACO can share in the "savings".

A year after the passage of the Affordable Care Act (first quarter 2011), hospital system-led ACOs outnumbered all other types at a rate of two to one, but there were still relatively few (71) ACOs. By the end of 2011, ACOs had doubled in number; hospitals still accounted for a majority of all ACOs, but physician groups and insurers saw faster relative growth. Since 2012 and the beginning of 2013, ACOs have nearly tripled in number again, with growth coming among all types of sponsoring entities. Of the 282 new ACOs in this period, 158 (56%) are sponsored by physician groups, 103 (36.5%) by hospital systems, 17 by insurers (6%), and four by community-based organizations (1.5%). The initial movement of ACOs was led by hospital systems, but physician groups have now surpassed them as the most common sponsoring entity among all ACOs (Muhlestein, 2013).

- **Physician Reaction to Above Changes, Especially Managed Care**

They formed independent practice associations (IPAs). Having medical groups with both primary care physicians (PCPs) and specialists enabled them to negotiate with health plans for better rates and risk-sharing arrangements. States, such as California, recognized these organizations and allowed them to carry risk provided that could meet financial viability standards. These are called Risk Bearing Organizations (RBOs).

- **Consumer and Employer Reactions**

As managed care plans, especially HMOs with restricted benefits and strict "gate keeper" policies, expanded, consumer protests against these HMOs arose alleging quality, access, and out-of-pocket cost problems.

Employers found it difficult to attract good employees when all they offered were restrictive HMO-type health benefits. Employers started demanding less restrictive managed care products such as Preferred Provider Organizations (PPOs) with larger networks of providers.

- **State Legislature Reactions**

Many state legislatures started imposing controls on managed care practices. For example, California established a separate department, the Department of Managed Health Care (DMHC) to oversee managed care organizations. New legislation was enacted permitting patients to receive care from physicians out of the health plan network of providers in some situations. Also provided were minimum hospital stays for procedures such as childbirth and enhanced appeal rights to patients and physicians.

- **Changes in Compensation Methods**

Over the past 30 years, the health care industry has seen major changes in compensation mechanisms. Health plans that usually paid physicians on a fee-for-service (FFS) basis, added capitation systems, risk pool sharing systems, and quality incentive systems (Pay for Performance or P4P systems).

Compensation for hospital services has changed from traditional per-diem systems to Diagnostic-Related Group (DRG) systems. The DRG systems group diagnostic categories drawn from the International Classification of Diseases (ICD) modified by the patient age, presence or absence of significant morbidities or complications, prognosis, treatment difficulty, need for intervention, and resource intensity. DRGs have been mandated for use in establishing payment amounts for individual admissions under Medicare's prospective hospital payment system.

Competition in the health care industry has caused many large health systems to adopt new strategies. Most notable in recent times have been the following mega mergers and joint ventures:

- Aetna acquired Humana for $37 billion.
- Centene acquired Health Net for $6.8 billion.
- Anthem acquired Cigna for $48 billion.
- CVS Health, the drugstore chain, and most recently Walmart, the giant retailer, are eyeing deals with Aetna and Humana, respectively, to use their stores to deliver medical care.

Mulero (2016), citing the 2016 Health Care Services Acquisition Report from Irving Levin Associates, points out that merger and acquisition activity among US hospitals and health systems increased from 2013 to 2015.

Studies also show that competition in the health care industry can increase quality of care and overall value to consumers/patients. For example, several studies have examined the relationships between competition and quality of health care (Chassin, 1997; Zwanziger and Melnick, 1996), between competition and health care system costs (Robinson and Luft, 1985; Zwanziger and Melnick, 1996), and between competition and patient satisfaction (Brook and Kosecoff, 1988; Miller, 1996). These studies show that competition is capable of increasing value for customers over time. Quality and process improvements lead to decreased costs, which in turn results in increased customer satisfaction.

In all industries, competition among businesses has long been encouraged as a mechanism to increase value for patients. In other words, competition ensures the provision of better products and services to satisfy the needs of customers. Rivers and Glover (2008) conducted a literature review of 50 items of literature related to competition in health care. Various perspectives of competition, the nature of service quality, health system costs, and patient satisfaction in health care were examined. Findings indicated *patient satisfaction as an outcome measure directly dependent on competition.* Quality of care and health care systems costs, while also directly dependent on the strategic mission and goals, are considered as determinants of customer satisfaction as well.

5.2.2. Competition among hospitals

Hospital competition in the US has reached an intense level causing many hospitals to make drastic strategic decisions like closing or merging with others.

More than 120 rural hospitals have gone out of business since 2005, and the trend has been accelerating since 2010 (Health Resources and Services Administration, 2017). The hotspot for closures and financial distress continues to be the South — particularly Florida, Alabama, Tennessee, Arkansas, Virginia, and Texas. A lot of states in the Midwest have no hospitals that are rural and at high risk of financial distress. Further, many of the closures in recent years affected Critical Access Hospitals, a designation by the Centers for Medicare and Medicaid Services for facilities that provide essential services in especially isolated communities. Most shut down amid financial woes tied to upkeep costs for things like leaking roofs, antiquated power supplies, and aging clinical equipment. Contributing factors included insufficient patient populations, high rates of uninsured patients, dwindling cash flow, and physician shortages.

The picture has not been much different in urban areas either. Nine urban hospitals closed during the first nine months of 2018 in cities, such as San Diego (California), Dallas and Webstar (Texas), Jacksonville (Alabama), and Florence and Gilbert (Arizona) (Ellison, 2018).

Also, see the following statistics for hospitals in USA (American Hospital Directory, 2018):

- As of July 2028, there were a total of 3,920 non-federal, short-term, acute care hospitals.
- Gross patient revenue was US$3,306,911,640,000.
- Competition is more intense in larger metropolitan areas. Number of hospitals in selected states are as follows:
    - California — 342
    - Texas — 367
    - New York — 190
    - Pennsylvania — 178
    - Ohio — 147.

How has competition among hospitals in California affected overall strategic planning of hospitals and their marketing strategies? In June 1982, California was the first state to enact legislation to encourage the formation of insurance plans able to contract with selected providers including hospitals. The legislation allowed the state's Medicaid program (Medi-Cal) and private insurance plans to contract with hospitals to which they would channel their beneficiaries in return for price (and other) concessions. Health plans adopted strategies to cope with this change (Zwanziger *et al.*, 1994).

- One health plan, Kaiser Permanente, has employed physicians and owns their hospitals.
- The majority of other health insurers contract with a selected group of providers including hospitals.
- In the latter model, hospitals have adopted the strategy of cost reduction and quality improvement.
- In a marketing sense, these hospitals have vastly improved their physician relations. Hospital selection is largely under physician control. Mersdorf (2018) states that 35–45% of referrals for adult inpatient care, as measured by revenue, go to a partner hospital. Therefore, hospitals compete for patients largely by trying to attract physicians. Since physicians generally are not price-sensitive, the demand for hospital services in this type of market is largely determined by a comparison of hospitals' quality and amenities. The availability of technically sophisticated services, modern facilities, and convenient parking are some of the critical dimensions of competition among hospitals.
- California hospitals have also realized that physician relations must be made an organization-wide initiative. These hospitals have begun to coordinate physician contracting, IT, and Provider Relation activities.

This does not mean that the only marketing strategy currently favored by hospital service marketers is in physician relations. There is evidence that they focus to a large extent on digital marketing as well.

> The point made in this discussion is how competition in the relevant health care market (hospitals in our discussion) eventually leads to redesigning marketing strategies.

5.2.3. Competition among health plans

Competition among health plans is fierce with a limited number of health plans having enormous market power in most states and metropolitan statistical areas (MSAs). AMA (2018) reports the extent of market concentration of health plans. High concentration means less competition. For example,

- 96% of the HMO markets are highly concentrated.
- 88% of the PPO markets are highly concentrated.

- In 91% of the MSAs, at least one insurer had a combined HMO + PPO + POS + Exchange products market share of 30% or greater.
- In 91% of the MSAs, at least one insurer had an HMO market share of 30% or greater.
- In 76% of the MSAs, at least one insurer had an HMO market share of 50% or greater.

This is a very significant factor in understanding competition among HMOs. Product differentiation among health plans is minimal.

California Healthline (2008) presents an analysis of how competition has intensified in the northern San Diego region health industry. It reports that competition is heating up among San Diego's health care systems to capture the area's most lucrative patient population. The northern part of the county, with its wealthier and better-insured population, has seen an expansion of services among a number of the region's health systems. Strategies, however, seem to vary among the region's big players:

- Sharp Healthcare is expanding its presence in San Diego's wealthier North Central, North Coastal, and North Inland regions by expanding exclusively through outpatient clinics.
- In terms of how they compete for market share under the Affordable Care Act, the University of California San Diego Health System is expanding its Thornton Hospital in La Jolla.
- The new Jacobs Medical Center will offer cardiovascular care, cancer care, specialty surgery, and women's and children's services. The system also has expanded its outpatient services in the northern part of the county with clinics in Encinitas, Vista, and Scripps Ranch, all of which will feed referrals to the new US$700 million hospital in La Jolla.

> What we see here is how patient characteristics and competition drive strategies of health care plans and providers. In turn, the chosen strategies will dictate their health care marketing plans.

5.2.4. Competition among pharmaceutical companies

Pharmaceutical subsector of the health care industry is dominated by large companies and competition is limited. A patent for a novel and effective drug is a barrier to competition in the short run. This barrier is created by the government to generate incentives for innovation. Morton and Boller (2017) highlight that over the past two decades, pharmaceutical innovation has shifted from chemically synthesized small molecule drugs toward more complex, bioengineered treatments grown from living tissue that are known as biologics often used to treat severe diseases that do not have effective small molecule treatments. The development of biologic medicines has represented a boon to many patients suffering from cancer, hepatitis, hemophilia, multiple sclerosis, autoimmune disorders, such as rheumatoid arthritis, or inflammatory diseases, such as Crohn's and ulcerative colitis. Other areas of new drug development have been chronic diseases like diabetes and asthma. Although total pharmaceutical spending has been increasing rapidly, with 29% cumulative growth between 2011 and 2015, utilization has remained roughly constant, with only a 1% increase in units sold over the same period (Price et al., 2017).

Modern trends in health care consumer/patient behavior affect all pharma companies. Consumers in the pharma industry comprise both patients who consume the drug as well as physicians who prescribe them. Thus, it is not surprising that marketing strategies among competing pharma companies are focused on:

- Direct advertising to consumers/patients, and
- Marketing to physicians.

Marketing to consumers/patients is not as simple as effective TV and other advertising. Many consumers/patients belong to HMO plans and the HMOs establish their own drug formularies together with multiple tiers. Therefore, even if a consumer/patient is convinced of a new drug that has come to the market, his/her health plan formulary may place the drug in a higher tier which will require payment of a higher out-of-pocket cost. In the end, generic versions of most drugs which are in no-cost or low-cost tiers will be the consumer/patient's final choice.

Morton and Boller (2017) explain how recent evidence shows that drug manufacturers use various techniques to make side payments to patients in order to undo the incentives described above, and thereby shift consumption toward more expensive branded drugs. These side payments can take the form of coupons, in-kind benefits provided under the guise of marketing, or charitable assistance programs.

Levy (1999) proposes the following reasons for this intense competition in the industry:

- Information technology has altered pharmacy-operating practices and has created intense competition among drug companies.

    Less than two decades ago, a pharmacist would fill each prescription as specified by the doctor. Retail pharmacies would manually order drugs from drug wholesalers.

    Today, pharmacies are typically part of the Pharmacy Benefit Manager (PBM) networks that administer the drug benefits portion of health insurer plans for employers and others. Computers linking network pharmacies to PBMs enable pharmacists to check which brand name or generic substitutions are required by the patient's health insurer, whether the doctor is prescribing according to the health plan policy, what copayment amount applies, and when drug stocks are low. The same computer technology allows pharmacies to manage their drug inventories.
- Competition among drug companies was focused on gaining the allegiance of prescribing physicians. While this traditional focus was on gaining the allegiance of prescribing physicians, drug companies now also compete for placement in health plan protocols and for contracts with HMOs.
- Information technology enables pharmaceutical companies to charge different prices from different groups of buyers, especially using copay structures of different health insurance programs.

Overall, among other findings, the report raises several possible antitrust concerns and a number of potential efficiency explanations involving the conduct of pharmaceutical companies.

5.2.5. Competition among physicians

The managed care model sets up one physician against another to drive down compensation. Managed care health plans use the capitation method (a fixed monthly payment per beneficiary assigned to the physician per month) to contract with PCPs. Specialists are usually paid on a FFS basis. However, specialists get paid only when a PCP refers a patient to the specialist. This requires specialists to depend on the goodwill of the PCPs for referrals and with health plans to get good FFS rates.

These reasons have led to physicians forming IPAs, which are able to negotiate with health plans for better rates and even risk-sharing arrangements.

Physicians were also affected by the adoption by managed care plans of the Medicare resource-based relative value scale.

5.3. Measuring Competition for Health Care Management and Marketing

Traditional competition in health care involves one or more elements (e.g., price, quality, convenience, and superior products or services). However, competition can also be based on new technology and innovation. A key role of competition in health care is the potential to provide a mechanism for reducing health care costs. Competition generally eliminates inefficiencies that would otherwise yield high production costs, which are ultimately transferred to patients via high health service and delivery costs (Rivers and Glover, 2008).

Competition faced by health care organizations is more complex than what meets the eye. For example, competition for a hospital is not just other hospitals a few miles away. It must be conscious of substitutes springing up like Urgent Care Centers, or a large medical group/IPA aligning itself with a rival hospital that is giving the medical group/IPA more favorable contracts.

There are several preliminary considerations in measuring the competition in health markets. These include the following (Baker, 2001):

- **Identifying the product or service, and the competitors providing the same service**

This is not always easy. For example, all specialists are not the same. A consultation provided by a world-renowned specialist may be very different from a visit to another physician in the same specialty but without the same reputation. Therefore, the two specialists, in reality, form two different markets. A small community hospital cannot be considered to be in the same market as, and competing with, an academic medical center.

In the model by Porter discussed below, this question comes under the analysis of "rivals". In other words, identifying the proper "rival" is the first step in analyzing competition for a product/service of a health care organization.

- **Identifying substitutes**

Sometimes, identifying the product/service to study the competition is made difficult due to similar, but not exactly the same, products/services. These are called "substitutes" in Porter's analysis. An example would be services offered by HMO and PPOs which are similar except for differences in the financing systems. Therefore, for an HMO, studying only rival HMOs, without studying relevant PPOs, would not be appropriate.

- **Identifying the geographic market area**

One strategy is to use standard geographic area definitions, such as those based on county borders or metropolitan statistical areas (MSAs), or even states. California Department of Health uses zip code collections to define the area to apply certain regulatory requirements (e.g., language assistance provision). We have already seen how AMA uses the MSAs to study market concentration of health plans.

California Department of Health (2018) also uses a Primary Care (adult and pediatric) 10 miles or 30 minutes from the beneficiary's residence for assigning Medicaid beneficiaries to a PCP, 15 miles or 30 minutes from beneficiary's residence for assigning beneficiaries for hospital services, and 10 miles or 30 minutes from beneficiary's residence for assigning beneficiaries to a pharmacy. Longer times and distances are allowed in rural areas. Physician practices and hospitals, especially those whose customer base comes from Medicaid, Children's Health and Medicare programs, might consider these standards in setting the geographic region to study competition.

This does not mean that all health care providers should define strict geographical areas by distance. Some providers adopt market area definition to vary with the provider size and firm's characteristics, giving rise to a "variable market area". For example, some hospitals use a variable radius using the residence zip codes of patients (Gruber, 1994; Robinson and Phibbs, 1989). Here, the length of the radius drawn around each hospital is set so that it encloses enough zip codes to capture some percentage (often 75%) of the hospital's patients. A similar method is used to define the set of standard geographic areas (e.g., zip codes or counties) from which a firm is observed to draw its patients and define the market area to include those areas (for hospitals, see Melnick *et al.*, 1992; for HMOs, see Wholey *et al.*, 1995).

- **Selecting the measures (methods) to study competition**

Here, we will review several methods used to analyze and understand the competition facing a health care organization. These are as follows:

- *Number of competing firms*: The simplest type of measure counts the number of competing firms (Baker, 2001). Baker comments on this simple approach as, "Easily implementable, and intuitive ... (but) does not capture the relative sizes of firms, which can play an important role in competition."

- *Herfindahl–Hirschman index (HHI)*: This index, which captures both the number of competitors and their size, is a commonly used measure of competition.

  HHI is the standard measure used by the Department of Justice (DOJ) and Federal Trade Commission in evaluating the degree of concentration in markets for anti-trust policy.

  The HHI for a market is the sum of the squared market shares of all of the firms competing in the market: for example, in a market with four firms, one with 40% market share, one with 30% market share, one with 20% market share, and the fourth with 10% market share, the HHI would be

  HHI = 0.5 squared + 0.4 squared + 0.3 squared + 0.1 squared = 0.3

  As the number of firms gets smaller, HHI increases indicating the concentration of the market by a fewer firms. The HHI computed as above is usually multiplied by 10,000, with 10,000 indicating no competition (monopoly).

- *Porter's five factor analysis of competition*: Porter's "five factor analysis of competition" is the best-known model to study competition for any business organization (Porter, 1979). Due to the fact that it is the most comprehensive method to study and understand from a health care management point of view, we will devote a separate section (see Section 5.4) to this method.

5.4. Porter's Five Forces Competition Analysis Applied to Health Care Organizations

The five factors, and *information to be gathered by market research* on each of these, are:

- **The Rivalry Among Existing Players in the Market**
  o Number of direct competitors;
  o Market shares: our company and rivals; and
  o Competitors' strategies, cost leadership/differentiation/focus strategies.

For example, a hospital may expand to an area where rival hospitals are not a great threat. In the East Los Angeles area, there are six to seven hospitals competing for the same Medicaid/Medicare population. The strategy employed by these hospitals is to provide generous contracts to physician groups.

- **Threat of Substitutes**
    - What are services that customers/patients can switch to?
    - What is the likelihood that customers will switch to a competitive product (e.g., a generic or competing pharmaceutical product) or a service (e.g., from hospital emergency care units to free-standing urgent care clinics)?
    - Switching costs.
    - Perceived level of product differentiation.

- **Entry of New Competitors**
    - How easy or difficult is it for new entrants to start to compete with our service?
    - Are there significant barriers (barriers to entry) to prevent competitors from doing so? Existing loyalty to major brands, capital requirements, learning curve advantages, Government restrictions, or legislation (e.g., health plan licenses).

- **Bargaining Power of Customers**
    - In the health care market, bargaining power of individual customers/patients is negligible.
    - In the B2B market of commercial insurance, larger employees have greater bargaining power. For example, in California, the largest buyer of group insurance, the California Public Employee Retirement System (CALPERS) has enormous power.
    - A common strategy of physicians is to enter into PPO contracts with large commercial HMOs.
    - Who are the powerful buyers?
    - What do they look for?

- **Bargaining Power of Suppliers** (e.g., physicians' role in health plan or hospital market)
    - Data on physician and medical groups.
    - Who they are contracted with (hospitals, HMOs)?
    - Prices they get from hospitals and HMOs.
    - Reasons for loyalty.

5.5. Porter's New Thinking on Competitive Analysis as Applied to Health Care Organizations

This discussion is based on Porter and Teisberg (2004).

- Presently, competition in health care occurs at the level of health plans, networks, and hospital groups.
- These entities focus on cost shifting rather than fundamental cost reduction. Costs are shifted from the payer to the patient, from the health plan to the hospital, from the hospital to the physician, from the insured to the uninsured, and so on.
- They strive for greater bargaining power rather than efforts to provide better care. Health plans, hospital groups, and physician groups have consolidated primarily to gain more clout and to cut better deals with suppliers or customers.
- The quality and efficiency gains from consolidation are quite modest.
- *Competition should occur in the prevention, diagnosis, and treatment of individual health conditions or cooccurring conditions.* It is at this level that true value is created — or destroyed — disease by disease and patient by patient. It is here where huge differences in cost and quality persist. And it is here where competition would drive improvements in efficiency and effectiveness, reduce errors, and spark innovation.
- Numerous studies show that when physicians or teams treat a high volume of patients who have a particular disease or condition, they create better outcomes and lower costs.
- Bargaining power of buyers should come into play. Employers should lead the way. Companies have a lot at stake in how the US health care system performs. Businesses' health care costs have outpaced inflation in 13 of the last 17 years, reaching more than US$6,200 per employee in 2003.

5.6. Sources of Information for Market Research of Competition in Health Care

Market research for competition must be guided by two concepts:

1. Porter's Five Factor Analysis of Competition

It is mandatory that the health care organization (physician, IPA/Medical Group, hospital, or pharmacy chain or pharmaceutical company) look for information on each of the five factors: The direct competitor rivals, substitutes, barriers to entry, partnerships with suppliers, and partnerships with customers/patients.

In modern times, attention must be devoted also to online options and choices available to customers/patients.

2. Elements of the Marketing Mix of the Health Care Organization

Walk along the seven elements of the organization's marketing mix for each segment/niche and gather as much information as possible on competitor's strategies to match your marketing mix. In other words, what products/services are competitors offering, prices and other value items, access improvements, promotional activities, staff capabilities, processes (e.g., wait times and appointment scheduling), and physical evidence (facilities, equipment, brochures, etc.).

> Focusing on Porter's five factors and the seven elements of the marketing mix, as applicable to the competitor, is the most effective way to direct a health care organization's search for information about its competitors' strengths, weaknesses, and strategies.

The information search about competition is easiest when it involves publicly traded companies. There are thousands of companies whose stocks are traded in public markets, and law requires that these companies share a significant amount of information with the public.

When the competition is small or local or private, the information about competition is harder to gather especially financial information and future business plans.

Health care marketers for physicians and small medical groups/IPAs can gather basic information from competitors, like services offered and prices, by calling them or visiting their offices. Time to get an appointment would be an approximate indicator of business volume.

Health care marketers can also talk to their customers. What do their customers like or dislike about each competitor? Why and how do customers decide between one competitor and another?

Directories of similar business are available from cities, chambers of commerce, and online sources. Economic census at www.census.gov has lists of types of businesses per county in the United States.

Health care marketers should certainly check competitors' websites. These websites will provide a lot of information about the competitors. If competition has no website, that also indicates their weakness in marketing and communication.

Marketing reports and mailing lists are available at a price from private companies. They are expensive.

Study advertisements and sales brochure of competitor medical practices, IPAs, and hospitals. These will provide an indication of your competitor's promotional strategies, programs, and budget. Study the content of competitor advertisements.

5.6.1. Summary of secondary sources of competitor information

- US Department of Health & Human Services, Agency for Health Care Research and Quality (AHRQ).
- American Hospital Association data for US Metropolitan Statistical Area hospitals.
- Kaiser Family Foundation has a large number of industry reports.
- Regional health plan associations' annual reports, e.g., The Annual Report of the California Association of Health Plans (CAHP) contains extensive enrollment data for each member plan by line of business and overall financial data.
- State records open to public: Information about Commercial and Medicaid HMOs. State agency publications such as industry directories, and statistics on local industry employment and business activity.
- CMS records (online): Information about Medicare HMOs and providers as well as star ratings.
- Census Bureau sources of statistics on health care and health care industry.
- Local competitive data from the City Clerk's office, the County Clerk's office, and the Chamber of Commerce.
- Dun & Bradstreet Million Dollar Database directory: This database includes over 1,600,000 businesses with a net worth of US$1 million or more. Data can be selected alphabetically, geographically, by line of business, and officers and directors. Financial ratios that can be used to compare your company's performance with competitors' performance are published in Almanac of Business and Industrial Financial Ratios by Leo Troy, the Dun & Bradstreet Industry Norms and Key Business Ratios, and RMA Annual Statement Studies.

- Ward's Business Directory of US Private and Public Companies (annual) provides profiles of over 100,000 companies (small and mid-size companies as well as large corporations, most privately held) across the US. Profiles include assets, gross earnings, revenues, and other pertinent information.
- Annual Reports: If the competitor is a publicly held company, many of its reports to the US Securities and Exchange Commission are available on the SEC-Edgar website. Annual reports provide financial information, including sales volume, revenue increases, and their total market share. 10-K reports provide still more detail and are supplemented by the quarterly 10-Qs. 8-Ks show significant events such as acquisitions and board membership changes when they occur between 10-K and 10-Q filings. Online versions of these products not only make their pertinent statistics easy to find. They often permit you to download data so you can combine it with other data to produce your own statistics.
- Online searches with Google, SpyFu, Google Trends, and Google Alerts.
- Private companies provide health care industry reports for a fee/subscription. For example, Report Linker claims to offer US Healthcare Industry 2018–2022 Reports on Demand, Social Conditions, Demographics, etc. Definitive Healthcare offers data on hospitals, physicians, and health care providers.
- Social media monitoring.
- Surveying customers and suppliers/physicians.

References

AMA (2018). "Competition in Health Insurance: A Comprehensive Study of U.S. Markets", https://www.ama-assn.org/system/files/2018-11/competition-health-insurance-us-markets_1.pdf. Accessed February 10, 2019.

American Hospital Directory (2018). https://www.ahd.com/state_statistics.html. Accessed October 17, 2018.

Arrow, K. J. (1963). "Uncertainty and the Welfare Economics of Medical Care", *American Economic Review*, 53 (5), 941–973.

Baker, L. C. (2001). "Measuring Competition in Health Care Markets", *Health Service Research*, 36 (1, Part 2), 223–251.

Berry, T. (2005). "Know Your Competition", July 11, https://www.entrepreneur.com/article/78596. Accessed October 16, 2018.

Brook, R. H. and Kosecoff, J. B. (1988). "Competition and Quality", *Health Affairs*, 7 (3), 150–161.

California Department of Health (2018). *Medicaid Managed Care Final Rule: Network Adequacy Standards*, March 26.

California Healthline (2008). "Competition Spurs Northern Expansion in San Diego", https://californiahealthline.org/news/competition-spurs-northern-growth-in-san-diego/. Accessed October 20, 2018.

Chassin, M. R. (1997). "Assessing Strategies for Quality Improvement", *Health Affairs*, 16 (3), 151–161.

Dayaratna, K. (2012). "Medicare Reform Debate: What Really Works in Health Care Competition", The Heritage Foundation, The Foundry, September 13, http://blog.heritage.org/2012/09/13/medicare-reform-debate-what-really-works-in-health-care-competition/. Accessed October 17, 2018.

Dayaratna, K. (2013). "Competitive Markets in Health Care: The Next Revolution", *Heritage Foundation Reports*, August 19, https://www.heritage.org/health-care-reform/report/competitive-markets-health-care-the-next-revolution#_ftn2. Accessed October 16, 2018.

Ellison, A. (2018). "9 Hospital Closures in 2018 So Far", *Becker's Hospital Report*, https://www.beckershospitalreview.com/finance/9-hospital-closures-in-2018-so-far.html. Accessed October 20, 2018.

Federal Trade Commission (2018). "Competition in the Health Care Marketplace", https://www.ftc.gov/tips-advice/competition-guidance/industry-guidance/health-care. Accessed October 18, 2018.

Gaynor, M. and Town, R. (2012). "Competition in Health Care Markets", in Mark Pauly, V., McGuire, T. G. and Barros, P. P. (Eds.), *Handbook of Health Economics*, Vol. 2, Oxford, UK: North Holland, pp. 499–637.

Ginsburg, P. B. (2005). "Competition in Health Care: Its Evolution Over the Past Decade", *Health Affairs*, 24 (6).

Gruber, J. (1994). "The Effects of Competitive Pressure on Charity: Hospital Responses to Price Shopping", *California Journal of Health Economics*, 13 (2), 183–212.

Health Resources and Services Administration (2017). "Hospital Closings Likely to Increase", https://www.hrsa.gov/enews/past-issues/2017/october-19/hospitals-closing-increase.html. Accessed October 20, 2018.

Heimlich, R. (2010). "Baby Boomers Retire", Pew Research Center, http://www.pewresearch.org/fact-tank/2010/12/29/baby-boomers-retire/. Accessed October 20, 2018.

Levy, R. (1999). "The Pharmaceutical Industry: A Discussion of Competitive and Antitrust Issues in an Environment of Change", Federal Trade Commission, Bureau of Economics.

Melnick, G. A., Zwanziger, J., Bamezai, A. and Pattison, R. (1992). "The Effects of Market Structure and Bargaining Position on Hospital Prices", *Journal of Health Economics*, 11 (3), 217–233.

Mersdorf, S. (2018). "Compelling Stats to Guide Your 2018 Healthcare Marketing Budget", February 28, https://www.evariant.com/blog/statistics-guide-your-2018-healthcare-marketing-budget. Accessed October 18, 2018.

Miller, R. H. (1996). "Competition in the Health System: Good News and Bad News", *Health Affairs*, 15 (2), 107–120.

Morton, F. S. and Boller, L. T. (2017). "Enabling Competition in Pharmaceutical Markets", Hutchins Center Working Paper #30, https://www.brookings.edu/wp-content/uploads/2017/05/wp30_scottmorton_competitioninpharma1.pdf. Accessed October 20, 2018.

Muhlestein, D. (2013). "Continued Growth of Public and Private Accountable Care Organizations", *Health Affairs*, February 19, https://www.healthaffairs.org/do/10.1377/hblog20130219.028313/full/. Accessed February 4, 2019.

Mulero, A. (2016). "Hospital Mergers and Acquisitions: Running List", https://www.healthcaredive.com/news/hospital-mergers-and-acquisitions-running-list/431136/. Accessed October 18, 2018.

Porter, M. E. (1979). "How Competitive Forces Shape Strategy", *Harvard Business Review*, 57 (2), 137–145.

Porter, M. E. and Teisberg, E. (2004). "Redefining Competition in Health Care", *Harvard Business Review*, 82 (6), 64–76.

Price, W., Nicholson, I. I. and Rai, A. K. (2015). "Manufacturing Barriers to Biologics Competition and Innovation", *Iowa Law Review*, 101, 1023.

Rivers, P. A. and Glover, S. H. (2008). "Health Care Competition, Strategic Mission, and Patient Satisfaction: Research Model and Propositions", *Journal of Health Organization and Management*, 22 (6), 627–641.

Robinson, J. C. and Luft, H. S. (1985). "The Impact of Hospital Market Structure on Patient Volume, Average Length of Stay, and the Cost of Care", *Health Economics*, 4 (4), 333–356.

Robinson, J. C. and Phibbs, C. S. (1989). "An Evaluation of Medicaid Selective Contracting in California", *Journal of Health Economics*, 8 (4), 437–455.

Thompson, A. and Strickland, A. J. (2003). *Strategic Management: Concepts and Cases*, 13th edn., McGraw-Hill.

Wholey, D. R., Feldman, R. B. and Christianson, J. B. (1995). "The Effect of Market Structure on HMO Premiums", *Journal of Health Economics*, 14 (1), 81–105.

Zwanziger, J., Melnick, G. A. and Bamezai, A. (1994). "Costs and Price Competition in California Hospitals, 1980–1990", *Health Affairs*, 13 (4).

Zwanziger, J. and Melnick, G. A. (1996). "Can Managed Care Plans Control Health Care Costs?", *Health Affairs*, 15 (2), 185–189.

Suggested Additional Readings

Chatterjee, H. (2018). "Competitive Strategy in the Pharmaceutical Industry", http://thought-leadership.top-consultant.com/UK/Competitive-Strategy-in-the-Pharmaceutical-Industry--978.html. Accessed October 20, 2018.

Gaynor, M., Mostashari, F. and Ginsburg, P. B. (2017). "Making Health Care Markets Work: Competition Policy for Health Care: Actionable Policy Proposals for the Executive Branch, Congress, and the States", Brookings Institute, https://www.brookings.edu/wp-content/uploads/2017/04/gaynor-et-al-final-report-v11.pdf. Accessed February 11, 2019.

Higher Study (2018). "Thompson and Strickland Strategic Management Model", http://higherstudy.org/thompson-and-strickland-strategic-management-model/. Accessed October 17, 2018.

Ibisworld (2018). "Hospitals in the US — US Industry Market Research Report", https://www.ibisworld.com/industry-trends/market-research-reports/health-care-social-assistance/hospitals/hospitals.html. Accessed October 14, 2018.

Senior Housing Business (2015). "Competition Heats Up in Home Healthcare and Services", January 16, http://seniorshousingbusiness.com/from-the-magazine/competition-heats-up-in-home-healthcare-and-services. Accessed October 14, 2018.

Small Business Encyclopedia (2018). https://www.entrepreneur.com/encyclopedia. Accessed October 13, 2018.

Chapter 6

Understanding Customer/Patient Characteristics and Behavior Affecting Health Care Marketing

In Chapter 3, we saw that health care marketing strategy and plans are derived from the health care organization's corporate and business line strategies. We also learnt that the first step in formulating corporate strategies was an analysis of the external environment faced by the organization, and that customer/patient demographics, other characteristics, and behavior were key elements of this external environment. Therefore, we will devote this chapter to learn what we need to know about our customers/patients, how to gather information toward this, and the sources of information on this subject.

What do health care managers and marketers need to know about customers/patients? This includes the following:

- Who are the customers of interest to the health care organizations (health plan, hospital, pharmaceutical companies, and physicians)?
- How do the customers/patients make decisions about health care, provider selection and retention?
- What are the characteristics and behavior patterns of health care customers/patients that would enable the health care organizations to segment the customers/patients in order to focus and communicate effectively? What are the conventional patterns, and what are the recent changes in their behavior patterns?

This chapter is organized to address these issues in that order.

6.1. Who are the Customers in Health Care?

In Section 1.4 of Chapter 1, we reviewed who the customers are from the point of view of health care marketing. We saw that marketing of health care products and services would appear to be directed at consumers/patients with the intention of influencing their decision to select a health care product, service or service provider. However, health care marketing, as this book continues to emphasize, is not only about mass advertising and promotion of health care products and services directly to consumers. It is also about communicating the value of a health care product or service. Sometimes this is possible to do more effectively by directing the message via other parties and stakeholders that influence the ultimate customer or user.

Therefore, in Section 1.4 of Chapter 1, we classified the health care customers broadly to include the following:

- Primary customers
    - End user customer: The patient;
    - The patient's family; and
    - The well person: The consumer (who is called a member or subscriber by health plans).
- Secondary customers
    - Physicians;
    - Pharmacists;
    - Care coordinators; and
    - Community of consumers, Community organizations, and Health Care Advocates.
- Internal customers
    - The staff of the health care organizations.

In this chapter, we focus on the primary customers in this classification, namely the patient, the patients' family and the health care consumer. Our interest is in understanding their behavior as consumers, and how such behavior affects the health care organizations' marketing.

We will study the characteristics of physicians and effects of such characteristics and physician behavior on marketing to physicians in Chapter 12. Similarly, in Chapter 11, we will study the internal customers (the staff of the organization) and their role and impact on effective health care marketing.

> Recall that we noted in Chapter 1 that two-thirds of an individual's interaction with a health care provider is as a customer for pre- and post-treatment. Only one-third of their encounter is as a patient during treatment (Krivich, 2011). This is why we will keep on using both these terms, i.e., customer and patient, in this chapter and throughout this book.

6.2. Why Study Health Care Customer/Patient Characteristics and Behavior?

In Chapter 3, we saw the importance of understanding the external environment of the health care organizations for formulating corporate, business line and health care marketing strategies. In Chapter 5, we studied one of the most important factors of the external environment, namely Competition. In this chapter, we address another equally important factor of the external environment of the health care organizations, the customer/patient.

As in any other industry, understanding customer demographics and behavior is important in the health care industry and for health care marketing. Additionally, there are several factors special to the health care industry that make understanding customers/patients important. These are as follows:

6.2.1. Health care marketing is no longer directed at mass markets

As noted earlier, health care marketing experts now agree with Weiss (2011) who states that, "Health care marketing today is about more than slick ads. It's about engaging with communities." Communities, broadly, include patients, consumers and other influencers of health care policy and decisions.

6.2.2. A trend in modern health care marketing is segmentation of consumers into narrow segments/ niches (Weiss, 2011)

Psychographic segmentation, discussed in Chapter 8 under Market Segmentation in Health Care Marketing, identifies groups of people according to their motivations, priorities and communication preferences. Psychographic segmentation enables health care organizations to customize patient communication and engagement by effective messaging.

This requires health care marketers to have a deep understanding of consumer/patient behavior in smaller segments/niches of the market. To perform segmentation of a health care organization's market and formulate the marketing mix for each segment/niche, the organization needs to understand its customers/patients' needs, expectations and behavior in detail, down to the segment/niche level.

6.2.3. The large number of product lines in health care, such as Medicare, Medicaid, Affordable Care Act (ACA) products, private commercial insurance, senior care services, mental health services, dental care and pharmaceuticals, requires understanding customer preferences and behaviors in each of these product lines

For example, how does a 70-year-old diabetic man become aware which new drugs are available in the market? Would this person use the same resources and decision-making process to select a hospital for his inpatient service needs?

6.2.4. Health care consumerism is on the rise

Health consumerism refers to a consumer trend where educated patients make informed decisions about health care options, with a particular focus on preventative care. Consumers are becoming less dependent on references and are becoming increasingly self-guided.

DataPath (2019) comments that today's consumers want to take responsibility for managing their own health, but the process of choosing and paying for medical services is complex and confusing.

C2b Solutions (2017) describes how this trend affects health care marketing. For example, health care providers must become more consumer-centric in a bid to succeed in this dynamic, experience-focused environment and change their mindset from patients to consumers. For example, health plans and health insurance companies that usually market to employers will have to focus on consumers who directly shop in markets such as Medicare Advantage plans and ACA exchanges.

What information these motivated health care consumers seek varies among consumer demographic groups and segments. This makes it important to understand what information is sought by different demographic and sociocultural ethnic groups.

6.2.5. Information seeking practices of health care customers/patients differ among demographic groups

A notable modern trend is more patients looking for information online before talking with their physicians (Hesse *et al.*, 2005 citing The Health Information National Trends Survey). Consumers/patients depend heavily on internet-based sources of information. Pew Research Center's (2013) Internet and American Life Project indicates that 80% of Internet users, or about 93 million Americans, have searched for a health-related topic online.

However, use of internet and internet-based sources for health information varies significantly across different demographic groups. According to a report by Deloitte (2016), use of health information, technology and online resources depend on personal health attitudes and behaviors. As such, consumer behavior relating to internet use for health information must be well understood for each relevant consumer/patient group.

Which Comes First, Consumer/Patient Analysis or Market Segmentation?

Should health care marketing first do market segmentation? This appears valid because we emphasize the need to understand customer behavior in key segments. On the other hand, we need to know customer demographics and behavior to form customer segments that we can use in formulating marketing strategy and programs.

In practice, these two concepts and related activities overlap. However, we need to discuss both concepts in this book in some order. We have chosen to first discuss understanding customer demographics and behavior in this chapter and examine market segmentation in Chapter 8.

Understanding consumer/patient behavior in health care would, thus, involve:

1. Identifying demographics of the target market population.
2. Understanding factors influencing health care and provider selection decisions of key population groups.

108 *Modern Health Care Marketing*

3. Understanding the health care consumer/patient decision-making process for each of the key population groups, including information relied on, and other parties, such as physicians, friends and family relied on, by the health care consumer/patient.
4. Understanding factors leading to retention, i.e., remaining with the same health care product or provider, by health care consumers/patients.

This chapter will discuss these issues. Finally, with respect to key target market segments, health care marketers should also know:

(a) Sources of information available to understand above issues.
(b) Methods to extract and analyze information from these sources.

Sources of information on customer/patient characteristics and behavior are discussed in Chapter 4.

> This highlights that the three concepts, understanding consumer/patient demographics and behavior, market and marketing research, and market segmentation are interrelated.

6.3. Role of Demographics in Planning Health Care Marketing

The most common basis for marketing segmentation in the health care industry is demographics. This is due to its simplicity as compared to psychographic segmentation (discussed in Chapter 8 under Market Segmentation in Health Care Marketing), which identifies groups of people according to their motivations, priorities and communication preferences. This approach requires a deep understanding of consumer behavior. Demographics, on the other hand, is plain statistics fairly easily obtained using primary or secondary data.

In this section, we discuss how demographic variations of health care consumers/patients impact health care management and marketing.

In the sections to follow, we will discuss how specific behaviors of health care consumers/patients affect health care management and marketing.

Ensocare (2017) highlights the importance of classifying target populations in health care marketing by demographics. Their arguments include the following:

- US population is getting bigger, older and more diverse, the ever-evolving composition of the population will have profound effects on the US health care system and the people in its care.
- Changes in population size, age, race and ethnicity affect the health services needed as these groups come up with varying health conditions and social and cultural beliefs.
- Health care organizations will have to adapt quickly to meet these patients' changing needs, in particular:
    - *An Aging Population*: In 1950, the population aged 65 and older represented 8.1% of the total US population. That percentage is projected to reach 20.2% by 2050.
    - *Racial Diversity*: While Latinos are the largest ethnic group, followed by African–Americans, population diversity has become more complicated. While many minority groups are still concentrated in specific areas of the country, many have moved around the US for economic reasons. Each population group has socioeconomic concerns that effect access to health services, and is predisposed to specific diseases. African–Americans face higher maternal mortality and are more likely to develop diabetes than whites. Latinos are far more likely than any other population to contract lupus.
    - *Cultural and Religious Differences*: In some cultures, female patients do not like to be seen by male physicians. Some cultures believe in alternative remedies that, when combined with traditional medicine, could have harmful consequences. Hindus and Buddhists believe in meditation and yoga as alternative or supplementary treatments for pain and mental illnesses.

These and other consumer/patient-related variables require health care organizations to understand their behaviors and formulate care and marketing/communication strategies accordingly.

What then are the key demographic variables useful for consumer/patient analysis in health care marketing?

6.3.1. Age

Price (2011) explains the notable effect of an aging population on health care delivery and marketing.

In 1950, the population aged 65 and older represented 8.1% of the total US population. That percentage is projected to reach 20.2% by 2050. This shift will place great demands on the nation's health care system.

How would this affect health care organizations' strategic planning? Price believes that hospitals and health systems will need to form more partnerships with other providers and payers to create a complete continuum of patient care. Hospitals will need more specialists in the diseases and conditions of aging — including chronic disease and palliative and hospice care — and health care professionals who can help patients address end-of-life care issues. Hospitals will also have to adopt new technologies to enhance care coordination. Health systems will also enhance services for chronic conditions and plan for increasing the workforce needed for elder care (Rowe *et al.*, 2016).

How would this affect health care marketing of hospitals? According to Rowe (2016), significant increase in communication and marketing efforts by senior living industry is already evident. Health care marketing will increasingly communicate the merits of social engagement for elderly consumers, and the advantages of arrangements to buy-in assisted living and skilled nursing care in what are called Continuing Care Retirement Communities (CCRC).

6.3.2. Racial diversity

While Latinos are the largest ethnic group, followed by African-Americans, population diversity has become more complicated, according to a two-part series, "Who We Are: Implications of the 2010 Census for Health Care" in Hospitals & Health Networks Daily. Americans have long-held beliefs that Latinos live in the Southwest and African-Americans live in the South.

But the 2010 census revealed that's not the case. While many minority groups are still concentrated in specific areas of the country, many have moved around the US, following jobs and cheaper housing. Each population group has socioeconomic concerns — lack of insurance or less access to health services, for example — and predispositions to specific diseases. African-Americans face higher maternal mortality and are more likely to develop diabetes than whites. Latinos are far more likely than any other population to develop lupus.

What does all of this mean? Hospitals and health systems must regularly assess their community's makeup to accommodate specific health needs and socioeconomic circumstances. Since the census is conducted every 10 years and population makeup can change rapidly due to economic downturns or natural disasters, health care organizations should rely on data from the American Community Survey, a mandatory annual sampling of the population conducted by the US Census Bureau, for their planning needs.

6.3.3. Cultural and religious differences

Cultural and religious diversity — well beyond communication barriers — is important as well. In some cultures, for example, a male physician won't see female patients. Other cultures have complementary and alternative remedies that, when combined with traditional medicine, could have harmful consequences.

Health care providers also need to keep patients' religious beliefs and traditions in mind. Buddhists, for example, place an importance on mindful awareness and often seek non-pharmacological pain management options. During the month of Ramadan, Muslims do not eat or drink from dawn to sundown, and this fasting could present harm to a patient (Associated Press, 2019). However, children, the elderly and the ill are exempted.

Health care professionals must be cognizant of these differences within their patient community. They need to communicate clearly, in a respectful manner, if and when cultural and religious preferences may put the patient in harm's way.

From patient age to religious preference, diversity is not going away. The once "one-size-fits-all" notion of health care has all but dissolved. Hospitals and other health care organizations will have to continually assess and plan for their changing patient populations' care needs.

Price (2011) presents the following examples of different approaches to study racial, cultural and ethnic variations in populations:

- According to county-level data from the 2007 US Census, Los Angeles County has more Hispanic residents (4.7 million), Asian residents (1.4 million), and Native American residents (146,500) than any other county in the nation. Consumer/patient behavior of these large cultural and ethnic groups is significantly different.

- Another approach is to look at the percentage of minorities in an area. By this measure, according to the online data repository City-Data, New York is the most diverse major city, with only 35% of residents identifying as "white only", followed by Dallas, Chicago, and Houston. However, City-Data's figures do not agree with the 2005 to 2009 US Census American Community Survey, which places the New York figure at 45.4, and Chicago's figure at 41.9%.
- Another useful classification is residents of a city born abroad. By that measure, according to the Migration Policy Institute (MPI), a think tank based in Washington, D.C., Miami, with its large population of immigrants from Cuba, as well as other countries in the Caribbean and South America, leads the nation with 36.5%. MPI also offers what might be the best measure of diversity. It defines "hyper diverse" cities as those with at least 9.5% foreign-born residents, with no one country of origin accounting for more than 25% of the foreign-born population, and immigrants coming from all regions of the world. The MPI highlights New York as one of the most "hyper diverse" cities in America, others being Washington, D.C.; San Francisco; and Seattle.

6.3.4. Income level

There are many surveys and studies confirming that income levels of the population are known to affect health conditions, access to health care and health care behavior of consumers/patients.

- CDC (2012) — Summary Health Statistics for US Adults: National Health Interview Survey 2011 — reports that people with lower incomes report poorer health and have a higher risk of disease. Poor adults are almost five times as likely to report being in fair or poor health as adults with family incomes at or above 400% of the federal poverty level and they are more than three times as likely to have activity limitations due to chronic illness. Low-income American adults also have higher rates of heart disease, diabetes, stroke, and other chronic disorders than wealthier Americans. Cited by Woolf *et al.* (2015).

  A similar continuous relation between income and mortality has been shown in Canada (Marmot, 2002).
- Cutler *et al.* (2006) show that the relationship between income and health is seen as a universal phenomenon. Mortality rates remain much

higher in poor countries, with a difference in life expectancy between rich and poor countries of about 30 years. This difference persists despite the remarkable progress in health improvement in the last half century, at least until the HIV/AIDS pandemic.

- Marmot (2002) argues that lower income affects population health in several ways.

    o First, it makes it more difficult for low income groups to acquire material conditions, such as clean water and good sanitation, adequate nutrition, and adequate housing and warmth that are necessary for good health.
    o Second, poverty often reduces chances of having a hobby or leisure activity, having friends or family around for a snack, taking children swimming, or having a family holiday. These are related to individual incomes to a greater or lesser extent, depending on purchasing power and public provision. They are not "material", in the sense that clean water and good sanitation are.
    o Third, people who are relatively poor are likely to have low levels of social participation.
    o Finally, income and education level seem to go together. Once education is included in the model, the effect of income on mortality is markedly reduced. This may be due to education affects health precisely because those with more education have higher incomes. It could, however, be because education is a better indicator than is income of some of the social factors, linked to social position, that are important for health.

6.3.5. Education level

National Bureau of Economic Research (2018) reports that there is a well-known, large, and persistent association between education and health. This has been observed in many countries and time periods, and for a wide variety of health measures. The differences between the more and the less educated are significant: in 1999, the age-adjusted mortality rate of high school dropouts ages 25–64 was more than twice as large as the mortality rate of those with some college education. The NBER report states,

> "An additional four years of education lowers five-year mortality by 1.8 percentage points; it also reduces the risk of heart disease by 2.16 percentage points, and the risk of diabetes by 1.3 percentage points."

Virginia Commonwealth University (2015) confirms these findings and also presents why education matters to health. Americans with fewer years of education have poorer health and shorter lives, and that has never been more true than today. In fact, since the 1990s, life expectancy has decreased for people without a high school education, especially white women.

What is the cause? Why does education matter more to health? In today's knowledge economy, education paves a path to good jobs: Completing more years of education confers health benefits after leaving school, such as better health insurance, access to medical care, and the resources to live a healthier lifestyle and to reside in healthier homes and neighborhoods.

6.3.6. Social relationships

Umberson and Montezl (2010) found that social relationships — both quantity and quality — affect mental health, health behavior, physical health, and mortality risk. Many types of scientific evidence show that involvement in social relationships benefits health. The most striking evidence comes from prospective studies of mortality across industrialized nations. These studies consistently show that individuals with the lowest level of involvement in social relationships are more likely to die than those with greater involvement. Risk of death among men and women with the fewest social ties was more than twice as high as the risk for adults with the most social ties. Moreover, this finding held even when socioeconomic status, health behaviors, and other variables that might influence mortality were taken into account. Social ties also reduce mortality risk among adults with documented medical conditions. For instance, House *et al.* (1988) confirm this by saying recent scientific work has established both a theoretical basis and strong empirical evidence for a causal impact of social relationships on health. Prospective studies, which control baseline health status, consistently show increased risk of death among persons with low quantity, and sometimes low quality, of social relationships.

Change *et al.* (2014) report a study using data for the period 2006–2010 from a US Health and Retirement Study. This study examined data on 2,965 older participants to determine if leisure activities mediated the link between social relationships and health in 2010, controlling for race, education level, and health in 2006. *Results:* The results demonstrated that leisure activities mediate the link between social relationships and health in these age groups. Perceptions of positive social relationships were associated with greater involvement in leisure activities, and greater involvement in leisure activities was associated with better health in older age. *Conclusion*: The contribution of leisure to health in these age groups is receiving increasing attention, and the results of this study add to the literature on this topic, by identifying the mediating effect of leisure activity on the link between social relationships and health. Future studies aimed at increasing leisure activity may contribute to improved health outcomes in older adults.

6.3.7. Gender

Gender segmentation is another common market strategy in almost every industry where customers are divided into categories of male and female. Examples include colognes, watches and sports shoes. Health disparities exist between men and women. For example, in 2007, life expectancy of US women was 80.4 while it was 75.3 for men (*Source*: National Center for Health Statistics cited by Harvard Men's Health Watch, 2010). This is a universal phenomenon shown by comparative statistics in almost every country.

Looking at diseases considered America's 10 leading killers, male:female death rate ratios (*Source*: National Center for Health Statistics cited by Harvard Men's Health Watch, 2010) are as follows:

1. Heart disease — 1.5
2. Cancer — 1.4
3. Stroke — 1.0
4. Chronic obstructive lung disease — 1.3
5. Accidents — 2.2
6. Diabetes — 1.4
7. Alzheimer's disease — 0.7
8. Influenza and pneumonia — 1.4
9. Kidney disease — 1.4
10. Septicemia (blood infection) — 1.2

All causes — 1.4

The reasons for this lag among men is accounted for by biological factors (such as sex chromosomes, hormones, reproductive anatomy and metabolism; social factors; work stress; behavioral factors; risky behavior; aggression and violence; smoking, alcohol and substance abuse; diet; lack of exercise; and lack of routine medical care (Harvard Men's Health Watch, 2010)).

Disparities exist between men and women in health behavior as well. Ek (2015) highlights how studies show that men often are unwilling and lack the motivation to engage with health-related information both in times of stressful life events and in everyday life generally. Mansfield *et al.* (2003) in an article titled "Why Won't He Go to the Doctor?" explain the reasons for such behavior by men. In their opinion, if a man greatly admires the people in his life who discourage or speak badly of seeking help, he will be less likely to seek help himself.

There is also a difference between genders in seeking health-related information. Ek (2015) argues that men, due to gender role strains and social constructions of masculinity, tend to be unaware of sources of health-related information and have inadequate competency to search for them because of either pure ignorance or reluctance, and accordingly low motivation, of seeking out what they do know to be available. Research, both prior to the internet and since the internet appeared, that have examined gender as a variable in health information-seeking behavior also clearly demonstrates that women are more active seekers of health-related information than men (Ek, 2015; Lorence and Park, 2007). Rice (2006) analyzed seven major US nationally representative datasets from the Pew Internet and American Life Project and found that one of the strongest and most consistent predictors of frequent health information seeking was being female. His extensive research also showed that "women are more likely to be health seekers, or not Internet users, than men, but less likely to be Internet users and not health seekers."

> "Women are the health care decision makers in our country — they make approximately 80% of the health care decisions in their families. Women take the lead role in choosing health plans, scheduling doctor's appointments, and making sure their loved ones are getting the care they need."
>
> National Partnership for Women and Families (2013)

6.3.8. Family size

The main effect on family size is in cost of insurance and health care. Health insurance plan costs increase with the number of persons in the family.

However, larger families with low income get certain subsidies to purchase health care. For example, if a family is seeking health care under an Affordable Care Act health insurance marketplace (called "exchanges"), they can receive a subsidy or premium tax credit in advance to help them pay monthly health insurance premiums. A subsidy is financial assistance from the government in the form of an advance premium tax credit. When calculating this subsidy amount, the total household income and family size are taken into account.

6.4. Understanding the Health Care Consumer/Patient Decision-Making Process

It is important for health care managers and marketers to have a basic understanding of the health care consumer/patient's decision-making process when it comes to decisions about health care, provider choice and retention with providers. We will address this issue in this section before proceeding in the next section to address specific factors and variables the health care consumer/patient takes into consideration in making these decisions.

Several writers and experts have analyzed the health care consumer/patient decision-making process.

In general, consumers are perceived as going through the following stages in making decisions to purchase goods and services (MSG, 2019):

- Need;
- Information gathering (search for information);
- Evaluation of alternatives;
- Purchasing product/service;
- Post-purchase evaluation leading to satisfaction/dissatisfaction, and retention decision.

Would this general decision-making process be valid for health care decisions?

At least, some writers believe in a similar process. For example, Gaynor (2016) identifies a four-stage decision-making process for health care consumer decisions as follows:

- Phase 1: Initial consideration;
- Phase 2: Active evaluation;
- Phase 3: Closure;
- Phase 4: Post-purchase.

> The importance of identifying stages of decision-making from a health care marketing perspective is that in each stage the health care consumer/patient seeks different types of information and depends on different sources for guidance.

For example, Gaynor (2016) claims that in the *initial consideration stage* of decision-making, for a patient considering elective knee surgery, the decision whether to have surgery and the choice of surgeon and hospital for surgery are likely to be driven by advertisements, informal referrals (from neighbor, co-worker or family member), formal referrals from a provider, and personal factors such as leave available from employer and geographic convenience.

Direct mail and print advertisements sent to the hospital's target consumer area may not have an effect in this case as these strategies are believed to have low response rates. Electronic and social media channels are more likely to create need and brand awareness in this initial consideration phase. Email messages about knee surgery directed at older populations may be a good strategy here.

During *active evaluation stage*, studies show that two-thirds of the sources used involve consumer-driven marketing activities, such as internet searches and reviews, word-of-mouth recommendations from friends and family, social media (posts, blogs and forums), as well as recollections of own past experiences.

During the next stage, *closure*, consumer/patient begins to seek detailed information on cost, insurance coverage, risks of surgery, provider credentials and post-surgical recovery. Health care marketing should be ready to provide convincing independent study/evaluation-based information to consumers/patients in this stage.

In the *post-purchase stage*, consumer/patient compares his or her outcomes, both physical and emotional outcomes, with pre-service expectations. Health care organization's management and marketing should be ready to provide information to convince consumer/patient that the outcome is as good as could have been expected using objective standards such as recovery time, cost and total patient experience.

The stage identified as "closure" in the above classification is also referred to by other researchers as "decision to seek care". Decision to seek care starts with initial and active evaluations and ends up when the consumer/patient decides to seek care from a health care provider and selects the health care provider. These stages are important for health care marketing as it is during these stages that the consumers/patients are seeking information from other persons and information sources such as print and online material. Health care marketing has a role here in identifying potential consumers/patients in these stages and providing effective communication and information.

Decision to seek care, as a health care consumer behavior, has received considerable attention among researchers. In a study of a group of men, Roberts *et al.* (1997) found that there was a significant association between propensity to seek care and physician utilization. Men with a high propensity to seek care were more likely to have had four or more physician visits, i.e., more engagement with one's primary care physician. Retirees also seem to be open to seeking care. These findings suggest that physician services marketing will benefit from focusing on senior consumers.

Berry *et al.* (2018) investigated the relationship between homophily and health care decision-making. Hemophily is a tendency for friendships to form between those who are alike in some designated respect, for example, among consumers/patients with a similar health concern such as high blood pressure. A tool that is available for health care researchers and markets to investigate the strength of homophilic association among target groups is the Perceived Homophily Scale (McCroskey *et al.*, 1975). Berry *et al.* studied a sample of 293 men with a new diagnosis of localized prostate cancer who reported relevant personal factors influencing the care management decision. One month later, participants reported how prepared they were for decision-making. One hundred twenty-three men (42%) reported friends and/or co-workers as information sources, of which 65 (53%) indicated that friends and/or co-workers influenced the care decision.

Studies on relationship between hemophily and patient decision-making have identified race/ethnicity as the strongest group affiliation in which homophily was evident. Family networks and occupational networks also were found to be homophilic. These groups provide forums for comfortable communication (McPherson *et al.*, 2001).

Modern practice of health education sessions often organized by health plans and public health organizations for promoting health behaviors in selected groups such as obese patients, African–American and Latina women are based on the concept of homophily, that is on the assumption that support and health-related information is more likely to be accepted from others in the same ethnic or racial community.

Technology can also be utilized by providers and their health marketers to provide opportunities for consumers/patients to connect with others with similar health care interests. Examples are online support groups, social media support groups using Facebook, and online health communities such as PatientsLikeMe.com.

Certainly, not all individuals will embrace electronically-mediated information. Credibility, quality and trustworthiness of the source, individuals' social connectedness, all influence information seeking behavior, and thus affect decision making. In Lee and Kim's 2015 survey, older Korean mothers trusted traditional media sources, whereas younger mothers trusted family, friends and the internet. Van Stee and Yang (2018) found skepticism of the utility of online cancer information from those of higher socioeconomic status in the Health Information National Trends Survey 4 Cycle 4, suggesting recognition of the range in quality of internet postings.

Information source selection by health care consumers is also an important factor for health care managers and marketers. MLA (2019) reports findings of a 2015 Pew Research Center Study which found that 73% of all those ages 16 and over say libraries contribute to people finding the health information they need. 42% of those who have gone online at a library using its computers, internet connections or Wi-Fi have done so for health-related searches. A previous 2013 Pew Research Internet Project reported that "59% of US adults say they have looked online for information about a range of health topics in the past year. 35% of US adults say they have gone online specifically to try to figure out what medical condition they or someone else might have." Whether the health information is needed for personal reasons or for a family member/friend, millions of health-related web pages are viewed by consumers.

Studies also show that media plays a powerful role in affecting patients' opinions and feelings; the physician–patient communication and the decision-making process. Media information influences consumer decision-making by adding to their level of education. Health care marketing should direct power of media and communications toward improving the scientific knowledge of health care consumers, in the target segments/areas, to encourage behavioral changes, particularly among individuals with lower levels of education (Passalacqua *et al.*, 2004).

Demographic variables also influence the health care consumer/patient decision-making process. For example, in certain groups, such as older people, seeking health care is affected by low expectations, resignation, and withdrawal. In addition, many conditions are attributed to ageing and not considered a medical condition. Some symptoms commonly experienced by older people are stigmatizing or embarrassing and are consequently neglected (Shaw et al., 2008).

Women are recognized as the health care decision makers of their families. According to Luce et al. (2015), 94% make decisions for themselves; 59% make decisions for others; and 94% of working moms make decisions for others.

Cultural and ethnic beliefs influence the health care decision-making process of minority ethnic groups (Euromed Info, 2019). The extended family has significant influence in their decision-making. Older family members are respected, and their authority is often unquestioned. Among Asian cultures, disagreement with the recommendations of health care professionals is avoided. However, this does not mean that the patient and family agree with or will follow treatment recommendations faithfully. Among Chinese patients, because the behavior of the individual reflects on the family, mental illness or any behavior that indicates lack of self-control may produce shame and guilt. As a result, Chinese patients may be reluctant to discuss symptoms of mental illness or depression. Some sub-populations of cultures, such as those from India and Pakistan, are reluctant to accept a diagnosis of severe emotional illness or mental retardation because it severely reduces the chances of other members of the family getting married. In Vietnamese culture, mystical beliefs explain physical and mental illness. Health is viewed as the result of a harmonious balance between the poles of hot and cold that govern bodily functions. Vietnamese do not readily accept Western mental health counseling and interventions, particularly when self-disclosure is expected. However, it is possible to accept assistance if trust has been gained.

Russian immigrants frequently view US medical care with a degree of mistrust. The Russian experience with medical practitioners has been an authoritarian relationship in which free exchange of information and open discussion was not usual. As a result, many Russian patients find it difficult to question a physician and to talk openly about medical concerns. Patients expect a paternalistic approach — the competent health care professional does not ask patients what they want to do, but tells them what to do. This reliance on physician expertise undermines a patient's motivation to learn more about self-care and preventive health behaviors.

Although Hispanics share a strong heritage that includes family and religion, each subgroup of the Hispanic population has distinct cultural beliefs and customs. Older family members and other relatives are respected and are often consulted on important matters involving health and illness.

Fatalistic views are shared by many Hispanic patients who view illness as God's will or divine punishment brought about by previous or current sinful behavior. Hispanic patients may prefer to use home remedies and may consult a folk healer, known as a *curandero*.

Many African–Americans participate in a culture that centers on the importance of family and church. There are extended kinship bonds with grandparents, aunts, uncles, cousins, or individuals who are not biologically related, but who play an important role in the family system. Usually, a key family member is consulted for important health-related decisions. The church is an important support system for many African–Americans.

Cultural aspects common to Native Americans usually include being oriented in the present and valuing cooperation. Native Americans also place great value on family and spiritual beliefs. They believe that a state of health exists when a person lives in total harmony with nature. Illness is viewed not as an alteration in a person's physiological state, but as an imbalance between the ill person and natural or supernatural forces. Native Americans may use a medicine man or woman, known as a shaman.

As can be seen, each ethnic group brings its own perspectives and values to the health care system, and many health care beliefs and health practices differ from those of the traditional American health care culture. Unfortunately, the expectation of many health care professionals has been that patients will conform to mainstream values. Such expectations have frequently created barriers to care that have been compounded by differences in language and education between patients and providers from different backgrounds.

Cultural differences affect patients' attitudes about medical care and their ability to understand, manage, and cope with the course of an illness, the meaning of a diagnosis, and the consequences of medical treatment. Patients and their families bring culture specific ideas and values related to concepts of health and illness, reporting of symptoms, expectations for how health care will be delivered, and beliefs concerning medication and treatments. In addition, culture specific values influence patient roles and expectations, how much information about illness and treatment is desired, how death and dying will be managed, bereavement patterns, gender and family roles, and processes for decision-making.

This discussion suggests that health care marketers should pay close attention to demographic and cultural/ethnic variations in selecting marketing/communication strategies.

6.5. Factors Influencing Provider Selection and Retention Decisions of Health Care Consumers/Patients

In this section, we will explore factors health care consumers/patients take into consideration in making health care provider selection and retention decisions. Studies show that a large number of factors and variables affect these decisions. These include structural factors such as insurance and payer coverage and policies, employer benefits and employer-provided health care plan choices, personal factors such as age and life cycle stage, occupation, income and economic situation, life style, social, group and cultural influences, social status, provider-related factors that include predicated outcome-related factors and service process-related factors.

First, we will discuss various research and survey findings that have identified such factors. Then, we will make a summary of these factors and also discuss implications for health care marketing.

Abraham *et al.* (2011) in a paper, "Selecting a Provider: What Factors Influence Patients' Decision-Making?" report results of a survey of 467 patients at four clinics in Minnesota. They found that the factors considered of greatest importance include reputation of the physician and reputation of the health care organization. Contractual and logistical factors also play a role, with respondents highlighting the importance of seeing a provider affiliated with their health plan and appointment availability. Few respondents indicated that advertisements or formal sources of quality information affected their decision-making.

The key implication for provider organizations is to carefully manage referral sources to ensure that they consistently meet the needs of referrers. Excellent service to existing patients and to the network of referring physicians yields patient and referrer satisfaction that is critical to attracting new patients. Finally, organizations more generally may want to explore the capabilities of new media and social networking sites for building reputation (Radulescu *et al.*, 2012).

The behavior of health services consumer is the result of the many factors both external (cultural factors, social factors, etc.) and internal (personal factor and psychological factors).

Decisions of health care consumers and patients in selecting physicians and hospitals seem to have significant differences.

Studies show that the search efforts for a physician by consumers/patients are limited. They do not depend on comprehensive quality studies, such as Consumer Assessment of Health Plans ("CAHPS") and Health Plan Employer Data and Information Set ("HEDIS") because they are hard to access and difficult to understand. They depend on information from family and friends and the judgments of individual doctors. This seems to stem from the difficulty of obtaining information with which to compare the quality of alternative physicians (Harris, 2003).

In a survey of a very large number of studies, Harris (2003; in a paper, "How Do Patients Choose Physicians?") found that a majority of respondents reported personal contacts as sources of information, with only one-third reporting that they had contacted more than one individual. Only 25% consulted another physician — most frequently in emergency situations. More than 75% of the respondents reported friends, colleagues, and relatives as information sources and less than 25% actively considered more than one physician; among those who considered alternative physicians, less than 60% actually visited or spoke with another physician.

Trust, existing trust or perceived trust, in the physician is a key element is selecting a physician and staying with the same physician. Older patients, like those on Medicare, appear to have long-standing relationships with their physicians which they do not like to change.

However, physicians seem to feel that patient trust, in general, in physicians is diminishing.

Liu *et al.* (2013) in their study found that the negative effect of Health Management Organizations (HMO) enrollment on patient trust declined significantly from 1996 to 2003. This finding is robust to bivariate analyses, multivariate analyses of cross-sectional data, and multivariate analyses of longitudinal data with interaction terms. Overall, patient trust increased over this time period, and our results suggest that this improvement may be solely due to HMOs.

They found wide variations in patient trust, not only by insurance status, but also by socioeconomic and demographic characteristics. Less educated people, minorities, and poorer individuals exhibit markedly less trust in their physicians. This may have very significant adverse implications for access to care and quality of care among these groups.

They also found that HMOs have begun to realize the limitations of restrictive practices and their negative effects on patient trust. During the past decade, patient trust on HMOs has been rising consistently.

Given limited information, many patients find it quite challenging to compare alternative complex insurance contracts and to judge the quality of medical services. Thus, HMO insurance plans are properly viewed as experience goods (Sloan and Hall, 2002). With more experience with HMOs, patient trust in their HMO providers may have improved (McGuire, 1983; Thom *et al.*, 2004). This could also help explain the improved trust among HMO enrollees over time.

At the same time, searching for health care information via the internet, media, and other sources, and greater patient participation in medical decision-making — a phenomenon referred to in the literature as "consumerism" — is on the rise (Bloche, 2006; Robinson, 2005).

Cohen (2016) in a paper, "How Do Patients Select a New Physician?" reports that:

- 59% of patients report using review sites at least often or sometimes, according to a report by the medical technology reviews company Software Advice.
- Only 16% of patients reported never using review sites; 25% said they rarely used them.
- A total of 77% of patients use online reviews before selecting a physician; 16% of patients use online reviews after selecting a physician.
- When looking at review sites, 47% of patients reported being interested in individual physician and entire practice reviews; 40% reported only being interested in individual physician reviews and 13% reported only being interested in entire practice reviews.
- A plurality of patients, 28%, said quality of care is the most important factor of online reviews while 26% said ratings are most important.
- Almost half of patients, 47%, said they would go out-of-network for a physician who has similar qualifications to an in-network physician, but who has better reviews.
- A total of 60% of patients said it is "very important" or "moderately important" for physicians to respond to poor reviews.
- Only 7% of patients use online reviews to evaluate a current physician.

Healthcare Success (2019) reports findings from (a) 2014 Healthgrades American Hospital Quality Report to the Nation, (b) Consumer Research: America's Readiness to Choose a Doctor or Hospital; Prepared by Harris Interactive; October 2012, and (c) a survey by the American Osteopathic Association (AOA), on consumer/patient choice of physicians and hospitals. The conclusions reported in these studies are as follows:

- **Choice of Physician:** Consumers who have selected a physician in the past three years are more concerned about convenient location (62%) and friendly office staff (56%) than success rates (22%).

- **Factors Most Often Considered When Selecting a Physician:**
    - Whether my physician is covered by my health insurance plan (72%);
    - The physician's office location (69%);
    - Which hospital he/she is affiliated with (49%);
    - How long it takes to get an appointment with that physician (47%);
    - Acceptance of insurance plan (83.3%);
    - Bedside manner/empathy (60.5%);
    - Proximity of office to home, work or school (57.4%);
    - Convenient office hours (42.9%); and
    - Medical specialty (37.5%).
- **Resources When Finding a Physician:**
    - Word of mouth, i.e., family, friends, co-workers (65.9%);
    - Insurance provider directory (51.9%);
    - Physician rating websites, i.e., Vitals, Healthgrades (22.8%);
    - Hospital website (10.8%); and
    - Consumer review websites, i.e., Yelp (10.5%).

6.5.1. Factors influencing selection of hospitals by consumers and patients

Unlike selection of physicians, consumers and patients seem to depend on physician recommendation and referral in selecting a hospital for inpatient services. Typically, they depend on their primary care physician for referrals to specialists, and in turn, the specialist usually recommends a hospital where the specialist has admitting privileges. Within those hospitals, the patient then takes into consideration other factors such as the following:

- **Convenient location:** Healthcare Success (2019) and Johnston (2017).
- **Outcomes information and reputation:** Healthcare Success (2019) and Johnston (2017).
- **Patient experience; word of mouth recommendations:** Johnston (2017).
- **Insurance coverage and out-of-pocket costs:** Keehn (2017) and Healthcare Success (2019).

Consumer Reports, a reputed independent rating organization, bases its hospital ratings on the following factors (Keehn, 2017): Statistics submitted by hospitals to government agencies and accreditation agencies are the source for most rating factors.

- Patient experience.
- Patient outcomes, including readmissions.
- Hospital practices — two measures are included under this heading, the use of electronic health records, and the appropriate use of Computed Tomography (CT) scanning.
- Safety score — a summary of several key categories related to hospital safety, such as avoiding infections, avoiding readmissions, communicating about new medications and discharge, appropriate use of chest and abdominal CT scanning, avoiding serious complications, and avoiding mortality.
- Avoiding adverse events in surgical patients.

Other sources available to evaluate hospitals are as follows:

- **Hospital Compare, a US Government (CMS) website:** Comparisons of hospitals based on government surveys of patient experience. https://www.cms.gov/.../hospitalqualityinits/hospitalcompare.html.
- **The Commonwealth Fund:** Performance data on hospitals nationwide.
- **The Joint Commission Data:** Joint Commission is the most reputed accreditation agency that evaluates hospital performance.
- **The Leapfrog Group Information:** A non-profit employer-advocacy group on overall patient safety and the safety of selected procedures. Their evaluations are based on a survey of over 1,000 hospitals.
- The US News & World Report Information on hospitals.

Service management literature provides another source for us to understand dimensions taken into consideration by consumers in evaluating a service provider. These come from a five-dimension approach, called SERVQUAL, well known in Service Management literature (Parasuraman et al., 1985, 1988). These five dimensions are as follows:

1. **Reliability:** Ability to perform the promised service dependably and accurately.
2. **Responsiveness:** Willingness to help customers/patients and provide prompt service.

3. **Assurance:** Knowledge and courtesy of employees and their ability to inspire trust and confidence.
4. **Empathy:** Caring, individualized attention the provider and staff provide its customers.
5. **Tangibles:** Physical facilities, equipment, and the appearance of the personnel.

Studies show that these five dimensions are present in consumer/patient decision-making in health care services (Chowdhury, 2008; Headley and Miller, 1993; Licata *et al.*, 1995; Lytle and Mokwa, 1992; Quader, 2009).

Studies focusing on health care environment have shown the following factors considered by consumers/patients as most important to them:

- **Cho *et al.* (2004):** Convenience, Physician concern, Non-physician (staff) concern, Tangibles.
- **Alden *et al.* (2004):** Tangibles, Access to services, Staff expertise, Personal care.
- **McCarthy *et al.* (2005):** Clear diagnosis, Effective treatment, Information, Communication, Assurance, Access, Post-care advice.
- **Kilbourne *et al.* (2004):** Tangibles, Reliability, Response, Empathy.
- **Gabbot and Hogg (1995):** Empathy, Credibility of physician, Range of services, Physical access, Situational factors, Responsiveness.
- **Brown and Schwartz (1989):** Professionalism, Skill of health professionals.
- **Lee *et al.* (2000):** Assurance, Empathy, Reliability, Responsiveness, Tangibles, Core medical service, Professionalism/Skill.
- **Jun *et al.* (1998):** Tangibles, Courtesy, Reliability, Communication, Competence, Understanding, Access, Responsiveness, Caring, Clinical outcomes, Collaboration.
- **Taylor (1994) and Babakus and Mangold (1992):** Post-service perception (single dimension).
- **Walbridge and Delene (1993):** Reliability, Professionalism/Skill, Empathy, Assurance, Core medical services, Responsiveness, Tangibles.
- **US Department of Health & Human Services (2018):** CAHPS Health Plan measures: Getting Needed Care, Getting Care Quickly; How Well Doctors Communicate; and Health Plan Customer Service.
- **Williams and Brown (2014):** Size and service mix, Resource levels, Location, Governance structures, Participation and connectedness, Culture and strategic orientation, Absorptive capacity.

Understanding factors leading to retention by health care consumers/patients

McKinsey (2015) explains that patients with high patient satisfaction tend to remain with the same hospital. Most health systems currently use a survey developed by the Centers for Medicare and Medicaid Services (CMS) — the Hospital Consumer Assessment of Healthcare Providers and Systems (HCAHPS) — to gauge how inpatients perceive their hospital stay as their basis for understanding patient satisfaction. McKinsey (2015) argues that while HCAHPS does provide important insights into the patient experience, it does not assess all of the important aspects of that experience.

Older Americans have long-standing ties with their physicians; among those with a usual source of care, 35.8% had ties enduring 10 years or more. Longer ties were associated with a decreased likelihood of hospitalization and lower costs. Compared with patients with a tie of one year or less, patients with ties of 10 years or more incurred US$316.78 less in Part B Medicare costs, after adjustment for key demographic and health characteristics. However, substantial impacts on the use of selected preventive care services and the adoption of certain healthy behaviors were not observed. *Conclusions*: This preliminary study suggests that long-standing physician–patient ties foster less expensive, less intensive medical care. Further studies are needed to confirm these findings and to understand how duration of tie influences the processes and outcomes of care (Weiss and Blustein, 1996).

6.6. Recent Trends in Health Care Consumer/ Patient Behavior Affecting Health Care Marketing

Industry experts and researchers have identified the following major recent changes in health care consumer/patient behavior.

6.6.1. Health care consumerism

In modern times, more consumers/patients are taking an active role in managing their health. Health consumerism is an approach to health care where educated patients make informed decisions about health care options. Some reasons for this are the escalating health care costs, complexity of the health care systems, lack of clear and easy information sources to understand these complexities, vast amounts of information available via internet-based sources, and diminished trust in physicians, hospitals and other providers in a mostly managed care environment.

C2b Solutions (2017) explains health care consumerism as the concept that patients are savvy consumers who take an active role in purchasing and consuming health care services, and also bear more of the cost burden. In the wake of nationwide health care reforms, patients have more choices, buying power and control over their own health care decisions than ever before. Patients can now shop for their own health insurance, just as they would shop for other goods.

Franklin Street (2018) in their *2018 Health Care Marketing Trends Report*, summarizes this phenomenon by saying, "Health care has moved out of the hospital and into the patient's hands."

Increase in health care consumerism can also be seen in a movement known as Consumer Driven Healthcare (CDH). Many working Americans now explore participating in Consumer Directed Health Care (CDHC) programs such as Health Reimbursement Arrangements (HRA), Health Savings Accounts (HSA), and Flexible Savings Accounts (FSA). These programs provide flexibility to employees in selecting health insurance programs that suit their age, needs, and budget.

Implications on health care marketing

Today's health care consumers want to manage their own health. For this, they need all the information and analysis. Health care marketing's first duty is to provide such information to target consumer groups. This information includes available choices, cost information, insurance coverage and out-of-pocket expense information, quality and performance data, and patient satisfaction data.

Today's health care marketing should exploit the opportunities created by employer sponsored consumer directed health care accounts such as Flexible Spending Accounts (FSAs), Health Reimbursement Arrangements (HRAs), and Health Savings Accounts (HSAs). Effective communication of advantages of these choices and tax implications must be done by health care marketing.

Health care marketing must increasingly communicate patient ratings and provider reviews to help consumers appreciate the value of services marketed.

6.6.2. Health care consumers have become avid researchers (DMN3, 2017)

Consumers/patients have become, or have the opportunities to become, more informed.

They are no longer content to blindly accept what a doctor tells them. They do their homework before visiting a doctor. They research their conditions and treatment options after visiting a doctor as well. Access to health information, cost and quality measures has become more readily available to consumers/patients.

According to Pew Research (DMN3, 2017):

- One in three American adults have gone online to figure out a medical condition.
- 72% of internet users say they looked online for health information within the past year.
- 47% of internet users search for information about doctors or other health professionals.
- 38% of internet users search for information about hospitals and other medical facilities.
- The most commonly researched topics are specific diseases or conditions; treatments or procedures; and doctors or other health professionals (NRC Health, 2019).
- In employer-provided health insurance, 76% of the employees relied on information from their employer when selecting their current care system. Older and low-income workers were more likely to use information from advertisements.

The implications on health care marketing have become obvious as stated by Whitler (2017) and Gallagher (2017, in a paper, "How Has Healthcare Marketing Changed in the Last Decade?"), "The patients have become more informed. When you have an informed patient, it's very difficult to market the same way that you (did) in the past."

6.6.3. US health care consumers are more diverse than ever before. Information and reference sources they depend on vary according to their demographic and ethnic backgrounds

Minority Americans tend to see physicians of their own race. Using data from the Commonwealth Fund 1994 National Comparative Survey of Minority Health Care, Saha *et al.* (2000) found that black and Hispanic Americans sought care from physicians of their own race because of personal preference and language, not solely because of geographic accessibility.

6.6.4. Millennials are about to surpass baby boomers as the nation's largest living adult generation

According to population projections from the US Census Bureau, as of July 1, 2016, Millennials (defined as those in ages 20 to 35 in 2016), numbered 71 million, and Boomers (ages 52–70) numbered 74 million. Millennials were expected to overtake Boomers in population in 2019 as their numbers would swell to 73 million and Boomers would decline to 72 million. Generation X (ages 36–51 in 2016) is projected to pass the Boomers in population by 2028 (Fry, 2016).

EBRI/Greenwald & Associates Consumer Engagement Health Care Survey, 2017 (https://www.ebri.org/health/ebri-greenwald-consumer-engagement-healthcare-survey) reveals that Millennials are as follows:

- Far less likely to have a primary care provider. Two-thirds of Millennials have a Primary Care Physician (PCP), compared with 85% among Baby Boomers and 78% among Gen Xers.
- More than twice as likely as Baby Boomers to use a walk-in clinic. 30% of Millennials have used a walk-in clinic, compared with 14% among Baby Boomers and 18% among Gen Xers.
- More than twice as likely to be interested in telemedicine as Baby Boomers. 40% of Millennials are interested in telemedicine compared with 19% among Baby Boomers and 27% among Gen Xers.
- More likely than other generations to have researched health care options, such as checking the quality or rating of a doctor or hospital (51% Millennial vs. 34% Gen X and 31% Baby Boomers); using an online health cost tracking tool (28% Millennial vs. 17% Gen X and 10% Baby Boomers); or otherwise finding health cost information (72% Millennial vs. 65% Gen X and 64% Baby Boomers).

- Generally, more likely to participate in wellness programs: for example, Millennials are more than twice as likely than Baby Boomers to participate in counseling on stress management, mindfulness classes, and resiliency training (33% Millennial vs. 21% Gen X and 15% Baby Boomers).
- Significantly more likely to be satisfied with various aspects of their health plan choices, such as ease of selecting a plan (56% Millennial vs. 46% Gen X and 43% Baby Boomers); information available to help understand health plan choices (56% Millennial vs. 46% Gen X and 46% Baby Boomers); number of health plans to choose from (47% Millennials vs. 34% Gen X and 32% Baby Boomers); and availability and affordability of health plans (46% Millennial vs. 33% Gen X and 29% Baby Boomers).
- Appear to bring their online shopping habits, and do-it-yourself consumer behaviors to health care interactions.

Family influences in health care decisions, which are often a family affair with input from boomers, Gen X and millennials (Carmichael, 2012).

6.6.5. Women's role in health care decision-making

Luce and Kennedy (2015) explain how, according to their report *The Power of the Purse: Engaging Women Decision Makers for Healthy Outcomes*, based on a multi-market survey of 9,218 respondents in the US, UK, Germany, Japan, and Brazil, health care consumers are overwhelmingly female and have huge unmet needs.

Women seem to need help with clear information sources. 53% think they can get the best health information online while only 31% of these women trust online sources. They do not trust the professionals who try to serve them. Of the women surveyed, 78% did not fully trust their insurance provider, 83% did not fully trust the pharmaceutical company that makes their medicine, and 35% did not fully trust their physician. Under these circumstances, i.e., lack of time, information, and trusted relationships, the researchers found that more than half (58%) of women surveyed lack confidence in their ability to make good health care decisions for themselves and their families.

6.6.6. Decline of institutional trust

Health care customers/patients are believed to have lost the trust in health care systems and services. For example,

- "Mistrust among patients, providers and insurers continues to grow" Nauert (2009).
- "Decline of institutional trust; related to medical system; billing; ethics" (Franklin Street, 2018).

6.6.7. Increased search for, and use of, digital technology-based information by health care consumers and patients

Today's health care consumers are no longer reliant on traditional methods of communication to get their information, e.g., billboards, direct mail, radio ads, etc. Mobile technology and the rise of smartphones have made information easily accessible (Hambelton, chief marketing officer at Evariant, August 26, 2016).

Today, more patients look for information online before talking with their physicians (Hesse *et al.*, 2005 citing The Health Information National Trends Survey). Consumers/patients depend heavily on internet-based sources of information. Pew Research (2013) in their Internet and American Life Project (2013) found that 80% of internet users, or about 93 million Americans, have searched for a health-related topic online.

There is a vast amount of survey findings on consumer/patient use of digital technology-based health information. We present here a few such findings:

- Use of health information, technology and online resources depend on personal health attitudes and behaviors (Deloitte, 2016). Use varies among each category in the Deloitte classification of health care consumers, i.e., "content and compliant", "sick and savvy", "casual and cautious", "online and onboard", "shop and save", and "out and about". See Section 7.5 of Chapter 7 for its classification used in market segmentation in health care marketing.
- Most frequently, people went online to look up information about a specific disease or medical problem (63%) or a particular medical treatment or procedure (47%). They were also interested in diet, nutrition, and vitamins (44%) and exercise or fitness information (36%). Other popular health topics include prescription or over-the-counter drugs (34%); alternative treatments (28%); health insurance (25%); depression, anxiety, or stress (21%) and a particular doctor or hospital (21%) (Deloitte, 2016).
- Four times as many customers would rather watch a video about a product than read about it (Franklin Street, 2018).

- Women are more likely to seek health information online than men (85% compared with 75%).
- Younger consumers are more likely to research health topics online.
  - Digital content is key to modern health care consumer decision process (DMN3, 2017). Prior to booking an appointment, 77% of patients used search engines, 83% used hospital sites, 54% used health insurance company sites, 50% used health information sites, and 26% used consumer-generated reviews.
  - Married couples, 25–34 years of age, are nearly 80% more likely to use the Web for health information than adults over 65.
  - (Google) One in 20 Google searches are for health-related information.
  - 62% of smartphone owners have used their phone in the past year to look up information about a health condition (Pew Research Center).
  - According to the 5th Annual "Pulse of Online Health" survey published by Makovsky and Kelton, 79% of Americans would be willing to use a wearable device to manage their health and 66% would be willing to use a mobile app to manage their health (Wellable, 2015).
  - 52% of patients want access to Electronic Medical Records (EMR) data related to physician notes (Accenture).
  - 64% of Americans would be willing to have a video visit with a doctor (American Well, 2016).

6.6.8. Modern health care consumers/patients focus on their total experience with health care providers

Patients, with more choices and more of their own money at stake, are demanding a more customer-friendly experience. More satisfied patients are going to be more engaged in their care and for that reason more likely to be healthier (Barr, 2016).

AHRQ (2018) defines Patient Experience as follows:

"Patient experience encompasses the range of interactions that patients have with the health care system, including their care from health plans, and from doctors, nurses, and staff in hospitals, physician practices, and other health care facilities. As an integral component of health care quality, patient experience includes several aspects of health care delivery that patients value highly when they seek and receive care, such as getting timely appointments, easy access to information, and good communication with health care providers."

Improving patient experience has many advantages (AHRQ, 2018).

- Enhances satisfaction of patients and their families.
- Is associated with important clinical processes and outcomes.
- Is correlated with key financial indicators, making it good for business as well as for patients.
- Is associated with lower medical malpractice risk.
- Results in greater employee satisfaction reducing turnover.
- Improves patient retention with the same physician or hospital.
- Improves the chances of the patient being an advocate in promoting the health care provider to other consumers/patients.

6.6.9. Implications for health marketing

Connolly (2017) states, "Health care marketing of the past focused on what a person felt internally during a physical ailment ... (now) smart health care marketers are recognizing a commonality between their patients/consumers that can be used to connect with them emotionally ... a sense of understanding from their peers," in the paper "Why Authenticity is the Prescription for Modern Healthcare Marketing". The following are some other findings:

- "The decline of traditional health care marketing — Word of mouth marketing is more relevant than ever" (Fredricks, 2011).
- "Yesterday's customer is not tomorrow's customer. Suddenly, health care marketers are expected to deeply understand consumer preferences" (Whitler, 2015).
- "Content marketing ... health explanatory videos ... mobile-friendly websites ... health apps ... social media presence ..." in Six Healthcare Marketing Trends in 2018 (Prasad, 2017).
- Recognition of the importance of customer/patient experience in health care by health care marketers.
    o "2018 Healthcare Marketing Trend #1: Customer Experience" (Kernan, 2017).
    o For health care consumers, personal experience is the number one reason for choosing a doctor or hospital. "Patient Experience: The Forgotten "P" in Your Medical Marketing Plan" (Gandolf, 2013).

○ Hospitals and health systems are following the trend predicated that by 2018, more than 50% of organizations will focus their efforts on improving customer/patient experience (Kernan, 2017).
○ More than two-thirds of health systems expect their marketing departments to spend more time and resources influencing patient behavior over the next few years (Greene, 2015; citing survey by Advisory Board Company, a Washington, D.C.-based health care consulting company).
○ "How the patients perceive the overall hospital experience has a significant impact on the success of the hospital in attracting more patients" (Jha *et al.*, 2008).

6.7. Sources of Information on Customer Characteristics and Behavior: Primary Data

There are several sources of data relating to patients that exist within many health care organizations, collected or created as part of their regular operations. These must be used first in analyzing consumer/patient characteristics and behaviors before seeking secondary data. Such internally available primary data include data on patient encounters, claims, utilization review, complaints and grievance data. However, extreme care must be taken in using such internal data to avoid violation of privacy laws. Only aggregate data should be used.

Other methods of collecting primary data directly from current and potential health care consumers/patients were discussed earlier in Chapter 3. These include the following:

- Primary data collected as per mandates from federal/state/accreditation (e.g., NCQA) agencies on race, ethnicity, and primary language,
- Focus groups,
- Depth interviewing,
- Observation, and
- Customer/patient satisfaction surveys, including online surveys.

6.8. Sources of Information on Customer Characteristics and Behavior: Secondary Data

Following is a list of sources of secondary data available for analyzing consumer/patient characteristics and behavior in health care.

- General search engines like Google, Bing, or Yahoo. Pew Research Center uses these frequently.
- Federal government health websites such as PubMed, CDC.gov, Medline, HHS.gov, and Medicare.gov.
- The Agency for Healthcare Research and Quality (AHRQ). https://www.ahrq.gov/research/data/dataresources/index.html
  - Compendium of US Health Systems, 2016.
  - Consumer Assessment of Healthcare Providers and Systems (CAHPS).
  - Healthcare Cost and Utilization Project (HCUP) Statistical Briefs on adverse events, cost of hospital stays, emergency department visits, hospital stays, hospitalization by insurer types, mental health and substance use treatments, readmissions, surgeries, and women's admissions.
  - Medical Expenditure Panel Surveys (MEPS) on over 30 expenditure categories.
- Online, searchable databases. Data on topics such as the use of health care, the costs of care, health care systems, trends in hospital care, health insurance coverage, out-of-pocket spending, patient satisfaction, accessibility of care, ambulatory surgeries, emergency department visits, health care disparities, health care quality, health care spending, hospitalizations, and state-specific health care information.
- National Information Center on Health Services Research and Health Care Technology (NICHSR). https://www.nlm.nih.gov/nichsr/usestats/sources.html
  - Health and population statistics from over 30 sources.
- CMS Program Statistics (Centers for Medicare & Medicaid Services (CMS), HHS).
- CMS Research, Statistics, Data & Systems (Centers for Medicare & Medicaid Services (CMS), HHS).
- Medicare Enrollment Dashboard (Centers for Medicare & Medicaid Services (CMS), HHS).
- Centers for Disease Control and Prevention (CDC) reports.
- AgingStats.gov (National Center for Health Statistics, CDC (NCHS), National Institute on Aging (NIA), NIH).
- Ambulatory Health Care Data — National Center for Health Statistics, CDC (NCHS).

- Behavioral Health Barometers — Substance Abuse & Mental Health Services Administration (SAMHSA), HHS.
- Bureau of Justice Statistics — US Department of Justice (DOJ) USA.
- Bureau of Labor Statistics — US Department of Labor (DOL).
- County Health Rankings & Roadmaps — Robert Wood Johnson Foundation (RWJF), University of Wisconsin.
- Emergency Department Visits — National Center for Health Statistics, CDC (NCHS).
- Global Health Atlas — World Health Organization (WHO).
- Health Insurance Data — US Census Bureau, ESA:

  o An annual report of United States health statistics. Health, United States (National Center for Health Statistics, (NCHS)).

- Kaiser State Health Facts — Kaiser Family Foundation (KFF) USA:

  o Provides health data on more than 700 health topics including demographics, health insurance coverage, health costs, minority health, and women's health for all 50 states.

- Multinational Comparisons of Health Systems Data, 2014 — Commonwealth Fund. https://www.commonwealthfund.org/trending/multinational-comparisons-health-system-data.

References

Abraham, J., Sick, B., Anderson, J., Berg, A., Dehmer, C. and Tufano, A. (2011). "Selecting a Provider: What Factors Influence Patients' Decision-Making?", *Journal of Healthcare Management*, 56 (2), 99–114.

AHRQ, Agency for Healthcare Research and Quality (2018). Section 2: Why Improve Patient Experience?, http://www.ahrq.gov/cahps/quality-improvement/improvement-guide/2-why-improve/index.html. Accessed November 12, 2018.

Alden, D. L., Hoa, D. M. and Bhawuk, D. (2004). "Client Satisfaction with Reproductive Health Care Quality", *Social Science & Medicine*, 59, 219–232.

American Well (2016). "2015 Telehealth Survey", https://www.americanwell.com/press-release/american-well-2015-telehealth-survey-64-of-consumers-would-see-a-doctor-via-video/. Accessed February 19, 2019.

Associated Press (2019). "Everything You Need to Know About the Muslim Fasting Month of Ramadan", May 5, 2019, https://www.bloomberg.com/news/articles/2019-05-06/a-look-at-the-muslim-fasting-month-of-ramadan.

Babakus, E. and Mangold, W.G. (1992). "Adapting the SERVQUAL Scale to Hospital Services: An Empirical Investigation", *Health Services Research*, 26, 767–786.

Barr, P. (2016). "Patient Experience Is Increasingly Important", H&HN Hospitals & Health Networks. March 31, 2016. https://www.hhnmag.com/articles/7083-patient-experience-is-increasingly-important. Accessed February 20, 2019.

Berry, D. L., Traci, M. B., Rachel, P. and Manan, M. N. (2018). "Understanding Health Decision-Making: An Exploration Of Homophile", *Social Science & Medicine*, 214, 118–124.

Bloche, M. G. (2006). Consumer-Directed Health Care. *The New England Journal of Medicine*, 355 (17), 1756–1759.

Brown, S. W. and Swartz, T. A. (1989), "A Gap Analysis of Professional Service Quality", *Journal of Marketing*, 53 (April), 92–98.

C2b Solutions (2017). "Healthcare Consumerism: How to Adjust to a Changing Healthcare Marketplace", https://www.c2bsolutions.com/healthcare-consumerism. Accessed February 12, 2019.

Carmichael, M. (2012). "Why Health-Care Marketing Needs an Overhaul", *Advertising Age*, 83 (13)

CDC, Center for Disease Control and Prevention (2012). *Summary Health Statistics for U.S. Adults: National Health Interview Survey 2011*, https://www.cdc.gov/nchs/data/series/sr_10/sr10_256.pdf. Accessed February 13, 2019.

Chang P.-J., Wray, L. and Lin, Y. (2014). "Social Relationships, Leisure Activity, and Health in Older Adults", *Health Psychology*, 33 (6), 516–523.

Cho, W. H., Lee, H., Kim, C. and Lee, S. (2004). "The Impact of Visit Frequency on the Relationship between Service Quality and Outpatient Satisfaction: A South Korean Study", *Health Services Research*, 39 (1), 13–33.

Chowdhury, M. M. U. (2008). "Customer Expectations and Management Perceptions in Healthcare Services of Bangladesh", *Journal of Services Research*, 8(2), 121–140.

Cohen, J. K. (2016). "How Do Patients Select a New Physician?", Becker's Hospital Review, November 4, 2016, https://www.beckershospitalreview.com/healthcare-information-technology/how-do-patients-select-a-new-physician-77-say-online-reviews.html. Accessed February 14, 2019.

Connolly, B. (2017). "Why Authenticity Is the Prescription for Modern Healthcare Marketing", http://www.olapic.com/resources/authenticity-prescription-modern-healthcare-marketing_blog-p1aw-g1lo-v1hc/. Accessed September 23, 2018.

Cutler, D. M., Deaton, A. S. and Lleras-Muney, A. (2006). "The Determinants of Mortality", NBER Working Paper Series, Cambridge.

DataPath (2019). "What is Healthcare Consumerism and How Does It Affect Healthcare?", https://dpath.com/what-is-healthcare-consumerism/. Accessed February 12, 2019.

Deloitte (2016). "Elevating the Health Care Consumer Experience Insights for the Future", https://www2.deloitte.com/us/en/pages/life-sciences-and-health-

care/articles/elevating-health-care-consumer-experience.html. Accessed October 20, 2018.
DMN3 (2017). "5 Healthcare Marketing Trends to Watch in 2017", https://www.dmn3.com/dmn3-blog/5-healthcare-marketing-trends-you-should-know-about/. Accessed January 23, 2019.
Ek, S. (2015). "Gender Differences in Health Information Behaviour: A Finnish Population-Based Survey", *Health Promotion International*, 30 (3), 736–745.
Ensocare (2017). "How Demographics Impact Healthcare Delivery", https://www.ensocare.com/resource-center/how-demographics-impact-health-care-delivery. Accessed October 27, 2018.
Euromed Info (2019). "How Culture Influences Health Beliefs", https://www.euromedinfo.eu/how-culture-influences-health-beliefs.html/. Accessed February 14, 2019.
Evariant (2016). "Why is Digital Marketing Important to Healthcare?", http://www.evariant.com/blog/digital-marketing-important-to-healthcare. Accessed January 15, 2019.
Feldman, R., Jon, C. and Jennifer, S. (2000). "Do Consumers Use Information to Choose a Health-Care Provider System?", *Milbank Quarterly*, 78 (1), 47–77.
Franklin Street (2018). *2018 Health Care Marketing Trends Report*, http://www.franklinstreet.com/2018-health-care-marketing-trends-report.
Fredricks, D. (2011). "The Decline of Traditional Health Care Marketing", *Marketing Health Services*, 31 (3), 3–5.
Fry, R. (2018). "Millennials Projected to Overtake Baby Boomers as America's Largest Generation", http://www.pewresearch.org/fact-tank/2018/03/01/millennials-overtake-baby-boomers/. Accessed February 15, 2019.
Fry, R. (2018). "Millennials Projected to Overtake Baby Boomers as America's Largest Generation", Fact Tank, https://www.pewresearch.org/fact-tank/2018/03/01/millennials-overtake-baby-boomers/. Accessed September 25, 2018.
Gabbot, M. and Hogg, G. (1995), "Grounds for Discrimination: Establishing Criteria for Evaluating Health Services", *The Service Industries Journal*, 15 (1), 90–101.
Gallagher, B. (2017). "How Has Healthcare Marketing Changed in the Last Decade?", https://www.Gallagher.sharecare.com/video/healthmakers/brendan-gallagher/what-is-the-future-of-healthcare-marketing. Accessed June 1, 2018.
Gandolf, S. (2013). "The Forgotten "P" in Your Medical Marketing Plan", Home » Blog » Healthcare Marketing » Patient Experience. Last Updated on August 2, 2013.
Gaynor, B. (2016). "Health Care Consumer Behaviors: 4 Stages of Consumer Decision-Making Applied to Health Care Shopping and Digital Transformation", https://www.linkedin.com/pulse/health-care-consumer-behaviors-4-stages-decision-making-bill-gaynor. Accessed February 12, 2019.

Greene, J. (2015). "Healthcare Marketers Reshape Ad Strategies", *Modern Healthcare*, http://www.modernhealthcare.com/article/20151030/MAGAZINE/310309995. Accessed October 1, 2018.

Harris, K. M. (2003). "How Do Patients Choose Physicians? Evidence from a National Survey of Enrollees in Employment-Related Health Plans", *Health Services Research*, 38 (2), 711–732.

Harvard Men's Health Watch (2010). "Mars vs. Venus: The Gender Gap in Health", https://www.health.harvard.edu/newsletter_article/mars-vs-venus-the-gender-gap-in-health. Accessed November 1, 2018.

Headley, D. E. and Miller, S. (1993), "Measuring Service Quality and Its Relationship to Future Consumer Behavior", *Journal of Health Care Marketing*, 13 (4), 32–41.

Healthcare Success (2019). "6 of 10 People Choose a Doctor Based on a Convenient Location", https://www.healthcaresuccess.com/blog/hospital-marketing/6-10-people-choose-doctor-based-convenient-location.html. Accessed February 14, 2019.

Hesse, B. W., Nelson, D. E., Kreps, G. L., Croyle, R. T., Arora, N. K., Rimer, B. K. and Viswanath, K. (2005). "Trust and Sources of Health Information: The Impact of the Internet and its Implications for Health Care Providers: Findings from the First Health Information National Trends Survey", *Arch Intern Med.*, 165 (22), 2618–2624.

House, J. S., Landis, K. R. and Umberson, D. (1988). "Social Relationships and Health", *Science*, 241 (4865), 540–545.

Jha, A. K., Orav, J., Zheng, J. and Epstein, A. M. (2008). "Patients' Perception of Hospital Care in the United States". *New England Journal of Medicine*, 359, 1921–1931.

Johnston, S. (2017). "3 Factors Patients Use to Choose a Hospital", DH, https://www.wearedh.com/blog/3-factors-patients-use-to-choose-a-hospital/. Accessed February 13, 2019.

Jun, M., Peterson, R. T. and Zsidisin, G. A. (1998), "The Identification and Measurement of Quality Dimensions in Health Care: Focus Group Interview Results", *Health Care Management Review*, 23(4), 81–96.

Keehn, J. (2017). "How to Choose a Hospital", *Consumer Reports*, https://www.consumerreports.org/hospitals/HowToChooseAHospital/. Accessed February 15, 2019.

Kernan, J. (2017). "2018 Healthcare Marketing Trend #1: Customer Experience", Smith Jones, https://smithandjones.com/resources/blog/2018-healthcare-marketing-trends-customer-experience. Accessed September 27, 2018.

Kilbourne, W. E., Duffy, J. A., Duffy, M. and Giarchi, G. (2004), "The Applicability of SERVQUAL in Cross-National Measurements of Health-Care Quality", *Journal of Services Marketing*, 18 (7), 524–533.

Krivich, M. (2011). "Customer Experience Management Applied to Healthcare", Healthcare Marketing Matters, http://healthcaremarketingmatters.blogspot.com/2011/01/customer-experience-management-applied.html. Accessed September 24, 2018.

Lee, H., Delene, L. M., Bunda, M. A. and Kim, C. (2000), "Methods of Measuring Health Care Service Quality", *Journal of Business Research*, 48, 233–246.

Licata, J. W., Mowen, J. C. and Chakraborty, G. (1995). "Diagnosing Perceived Quality in the Medical Service Channel", *Journal of Health Care Marketing*, 15 (4), 42–49.

Liu, H., Fang H. and Rizzo, J. A. (2013). "HMOs and Patient Trust in Physicians: A Longitudinal Study", *International Journal of Applied Economics*, 10 (1), 1–21.

Lorence, D. and Park, H. (2007). "Gender and Online Health Information: A Partitioned Technology Assessment", *Health Information and Libraries Journal*, 24, 204–209.

Luce, C. B. and Kennedy, J. T. (2015). "The Health Care Industry Needs to Start Taking Women Seriously", *Harvard Business Review* (on line), https://hbr.org/2015/05/the-health-care-industry-needs-to-start-taking-women-seriously. Accessed February 20, 2019.

Luce, C. B., Sylvia, A. H., Julia, T. K. and Laura, S. (2015). "The Power of the Purse: Engaging Women Decision Makers for Healthy Outcomes", *Center for Talent Innovation*, https://www.talentinnovation.org/_private/assets/PopHealthcare_ExecSumm-CTI.pdf. Accessed February 14, 2019.

Lytle, R. S. and Mokwa, M. P. (1992), "Evaluating Health Care Quality: Moderating Role of Outcomes", *Journal of Health Care Marketing*, 12 (1), 4–14.

Mansfield, A., Addis, M. and Mahalik, J. (2003). "Why Won't He Go to the Doctor? The Psychology of Men's Help Seeking", *International Journal of Men's Health*, 2 (2), 93.

Marmot, M. (2002). "The Determinants of Health: The Influence of Income on Health: Views of an Epidemiologist", *Health Affairs*, 21 (2).

McCarthy, C. J., Oldham, J. A. and Sephton, R. (2005). "Expectations and Satisfaction of Patients with Low Back Pain Attending a Multidisciplinary Rehabilitation Service", *Physiotherapy Research International*, 10 (1), 23–31.

McCroskey, J. C., Richmond, V. P. and Daly, J. A. (1975). "The Development of a Measure of Perceived Homophily in Interpersonal Communication", *Human Communication Research*, 1 (4), 323–332.

McDonough, P., Duncan, G. J., Williams, D. and House, J. (1997). "Income Dynamics and Adult Mortality in The United States, 1972 through 1989", *American Journal of Public Health*, 87 (9), 1476–1483.

McGuire, T. G. (1983). "Patients' Trust and the Quality of Physicians", *Economic Inquiry*, 21 (2), 203–222.

McKinsey (2015). A Comprehensive Approach Health Systems Can Use to Better Understand the Patient Experience and Thereby Improve Patient Satisfaction. August 2015.

McPherson, M., Smith-Lovin, L. and Cook, J. M. (2001). "Birds of a Feather: Homophily in Social Networks", *Annual Review of Sociology*, 27, 415–444.

MLA, Medical Library Association (2019). "Find Good Health Information", https://www.mlanet.org/page/find-good-health-information. Accessed February 13, 2019.

MSG, Management Study Guides (2019). "Stages in Consumer Decision-Making Process", https://www.managementstudyguide.com/consumer-decision-making-process.htm. Accessed February 14, 2019.

National Bureau of Economic Research (2018). "The Effects of Education on Health", https://www.nber.org/digest/mar07/w12352.html. Accessed October 30, 2018.

National Partnership for Women and Families (2013). "Women: Health Care Decision Makers", http://www.nationalpartnership.org/research-library/health-care/aca-enrollment-event-toolkit.pdf. Accessed October 30, 2018.

Nauert, R. (2009). "Trust in Health Care System Continues To Decline", https://psychcentral.com/news/2009/09/02/trust-in-health-care-system-continues-to-decline/8125.html. Accessed January 39, 2019.

NRC Health (2019). *2019 Health Care Consumer Trends Report*, https://nrchealth.com/wp-content/uploads/2018/12/2019-Healthcare-Consumer-Trends-Report.pdf. Accessed February 16, 2019.

Parasuraman, A., Berry, L. L. and Zeithaml, V. A. (1985). "A Conceptual Model of Service Quality and Its Implications for Future Research", *Journal of Marketing*, 49 (4), 41–50.

Parasuraman, A., Berry, L. L. and Zeithaml, V. A. (1988). "SERVQUAL: A Multiple-Item Scale for Measuring Consumer Perceptions of Service Quality", *Journal of Retailing*, 64 (1), 12–40.

Passalacqua, R., Caterina, C., Stefania, S., Sandro, B., Giordano, D. B., Paolo, C., Antonio, C., Francesco, D. C., Lucia, T. and Francesco, C. (2004). "Effects of Media Information on Cancer Patients' Opinions, Feelings, Decision-Making Process and Physician-Patient Communication", *Cancer*, 100 (5), https://onlinelibrary-wiley-com.lib-proxy.fullerton.edu/doi/epdf/10.1002/cncr.20050. Accessed February 12, 2019.

Patient Engagement (2019). "How Do Healthcare Consumers Define Value in Patient-Centered Care?", https://patientengagementhit.com/news/how-do-healthcare-consumers-define-value-in-patient-centered-care. Accessed February 14, 2019.

Pew Research Center (2013). "Health Online 2013" by Susannah Fox and Maeve Duggan, http://www.pewinternet.org/2013/01/15/health-online-2013/. Accessed June 23, 2018.

Prasad, A. (2017). "6 Healthcare Marketing Trends in 2018: How to Leverage Them", https://blog.gmrwebteam.com/2018-healthcare-marketing-trends-how-to-leverage-them/ Accessed January 12, 2019.

Price, A. (2011). "Is Los Angeles the Most Diverse City in America?", https://www.good.is/articles/is-los-angeles-the-most-diverse-city-in-america. Accessed October 26, 2018.

Quader, M. S. (2009). "Manager and Patient Perceptions of a Quality Outpatient Service", *Journal of Services Research*, 9 (1), 109–137.

Radulescu, V., Cetina, I. and Orzan, G. (2012). "Key Factors that Influence Behavior of Health Care Consumer, the Basis of Health Care Strategies", *Contemporary Readings in Law and Social Justice*, 4 (2), 992–1001.

Rice, R. E. (2006). "Influences, Usage, and Outcomes of Internet Health Information Searching: Multivariate Results from the Pew Surveys". *International Journal of Medical Informatics*, 75, 8–28.

Roberts, R. O., Rhodes, T., Girman, C. J., Guess, H. A., Oesterling, J. E., Lieber, M. M. and Jacobsen, S. J. (1997). "The Decision to Seek Care: Factors Associated with the Propensity to Seek Care in a Community-Based Cohort of Men", *Archives of Family Medicine*, 6 (3), 218–222.

Robinson, J. (2005). "Managed Consumerism in Health Care", *Health Affairs (Project Hope)*, 24 (6), 478–489.

Rowe, J. W., Fulmer, T. and Fried, L. (2016). "Preparing for Better Health and Health Care for an Aging Population", *JAMA*, 316 (16), 1643–1644.

Saha, S. L., Taggart, S. H., Komaromy, M. and Bindman, A. B. (2000). "Do Patients Choose Physicians of Their Own Race?", *Health Affairs*, 19 (4), 76–83.

Shaw, C., Brittain, K., Tansey, R. and Williams, K. (2008). "How People Decide to Seek Health Care: A Qualitative Study", *International Journal of Nursing Studies*, 45(10), 1516–1524.

Sloan, F. A. and Hall, Mark A. (2002). "Market Failures and the Evolution of State Regulation of Managed Care", *Law and Contemporary Problems*, 65 (4), 169–206.

Taylor, S. A. (1994). "Distinguishing Service Quality from Patient Satisfaction in Developing Health Care Marketing Strategies", *Hospital and Health Services Administration*, 39 (2), 221–236.

Thom, D., Hall, M. and Pawlson, L. (2004). "Measuring Patients' Trust in Physicians When Assessing Quality of Care", *Health Affairs*, 23 (4), 124–132

US Department of Health & Human Services (2018). Agency for Healthcare Research and Quality, *CAHPS Health Plan Survey Measures*, http://www.ahrq.gov/cahps/surveys-guidance/hp/about/survey-measures.html. Accessed February 20, 2019.

Umberson, D. and Montezl, J. K. (2010). "Social Relationships and Health: A Flashpoint for Health Policy", *J. Health and Social Behavior*, 51 (Suppl), S54–S66.

Van Stee, S.K. and Yang, Q. (2018). "Online Cancer Information Seeking: Applying and Extending the Comprehensive Model of Information Seeking", *Health Communication*, 33 (12), 1583–1592.

Virginia Commonwealth University (2015). Center on Society and Health. "Education: It Matters More to Health than Ever Before", https://societyhealth.vcu.edu/work/the-projects/education-it-matters-more-to-health-than-ever-before.html. Accessed October 30, 2018.

Walbridge, S. W. and Delene, L. M. (1993), "Measuring Physician Attitudes of Service Quality", *Journal of Health Care Marketing*, Winter, 6–15.

Walter, U., Edvardsson, B. and Ostrom, A. (2010). "Drivers of Customer Service Experiences: A Study in the Restaurant Industry", *Managing Service Quality*, 20 (3), 236–258.

Weiss, L. J. and Blustein, J. (1996). "Faithful Patients: The Effect of Long-Term Physician-Patient Relationships on the Costs and Use of Health Care by Older Americans", *Am J Public Health*, 86 (12), 1742–1747.

Weiss, R. (2011). "Beyond Brochures: Health Care Marketing Today is About More Than Slick Ads. It's About Engaging with Communities", *Marketing Health Services*, Fall 2011.

Weiss, R. (2013). "Modern Marketing Defined: Health Care Marketing's Organizational Impact Cannot be Easily Labelled", *Marketing Health Services*, Winter.

Wellable (2015). "79% of Americans Willing to Use Wearable Devices to Manage Health", https://blog.wellable.co/2015/06/01/79-of-americans-willing-to-use-wearable-devices-to-manage-health. Accessed February 18, 2019.

Whitler, K. A. (2015) "The New World of Healthcare Marketing: A Framework for Adaptation", Forbes/CMO Network, https://www.forbes.com/sites/kimberlywhitler/2015/09/06/the-new-world-of-healthcare-marketing-a-framework-for-adaptation/#1685815a1c10. Accessed June 30, 2018.

Whitler, K. A. (2017): "The New World of Healthcare Marketing: Lessons from Across the World", https://www.forbes.com/sites/kimberlywhitler/2017/07/22/the-new-world-of-healthcare-marketing-lessons-from-across-the-world/#109f90546084. Accessed June 30, 2018.

Williams, I. and Brown, H. (2014). "Factors influencing decisions of value in health care: A review of the literature", University of Birmingham, Health Services Management Centre.

Woolf, S. H., Aron, L., Dubay, L., Simon, S. M., Zimmerman, E. and Luk, K. X. (2015). "How are Income and Wealth Linked to Health and Longevity?", Urban Institute. Center on Society and Health, https://www.urban.org/sites/default/files/publication/49116/2000178-How-are-Income-and-Wealth-Linked-to-Health-and-Longevity.pdf. Accessed February 2, 2019.

Suggested Additional Readings

Abraham, J., Sick, B., Anderson, J., Berg, A., Dehmer, C. and Tafano, A. (2011). "Selecting a Provider: What Factors Influence Patients' Decision-Making?", *Journal of Healthcare Management*, 56 (2), 99–115.

Chang, P.-J., Wray, L., Lin, Y. (2014). "Social Relationships, Leisure Activity, and Health in Older Adults", *Health Psychology*, 33 (6), 516–523.

Employee Benefit Research Institute (2018). "Millennials Bring Online and Do-It-Yourself Consumer Behaviors to Health Care Interactions", 297, March 5, https://www.ebri.org/pdf/2018-297-FF-Millennials.pdf. Accessed February 22, 2019.

Fadiman, A (1997). *The Spirit Catches You and You Fall Down*, Noonday.

Healthcare Success (2017). "6 Things You Need to Know about Millennials and Healthcare", https://www.healthcaresuccess.com/blog/healthcare-marketing/millennial-healthcare.html?

Mansfield, A., Addis, M. and Mahalik, J. (2003). "Why Won't He Go to the Doctor? The Psychology of Men's Help Seeking", *International Journal of Men's Health*, 2 (2), 93.

Marketing Strategies (2018). "Demographic Segmentation: Définition, Variables and Examples", https://www.marketingtutor.net/demographic-segmentation-definition-variables-examples/. Accessed October 25, 2018.

McKinsey (2015). A Comprehensive Approach Health Systems Can Use to Better Understand the Patient Experience and Thereby Improve Patient Satisfaction. August 2015.

Brandon, C., Jenny, C., Whitney, G. and Kevin, N. https://healthcare.mckinsey.com/measuring-patient-experience-lessons-other-industries. Accessed October 20, 2018.

Radulescu, V. and Cetina, I. (2012). "Key Factors that Influence Behavior of Health Care Consumer, the Basis of Health Care Strategies", *Contemporary Readings in Law and Social Justice*, July 1, 2012.

Statista (2014). "Distribution of Factors for U.S. Consumer Healthcare Purchasing Decisions as of 2014", https://www.statista.com/statistics/378824/consumer-factors-in-the-us-for-healthcare-purchasing/.

Weiss, R. (2011). "Beyond Brochures: Health Care Marketing Today is About More than Slick Ads. It's About Engaging with Communities", *Marketing Health Services*, Fall 2011.

Wortzel, L. H. (1976). "The Behavior of the Health Care Consumer: A Selective Review", *Advances in Consumer Research*, 3, 295–301.

Chapter 7

Customer/Patient Experience: Key Driver of Modern Health Care Marketing

7.1. Introduction to Customer Experience (CX) and Patient Experience (PX)

Enhancing customer/patient experience is probably the most discussed and researched topic in health care management, with a significant impact on health care marketing as well. For example, Deloitte (2017a) in their report *2018 Global Health Care Outlook* boldly predicted, "Engaging with consumers and improving patient experience is among the top five issues in health care in 2018." Other health care marketing experts like Kernan (2017) seem to agree: "2018 Healthcare Marketing Trend #1: Customer Experience."

Why Use Both Terms "Customer Experience" (CX) and "Patient Experience" (PX) in This Book?

As we saw in Chapter 1, two-thirds of an individual's interaction with a healthcare provider is as a "customer" (or consumer) during pre- and post-treatment periods. Only one-third of their encounter is as a "patient" during treatment. Therefore, focus of health care marketing is not limited to patients. Focus of health care marketing is toward both consumers/customers and patients.

Furthermore, as discussed earlier in the book, the term "customer" in health care includes others beyond the "patient". These include families, primary care physicians, care givers, and the community at large.

What function or department in a health care organization is responsible for improving customer/patient experience? The answer is "all functions/departments."

Does health care marketing have a role in improving customer/patient experience? The answer is in the affirmative. See, for example:

- Nausation *et al.* (2014) who emphasize, "The customer experience framework should be used as the baseline for strategy and implementation of services/health care marketing."
- Becker's Hospital Review (2013) highlights the importance of improving patient experience at hospitals and the role of marketing in such efforts. Citing Matt Hall, founder and CEO of Human Care Systems, a leading health care marketing agency, this paper states, "The way that hospitals can successfully grow their service lines, and possibly grow their enterprises, is by offering fundamentally better experiences, which should translate into marketing."

There are tangible financial benefits too for health plans that improve customer experience. Under Centers for Medicare and Medicaid's new value-based payment scheme under the Medicare Access and CHIP Reauthorization Act (MACRA), provider reimbursements will be based in part on patient engagement efforts such as promoting self-management and coaching patients.

Surveys show slow adoption of the significance of customer experience in the health care industry. The health care industry has typically been slower to adapt to practices that place a heavy focus on customer satisfaction (Matejka, 2017). Matejka also cites the American Customer Satisfaction Index's 2017 Utilities, Shipping, and Health Care Report, which reports that hospitals achieved a customer satisfaction score of 75 out of 100 for the second year in a row. This places the health care industry 32nd in customer satisfaction, behind banks, supermarkets, and gasoline stations.

Messinger (2014) cites from a PricewaterhouseCoopers' Health Research Institute report that when asked how well customers are treated in each industry, health care was ranked sixth out of eight industry choices — only ranking above the entertainment and airline industries. In 2012, the health care industry was ranked fifth. With the modern emphasis on consumer/patient-centric care, it is disquieting to see that patient experience rankings from health care providers are falling. Messinger recommends hospitals and health care providers to leverage digital channels to establish trust and create experiences for patients even before they arrive for health care at the physical facilities.

Beryl Institutes PX Report 2017 (Beryl Institute, 2018) covering US and non-US hospitals, long-term care facilities, and medical practices, reports that:

- 1% had not started any PX initiatives;
- 26% reported that they were well established;
- 56% reported that they have established/made some progress; and
- 18% reported that they were just beginning.

CX/PX is a prominent topic discussed in present-day health care marketing conferences. It is also a frequent topic in health care marketing and services marketing literature. Also notable is the advent in 2014 of a journal dedicated to the subject, *The Journal of Patient Experience*. This journal is easily accessible via *pxjournal.org*.

(a) What is Customer Experience (CX) and How is It Related to Customer Satisfaction (CS)?

Blake (2018) highlights that CX is one of the hottest buzzwords in business these days with companies pouring more resources than ever before into building a strong customer experience, and many expect to soon compete on experience more than on price or quality. She cites a study of brands in Forrester's Customer Experience Index that shows that companies that invest in customer experience had higher stock price growth and higher total returns.

Definitions of CX: We present below some definitions of CX from the literature:

- How customers perceive their interactions with your company (Manning, 2010).
- A mental journey that leaves the customer with memories of having performed something special, having learned something or just having fun (Sundbo and Hagedorn-Rasmussen, 2008).
- CX is the customer's direct and indirect experience of the service process, the organization, the facilities, and the interactions with the service organization's staff and other customers (Walter et al., 2010).

As the customer goes through the service process, he/she comes into contact with many "touchpoints". The significance of treating customer experience as a journey through the service process with many touchpoints is the modern view of customer experience.

How is CX different from CS (or Customer Care)? Blake (2018) explains as follows:

- CS is the advice or assistance a company gives its customers to increase customer satisfaction during pre-purchase and post-purchase stages.
- Customer care means how well customers are taken care of while they interact with the brand. Customer care moves one step beyond basic customer service by building an emotional connection.
- CX is the total journey of a customer's interactions with a brand. Customer experience is the sum of all contacts, from first discovering and researching a product to shopping and purchasing to actually using the product and following up with the brand afterwards. Customer experience measures how customers feel about a company overall and includes the emotional, physical, psychological connection customers have with a brand. It is not a one-off interaction, but rather includes the entire customer lifecycle and every touchpoint a customer has with a product or service.

> CX measures how the customer feels overall about the company and its products/services. Enhancing CX is a strategy to gain competitive advantage. CX has to be embedded in the organization's culture. Efforts to enhance CX must be based on extensive data analysis. Customer experience is usually measured by net promoter score (NPS), which tracks how likely a customer is to recommend the brand to a friend. CS, usually measured with satisfaction scores, really measures how satisfied customers are with the experience (CX).

(b) Patient Experience (PX) is the Health Care Industry Equivalent of Customer Experience (CX).
PX is defined by Wolf *et al.* (2014) and Beryl Institute (2017) as

> "The sum of all interactions, shaped by an organization's culture, that influence patient perceptions, across the continuum of care."

The emphasis is on "across the continuum of care", i.e., across the entire patient journey over a life time. For example, it is not a patient's satisfaction or dissatisfaction of one visit to the provider. It is the patient's experience with the physician, hospital, health plan, or other providers' total care including staff care and attributes of the facilities and systems, over repeated encounters that forms a lasting experience.

Other PX definitions:

- "Engaged healthcare is better healthcare, for everyone. And that's the best definition of the patient experience" Robison (2010).
- "The Patient Experience refers to the quality and value of all of the interactions — direct and indirect, clinical and non-clinical — spanning the entire duration of the patient/provider relationship" Fein *et al.* (2009).

Some PX definitions focus heavily on how *expectations* of the patients are met.

Bowling *et al.* (2012) conducted a comprehensive review of patient expectations from 2000–2009. They evaluated two concepts: (1) pre-visit expectations and (2) post-visit experience in general practitioner patients and hospital outpatients. The authors defined patients' experiences as "Their direct, personal observations of their healthcare", and measured patient experience in terms of whether patient "expectations" were met.

Expectations of experience included: cleanliness, easily available information about where to go, convenient and punctual appointments, being seen on time, choice of hospital/doctor, helpful reception staff, the doctor being respectful and knowledgeable, clear and easy to understand, and for the patient to be involved in treatment decisions and to experience a reduction in symptoms/problems, being given reassurance, receiving advice about health or condition, information about cause and management of condition and information about benefits/side effects of treatment, and being given an opportunity to discuss problems.

This type of Expectations vs. Perceptions view of customer satisfaction is well established in service management literature. In this well-known method, called SERVQUAL by the authors (Parasuraman *et al.*, 1988), two questionnaires are given to customers, one before they receive the service and the other after they have received the service. The questionnaires contain 22 statements representing the five dimensions of service quality, namely reliability, responsiveness, assurance, empathy, and tangibles SERVQUAL is probably the most applied model for measuring service quality all over the world. It has been applied and adapted to measure service quality in a variety of settings including health care environments.

7.2. Significance of CX/PX in Modern Health Care Marketing

Modern health care marketing acknowledges the significance of consumer/patient personal experience and their emotional ties with health care providers such as physicians and hospitals.

Connolly (2017, in a paper "Why Authenticity is the Prescription for Modern Healthcare Marketing") describes this well:

> "Healthcare marketing of the past focused on what a person felt internally during a physical ailment. (Now) smart healthcare marketers are recognizing a commonality between their patients/consumers that can be used to connect with them emotionally."

PricewaterhouseCoopers (2017) in their "Top Health Industry Issues of 2018. Patient Experience as a Priority and Not Just a Portal" says,

> "2018 will be about making significant strategic investments in patient experience so it changes behavior and improves outcomes — a critical goal as the industry turns toward paying more for value, not volume."

This report, reviewing current status of awareness and action on enhancing patient experience in health care organizations, states,

> "Some healthcare organizations also will begin to use patient experience to differentiate themselves in the market. Forty-nine percent of provider executives said revamping the patient experience is one of their organization's top three priorities over the next five years. Many already have or are building the role of chief patient experience officer. In a few organizations, including Texas Health Resources (THR) in Dallas–Fort Worth, this position reports directly to the CEO."

This report also emphasizes that "CX/PX" is the most important factor in the customer/patient mindset in selecting, and remaining with providers (physicians, hospitals and health plans).

Several other researchers and industry experts also have emphasized the significance of customer/patient experience in health care marketing. For example,

- Resnick (2018) in a paper, "5 Themes That Will Drive Healthcare Marketing in 2019", predicts,

    "Customer Experience, overused and underdelivered, often relabeled 'consumerism, empowerment, humanization, and engagement,' CX will go beyond journey mapping as healthcare companies commit to budgeted, cross-functional efforts across customer life cycle touchpoints."

    He also presents a key statistic: Health insurers' customer experience is among the lowest of all industries, ranking 15th of 19 US industries compared with a score that has not changed since 2016.
- Kernan (2017) states that, "Customer/patient experience is the leading driver of health care marketing," in "2018 Healthcare Marketing Trend #1: Customer Experience".

    Kernan cites industry research and advisory company prediction that by 2018, "more than 50 percent of organizations will focus their efforts on improving the customer experience". Hospitals will get higher payments from Medicare and Medicaid for better customer/patient experience scores.
- Haefner (2017) in his paper "8 Healthcare Marketing Trends for 2018" asserts, "Hospital marketers will be expected to enhance employee culture. More executives are moving into roles as heads of culture, as issues with hospital employees can plague hospitals with low satisfaction marks."
- Gallagher (2017) in a paper "How Has Healthcare Marketing Changed in the Last Decade?" writes, "Nowadays I think they have to put customer experience at the very top (of priorities)." He gives an example from the pharmaceutical industry where a pharmaceutical manufacturer might create a customer experience without associating or promoting a specific drug. It may just be digital communications like apps or text messages educating consumers/patients how to improve their health.
- Gandolf, (2013) in his paper, "Patient Experience: The Forgotten 'P' in Your Medical Marketing Plan" states, "For healthcare consumers, personal experience is the number one reason for choosing a doctor or hospital."
- Messinger (2014) in a paper in *Marketing Health Services* states that among health care marketing strategies, "Content is king, and connections are queen, but patient experiences rules."

Modern health care marketing is related to customer/patient experience in two complementary ways:

- When the customer's/patient's experience with health care services of the organization is great, that provides an additional competitive feature for the health care marketing function to publicize.
- Health care marketing has a role in working with functional areas of the health care organization such as operations, quality management, call centers, information systems/information technology, human resources, compliance, and finance to improve access and quality of service, enhance cost-benefit, improve service efficiency, and develop a customer-oriented culture, all of which contribute to improved customer/patient experience.

> **Relationship between Customer/Patient Experience and Health Care Marketing**
>
> Great customer/patient experience enables health care marketing to effectively communicate additional value of services to customers/patients.
>
> Conversely, health care marketing has a role in working with functional areas to improve customer/patient experience.

Modern health care marketing is aimed at communicating the value of the organization's health care product/services. This value is derived from superior quality, efficient operations, competitive costs, and excellent customer service/experience. As such, health care marketing benefits from improvements in quality, cost, operations, and service of the organization.

Improvements in customer experience contributes to many of these factors (Agency for Healthcare Research and Quality, 2018).

7.2.1. Customer/Patient experience and corporate image, recognition, and accreditation

Health plans are now evaluated by CMS and accreditation agencies on quality of services as well as patient satisfaction. The latter is measured using the Consumer Assessment of Health Plan Survey (CAHPS). The CAHPS scores are reported publicly together with other quality measures such as CMS "star ratings" that take into account current performance and initiatives to improve quality. Health plans are thus incentivized to implement performance-based compensation systems, board certification, and licensing requirements for physicians. The CAHPS Health Plan Survey is a mandatory part of health plan accreditation required by the National Committee for Quality Assurance (NCQA) for both commercial and Medicaid health plan product lines.

A similar survey called HCAHPS (Hospital Consumer Assessment of Healthcare Providers and Systems) Survey, also known as the CAHPS Hospital Survey or Hospital CAHPS, has been in use since 2006 to measure patients' perspectives on hospital care.

CAHPS and HCAHPS Surveys

CAHPS is a US Department of Health and Human Services' Agency for Healthcare Research and Quality (AHRQ) program that began in 1995. CAHPS surveys ask consumers and patients to report on and evaluate their experiences with health plans, providers, and health care facilities.

CAHPS surveys cover topics such as the communication skills of providers and ease of access to health care services. CAHPS states that Patient Experience encompasses the range of interactions that patients have with the health care system, including their care from health plans, and from doctors, nurses, and staff in hospitals, physician practices, and other health care facilities, and asserts that the terms "patient satisfaction" and "patient experience" are often used interchangeably, but they are not the same thing.

Hospital Consumer Assessment of Healthcare Providers and Systems (HCAHPS) Survey, also known as the CAHPS® Hospital Survey or Hospital CAHPS®, is a standardized survey instrument and data collection methodology that has been in use since 2006 to measure patients' perspectives on hospital care. The HCAHPS Survey is composed of 27 items including 18 items that encompass critical aspects of the hospital experience (communication with doctors, communication with nurses, responsiveness of hospital staff, cleanliness of the hospital environment, quietness of the hospital environment, pain management, communication about medicines, discharge information, overall rating of hospital, and recommendation of hospital).

Several US states require conducting and reporting of the Medicaid version of the CAHPS Health Plan Survey as part of performance-based managed care contracts for Medicaid and Children's Health Insurance Programs (CHIP) enrollees.

The Patient Protection and Affordable Care Act of 2010 (ACA) includes several new provisions for measuring and reporting patient experience of care. Clinician and Group Consumer Assessment of Healthcare Providers and Systems (CG CAHPS) survey is designed to measure patients' perception of care provided by physicians in an office setting.

Health systems choosing to participate in the Medicare Shared Savings Program are required to use the CAHPS Survey for Accountable Care Organizations (ACOs). The results of the ACO CAHPS Survey are used for public reporting on the Physician Compare website, as well as for calculating any "shared savings" to be earned by participating ACOs.

Similarly, the Physician Quality Reporting System (PQRS) program administered by CMS includes a patient experience survey component using the CAHPS for PQRS Survey. These survey results are reported on the Physician Compare website and used with other performance measures to adjust Medicare fee-for-service (FFS) payments to all participating physicians for 2017.

Starting in 2019, two new physician payment programs — a merit-based incentive payment system (MIPS) and eligible alternative payment models (APMs) — are likely to include some version of the CG CAHPS Survey as part of the quality measurement formula used for payment. These programs were created under the Medicare Access and CHIP Reauthorization Act (MACRA).

The National Committee for Quality Assurance's (NCQA) Patient-Centered Medical Home program includes optional recognition of patient experience. Physician practices seeking recognition are encouraged to use the CAHPS Clinician and Group Survey with the Patient-Centered Medical Home Item Set.

The American Board of Medical Specialties (ABMS), which oversees the Maintenance of Certification (MOC) process that 24 medical specialties use to confirm physicians' qualifications every five years, continues to explore requiring medical boards to use patient experience measures to assess the communication skills and professionalism of physicians with direct patient care responsibilities.

Health plans (such as Blue Cross Blue Shield of Massachusetts and HealthPlus of Michigan) and multi-stakeholder organizations (such as California's Integrated Healthcare Association) are incorporating patient experience scores into provider pay-for-performance incentives.

7.2.2. Customer/Patient experience and employee satisfaction

Larson (2012) reports a 2011 study published in *Health Affairs* by Matthew McHugh, an assistant professor of nursing at the University of Pennsylvania, and a team of researchers that found that the percentage of patients who reported they would "definitely recommend" a hospital to their loved ones decreased by 2% for every 10% of the nurses who expressed dissatisfaction with their jobs. This report concluded that environments that support nurses allow them to do their jobs well and provide the best possible care.

Larson (2012) also mentions a report published by John Griffith, a professor at the University of Michigan's School of Public Health. Griffith examined 34 community hospitals that had won the Malcolm Baldridge National Quality Award in the healthcare sector. He found that hospital employee morale was the biggest factor in patient satisfaction — and achieving that started with leadership at the very top.

Efforts to improve patient experience result in greater employee satisfaction, reducing turnover. Improving the experience of patients and families also requires improving work processes and systems that help employees perform their tasks better and with greater satisfaction.

7.2.3. Customer/Patient experience and retention

Patients keep or change providers based on experience. Relationship quality is a major predictor of patient loyalty; one study found that patients reporting the poorest-quality relationships with their physicians were three times more likely to voluntarily leave the physician's practice than patients with the highest-quality relationships (Safran *et al.*, 2001).

7.2.4. Customer/Patient experience and clinical outcomes

Patients with better care experiences often have better health outcomes (Stewart, 1995). Patient experience positively correlates to processes of care for both prevention and disease management (Sequist *et al.*, 2018). Diabetic patients are reported as developing greater self-management skills and quality of life when they report positive interactions with their providers (Greenfield *et al.*, 1988). Studies show that among patients hospitalized for heart attack, patients with more positive reports about their experiences with care had better health outcomes a year after discharge (Fremont *et al.*, 2001).

Deloitte (2017b) reports that hospitals with higher patient experience scores have higher clinical quality.

> "Hospitals with higher patient reported experience ratings have better process of care quality scores. Hospitals receiving 'excellent' (9 or 10 out of 10) patient experience ratings have better clinical quality scores for all 18 process of care measures that were analyzed compared to hospitals receiving 'low' (0 to 6 out of 10) ratings. For instance, a 10-percentage-point higher score in the number of respondents giving a hospital an 'excellent' experience rating is associated with a 20-minute lower emergency department (ED) wait time relative to hospitals receiving a 'low' rating."

Studies indicate that clinical quality measures that are more tangible and more visible to patients, such as ED wait times and readmissions, are more strongly associated with patient experience and their ratings.

Communication with nurses and relevant discharge information enhance patient experience, and are strongly associated with clinical quality. Experience scores pertaining to nurse communication and discharge information have the strongest association with the largest number of clinical quality measures.

Hospitals' participation in value-based care models, such as Accountable Care Organizations (ACO) affiliation and bundled-payment arrangements, may strengthen the association between patient experience and hospital clinical quality. Our regression analyses determined that ACO affiliation and payment incentives tied to quality — such as bundled payments — might strengthen and reinforce the association between patient experience and clinical care quality domains such as ED and surgical care.

Hospital executives face multiple priorities and resource demands, and may question the business value.

7.2.5. Customer/Patient experience improves financial performance of the health care organization

Good patient experience is associated with lower medical malpractice risk (Levinson *et al.*, 1997). Fullam *et al.* (2009) report a study that found for each drop in patient-reported scores along a five-step scale of "very good" to "very poor", the likelihood of a provider being named in a malpractice suit increased by 21.7%.

The Centers for Medicare & Medicaid Services (CMS) began withholding hospital's Medicare reimbursement based on their quality performance. 30%

of the decision is derived from how well hospitals score on the HCAHPS survey, a measure of customer satisfaction. Improved patient experience pays in CMS' new value-based payment scheme under the Medicare Access and CHIP Reauthorization Act (MACRA). Provider reimbursements will be based in part on patient engagement efforts such as promoting self-management and coaching patients between visits. Now, HCAHPS scores determine up to 2% of a hospital or health system's Medicare payments (Shute, 2017).

Several studies now indicate that hospitals that perform well on patient care experience surveys also do better on clinical metrics. The "Triple Aim" of reducing costs per capita, improving patient experience and population health all require an engaged patient to improve clinical outcomes (Luxford and Sutton, 2014).

Modern health care marketing is no longer about a one-way communication from the health care organizations to the consumers/patients using advertisements. It is about a marketing mix that emphasizes two-way communication, inviting consumer/patient feedback. As the group in the health care organization closest to the consumer/patient, next to the actual providers of care, health care marketing has a role in:

- Measuring what is important to the consumer/patient's formation of CX/PX,
- Establishing communication channels, including digital internet-based channels, to communicate to the consumer/patient,
- Measuring PX as an ongoing exercise, and
- Working with providers, CS and PX staff, and management in planning and implementing CX/PX enhancements.

7.3. Basic Principles of CX/PX

The literature is fast building up with research, industry expert discussions, and case studies on CX/PX. Through these efforts, certain principles on CX/PX, useful for health care marketing, have emerged. Some of these are discussed here.

7.3.1. Guiding principles of CX/PX

CX/PX is based on the customer's/patient's overall interactions with the service firm. In receiving a service, the customer/patient goes through a "journey" during which he/she comes across many "touchpoints". These concepts, "customer journey", "customer journey mapping", and "touchpoints" will be defined and discussed in detail later in this chapter.

- CX/PX is not a onetime impression or perception of the customer. Therefore, a one-time customer/patient satisfaction survey form will not help in measuring CX/PX.
- The customer/patient develops CX/PX over time. Afshar (2015) cites Paul Greenberg, a world-renowned expert on CX as saying, "CX is how a customer feels about a company over time."
- Experience is Perception (Walden, 2009).

Walden argues that, when it comes to customer experience, it is not the reality of an experience that matters, but how it is perceived, and that the customer will not pay attention to every aspect of what the service provider does, but instead gains an impression from the cues used by the provider. He gives the example of K-Mart and Walmart which are similar shops. The fact that Wal-Mart bagged shopper purchases in brown paper bags whereas K-Mart used plastic, he argues, has made shopping experience at Walmart feel different.

In other words, little things matter, and service and health care managers should try to identify innovative improvements at vital touchpoints.

Morgan (2017) confirms this view:

> "Customer experience can include a lot of elements, but it really boils down to the perception the customer has of your brand. Even if you think your brand and customer experience is one thing, if the customer perceives it as something different, that is what the actual customer experience is."

Thus, even if a health care provider believes that their services are of high quality to provide a strong customer experience, if a patient has a billing problem that is not resolved quickly causing the patient to undergo stress, the patient will perceive the quality of this health care provider's service as low, and that is what affects the patient's experience.

- The customer adjusts CX/PX every time there is a contact with the company (Inc.com, 2014). This is important because it implies that, over time, service managers can influence CX/PX.

Paul Conder, a consultant in leading multidisciplinary teams, bridging the fields of experience design, interior design, and product and retail strategy, who has led research and design projects for many leading brands, including Starbucks, Starwood, Canyon Ranch, Lululemon, Telus, Philips

Design, and the 2010 Olympic, presents several additional basic principles on CX (Conder, 2014). These include the following:

- CX is a personal and subjective thing composed of the customer's perceptions, feelings, memories, and associations with a product/service. A company cannot create customer experiences.
- A "Customer Journey" is the framework of customers' interactions and experiences while engaging with a brand. It includes interactions with digital media, social interactions, word of mouth, and service interactions. Mapping the Customer Journey across channels is the key to understanding how customer experiences can be enabled, communicated, and focused.
- Touchpoints are the physical or digital enablers in the Customer's Journey. Every touchpoint designed into a website, app, retail interior, hospital, office, store fixture, airport, smartphone, or table setting is put there to enable certain interactions, carry certain messages, and pattern certain behaviors. Service organizations should focus not only on making services at these touchpoints efficient but also on what the customer is actually thinking, feeling, saying, or doing.
- The modern customers/patients use multiple channels, physical and digital, to interact with the service organization. They see the whole organization via word of mouth reviews, websites, and blog comments. Therefore, it is important for the organization to understand what others comment about their service.
- Customer Experience is not about projecting a made-up or staged theme, which is likely to create a brand perception that is insincere and inauthentic.

  Modern consumers/patients are smart. They identify authenticity. Baltes (2017) comments, "Strong brands are based on a story that communicates who is the company; authenticity is to communicate what you really are."

PX/CX is personal and is related to the modern concept of patient-centered care. Patient-centered care is the practice of caring for patients (and their families) in ways that are meaningful and valuable to the individual patient (Oneview, 2015). It includes listening to, informing, and involving patients in their care.

The Institute of Medicine (IOM) defines patient-centered care as: "Providing care that is respectful of, and responsive to, individual patient preferences, needs, and values, and ensuring that patient values guide all clinical decisions."

Research conducted by Picker Institute and Harvard Medical School has identified eight principles of patient-centered care. These are (Oneview, 2015):

- **Respect for patients' values, preferences, and expressed needs.**
- **Coordination and integration of care:** Coordination of clinical care, ancillary and support services, and front-line patient care.
- **Information and education:** Information on clinical status, progress, and prognosis; on processes of care; and information to facilitate autonomy, self-care, and health promotion.
- **Physical comfort:** Pain management, assistance with activities and daily living needs, and hospital surroundings and environment.
- **Emotional support and alleviation of fear and anxiety:** Anxiety over physical status, treatment and prognosis, over the impact of the illness on themselves and family, and over the financial impact of the illness.
- **Involvement of family and friends:** The role of family and friends in the patient experience. Family dimensions of patient-centered care include providing accommodations for family and friends; involving family and close friends in decision making; supporting family members as caregivers; and recognizing the needs of family and friends.
- **Continuity of care and transition between care levels:** Post-discharge care information; understandable, detailed information regarding medications, physical limitations, dietary needs, etc.; coordinate and plan ongoing treatment and services after discharge; and information regarding access to clinical, social, physical, and financial support on a continuing basis.
- **Access to care:** Access to the location of hospitals, clinics, and physician offices; availability of transportation; scheduling appointments; availability of appointments when needed; accessibility to specialists or specialty services when a referral is made; clear instructions provided on when and how to get referrals.

Effective patient-centered care requires health care organizations and systems to focus on patient experience, communications, workflow and patient portals providing information. Use of modern digital technology is essential to implement patient-centered care.

7.3.2. Guiding principles of PX

The leading institute in the field of patient experience which is "dedicated to improving the patient experience through collaboration and shared knowledge", is The Beryl Institute (www.theberylinstitute.org/). The definition of PX we adopted earlier in the chapter ("The sum of all interactions, shaped by an organization's culture, that influence patient perceptions, across the continuum of care.") was developed by the Beryl Institute. Beryl Institute is also the publisher of *The Journal of Patient Experience*.

Beryl Institute's *guiding principles on PX Excellence* for health care organizations are (Beryl Institute, 2019):

- Identify and support accountable leadership with committed time and focused intent to shape and guide experience strategy.
- Establish and reinforce a strong, vibrant, and positive organizational culture and all it comprises.
- Develop a formal definition for what the experience is to their organization.
- Implement a defined process for continuous patient and family input and engagement.
- Engage all voices in driving comprehensive, systemic, and lasting solutions.
- Look beyond clinical experience of care to all interactions and touchpoints.
- Focus on alignment across all segments of the continuum and the spaces in between.
- Encompass both a focus on healing and a commitment to well-being.

7.4. Factors Influencing Customer/Patient Experience

Many studies and surveys have studied factors customers/patients focus on in deciding the level of customer/patient experience. A summary of these factors is presented in Table 7.1.

Consumer expectations of value are reported to be evolving (Deloitte, 2016). This paper identifies five main characteristics customers look for in their health care interactions. These are as follows:

- They want things to be personal;
- They yearn for simplicity (customers typically do not care how a hospital or physician practice is organized internally);

Table 7.1. Factors Affecting Customer/Patient Experience in Health Care Settings.

Author/s (see full citations in chapter end references)	Factors identified
Shah et al. (2010)	Wait time in triage; Lack of information about delays.
Jha (2017)	Patient engagement, satisfactory interaction between patient and staff, clinical effectiveness, personalization, patient safety, and admission and discharge process.
Robison (2010)	Four basic emotional needs: confidence, integrity, pride, and passion.
Bowling et al. (2012)	Difference between pre-encounter expectations and post-encounter perceptions.
McCance et al. (2015)	Consistent delivery of nursing/midwifery care against identified need.
	Patient's confidence in the knowledge and skills of the nurse/midwife.
	Patient's sense of safety while under the care of the nurse/midwife.
	Patient involvement in decisions made about his/her nursing/midwifery care.
	Time spent by nurses/midwives with the patient.
	Respect from the nurse/midwife for patient's preference and choice.
	Nurse's/midwife's support for patients to care for themselves where appropriate.
	Nurse's/midwife's understanding of what is important to the patient.
Moss et al. (2014)	Repeat patients at emergency care: Health professionals' sustained and enmeshed ethic and duty of care.
	Respect for patient dignity, acknowledge their knowledge of themselves and respond sensitively to their vulnerability.
Junewicz and Youngner (2015)	Provision of interventions that patients or their families desire (but may be medically unnecessary or potentially wrong or harmful).
	The provision of medically necessary care that improves outcomes.
	Attention to human experience, such as being treated with respect, good communication, clean and beautiful facilities, and conveniences, such as good parking.

Table 7.1. (*Continued*)

Author/s (see full citations in chapter end references)	Factors identified
Fustino *et al.* (2018)	Superior medical outcomes, clinical quality, patient safety measures, physician job satisfaction, doctor–patient communication, and patient compliance with treatment recommendations.

- Patients do not want to be left waiting;
- They desire transparency; and
- They require security.

Ellis (2016) presents five dimensions consumers want in the healthcare experience (five E's) set forth by John Quelch, Professor at Health Policy and Management at Harvard T.H. Chan School of Public Health, Charles Edward Wilson Professor of Business Administration at Harvard Business School, and author of *Consumers, Corporations, and Public Health: A Case-based Approach to Sustainable Business*. These are as follows

- Experience that will lead to a cure.
- Empathy to make them feel that the provider cares.
- Efficiency so that they will not be kept waiting.
- Economy to ensure they are getting fair value.
- Empowerment that gives them some degree of choice around their treatment plans.

Ellis quotes Quelch as commenting that very few hospitals have done significant research to understand what different segments of consumers want.

7.5. Marketing's Role in Improving CX/PX

CX/PX is key to customer/patient satisfaction. This helps health care marketing attract new customers/patients and retain current customers/patients.

On the surface, it might appear that it is the operations, processes, quality assurance, and staff that contribute to CX/PX. Does health care marketing have a role in improving CX/PX? In this section, we explore this key question.

Which function in the organization is responsible for improving CX/PX? Meyer and Schwager (2007) in a Harvard Business Review article, says, "All hands on board", meaning all departments and functions of the organization. They comment,

> "Many organizations place responsibility for collecting and assessing customer experience data within a single, IT-supported, customer-facing group. But it is a mistake to assign to customer-facing groups overall accountability for the design, delivery, and creation of a superior customer experience, thereby excusing those more distant from the customer from understanding it. **Every function has a role to play.**"

Here is a summary of roles key departments/functions have to play in enhancing customer/patient_experience:

- **Top management/leadership:** Chris Woods, Patient Experience Officer at Murphy Medical Center, Murphy, says (Woods, 2016), "Leadership is the driving force of customer/patient experience." She highlights that leadership is responsible for:
    o Setting goals and strategies of the organization,
    o Establishing programs for employee engagement, and
    o Creating and maintaining a customer-oriented culture.

Extracts from Job Description of Chief Patient Experience Officer at Johns Hopkins Healthcare

This executive will drive and foster a culture of patient- and family-centered care and service excellence, while improving patient and family experience and patient relations across the enterprise. The Chief Patient Experience Officer will work directly with the Executive Teams at all the Johns Hopkins Health System affiliates to assess and communicate performance and to create change at all levels of the organization. This position will also be accountable to supporting and managing the organizational needs, as well as the design, implementation, and evaluation of programs that facilitate the professional development and continuous learning of all team members. Tasked with translating the concepts of service excellence, patient experience, and patient relations into actionable behaviors, this individual will take a culture steeped in clinical excellence into the ever-evolving world of patient- and family-centered care.

(Continued)

> Important areas of practice knowledge will include:
>
> - Patient/Consumer Experience, Patient Relations, and Measurement Tools,
> - Organizational Change Management,
> - Best Service Practices, and Protocols,
> - Workforce Engagement, and Performance,
> - Surveys, Metrics, and Standards, and
> - Data Analysis and Interpretative skill.
>
> This Leader will be the system expert on patient satisfaction and service excellence.
>
> *Source*: https://www.patient-experience.org/PDFs/Johns-Hopkins-Chief-Patient-Experience-Officer.aspx.

- **Marketing:** Has to capture the needs and expectations of every one of its targeted market segments, circulate that knowledge within the company, and then tailor all customer/patient communications accordingly.
- **Service operations:** Must ensure that processes, skills, and practices are optimized at every touchpoint.
- **Service design and development:** Should design processes to maximize PX/CX at every touchpoint.
- **Information technology:** Must collect, analyze, and distribute customer experience data and monitor progress.
- **Human resources:** Since the front line determines the bulk of customer experience, capabilities and customer orientation of contact employees must be enhanced.

Who at leadership level has the primary responsibility and accountability for addressing PX?

Gambie (2013) reports results of a survey based on responses from more than 1,000 hospitals or hospital systems representing 672 unique organizations. The responses to the above question include the following:

- Committee: 26%,
- Chief experience officer or patient experience director: 22%,

- Chief nursing officer: 14%,
- CEO or senior administrator: 8%,
- Chief quality officer: 8%,
- COO: 3%,
- Physician, nurse, or clinical staff: 3%,
- CMO: 1%,
- Chief marketing officer: 1%,
- No one in particular: 1%, and
- Other: 12%.

7.5.1. Need for an integrative approach

In modern health care organizations, PX/CX improvement is recognized as one needing an integrative approach, integrating quality/safety improvement, service improvement via employee engagement, health care marketing, and IT (for big data analytics).

Hall (2013) in a paper "Incorporating Patient Experience into Healthcare Marketing", states, "Hospital marketing should be integrally tied to the whole patient experience."

> In summary, health care marketing has a role in improving CX/PX ideally integrated with all other functions.

7.6. Customer Experience Management (CXM) and Customer Relationship Management (CRM)

The concept of Customer Relations Management or CRM has been around for a longer time than CXM.

What are the differences between CRM and CXM?

- **CRM**
    - Practices, strategies, and technologies that companies use to manage and analyze customer interactions and data throughout the customer lifecycle.
    - CRM software helps a business integrate sales, marketing, and customer support by analyzing customer data.

- **CXM**
    - Collection of processes a company uses to track, oversee, and organize every interaction between a customer and the organization throughout the customer lifecycle.
- **Difference between CRM and CXM?**
    - A CRM tool is inclined toward capturing transactional data. It does not tell you what the customer "feels" while engaging or interacting with your brand. For example, using a CRM software tool we can find out, for instance, how many patients used oncology services in the hospital. But this data does not tell us how happy or satisfied they were with their experience at the hospital.
    - A Customer Experience Management (CXM) platform is expected to capture and analyze experiential data or the "Voice of the Customer" to find out which aspects of the service experience the health care organization is falling behind on, and what they need to do to rectify it.
    - The key difference, thus, is the focus.
        - Focus of CRM systems is on capturing the key transactional data. Thus, CRM is a "customer card".
        - The focus of CXM is not the service company or staff but the customer. CXM means getting to know your customers well by collecting data from all touchpoints, analyzing the data, and using it to deliver personalized engagement back to those touchpoints. CXM ensures the experience for the customer is efficient and effective.

An example from Hoag Imaging Center in Newport Beach, California: Long waits on the phone to talk to a customer representative may be inevitable, given the resources available. An alternative is offered to call the patient back. Even a better example can be found at American Airlines Advantage Member call services, though not a health care organization. This call service informs the customers the exact time (within a five-minute window) they would be called back.

7.6.1. What should health care organizations implement, CRM or CXM?

Health care organizations should implement both CRM and CXM. The two work together to ensure an optimal outcome for customers.

CRM software supports CXM by:

- Recording service interactions with customers/patients;
- Allowing recording of potential marketing and communication opportunities; and
- Providing automated pipelines for moving patients through the health care service process.

7.7. Current Status of Customer/Patient Experience Management (CXM/PXM) in Health Care Organizations

Wolf (2017) presents results from a Beryl Institute survey of 944 US hospitals, 106 practices, and 64 long-term care providers on current PX efforts. Results show that 26% reported well-established PX practices and 56% reported established/making some progress. Also reported was that priorities in PX over the next 3 years would focus on improving quality, safety, and service.

Gambie (2013) discusses results of a survey from Catalyst Healthcare Research and the Beryl Institute based on more than 1,000 hospitals or hospital systems representing 672 unique organizations. Chief experience officers accounted for 25% of the respondent base, along with chief quality officers, chief nursing officers, CEOs, COOs, and clinical staff members. Respondents ranked the following as their top priorities for the next three years:

- Patient experience and satisfaction: 70%,
- Quality and patient safety: 63%,
- Cost management and/or reduction: 37%,
- Electronic health records, meaningful use, and health information technology: 35%,
- Employee engagement and satisfaction: 22%,
- Accountable care organizations' development and/or implementation: 18%,
- Physician recruitment/retention: 17%, and
- Construction and/or capital improvements: 11%.

The Cleveland Clinic is recognized as the first major academic medical center to make patient experience a strategic goal and appoint a Chief Experience Officer. It was also one of the first to establish an Office of Patient Experience.

Other case studies of established PX programs are reported from Johns Hopkins Hospital, Baptist Memorial Health Care, and Southern Hills Hospital in Las Vegas (Swaney, 2017, in a paper on "Improving the Patient Experience through Hospital Room Technology").

7.8. Customer/Patient Journey Mapping (CJM); Touchpoints; Moments of Truth

CJM is the technique used to record the patient/customer experience across all touchpoints between the patient/customer and the health care provider/ organization, from "awareness" of the service, initial contact, through receiving the service, after-service follow-up, and hopefully staying with the provider/organization for future health care needs. Table 7.2 shows a CJM of a new patient journey in summary form.

Mayo Clinic has been using CJM since 2012. According to James Oliver, the Experience Design Lead at Mayo Clinic, there are four components used to design patient-centric experiences at Mayo Clinic (Seton — Ascension, 2017).

1. Patient Journey Maps to understand different mental states across the health care experience.
2. Behavior Mapping charts to cross-reference user state with needs.
3. Multi-user schematics to map out goals across audiences.
4. Mobile Wellness assessment to focus the information delivery to patients.

The more the touchpoints in a customer interaction with the health care provider, the more complex the CJM gets.

Davey (2016, in a paper, "How to Create a Customer Journey Map") outlines elements of a CJM. These are:

- Context or stakeholder (patient, family, providers).
- **Persona** (a patient/customer profile): identify segments of patients/ customers.
- Outcomes and emotions expected by patient/customer.
- Steps before receiving the health care service, e.g., online research; provider search.
- **Touchpoints:** All stages (before: new awareness, research, and consideration; selection of provider/organization; during the service process; and afterwards) (Jones, 2015).

Table 7.2. A Summary Form CJM for a New Patient Journey.

Activities	Touchpoints	Emotions/Experiences
Searches and finds a physician	References Advertisements Websites	Uncertainty Anxiety Helpful/not helpful
Makes appointment	Staff Phone contact Online system	Courtesy, respect Empathy Fairness in scheduling Flexibility User-friendly systems
Arrives at clinic	Reception Cashier Nurses	Feels welcome/not so Instructions clear/not so
Waits for physician	Nurses Staff Waiting areas Other patients	Long wait time Facility cleanliness Courtesy Scheduling fairness
Consults physician	Physician Nurses Equipment	Feels respected/not Feels caring/not Feels assured/not Nervous and anxious Equipment modern/old
Receives prescriptions and instructions	Nurses Staff Lab X-ray unit	Instructions clear/not clear Feels relieved/still anxious Feels assured/not so
Post-visit interactions	Nurses Staff	Response time to calls Empathy felt/no Information useful/not

- **Moments of truth:** These are moments wherein the patient/customer and the health care provider/organization come into contact with one another in a manner that gives the patient/customer an opportunity to either form or change an impression about the provider/organization; moments in which there is an opportunity for the health care provider/organization to make a difference when interacting with a patient/customer.
- **Staff roles:** Who delivers service at each touchpoint; who is directly responsible (e.g., front office personal)? Assign ownership of key touchpoints to internal departments.

- **Blueprint:** A complete picture of the working of the organization and emotional journey, from the outside in.
- **Integration of departments:** Break down silos (department barriers) to create one shared, organization-wide vision.
- Involve and engage all departments and managers in the process and with the end product in mind.

There are several mistakes experts have identified which should be avoided in patient/customer journey mapping (Fish, 2016)

- Insufficient focus on "outside to in" customer understanding:

It is not what management thinks the journey is. It is what the customer is exposed to in moments of truth. No CJM should depend entirely on internal inputs. Customer/patient input is essential to CJM.

- Confusing process mapping with journey mapping:

Process maps are merely flow charts of the process. The focus is not on customer's important touchpoints.

- Only considering status quo:

CJM should be flexible to accommodate possible future changes in the customer/patient journey as well.

- Believe the customer journey is linear and non-recursive:

There are many looping and sometimes repeating steps in a customer/patient journey.

- Over complicating.
- Stopping at point service ends.
- Not communicating the CJM well to staff.
- Not taking corrective action with the findings of a CJM.

7.9. Measuring CX/PX

Over the last two decades, there has been much research and discussion on measuring and improving the health care experience of patients. This interest is believed to have been prompted by movements for public reporting of quality measures, which later adopted measures on health plan member and patient satisfaction. The Institute of Medicine report, *Crossing the Quality Chasm* (Institute of Medicine, 2001) and the Hospital Consumer Assessment of Healthcare Providers and Systems (HCAHPS, CMS, 2013) encouraged public reporting of health care quality measures. Patient experience (PX) measures are also now used for accreditation and pay-for-performance programs (Lavela and Gallan, 2014).

This brings up the question of measuring CX/PX. Despite various discussions on the subject, measuring PX is not easy. This is due to the fact that PX does not depend only on objective measures such as clinical outcomes but also on customers'/patients' subjective and emotional factors.

Like almost all measures of consumer behavior, patient experience can also be measured using qualitative methods, quantitative methods, or mixed methods. In Chapter 4, we saw that use of mixed methods that rely on qualitative data and quantitative data, and subsequent data analysis using qualitative as well as quantitative techniques, seem to be more useful in health care market/marketing research. The same is true in measuring CX/PX.

> One of the most common fallacies in measuring CX/PX is that it is often equated to CS/PS discussed earlier in this chapter. We saw earlier that CS/PS is not the same as CX/PX. The latter encompasses a long-term, actually life-time, experience with the health care provider or organization.

We present below several methods of measuring PX found in the literature. These include:

- Patient Reported Experience Measures (PREM);
- HCAHPS (Hospital Consumer Assessment of Healthcare Providers and Systems) Survey;
- CAHPS Survey to Measure PX with Health Care Providers and Health Plans;
- Traditional Customer Satisfaction (CS) Measurement Methods;
- Net Promotor Score (NPS);
- Overall Patient Experience Score;
- Patient Memorability Based Scores; and
- Customer Effort Score (CES).

7.9.1. Patient-reported measures

Patient-Reported Experience Measures (PREMs) are used to evaluate a wide range of interactions of the patient within the health care system. Information can be collected using phone, mail, online, and in person. Many formats are used such as surveys, interviews, and focus groups. Both quantitative and qualitative data are usually collected.

PREMs typically focus on specific activities (called "touchpoints" in CX/PX terminology) within the health care system, such as waiting times, convenience in accessing services, ease of movement between departments, information provided on treatment and care, quality of communication of physicians, nurses and staff, and courtesy and efficiency of reception and administrative staff. Questions in PREM surveys are typically tailored to suit specific health care settings, such as clinics, hospitals, and long-term care facilities.

Some writers recommend PREMs in health care settings claiming that they would markedly improve measurement of the "total" patient experience and would heighten the health care organization's understanding of the patient experience (Lavela and Gallan, 2014).

There are limitations to PREMs as well. Manary et al. (2013) highlight concerns with patient-reported measures. Their concerns are that (1) PX feedback may not reflect medical outcome and quality of processes and might express only subjective assessments of their current health status, regardless of the care experience, and (2) patient-experience measures may reflect fulfillment of patients' immediate desires, for instance, short waiting time. These criticisms do not make much sense because PX is, in fact, supposed to take into account non-outcome-based subjective factors.

Sandager et al. (2016) claim that PX measures are affected by loyalty to health care professionals. Patients are generally loyal to the health care professionals and are reluctant to criticize. Patients evaluate treatment and care relative to difficulties experienced by health care professionals, such as time availability, and adequacy of facilities and supporting staff. Patients report a negative experience only if they believe that a negative outcome is under direct control and responsibility of the health care professional.

PREMs are often confused with PROMs, i.e., Patient Reported Outcome Measures, which are measures on clinical outcomes. Verma (2018) explains the difference as follows:

- PROM Short term is to get feedback on immediate individual care.
- PROM Long term is to get feedback on longer term clinical outcomes.
- PREM Short term is to get feedback on current integration of care.
- PREM Long term is to get feedback on system of integrated care.

> It must be remembered that PREMs do not intend to ignore patient's evaluation of outcomes (such as clinical outcomes). PREMS are intended to capture patient's evaluation of BOTH, outcome and process measures.

For a comprehensive discussion of PROMs and PREMs, see Reay (2010) "How to Measure Patient Experience and Outcomes to Demonstrate Quality in Care".

7.9.2. Hospital consumer assessment of healthcare providers and systems survey

Centers for Medicare and Medicaid Services (CMS, 2017) explain that three broad goals have shaped HCAHPS.

- The survey is designed to produce data about patients' perspectives of care that allow objective and meaningful comparisons of hospitals on topics that are important to consumers.
- Public reporting of the survey results creates new incentives for hospitals to improve quality of care.
- Public reporting serves to enhance accountability in health care by increasing transparency of the quality of hospital care provided in return for the huge payments made by CMS or care rendered to Medicare and Medicaid beneficiaries.

The HCAHPS survey asks recently discharged hospital patients 27 questions about their hospital stay. The survey contains 18 core questions about critical aspects of patients' hospital experiences (communication with nurses and doctors, the responsiveness of hospital staff, the cleanliness and quietness of the hospital environment, pain management, communication about medicines, discharge information, overall rating of hospital, and whether they would recommend the hospital).

The survey is administered to a random sample of adult patients across medical conditions between 48 hours and six weeks after discharge. It is not limited to Medicare beneficiaries. Data can be collected by mail, telephone, mail with telephone follow-up, or phone. Hospitals must survey patients each month of the year. The survey is available in official English, Spanish, Chinese, Russian, and Vietnamese versions.

The survey and its protocols for sampling, data collection and coding, and file submission can be found in the current HCAHPS Quality Assurance Guidelines, which is available on the official HCAHPS website, www.hcahpsonline.org.

7.9.3. CAHPS survey to measure PX with health care providers and health plans

The Consumer Assessment of Healthcare Providers and Systems (CAHPS) program is managed by the Agency for Healthcare Research and Quality (AHRQ). It aims to measure patient experience and report survey results.

CAHPS surveys ask patients about their experiences with providers, such as medical groups, Accountable Care Organizations (ACO) participating in Medicare initiatives, and health plans. There are CAHPS surveys focusing on experiences with care delivered in facilities, including hospitals, dialysis centers, and nursing homes (although, HCAHPS, described above, is the survey most applicable for hospitals).

The Medicare version of the CAHPS survey uses the following composite measures:

- Getting Needed Care
- Getting Appointments and Care Quickly
- Doctors Who Communicate Well
- Customer Service
- Getting Needed Prescription Drugs
- Care Coordination.

The survey reports scores on three rating measures:

- Rating of Health Plan
- Rating of Health Care Quality
- Rating of Drug Plan for health plans offering Medicare Advantage — Prescription Drug (MA-PD) plans and stand-alone Prescription Drug Plans (PDP).

The Medicare Advantage and Prescription Drug Plan CAHPS Survey uses two survey mailings and telephone follow-up of non-respondents to the mailed questionnaire.

The results from the Medicare CAHPS surveys are published in the *Medicare & You Handbook* made available annually to each Medicare beneficiary.

CAHPS Health Plan Survey Measures
Version 4.0

Getting Needed Care

Q17   In the last 12 months, how often was it easy to get appointments with specialists?

Q21   In the last 12 months, how often was it easy to get the care, tests, or treatment you thought you needed through your health plan?

Getting Care Quickly

Q4   In the last 12 months, when you needed care right away, how often did you get care as soon as you thought you needed it?

Q6   In the last 12 months, not counting the times you needed care right away, how often did you get an appointment for your health care at a doctor's office or clinic as soon as you thought you needed it?

How Well Doctors Communicate

Q11   In the last 12 months, how often did your personal doctor explain things in a way that was easy to understand?

Q12   In the last 12 months, how often did your personal doctor listen carefully to you?

Q13   In the last 12 months, how often did your personal doctor show respect for what you had to say?

Q14   In the last 12 months, how often did your personal doctor spend enough time with you?

Health Plan Information and Customer Service

Q23   In the last 12 months, how often did your health plan's customer service staff give you the information or help you needed?

Q24   In the last 12 months, how often did your health plan's customer service staff treat you with courtesy and respect?

(Continued)

Overall Ratings

Q8 Using any number from 0 to 10, where 0 is the worst health care possible and 10 is the best health care possible, what number would you use to rate all your health care in the last 12 months?

Q15 Using any number from 0 to 10, where 0 is the worst personal doctor possible and 10 is the best personal doctor possible, what number would you use to rate your personal doctor?

Q19 We want to know your rating of the specialist you saw most often in the last 12 months. Using any number from 0 to 10, where 0 is the worst specialist possible and 10 is the best specialist possible, what number would you use to rate the specialist?

Q27 Using any number from 0 to 10, where 0 is the worst health plan possible and 10 is the best health plan possible, what number would you use to rate your health plan?

Source: https://www.ahrq.gov/cahps/surveys-guidance/hp/about/survey-measures.html.

7.9.4. Traditional customer satisfaction (CS) measurement methods

Often service organizations, including health care organizations, resort to basic traditional CS measurements interpreting them as measures of CX. We have, however, seen previously that CS is not the same as CX, and as such, results of traditional CS surveys are not proper substitutes to evaluate CX.

Measuring customer satisfaction with services has been the most researched and discussed subject in the field of service management in the last 40 years. Various theories have been developed on how to measure customer satisfaction.

For example, Farris *et al.* (2010) define CS as "the number of customers, or percentage of total customers, whose reported experience with a firm, its products, or its services (ratings) exceeds specified satisfaction goals." This definition provides a measure or a metric of CS for an organization. These authors also claim that in a survey of nearly 200 senior marketing managers, 71% responded that they found a customer satisfaction metric very useful in managing and monitoring their businesses.

However, the prevailing theory on CS is that it is the difference between a customer's pre-service expectations and post-service perceptions of a service (Parasuraman *et al.*, 1988). Customer Satisfaction is the extent to which a customer is happy with the products and services provided by a particular business firm. In other words, it is a measure of how the goods or services provided by the said company meet the customer's expectations (Business Zeal, 2018).

According to Parasuraman *et al.* (1988),

Customer Satisfaction = Post-service perceptions of the customer − Pre-service expectations of the customer.

Their method of measuring CS, known as the SERVQUAL method, was discussed in Section 7.1.

Customers/patients have a specific set of expectations about the health care service as they arrive for the service. Those expectations are based on three factors:

- Personal past experience of the same or similar service,
- Word of mouth, i.e., experience of others, and
- Communications of the service organization such as advertisements and promotions.

Often customer/patient expectations are not realistic and not even reasonable. This makes it difficult for the health care organization to meet their expectations.

Health Care Marketing has a significant role in creating reasonable and valid expectations in the customer/patient. This could be done by:

- Encouraging satisfied customers to act as brand ambassadors spreading word of mouth recommendations of services provided by this organization.
- Ensuring that advertising and promotional communications are honest and create only valid and reasonable expectations in customers/patients.

If the service organization can consistently exceed customer service expectations, many of these satisfied customers will convey positive information to friends, relatives, neighbors, and co-workers. Such recommendations are worth a whole lot more than the marketing and advertising health care organizations pay for (Manternach, 2012).

However, customer expectations are difficult to understand in a usable way because they:

- Differ from one customer to another. Research shows variations in expectations across demographic factors such as age, gender, and ethnicity.
- Vary among the dimensions. In children's health care services, research show that mothers did not care much about the comfort of the facilities as much as they did about the actual care received from doctors and nursing staff.
- Change over time. Gunawardane (2010) has shown how patient expectations and priorities change with repeated visits to health care providers.

As discussed previously, these traditional CS measurements are not the most suitable for measuring experiences, i.e., CX/PX.

Still, 80% of customer service organizations use customer satisfaction (CSAT) scores as the primary metric for gauging the customer's experience (GFK, 2015: "Customer Satisfaction v Customer Experience: From Satisfaction and Loyalty, to Experiences and Relationships"). The ineffectiveness of these surveys is indicated by the fact that 20% of "satisfied" customers intended to leave; while 28% of the "dissatisfied" customers intended to stay.

PricewaterhouseCoopers (2017) agrees:

> "Organizations have traditionally built patient experience efforts around the industry's satisfaction surveys and measured performance based on satisfaction scores, service volume, and revenue. Though they're important, these measurements don't get to the root of what patients value most or what motivates them to get and stay healthy."

7.9.5. Net promotor score (Reichheld, 2003)

This very popular measure asks customers/patients a question of the form, "How likely is it that you would recommend (health care provider/plan/hospital/organization/system) to a friend or colleague?" The responses are scored on a 0 to 10 (11 point) scale, and customers are categorized as promoters (those who responded with a 9 or 10), passives (7 or 8), or detractors (0 to 6). NPS is then computed by subtracting the percent of detractors from the percent of promoters.

> **Net Promoter Score (NPS) to Measure CX/PX**
>
> Net Promoter Score = Percentage of customers who are promoters of a health care service or system *minus* the percentage who are detractors.

Though NPS is a popular and easy-to-use measure, it is not without criticism from researchers. In several industries it has been shown to be inferior to customer satisfaction measures in predicting future business performance (Morgan and Lopo, 2006). Nonetheless, NPS continues to be widely used by organizations across many industries (Health Outcomes Insights, 2012).

Health Outcomes Insights (2012) also cautions users of NPS in health care. The usual time between health care encounters affects patients' fading memory and actual behavior. Discovering a patient's intent to refer a friend to a health care provider may not always translate into one's own behavior, like retention with the same provider.

7.9.6. Overall patient experience score

Overall Patient Experience Scores are used by some health care organizations such as the National Health Service (NHS) in the United Kingdom. The Overall Patient Experience Scores are a statistical series measuring overall patient views of care and services provided by the NHS. The statistics are composite scores constructed using results taken from the NHS Patient Survey Program (NHS, 2018).

NHS asks patients questions on the following categories:

- **Access and waiting:** Two survey questions — these questions ask how long the patient had to wait after the stated appointment time.
- **Safe, high quality coordinated care:** Five survey questions — this category includes questions about whether patients received clear messages and whether they trusted the staff.
- **Better information, more choice:** Five survey questions — questions aim to get feedback on communication in terms of involving the patient in their care and telling patients what they need to know clearly.
- **Building close relationships:** Five survey questions — this category assesses whether patients got the opportunity to discuss their problems with staff, whether patients received clear answers to questions, and whether staff avoided talking about a patient as if s/he were not there.

- **Clean, comfortable, friendly place to be:** Three survey questions — on cleanliness, being treated with respect and dignity, and being told why any delays arose.

The Overall Patient Experience Scores are computed from answers to these questions. Patients do not answer a question asking for their "overall experience".

7.9.7. Patient memorability-based scores

Solis (2019) describes how good customer experience ends up as good memories:

> "Customer experience is a matter of perspective and empathy. It's possessive. It's theirs. It's the customer's experience, with an emphasis on the apostrophe. Their experiences become memories. Whether they're good or bad, it's what they remember that becomes your brand and what they recall or share with others in critical moments of truth. Anything that's forgettable is also your brand."

Vibe Vision (2017) adds:

> "Some experts see CX essentially as a memory of the experience that customers have. No matter how smoothly does the experience go in reality, if the customer for some reason remembers it differently, that's what it is! And many of us know from psychology classes how emotions affect our memories — the stronger the emotion related to the memory, the deeper the memory itself."

The measure of customer/patient experience we discuss here is based on this concept. It asks the customer/patient whether they have a "positive memorable" or "neutral" or "negative memorable" experience with the health care service/provider/organization.

The CX/PX score is then computed as % positive memorable minus % negative memorable.

Studies claim that this score is highly correlated to NPS.

7.9.8. Customer effort score (Dixon *et al.*, 2010)

Customer Effort Score (CES) is a type of customer satisfaction metric that measures the ease of an experience with a company by asking customers, on a five-point scale of "Very Difficult" to "Very Easy", how much effort was required on the part of the customer to use the product or service, and how much effort it took to get problems resolved.

CES is then computed as the difference between percentage of people who said "easy" from the percentage of those who said "difficult", i.e., CES = % Responses "Easy" – % Responses "Difficult".

7.10. Guidelines for Effective Customer/Patient Experience Management

There is no shortage of management views and discussions on customer satisfaction and experience, but many of these are rhetorical punch lines such as "delight the customer" and "exceed customer expectations". Use of terms like "quality", "efficiency", and "customer service" are also thrown in without explaining how to achieve them.

An excellent analysis of management rhetoric vs. effective practices in customer satisfaction/experience appears in a paper in the Harvard Business Review on "Stop Trying to Delight Your Customers" by Dixon *et al.* (2010). In this paper, the authors present a few simple realities in, and good guides to, customer service/experience management. They include the following:

- Simply telling reps to exceed customers' expectations is apt to yield confusion, wasted time and effort, and costly giveaways.
- To really win their loyalty, forget the bells and whistles and just solve their problems.
- In a study of more than 75,000 people interacting with contact-center representatives or using self-service channels, it was found that over-the-top efforts make little difference: All customers really want is a simple, quick solution to their problem.
- Reduce the need for repeat calls by anticipating and dealing with related downstream issues.
- Arm reps to address the emotional side of customer interactions; minimize the need for customers to switch service channels.
- Elicit and use feedback from disgruntled or struggling customers.
- Focus on problem solving, not speed.
- When it comes to service, companies create loyal customers primarily by helping them solve their problems quickly and easily.
- In fact, the study quoted in the paper found little correlation between satisfaction and loyalty, which begs the question: Why measure satisfaction if it does not predict retention and increase lifetime value?

Edwards *et al.* (2015) in a paper on, "Instruments to Measure the Inpatient Hospital Experience: A Literature Review", in the *Patient Experience Journal*, highlight several factors health care managers should focus on to enhance CX/PX. These are as follows:

- Respect for patients' values, preferences, and expressed needs;
- Coordination and integration of care;
- Information, communication, and education;
- Physical comfort;
- Emotional support and alleviation of fear and anxiety;
- Involvement of family and friends; and
- Support during transition (e.g., discharge) and continuity.

Swaney (2017) recalls how Johns Hopkins Hospital held a patient town hall in 2015, and discovered that one of the most common pieces of feedback from patients was that they wanted better and up-to-date communications about their care. Technology now exists that enables fulfillment of this request.

Gambie (2013) summarizes key components for organizations' patient experience initiatives as follows:

1. Sharing patient satisfaction and experience scores: 52%,
2. Regular or hourly rounding by clinical team members: 50%,
3. Leadership rounding by members of senior management: 49%,
4. Staffing training programs for customer service or other behaviors: 49%, and
5. Special initiatives to improve specific Hospital Consumer Assessment of Healthcare Providers and System domains: 38%.

Should health care marketing select different strategies across all customers of a health care practice, hospital, or provider? The answer seems to be — No. Health care organization's management and marketing should segment their customers/patients according to patient satisfaction/experience scores and distribute their retention efforts over these segments rather than adopting same strategies with all customers (Meyer and Schwager, 2007). The segmentation of customers could be as follows:

- Model customers: good summary scores; good revenue.
- Growth customers: good summary scores; higher potential revenue.
- At-risk customers: low scores; good revenue. Demanding decisive intervention.

- Dangling customers: low scores; low revenue. To be rescued or abandoned.

Reichheld (2003) reports that: CX scores drop after just one failure for those in the "at-risk" category.

7.10.1. Focus on relationships with customers/patients, not just encounters one at a time

Consider every customer interaction (touchpoint) as just one small piece of an ongoing relationship. Building beyond a transaction or a visit inevitably leads to better service for patients.

7.10.2. Memories build relationships (GFK, 2015)

The best way to build strong, positive relationships with your customers is to *create positive memorable experiences* (and avoiding/recovering from negative memorable experiences).

What are some guidelines for creating memorable experiences?

- Barrows (2010, in a paper on "Six Ways to Create Memorable Experiences") emphasizes: Attentiveness; Recognition; Personalization; Consideration; Appreciation; Delight.
- Fileboard (2010, in a paper on "9 Ways to Create a Memorable Experience for Your Customers" recommends:
    - Listen to customers' problems sincerely.
    - Create a great internal corporate culture that puts employees at the top. Happy employees create happy customers.
    - Make it very easy to work with your product or service. In our case, the health care service.
    - Make customers/patients feel special and personal. Smart organizations use available data to make customers feel special (like cards or text messages on birthdays).
    - Constantly strive to learn more about your customers and build personalization in your products and branding messages.
    - Have the leadership team put customer experience at the top of their priorities.
    - Measure customer satisfaction, experience, and engagement.

7.10.3. Adopt appropriate modern digital technology (Luxford and Sutton, 2014)

- 88% of health insurers are investing in technology to improve the member experience. E.g., Humana's Analytics. Common applications are patient portals and electronic medical records (EMR).
- Lakdawala (2015) recommends encouraging the use of, and maximizing information flow, with mobile apps.
- Data analysis: Accolade, a company that helps employees and health plan members navigate the health system, uses machine learning to find patterns in the information patients provide and use that knowledge to predict behaviors.
- PricewaterhouseCoopers (PWC, 2018) suggests using technology to enable patients help themselves at every touchpoint — from making an appointment, to getting a question answered, to finding out coverage by their health insurance plan, etc. PWC surveys have shown that 50% of consumers said they would like to see scheduling appointments more digitized.

7.10.4. Employee experience

Employees must perceive top management as seriously involved in enhancing customer/patient experience. Say Meyer and Schwager (2007),

> "Customer experience does not improve until it becomes a top priority and a company's work processes, systems, and structure change to reflect that. When employees observe senior managers persistently demanding experience information and using it to make tough decisions, their own decisions are conditioned by that awareness."

This concept is sometimes called "Employee Experience".

71% of consumers say employees have a significant impact on customer experience. 59% of consumers say companies and organizations have lost touch with the human element of customer experience (PWC, 2018).

Despite the increased use of digital technology, iPhones, and tablets, PWC's surveys have found that 71% of Americans would rather interact with a human than an automated process. Health care is a special service close to the patient's heart and one that makes the patients anxious and needing comfort from health care organization's providers and staff.

References

Afshar, V. (2015). "50 Important Customer Experience Stats for Business Leaders", *Huffington Post*, October 15, 2015.

Agency for Healthcare Research and Quality (2018). "Why Improve Patient Experience?", Content last reviewed, http://www.ahrq.gov/cahps/quality-improvement/improvement-guide/2-why-improve/index.html. Accessed November 12, 2018.

Baltes, L. P. (2015). "Content Marketing — The Fundamental Tool of Digital Marketing", *Bulletin of the Transylvania University of Brasov. Economic Sciences. Series V*, 8 (2), 111–118.

Barrows, S. (2010). "Six Ways to Create a Memorable Customer Experience", https://www.entrepreneur.com/article/206760. Accessed March 1, 2019.

Becker's Hospital Review (2013). "Incorporating Patient Experience into Healthcare Marketing", https://www.beckershospitalreview.com/strategic-planning/incorporating-patient-experience-into-healthcare-marketing.html. Accessed February 20, 2019.

Beryl Institute (2017). "Defining Patient Experience", https://www.theberylinstitute.org/page/definingpatientexp. Accessed July 25, 2018.

Beryl Institute (2018). "A Report on the Beryl Institute Benchmarking Study, the State of Patient Experience 2017: A Return to Purpose", https://cdn.ymaws.com/www.theberylinstitute.org/resource/resmgr/benchmarking_study/2017_Benchmarking_Report.pdf. Accessed November 8, 2018.

Beryl Institute (2019). "Guiding Principles of Patient Experience", https://www.theberylinstitute.org/page/GuidingPrinciples. Accessed February 25, 2019.

Blake, M. (2018). "Customer Experience vs. Customer Service vs. Customer Care", https://www.forbes.com/sites/blakemorgan/2018/03/05/customer-experience-vs-customer-service-vs-customer-care/#703fda694167. Accessed November 6, 2018.

Bowling, A., Rowe, G., Lambert, N., Waddington, M., Mahtani, K. R., Kenten, C. et al. (2012). "The Measurement of Patients' Expectations for Health Care: A Review and Psychometric Testing of a Measure of Patients' Expectations", *Health Technology Assessment*, 16 (30).

Business Zeal (2018). "Why is Customer Satisfaction Important?", https://businesszeal.com/why-is-customer-satisfaction-important. Accessed November 4, 2018.

CMS (2017). "HCAHPS: Patients' Perspectives of Care Survey. HCAHPS Overview", https://www.cms.gov/Medicare/Quality-Initiatives-Patient-Assessment-Instruments/HospitalQualityInits/HospitalHCAHPS.html. Accessed February 22, 2019.

CMS, Centers for Medicare & Medicaid Services (2013). "Hospital Consumer Assessment of Healthcare Providers and Systems (HCAPS) Fact Sheet", Baltimore, MD: CMS, www.hcahpsonline.org. Accessed March 4, 2019.

Conder, P. (2014). "Ten Guiding Principles of Customer Experience", http://www.lenati.com/blog/2014/06/ten-guiding-principles-customer-experience/. Accessed February 26, 2019.

Connolly, B. (2017). "Why Authenticity is the Prescription for Modern Healthcare Marketing", http://www.olapic.com/resources/authenticity-prescription-modern-healthcare-marketing_blog-p1aw-g1lo-v1hc/. Accessed September 23, 2018.

Davey, N. (2016). "How to Create a Customer Journey Map", MyCustomer.com. Accessed February 28, 2019.

Deloitte (2016). "Elevating the Health Care Consumer Experience Insights for the Future," https://www2.deloitte.com/us/en/pages/life-sciences-and-healthcare/articles/elevating-health-care-consumer-experience.html. Accessed October 20, 2018.

Deloitte (2017a). "2018 Global Health Care Outlook: The Evolution of Smart Health Care", https://www2.deloitte.com/global/en/pages/life-sciences-and-healthcare/articles/global-health-care-sector-outlook.html. Accessed October 1, 2018.

Deloitte (2017b). "Value of Patient Experience: Hospitals with Higher Patient Experience Scores Have Higher Clinical Quality", https://www2.deloitte.com/content/dam/Deloitte/us/Documents/life-sciences-health-care/us-value-patient-experience-050517.pdf. Accessed February 22, 2019.

Dixon, M., Freeman, K. and Toman, N. (2010). "Stop Trying to Delight Your Customers", *Harvard Business Review*, July–August.

Edwards, K. J., Walker, K. and Duff, J. (2015) "Instruments to Measure the Inpatient Hospital Experience: A Literature Review", *Patient Experience Journal*, 2 (2), Article 11.

Ellis, L. (2016). "A Roadmap to Improve Customer-Centricity in Health Care", https://www.hsph.harvard.edu/ecpe/a-roadmap-to-improve-customer-centricity-in-health-care/. Accessed August 24, 2018.

Farris, P. W., Neil, Bendle, T., Pfeifer, P. E., Reibstein, D. J. (2010). *Marketing Metrics: The Definitive Guide to Measuring Marketing Performance*. Upper Saddle River, New Jersey: Pearson Education, Inc.

Feirn, A., Betts, D. and Tribble, T. (2009). "The Patient Experience: Strategies and Approaches for Providers to Achieve and Maintain a Competitive Advantage", Deloitte LLP's Health Sciences Practice White Paper, https://www.deloitte.com/assets/DcomUnitedStates/Local%20Assets/Documents/us_lshc_ThePatientExperience_072809.pdf. Accessed April 10, 2014.

Fileboard (2012). "9 Ways to Create a Memorable Experience for Your Customers", https://blog.fileboard.com/blog/2012/08/06/9-ways-to-create-a-memorable-experience-for-your-customers/. Accessed March 1, 2019.

Fish, D. (2016). "Ten Mistakes to Avoid in Journey Mapping", e-Commerce, http://www.dckap.com/blog/ten-mistakes-avoid-journey-mapping/. Accessed March 1, 2019.

Fremont, A. M., Clearly, P. D. and Hargraves, J. L. (2001). "Patient-Centered Processes of Care and Long-Term Outcomes of Acute Myocardial Infarction", *J Gen Intern Med*, 14, 800–808.

Fullam, F., Garman, A. N. and Johnson, T. J. (2009). "The Use of Patient Satisfaction Surveys and Alternate Coding Procedures to Predict Malpractice Risk", *Medical Care*, 47 (45), 1–7.

Fustino, N. J., Moore, P. and Viers. S. (2018). "Improving Patient Experience of Care Providers in a Multispecialty Ambulatory Pediatrics Practice", https://doi.org/10.1177/0009922818806309. Accessed February 28, 2019.

Gallagher, B. (2017). "How Has Healthcare Marketing Changed in the Last Decade?", https://www.Gallagher.sharecare.com/video/healthmakers/brendan-gallagher/what-is-the-future-of-healthcare-marketing. Accessed June 1, 2018.

Gambie, M. (2013). "28 Statistics on Hospitals' Patient Experience Strategies", https://www.beckershospitalreview.com/hospital-management-administration/28-statistics-on-hospitals-patient-experience-strategies.html. Accessed February 27, 2019.

Gandolf, S. (2013). "The Forgotten 'P' in Your Medical Marketing Plan", Home » Blog » Healthcare Marketing » Patient Experience. Last Updated on August 2, 2013.

GFK (2015). "Customer Satisfaction v Customer Experience: From Satisfaction and Loyalty, to Experiences and Relationships", http://www.gfk.com/fileadmin/user_upload/dyna_content_import/2015-11-24_news/data/au/news-and-events/News/Documents/GfK%20-%20Customer%20Satisfaction%20v%20Customer%20Experience.pdf. Accessed March 1, 2019.

Greenfield, S., Kaplan, H. S. and Ware, J. E. Jr. (1988). "Patients' Participation in Medical Care: Effects on Blood Sugar Control and Quality of Life in Diabetes", *J Gen Intern Med*, 3, 448–457.

Gunawardane, G (2010). "An Assessment of the Dynamic Nature of Customer Expectations in Service Encounters", *California Journal of Operations Management*, 8 (1).

Haefner, M. (2017). "8 Healthcare Marketing Trends for 2018", *Becker's Hospital Review*, https://www.beckershospitalreview.com/hospital-management-administration/8-healthcare-marketing-trends-for-2018.html. Accessed February 25, 2019.

Hall, M. (2013). "Incorporating Patient Experience into Healthcare Marketing", *ASC Communications*.

Health Outcomes Insights (2012). "Net Promoter Score in Health Care", https://thepatientoutcomesblog.com/2012/11/12/net-promoter-score-in-health-care/. Accessed February 22, 2019.

Inc.com (2014). "What is Customer Experience? An interview with Estaban Kolsky", https://www.inc.com/disneyinstitute/afshar/what-is-customer-experience.html. Accessed February 24, 2019.

Institute of Medicine (2001). *Crossing the Quality Chasm: A New Health System for the 21st Century*. Washington, DC: The National Academies Press, 2001.

Jha. S. M. (2000). *Services Marketing*, Mumbai: Himalaya Publishing House, 2000, 10.

Jones, J. (2015). "Touch-Points in the Customer Journey", Training — Industry website, https://www.trainingindustry.com/sales-training/articles/touch-points-in-the-customer-journey.aspx, July 1, 2015. Accessed February 28, 2019.

Junewicz, A. and Youngner, S. J. (2015). "Patient-Satisfaction Surveys on a Scale of 0 to 10: Improving Health Care or Leading It Astray?", *Hastings Cent Rep*, 45, 43–51.

Kernan, J. (2017). "2018 Healthcare Marketing Trend #1: Customer Experience", https://smithandjones.com/resources/blog/2018-healthcare-marketing-trends-customer-experience. Accessed September 27, 2018.

Lakdawala, M. (2015). "Beacons Brighten the Patient Experience. Eight Ways Beacon Technology Can Improve Patient Care — And Health Outcomes", PricewaterhouseCoopers, http://usblogs.pwc.com/emerging-technology/beacons-brighten-the-patient-experience/. Accessed January 23, 2018.

Larson, J. (2012). "The Connection between Employee Satisfaction and Patient Satisfaction", *Healthcare News*, https://www.amnhealthcare.com/latest-healthcare-news/459/1033/. Accessed February 22, 2019.

LaVela, S. L. and Gallan, A. S. (2014). "Evaluation and Measurement of Patient Experience", *Patient Experience Journal*, 1 (1), Article 5.

Levinson, W., Roter, D. L. and Mullooly, J. P. (1997). 'Physician-Patient Communication: The Relationship with Malpractice Claims among Primary Care Physicians and Surgeons", *JAMA*, 277, 553–559.

Luxford, K. and Sutton, S. (2014). "How Does Patient Experience Fit into the Overall Healthcare Picture?", *Patient Experience Journal*, 1 (1), Article 4.

Manary, M. P., Boulding, W., Staelin, R. and Glickman, S. W. (2013). "The Patient Experience and Health Outcomes", *New England Journal of Medicine*, 3 (368), 201–203.

Manning, H. (2010). "Customer Experience Defined", http://blogs.forrester.com/harley_manning/10-11-23-customer_experience_defined. Accessed February 22, 2019.

Manternach, L. (2012). "When It Comes to Service, Perception is Reality", *Corridor Business Journal*, 8 (51), 25.

Matejka, R. (2017). "Promoting Customer Satisfaction in Healthcare", *Healthcare Business Insights*, https://www.healthcarebusinessinsights.com/blog/information-technology/promoting-customer-satisfaction-healthcare/. Accessed November 5, 2018.

McCance, T., Hastings, J. and Dowler, H. (2015). "Evaluating the Use of Key Performance Indicators to Evidence the Patient Experience", *Journal of Clinical Nursing*, First published: 10 August 2015. Also available on Wiley on line library.

Messinger, B. (2014) "Content is King and Connections are Queen, but Patient Experiences Rule", *Marketing Health Services*, 34 (1), 20–23.

Meyer, C. and Schwager, A. (2007), "Understanding Customer Experience", *Harvard Business Review*, February, 117–126.

Morgan, B. (2017). "What is Customer Experience?", *Forbes*, https://www.forbes.com/sites/blakemorgan/2017/04/20/what-is-customer-experience-2/#22b3d09270c2. Accessed February 27, 2019.

Morgan, N. A. and Lopo, L. R. (2006), "The Value of Different Customer Satisfaction and Loyalty Metrics in Predicting Business Performance", *Marketing Science*, 25 (5), 426-439.

Morgan, N. A. and Rego, L. (2006), "The Value of Different Customer Satisfaction and Loyalty Metrics in Predicting Business Performance", *Marketing Science*, 25 (5), 426–439.

Moss, C., Nelson, K., Connor, M., Wensley, C., McKinlay, E. and Boulton, A. (2014). "Patient Experience in the Emergency Department: Inconsistencies in the Ethic and Duty of Care", *Journal of Clinical Nursing*, First published: 19 May 2014. Also available on Wiley on line library.

Nasution, R. A., Sembada, A. Y., Miliani, L., Resti, N. D. and Prawono, D. A. (2014). "The Customer Experience Framework as Baseline for Strategy and Implementation in Services Marketing", *Proceedia Social and Behavioral Sciences*, 148, 254–261.

NHS (2018). "Overall Patient Experience Scores", NHS England, https://www.england.nhs.uk/statistics/statistical-work-areas/pat-exp/. Accessed February 24, 2019.

Oneview (2015). "The Eight Principles of Patient-Centered Care", https://www.oneviewhealthcare.com/the-eight-principles-of-patient-centered-care/. Accessed February 24, 2019.

Parasuraman, A., Berry, L. L. and Zeithaml, V. A. (1988). "SERVQUAL: A Multiple-Item Scale for Measuring Consumer Perceptions of Service Quality", *Journal of Retailing*, 64 (1) 12–40.

PricewaterhouseCoopers (2017). "Top Health Industry Issues of 2018. Patient Experience as a Priority and Not Just a Portal", https://www.pwc.com/us/en/health-industries/top-health-industry-issues/patient-experience.html. Accessed November 7, 2018.

PricewaterhouseCoopers (2018). "Healthcare Companies Can Improve the Patient Experience and Make Healthcare Work Better for Everyone", http://usblogs.pwc.com/emerging-technology/four-ways-healthcare-can-improve-customer-experience/. Accessed January 23, 2019.

Reay, N. (2010). "How to Measure Patient Experience and Outcomes to Demonstrate Quality in Care", *Nursing Times*, 106 (7).

Reichheld, F. (2003). "The One Number You Need to Grow", *Harvard Business Review*, December.

Resnick, L. (2018). "5 Themes that Will Drive Healthcare Marketing in 2019", https://www.cmo.com/opinion/articles/2018/10/23/themes-that-will-drive-healthcare-marketing-in-2019.html#gs.JDHEUpMN. Accessed February 23, 2019.

Robison J. (2010). "What is the 'Patient Experience'?", *Gallup Management Journal Online*, http://businessjournal.gallup.com/content/14 3258/patient-experience.aspx. 2010. Accessed March 15, 2018.

Safran, D. G., Montgomery, J. E. and Chang, H. (2001). "Switching Doctors: Predictors of Voluntary Disenrollment from a Primary Physician's Practice", *Journal of Family Practice* 50 (2), 130–136.

Sandager, M., Freil, M. and Knudsen, J. L. (2016). "Please Tick the Appropriate Box: Perspectives on Patient Reported Experience", *Patient Experience Journal*, 3 (1), Article 10.

Sequist, T. D., Schneider, E. C., Anastario, M. *et al.* (2008). "Quality Monitoring of Physicians: Linking Patients' Experiences of Care to Clinical Quality and Outcomes", *J Gen Intern Med*, 23 (11), 1784–1790.

Seton — Ascension (2017). "Healthcare Journey Mapping is in for 2016", https://www.seton.net/medical-services-and-programs/innovation/healthcare-journey-mapping/. Accessed February 28, 2019.

Shah, S., Patel, A., Rumoro, D. P., Hohmann, S. and Fullam, F. (2015). "Managing Patient Expectations at Emergency Department Triage", *Patient Experience Journal*, 2 (2), Article 6.

Shute, D. (2017). "The ROI of Patient Experience", *Health Leaders Media*, http://www.healthleadersmedia.com/finance/roi-patient-experience?page=0%2C1. Accessed February 22, 2019.

Solis, B. (2019). "Customer Experiences Become Memories, Good or Bad, and They Add Up to Your Brand", https://www.briansolis.com/2019/02/customer-experiences-become-memories-good-or-bad-and-they-add-up-to-your-brand/. Accessed February 24, 2019.

Stewart, M. A. (1995). "Effective Physician-Patient Communication and Health Outcomes: A Review", *Canadian Medical Association Journal*, 152 (9), 1423–1433.

Sundbo, J. and Hagedorn-Rasmussen, P. (2008). "The Backstaging of Experience Production." In Sundbo, J. and Darmer, P. (Eds.), *Creating Experiences in the Experience Economy*, Cheltenham: Elgar.

Swaney, R. (2017). "Improving the Patient Experience through Hospital Room Technology", https://insights.samsung.com/2017/07/12/improving-the-patient-experience-through-hospital-room-technology/. Accessed February 28, 2019.

Verma, R. (2018). "Overview: What are PROMs and PREMs?", ACI NSW Agency for Clinical Innovation, https://www.aci.health.nsw.gov.au/__data/assets/pdf_file/0003/253164/Overview-What_are_PROMs_and_PREMs.pdf. Accessed February 22, 2019.

Vibe Vision (2017). "Customer Experience — Creating Outstanding Memories", https://www.vibevision.fi/l/customer-experience-creating-outstanding-memories/. Accessed August 25, 2018.

Walden, S. (2014). "Experience is Perception", *Customer Think*, http://customerthink.com/experience_is_perception/. Accessed February 26, 2019.

Walter, U., Edvardsson, B. and Ostrom, A. (2010). "Drivers of Customer Service Experiences: A Study in the Restaurant Industry." *Managing Service Quality*, 20 (3), 236–258.

Wolf, J. A. (2017). "The Patchwork Perspective: A New View for Patient Experience", *Patient Experience Journal*, 4 (3), Article 1.

Wolf, J. A., Niederhauser, V., Marshburn, D. and LaVela, S. L. (2014). "Defining Patient Experience", *Patient Experience Journal*, 1 (1), Article 3.

Woods, C. (2016). "The Role of Leadership in Patient Experience", https://www.languageofcaring.com/blog-post/role-of-leadership-in-patient-experience/. Accessed February 27, 2019.

Suggested Additional Readings

Ensocare (2017). "How Demographics Impact Healthcare Delivery", https://www.ensocare.com/resource-center/how-demographics-impact-health-care-delivery. Accessed October 27, 2018.

Krivich, M. (2011). "Customer Experience Management Applied to Healthcare", *Healthcare Marketing Matters*, http://healthcaremarketingmatters.blogspot.com/2011/01/customer-experience-management-applied.html. Accessed September 24, 2018.

Chapter 8

Market Segmentation in Health Care Marketing

8.1. Market Segmentation — Definition and Overview

It is not effective, and virtually impossible, to plan and implement the same marketing strategies and methods to all products and services offered by the health care organization. It is also not effective to market even one product or service to all customers within a certain geographical area or market.

An obvious example is a health plan offering both Medicare and Medicaid managed care products. This plan has to promote its Medicare plans to seniors who have characteristics and behaviors much different from low-income and usually younger consumers seeking health care under Medicaid.

Another less straightforward example is a physician or a physician group offering primary care and specialist services to consumers whose age, income, and education characteristics are different. The physician or physician group will be developing different marketing strategies and plans for the different demographic groups.

Therefore, it is essential for the health care organization to identify appropriate market segments and niches. This process is called *market segmentation*.

Let us first look at some formal definitions of market segmentation:

- A process of dividing the entire marketplace into separate groups, consisting of individuals who have similar products or service needs. When a

- segment is divided into smaller subsegments, one of these smaller subsegments is called a "niche" (Kotler et al., 2008).
- Market segmentation describes the division of a market into homogeneous groups which will respond differently to promotions, communications, advertising, and other marketing mix variables. Each group, or "segment", can be targeted by a different marketing mix (DSS Research, 2016).
- Market segmentation was first described in the 1950s, when product differentiation was the primary marketing strategy used. In the 1970s and 1980s, market segmentation began to take off as a means of expanding sales and obtaining competitive advantages (Kotler et al., 2008).

The practice of market segmentation has been traced back to as far back as the 16th century. Traders at that time are known to have focused on customers by income levels to facilitate marketing and selling their goods. Researchers claim that contemporary market segmentation emerged in the first few decades of the 20th century as marketers began to have access to demographic and purchasing data for significant groups. At the same time, newer advertising and distribution channels to reach these groups also became available for groups, but rarely for single consumers. Use of US tax registers and census data to identify consumers by educational levels and income also came into practice in the early 1900s. By the 1930s, market researchers are reported to have realized that demographics alone were insufficient to explain purchasing behavior of different segments, which led to exploring the use of lifestyles, attitudes, values, beliefs, and culture to segment markets.

Wendell R. Smith is generally credited with being the first to introduce the concept of market segmentation into the marketing literature in 1956 with the publication of his article, "Product Differentiation and Market Segmentation as Alternative Marketing Strategies" (Smith, 1956). Early segmentation approaches focused primarily on short-term tactical advantages, e.g., an immediate marketing campaign.

With the advent of modern mass data availability and digital communications, it has now become possible for marketers to segment markets to smaller niches and even individual customer levels. This permits marketers to come up with customized communications and offers. This concept vastly benefits the modern health care concept of patient-centered care.

For a comprehensive coverage of history of market segmentations, see Lockley (1950), Fullerton (2016), Cox and Dannehl (2007), McKendrick et al. (1982), and Jones and Tadajewski (2016).

Chand (2018) summarizes the evolution of market segmentation by identifying the following sequential stages:

- *Mass marketing*: Treats whole market as one segment.
- *Product variety marketing* (we referred to this earlier as product differentiation).
- *Target marketing*: Focuses on the total market in a given segment.
- *Micro marketing*: This serves one or more selected segments in a market.
- *Customized marketing*: This focuses on individual-level customer needs, but designs and delivers products/services as a standard product/service for the group of individuals. Thus, the target is still a group of customers, not specific individuals (which is addressed in the next category).
- *Personalized marketing*: This focuses on personal customer needs at the specific customer/patient level. See, patient-centered care discussed elsewhere is this book.

8.1.1. Market segmentation as a technique in health care marketing

Market segmentation in health care marketing is fairly recent. Dey (2013) recalls a series of early studies on market segmentation in health care to trace the evolution of market segmentation in health care. These include the following:

- In their study, Flnn and Lamb (1987) showed that hospitals can have benefit segments depending on different clientele using their services. Using tools like exploratory factor analysis and cluster analysis, they identified four clusters or segments of consumers based on services sought from the hospital. They named them as *Take care of me*, *Cure me*, *Pamper me*, and *Cognitive*. These segments were separate in terms of their need of infrastructure, medical knowledge, customized service, and administrative issues from the hospital.
- In their study, Dolinsky and Stinerock (1998) argued that cultural differences within the consumers lead to different importance being accorded by them to various health care attributes. They studied three main ethnic groups of USA, namely Anglo Americans, Afro Americans, and Hispanics. They had chosen 16 health care attributes representing five health care constructs including physician quality, health care economics, quality of

nurses and other medical staff, access to health care, and non-medically related aspects. Education, gender, health status, marital status, age, and number of household members were used as the independent variables, whereas ethnicity was the dependent variable. The authors even explore differences within each race.

- An investigation was conducted by Johnson et al. (2004) into the racial and ethnic differences in patients' perceptions of bias and cultural competence in health care. They used a three-stage model based on demographic characteristics, self-reported health status, primary source of medical care, patient–physician communication, and respondents' health literacy. The authors chose Anglo Americans, Afro Americans, Asians, and Hispanics for their study, and their self-reported ethnicities were used as dependent variables for the study. Their results revealed that Hispanics considered themselves to be treated with more respect and dignity as compared to their white counterparts by their physicians, whereas Asians perceived themselves to be looked down upon by their physicians because of their way of living. All the three races perceived that the health system in place has a bias against them as compared to whites, and they perceive that had they been whites then they would have received better medical care, fair treatment from medical staff, and better judgment from the medical staff.
- Lynn et al. (2007) suggested a conceptual framework for population stratification based on health prospects and priorities rather than on health care providers. They took into consideration three conditions for formation of these segments. These were limited number of segments, all-inclusive but mutually exclusive, and justification ability of the segment in terms of size and reach. Based on the above conditions, they proposed eight segments, namely (1) healthy, (2) maternal and infant health, (3) acutely ill with likely return to health, (4) chronic conditions with generally normal function, (5) significant but relatively stable disability, (6) dying, (7) limited reserve and serious exacerbations, and (8) long course of decline. They also proposed the priority concerns for these populations as well as the major components of health care associated with each of these segments. They called this framework as a bridge to the health model. They argued that correlating each of these segments with the Institute of Medicine's goals for quality can ultimately lead to better resource planning, care arrangements, and health service delivery.
- Moschis and Friend (2008) focused on the growing number of mature consumers in the US health care market using the Gerontographic

segmentation technique. Using factor analysis and cluster analysis, they identified four segments, namely (1) healthy hermits, (2) ailing outgoers, (3) frail reclusives, and (4) healthy indulgers. They empirically proved that as compared to simple age-based segmentation, their segmentation technique gave clearer and precise results. They argued that by using Gerontographic segmentation, the preference of consumers can be gauged on a more accurate basis as compared to other conventional modes of segmentation techniques used.
- The importance of the emerging technique of data mining for segmentation of health care industry was investigated by Liu and Chen (2009). They performed two types of data analysis. In the first method, they found out six clusters performing cluster analysis directly on all the 24 variables they had chosen, wherein, in the second method, they first performed a factor analysis. They identified five factors and performed cluster analysis on the factor scores and found out three clusters, namely (1) reputation driven, (2) performance driven, and (3) empowerment driven.

8.2. Need for Market Segmentation in Health Care Marketing

In health care organizations, market segmentation serves multiple objectives. Market segmentation is not only used to identify consumer segments to sell health care services but also used as a marketing sales tool.

Market segmentation is essential to effectively perform all activities of modern health care marketing. Modern health care marketing (see Chapter 2) involves the exchange of information between the health care organization and its customers/patients, potential customers (market), society at large, health care providers and suppliers, government regulators and employees with the primary focus on customer/patient life time engagement and enhancing customer/patient life time experience. This exchange of information and customer engagement to enhance customer experience can be done more efficiently and effectively by identifying customer segments and focusing on appropriate communication and engagement strategies in each segment.

Butcher (2016) states, "On the one hand, segmentation is all about the patients." He presents the following three informative examples:

1. **TriHealth Corporate Health**, based in Cincinnati, a pioneer in the use of consumer segmentation to improve patient engagement in their health status and health care.

    a. TriHealth conducted a three-month pilot program involving 210 individuals who work with health coaches to manage either diabetes or musculoskeletal disorders. Through this work, TriHealth classifies each individual into one of five psychographic segments, based on the participant's responses to a 12-question survey. (This psychographic segmentation method will be explained later in the chapter.)

    b. TriHealth's coaches are trained to use their knowledge about segmentation to tailor their communications. The pilot program demonstrated that the consumer segmentation strategy improved goal attainment, which is how health coaches measure success. It also improved satisfaction for both participants and coaches.

2. **Carolinas HealthCare System (CHS)** operates in more than 900 locations throughout North and South Carolina.

    a. This system is reported as using an entirely different approach to segment its patients. It employs a population health analytics team of data scientists, statisticians, business intelligence specialists, epidemiologists, and others. Using data from a three-year period, covering 2.2 million patients, they segmented these patients into seven segments to inform the health system's care management strategy.

    b. The team aggregated data from CHS's electronic health record system and its billing system supplemented with behavior, consumer, and geospatial data that identify the census tract in which each patient lives. Instead of segmenting patients by conventional basis like cost or diagnosis, the analysts used a sophisticated hierarchical cluster analysis. This segmented the patients into seven mutually exclusive groups: (1) advanced cancer, (2) complex chronic conditions, (3) aging, (4) high risk, (5) mental health, (6) pregnancies and deliveries, (7) newborns and toddlers.

    c. They were also able to divide, for example, those complex chronic patients by long-term changes in health, certain combination of diagnoses, those who have had avoidable utilization, and those who belong to certain demographics. These are what we previously called smaller segments or niches.

3. **Novant Health**, a four-state network based in Winston-Salem, NC, deploys a segmentation strategy that will inform the system's interactions with its patients.

a. Novant Health segments patients into six distinct groups. The organizing principle is patients' varying levels of engagement with health care. One segment includes individuals, many of whom are caregivers for other patients, who are highly engaged with the health care system. Patients in another segment tend to avoid interacting with health care providers unless it is necessary.

> These examples show that there are multiple methods for segmentation available to health care organizations. Each organization must develop the best segmentation method suitable for it. A single marketing strategy and plan will not work for marketing all the health care products and services.

Examples of health care organizations and their market segmentation methods are as follows:

- A Health Maintenance Organization (HMO)/Health Plan offering multiple services such as Medicare and Medicaid managed care products.
- A hospital offering services for older patients as well as younger patients.
- Provider of a single health care service (e.g., private insurance or Affordable Care Act (ACA) exchange insurance plans) to consumers of different health conditions such as those who are healthy and stable vs. those with chronic diseases.

8.2.1. Benefits of market segmentation in health care marketing (DSS Research, 2016; Pinnell, 2003)

- Understanding customers/patients and their unique needs and characteristics allows healthcare marketers to:
    o Retain current customers/patients,
    o Develop new products and services, and
    o Acquire new customers/patients.
- Easier marketing: It is easier to address the needs of smaller groups of customers, particularly if they have many characteristics in common (e.g., seek the same benefits, same age, and gender) (DSS Research, 2016).
- Enables health care marketers to find niches: Identify underserved or unserved markets. Using "niche marketing", segmentation can allow a

new company or new product to target less contested buyers and help a mature product seek new buyers.
- Efficiency: More efficient use of marketing resources by focusing on the best product/service mix for each segment/niche.
- Effective communication: Segmentation can help you avoid sending the wrong message or conveying your message to the wrong people.

8.3. Characteristics of a Segment to be Useful in Formulating Health Care Marketing Strategy

An arbitrary division of a health care consumer/patient market into a few segments does not help a health care organization to effectively market its products/services. A useful market segment should be large enough to earn worthwhile patient enrollments, revenue, and profits. It should be one accessible to the organization via its promotion and distribution channels. For example, rural low-income population in a particular county can be considered an easily identifiable segment by a health plan. However, if the health plan's provider network does not have a sufficient number of physicians and hospitals in this county, focusing on this segment for promoting the value of the organization's health services will have a negative effect on its resources. Also, marketing efforts should be directed at stable segments. A consumer segment in health care could be considered unstable for many reasons. The population in the segment may be migratory or continuity of benefits presently available through government programs may be uncertain if political changes take place.

Researchers and industry experts have identified several characteristics in a market segment for it to be useful. These include the following:

- Khanna (2013) posits that a segment is only useful if:
    - It is possible to measure;
    - It is large enough to earn a profit;
    - It is stable enough that it does not vanish after some time; and
    - It is possible to reach potential customers via the organization's promotion and distribution channel.
- Kotler et al. (2008) add two more characteristics as follows:
    - Differentiable and
    - Actionable.

- Jadczaková (2013) presents the summary of these essential characteristics of a market segment as follows:

    o *Identifiability*: Segments should be recognized easily so that they allow for measurement.
    o *Substantiality*: Each segment should have sufficient size to be profitable enough.
    o *Stability*: Each segment should be relatively stable over time.
    o *Actionability*: Each segment should be easily communicated with distinctive promotion, selling, and advertising strategy.
    o *Accessibility*: Each segment should be easily addressed through trade journals, mailing lists, industrial directories, and other media.
    o *Responsiveness*: Each segment should differently respond (in terms of product/brand choice) to a marketing mix.

> **Discussion**
>
> The commercial insurance market is often further divided into individual plans and group plans. Do these meet the above tests to be recognized as market segments by a health plan operating in such an area?

8.3.1. Difference between product differentiation and market segmentation (Smith, 1956)

Earlier in this chapter we saw that market segmentation was first described in the 1950s, when product differentiation was the primary marketing strategy used. Product differentiation is the process of distinguishing a product or service from others to make it more attractive to a particular target market. Differentiation could be between products/services of the organization and products/services of competitors. This concept was discussed in Chapter 3. Differentiation can be made between products/services of this organization itself. This is what is referred to as a segmentation technique. Under this strategy, the organization will focus on customer segments to whom different variations of a product/service of the organization may be appealing.

An example of using product differentiation to segment a market in the health care industry is seen with Medicare managed care health plans often offering multiple Medicare Advantage programs. Health plans distinguish them with attractive names such as "Silver Plan" or "Platinum Plan". These plans within a Medicare health care plan will differ by premium, size of provider network, additional benefits, co-payments, deductibles, and Maximum Out-of-Pocket (MOOP) amount. Higher annual deductibles often mean lower monthly plan premiums.

How does all this apply to market segmentation? Health plans offering multiple Medicare Advantage insurance products will use market research to identify segments of the Medicare population that consider themselves fairly healthy and prefer lower current premiums in exchange for higher co-pays (that occur only when they visit a health care provider). Similarly, the health plan could identify Medicare beneficiaries who have higher retirement income and prefer name brand prescription drugs at a higher out-of-pocket cost than generic drugs.

Product differentiation and market segmentation is a two-way street. A health care organization can create new products/services within a product/service category to meet the demands of consumer segments with varying demands and behavior identified by the organization in its market research, or it can do the reverse, that is, it can research to identify segments of consumers who will fit into each of their multiple products.

However, the process usually followed is the first of these, that is, segmentation is based upon developments on the demand side of the market and represents a rational and more precise adjustment of product and marketing effort to consumer or user requirements. Usually, health care organizations will segment a market with product differentiation by making different versions of the same product.

8.4. Generic Market Segmentation Methods

Before we discuss market segmentation methods usually adopted by health care organizations, let us discuss two generic approaches to market segmentation. These are "*A Priori* Segmentation" and "*Post Hoc* Segmentation".

- *A priori segmentation* involves dividing a market into segments without the benefit of primary market research. In this segmentation approach, variables, such as age or income, are selected first and then customers are classified accordingly. Manager intuition, analysis of secondary data sources, analysis of internal customer databases, or other methods are used to group people into various segments. In summary, basis for segmentation is decided before data collection by the organization.

For example, a health care plan deduces that older adults over 50 are not as familiar with computer and internet-based technology compared to younger consumers. This is based on secondary research available from surveys conducted by industry publications. Therefore, the health plan segments consumers into two segments — consumers over 50 years of age and consumers under 50 years of age — and implements an email and text messaging campaign promoting the organizations' services to only the second group. Note that this basis of segmentation may not be valid in the future as the older population dwindles into an insignificant portion of the market.

- *Post hoc segmentation* uses market research to collect classification and descriptor variables for members of the target market. The number of segments and characteristics of each segment are determined by the data collected by, or is internally available at, the health care organization.

8.4.1. Hybrid/Nested segmentation

A third alternative is a hybrid/nested segmentation method consisting of two steps. First, an *a priori* segmentation based on generic variables (such as age or income) is done. This is followed by a second phase of segmentation, where *a priori* segments are further clustered based on other variables (Kazbare *et al.*, 2010).

Kazbare *et al.* (2010) claim that most health behavior research employs *a priori* segmentation with observable consumer characteristic variables such as demographic and geodemographic segmentation (with emphasis on age, gender, and race) with some attempts to apply psychographic segmentation. They add that behavioral segmentation in health behavior studies usually focus on single-variable segmentation, e.g., age.

In a study evaluating the use of different segmentation methods in the design of healthy eating campaigns among youth, these authors tested four segmentation methods followed by a self-administered survey among 923 seventh- and eighth-grade pupils (13–15 years old) from nine primary and lower-secondary schools in five regions of Denmark. The following four segmentation models were valuated with responses received:

- *Model 1*: One-segment model (entire population considered as one segment).
- *Model 2*: *A priori* predictive method based on demographic segmentation.

- *Model 3*: *A priori* predictive method based on behavioral segmentation.
- *Model 4*: *Post hoc* predictive segmentation.

Demographic characteristics measured were gender, age, and number of siblings. Target behaviors selected were increasing consumption of fruits and vegetables and decreasing consumption of soft drinks.

The author's conclusion was that all four methods of segmentation had their strengths and that different behaviors may require separate segmentation studies because the same respondents may have different attitudes and intentions about two different behaviors (such as increasing consumption of fruits and vegetables and decreasing consumption of soft drinks). This suggests that in health care marketing, product/service-specific and domain-specific segmentations provide more insightful results. Other conclusions of the study were as follows:

- If there is evidence that certain demographic, psychographic, or behavioral variables are important for health behavior (healthy eating behavior in this study), then *a priori* predictive segmentation could be useful.
- *A priori* segmentation, based on demographic or behavioral variables, results in segments that are substantial and, in most cases, accessible.
- *Post hoc* segmentation, on the other hand, allows maximizing the differentiability of the segments, providing valuable insight for planning the design of healthy eating campaigns.
- Important insight can be generated using predictive segmentation methods that are based on theory and to address those issues that are directly related to the behavior of interest.

8.5. Types of Market Segmentation Commonly Used in Health Care Marketing

There are several well-known segmentation methods used in the health care industry. These are summarized as follows:

Product/payer segmentation: This is probably the most common broad classification used by health plans, physicians, and hospitals. With the growth of managed care, marketing is most efficient when directed at distinct products such as:

- Medicare (payer: CMS);
- Medicaid (payer: state agencies);

- Commercial subscribers — usually further segmented into individual markets and group markets; and
- ACA exchange products.

Demographic segmentation: This involves segmenting a market by demographics such as gender, age, income, education, and socioeconomic status. A physician group practice might divide its patients into three classes: children, adults, and seniors.

Geographic segmentation: An example of this is a health plan (HMO) in California identifying, at the business unit (product line) level, its Medicare business in California and Texas as two separate segments, although certain key aspects applicable to both, such as CMS regulations, are exactly the same.

B2C and B2B segmentation: Hospital services and pharmaceuticals are marketed directly to the consumers as well as to physicians. These form two distinct segments as the decision-making patterns of these groups are different.

Commercial insurance products are marketed to individuals as well as employers, thus creating two segments that are efficient to manage.

Segmentation based on health status/risk of consumers: Butcher (2016) illustrates this with the case study of the Carolinas HealthCare System (CHS) which has 900 locations throughout North and South Carolina.

Using data from a three-year period, CHS segmented 2.2 million patients into seven segments to inform the health system's care management strategy. CHS aggregated data from its electronic health record system and its billing system supplemented with behavior, consumer, and geospatial data that identify the census tract in which each patient lives. The analytical techniques sorted all patients into seven mutually exclusive groups. In six of those groups, patients "clustered" together because of the following traits they shared:

- *Advanced cancer*: These patients, who account for 0.6% of CHS's patient population, clustered together on the basis of their high billed charges (a proxy for resource utilization) and cancer diagnoses.
- *Complex chronic*: These patients — typically older, having low income, covered by Medicare, widowed, and struggling with behavioral health

problems and multiple chronic conditions — account for 6.6% of the patient population.
- *Aging rising risk*: Younger than patients in the "complex chronic" segment, these people typically are married, commercially insured, and have just one chronic condition, such as Type-2 diabetes, that is under control. They make up 16.7% of the patient population.
- *Mental health*: A large percentage of patients have a mental health diagnosis, of course, but the 0.1% who clustered to create this segment share some specific commonalities. They are older teens and young adults, most of whom are male and who have serious mental health conditions that require a great deal of support.
- *Pregnancies and deliveries*: These are healthy women who make up 2.6% of the system's patients.
- *Newborns and toddlers*: In general, these are healthy children under age three who account for 2.5% of CHS's patients.

Psychographics segmentation: Segmentation based on personality characteristics of people

- The "Gerontographic" segmentation analysis provided by Moschis *et al.* (2004).

In this method, four consumer segments for those aged 55 years and older are used. The population figures are as of 2004. The four groups are:

- o *Healthy hermits*: Individuals in relatively good health, yet somewhat withdrawn socially. Estimate: 20 million American seniors in this category.
- o *Ailing outgoers*: Individuals in relatively poor health yet determined to remain socially active. Estimate: 18 million mature adults in this segment.
- o *Frail reclusives*: Inactive individuals usually burdened with health problems. They spend most of their time at home and are very concerned with personal and physical security. Estimate: 18 million older Americans.
- o *Healthy indulgers*: This group has more in common with the baby boomers than any other segment. They are relatively wealthy and focused on making the most of life. Estimate: 7 million adults in this rapidly growing segment.

- The PATH Institute's PATH "Valuegraphic" profiles of health care consumers (Navarro and Wilkins, 2001).

Studies show that 90% of adults across the US can be classified into one of the following nine groups:

- *Clinic Cynic*: Generally distrustful of the medical profession.
- *Avoider*: Refrains from using health care services until very sick or injured.
- *Generic*: Tends to balance a concern for cost with a concern for quality.
- *Family-centered*: Puts family health above all other matters.
- *Traditionalist*: Willing to pay more for quality and tends to use the same providers.
- *Loyalist*: Characterized by moderation in health care opinions and behaviors.
- *Ready User*: Actively seeks and uses health care services of all kinds
- *Independently Healthy*: Very actively involved in their own health.

Psychographic segmentation identifies groups of people according to their motivations, priorities, and communication preferences. Psychographic segmentation enables healthcare organizations to customize patient communication and engagement by effective messaging.

Behavioral segmentation: Segmentation based on consumer usage or behavior patterns. One criterion used commonly by health plans and large medical groups is "loyalty to the brand". Health plans and large medical groups typically monitor how long subscribers/members have stayed with the plan without disenrollment (switching).

Such a segmentation is used to differentiate the health care marketing effort among the segments. Typically,

- Long-term enrollees are focused for aggressive customer relationships and retention; and
- Enrollees who switch health plans are focused for customer engagement to prevent switching.

Before addressing market segmentation using health care behavioral factors for use in health care marketing, let us look to get an understanding of some consumer behavioral factors in market segmentation, in general. A comprehensive description of this is presented by DeAsi (2018). DeAsi lists several behavioral segmentation methods. A version of this classification revised by grouping overlapping and similar items is given as follows:

- *Purchasing behavior*: Behavior prior to purchase, and behavior in information search and evaluation of option.

    DeAsi classifies consumers in a market into "price-conscious" buyers, the "smart" buyers, the "risk-averse" buyers, the "needs-proof" buyers, the "I'll get it later" buyers, and the "persuadable" buyers.

> A classification of health care consumers by Deloitte (2012) along the same lines is described in the discussion that follows, where consumers are classified as "casual and cautions", "content and compliant", "online and onboard", "sick and savvy", "out and about", and "shop and save". Note the similarities in the two classifications.

- *Benefits sought*: Primary benefit sought in a product/service, e.g., lower cost or higher quality.
- *Customer journey stage*: Preliminary search stage or awareness stage through serious consideration, purchase and retention, and "user status" — Non-users, prospects, new customers, frequent users, and customers who have defaulted.
- *Usage*: Frequency of use of product/service, manner of use, and "occasion or timing", times of day product/service used, and time elapsed between use.
- *Customer satisfaction*: High and low satisfaction customers, customers low and high on measurement scales (e.g., Net Promoter Score (NPS)), "customer loyalty", "interest", and "engagement level".

A well-known study on market segmentation by health behavior of consumers is the Deloitte (2012) study of 4,012 US adults. This study identified six behavior/attitude patterns.

(1) Casual and cautious
These are consumers who have made fewer wellness visits, had lower participation and interest in wellness programs, low vitamin use, low use of the system, and low compliance with treatment when treatment is needed. They are less likely than other segments to have health insurance, least prepared

financially to handle future health care costs, and least satisfied with their health plan if insured. They are not likely to spend time and effort to shop for alternative insurance options. (Estimated share of population: 34%. Growth of this segment is reported to be very high.)

(2) Content and compliant
Satisfied with their primary care provider and health plan. They follow a "passive patient" approach relying on doctors to make decisions, follow through on recommended treatment, and adhere strictly to medication labels. They prefer traditional doctors, standard treatments, and conventional care settings. They are very trusting of doctors, least trusting of online sources for information, and least interested in shopping for insurance and health plan options. (Estimated share of population in 2012: 22%. This segment is reported to be declining.)

(3) Online and onboard
This group displays a high use of the system and medications; is most likely to use a health plan and provider websites, self-monitoring tools, and electronic personal health records; and makes high use of quality and price information to compare providers and health plan options. Yet, they prefer traditional doctors and standard treatment approaches, but are open to receiving care in non-conventional settings like retail clinics. (Estimated share of population in 2012: 17%. This segment is reported to be growing.)

(4) Sick and savvy
This group displays the highest use of the system and medications; is the most proactive, preventive, and prepared; and regularly seeks information to compare providers and identify treatment options. They like to partner with doctors in making decisions and adhere to treatment plans. Open to buying prescription medications online or through mail order. Show average level of interest in shopping on their own for insurance and health plan options. (Estimated share of population in 2012: 14%. This segment is also reported as declining.)

(5) Out and about
This segment seems to prefer providers who use alternative treatment approaches and is most likely to use and substitute alternative/natural therapies for prescribed medication. They often search online for information and

guidance from experts. Yet, they prefer to make health care decisions independently and adhere less strictly to recommended plans. They seem to be least satisfied with their primary care provider and thus more likely to switch doctors, to travel outside the area or US for health care, and prefer to shop on their own for insurance and health plan options. (Estimated share of population in 2012: 9%. This segment is also reported to be declining.)

(6) Shop and save
This segment is most likely to switch health plans, providers, and medications; most likely to seek care at retail clinics and travel out of the area or US for health care; and more likely to buy prescription medications online or through mail order. They are interested in comparing plans, providers, and treatments on price/quality, and interested in shopping on their own for insurance and health plan options. Yet, they prefer traditional doctors and standard treatment approaches, but are open to using alternative/natural therapies and open to not adhering to treatment plans. (Estimated share of population in 2012: 4%. This segment is reported to be stable.)

Deloitte cautions that demographics influences the six health care consumer segments but do not define them exactly, that health care consumers are not homogenous, and that each demographic group has a unique segment profile. For example,

- Less than half of all millennials are "casual and cautious".
- The youngest generation includes the highest percentage of "shop and save".
- Thus, the value-seeking segment may grow as millennials grow older and need more health care services.
- The largest segment among seniors is "content and compliant".
- Considerable proportions are "sick and savvy" and "online and onboard".
- Nearly seven in 10 uninsured consumers are currently "casual and cautious".
- Enrollees in employer plans are generally more active consumers than enrollees in Medicare and Medicaid.
- Each of Medicare and Medicaid programs includes sizeable proportions of "sick and savvy", "online and onboard", and "out and about" consumers.
- Direct purchasers of health care, i.e., those who buy health insurance on their own from managed care health plans and ACA exchanges include the highest percentage of "shop and save" consumers.

For complete description of the survey and findings, see Deloitte (2012).

8.6. Customer-Centric Segmentation

Customer-centric marketing is a strategy that places the individual customer at the center of marketing design and delivery. It starts from the realization that there is no "average" customer. Customers have different behaviors and preferences. Therefore, "one-size-fits-all" marketing strategies and programs will not appeal to customers/patients.

Customers/patients differ from health care-related behaviors including interaction with health care-related information. Some are savvy computer, internet, and social media users interacting with health care-related messages and communications almost on a daily basis. Others use internet only when they want to search for health information and products/services.

Klein (2013) introduces two contrasting approaches to marketing — customer-centric and product-centric. Product-centric marketing, which is the most common approach, focuses on products/services currently available. A pharmaceutical company promoting a drug on TV or a health plan promoting its Medicare Advantage products during the open enrollment period is using product-centric marketing.

> Currently, there is much interest and discussion in health care marketing about better segmentation into (smaller) niches and customer-centric segmentation (Resnick, 2017).

Customer-centric segmentation starts with data on customer behavior and decides which customers to target.

Grenier (2018) cites Bill Macaitis, who is well known in the health care industry having been associated with tech giants Salesforce (Senior Vice President of Marketing), Zendesk (Chief Marketing Officer), and Slack (Chief Marketing Officer and Board Advisor), as saying,

> "Use the insightful long-term metrics to understand your customers. Without the right data, it's difficult to understand your customers at all."

In other words, customer-centric segmentation (for customer-centric marketing) should be data driven, and not driven by management hunches.

> **How Do You Start?**
>
> Health care marketers interested in customer-centric marketing should start organizing data collected from individual customers' transactions with you, over time, as well as related data from industry databases, around customer groups rather than around products or services. Traditional analysis of past aggregate measurements at a product/service or event level must be replaced by analysis at the individual customer level to understand a customer's behavior over time.

Elkind (2014) explains that it is easy to know what to look for in aggregate-level data such as overall sales trends but what to look for in data at the individual customer level is not so clear. He suggests looking for patterns in new customers and long-standing customers. For example, how has a health plan communicating in different manners and/or with different communication content with customers who leave the health plan soon compared to customers who have stayed with the health plan for several years? Such analysis leads to the discovery of customer segments whose key behaviors at a smaller group level can be used to decide how often to contact them and what message(s) should be conveyed. The same message conveyed, say via social media, at the same frequency is not the basis of customer-centric marketing.

> By now, it must be clear that customer-centric segmentation does not always mean identifying individual customers/patients individually. From a practical standpoint, it really means identifying smaller groups of customers/patients whose behaviors are identical or similar. Thus, the concept of customer-centric segmentation discussed here is somewhat different from identifying health care needs and environment of individual patients discussed under patient-centered care elsewhere in this book.

Robinson (2011), in an article "Customer Centric Segmentation", presents examples of application of this concept in health care marketing. He explains,

> "Marketers are zeroing in on physician and patient targets with new media, new segmentation techniques, and new analytics. Segmentation has gone micro these days, and the ability to target a very specific audience is easier

than ever. Brand teams are diving deeper into the more granular individual needs of these customers — patients, physicians, and payers. This customer-centric focus creates a greater need for tools and techniques that can support the delivery of a very targeted message to the right client at the right time with the right content."

He presents the following examples from the health care industry:

- **Customer/patient direct marketing**

Need for health care marketing to go beyond demographic and psychographic segmentations and leverage patients' behavioral styles in ways that reach each individual.

For example, behavior analysis of patients with breast care reveals that compliance with treatment and medication (referred to as "adherence") is not related to demographic variables such as age of the patient or stage of the disease. Adherence appears to depend on patient's attitudes regarding coping up with cancer. Understanding a patient at this human thinking process level helps health care marketing to design communications and arrange to offer support satisfying the patient's outcome and emotional needs.

Some modern aspects of health care customer/patient behavior also necessitate segmentation of patients in a physician practice into smaller groups/niches. Emerging is a segment of people who are connected to medical devices and wearables to monitor health conditions and healthy practices. The people in this segment like to self-manage their health. Another segment consists of younger customers who are avid users of real-time internet/mobile sources for health and wellness information. Physicians can be assisted by development of analytically based microsegments that can be used to communicate appropriate messages with these segments that promote enhanced engagement and retention.

- **Physician services marketing**

Patients in a physician practice can be segmented into smaller groups based on their attitudes and behavior. Studies show that usually a segment of patients favor adherence/compliance and prefer traditional providers while another segment is open for new options of care and providers and health plans. For the latter segment, the physician should research and identify their needs such as experience with his practice and office and protocols that may suggest changes in processes and protocols. For both segments, particularly the latter segment, communications to educate them on the need for current processes (such as those required for health plan and regulatory compliance) and opportunities and channels to communicate with the physician could be considered.

- **Pharmaceutical marketing**

Traditionally, physicians are segmented by prescribing behaviors and their experience with previously used drugs. In a customer-centric segmentation, they can also be segmented by origin of education (US vs. foreign medical schools), dates of graduation, and medical schools attended. Also important in a customer-centric segmentation of physician is their reference base such as hospital privileges and hospital they admit patients to. These other physicians they associate are often a source for information and advice.

Robinson cites Wendy Blackburn, a health care consultant and expert from Intouch Solutions, who states, "It's a new world, and customer-centric is the buzzword of the day. This trend is definitely hot, evidenced by the fact that entire pharmaceutical conferences are being specifically designed around the topic."

Physician segments display varying levels of digital behaviors and preferences. Some physicians are tech savvy and they are often not so accessible through traditional channels. Additionally, these physicians seek information online and have different expectations for content of information they seek. These physicians usually need different messaging approaches.

Customers' behavior, whether it is consumers, patients, or physicians, change over time. Therefore, segmentation grouping must be reviewed from time to time.

The motivation for smaller group-centric segmentation should not only be profit that can be generated from such a segmentation and subsequent focused communications. For example, identifying patients who are dependent on multiple medications as a segment, and messaging them reminders on compliance on time, may not yield much in terms of revenue and profit. However, this type of adherence programs will promote loyalty and retention with current physicians and drugs.

As with almost every concept discussed in this book, the main objective of customer-centric segmentation and customer-centric marketing is enhancing customer/patient experience. Brinker (2009) in an article, "Customer-Centric Segmentation", says,

> "Very often, you're trying to not only uncover the immediate need, but to get some insight into the longer-term relationship — to learn how you can

tailor the experience this customer will have with your company moving forward in ways that will maximize their delight. *That is the customer-centric goal of segmentation.*" (Italics added).

8.7. Analytical Techniques for Segmenting a Health Care Market

There are several analytical techniques used in market segmentation suitable to segment a health care market.

The level of mathematical and statistical basis of these techniques is quite advanced and beyond a health care marketing book such as this one in terms of both volume (pages) that would have been needed for a full coverage of these techniques and the mathematical sophistication. As such, we will present here a discussion enough for an appreciation of these techniques by health care managers and marketers.

There are three main stages in market segmentation where statistical techniques are used (DSS Research, 2016). These stages are data preparation, data analysis, and classification.

8.7.1. Techniques used in data preparation — Factor analysis and conjoint analysis

Popular statistical programs to apply these techniques are SAS and SPSS. Others include BMDP, Statistica, and SYSTAT.

The first step here is the design of questionnaires to gather information from a sample of customers/patients.

For example, let us assume that a statistically determined sample of 150 previous patients were asked to select on a Likert scale of 1–5 factors important to them in selecting a specialist provider. As an example, let us say that the questionnaire had 20 questions such as years of experience of specialist, main hospital attended by the specialist, and quality of residency program completed by specialist. Responses from the 150 patients will display several characteristics. Answers to several questions may be consistent indicating that perhaps they all mean the same to the respondents.

Factor analysis, usually done with statistical software programs such as SAS and SPSS, will identify similarities between responses. Questions which belong to one factor may be found to be highly correlated with each other. Factor analysis groups variables. Factor analysis can be used to establish whether multiple questions mean the same thing to respondents and measure the same thing. This will be useful to shorten a long questionnaire. More importantly, it reveals to marketers correlations between customer beliefs and attitudes which otherwise may appear to be different attributes of customer behavior. Factor analysis identifies which relations are strongest. A market researcher who wants to know what combination of variables (or factors) is most appealing to a consumer in a target group can use factor analysis to reduce the data down to just a few variables.

There are two types of factor analyses in marketing research: exploratory and confirmatory. Exploratory factor analysis determines the factors. Confirmatory factor analysis tests and confirms hypotheses.

For details, interested readers are referred to "Specialized Texts on Statistical Techniques for Market Research and Market Segmentation" section at the end of this chapter.

Conjoint analysis was discussed previously in Section 4.5.

In a survey-based market research study, it helps determine how consumers value different attributes (feature, function, and benefits) that make up an individual product or service. Conjoint analysis methods ask customers/patients on what they would be willing to sacrifice in the real world and trade off, and what they are likely to weigh, for example, weights assigned when selecting a hospital to factors such as location, physicians, technology, personal care, and hospital reputation.

8.7.2. Techniques used in data analysis

Statistical techniques used in this stage aim to identify groups according to segmentation variable(s) selected.

The most commonly used analytical technique in this step is cluster analysis. (We omit discussions on other advanced statistical methods such as Chi-square Automatic Interaction Detection (CHAID) or Classification and Regression Trees (CART), Artificial neural networks, and Latent class structure models.)

Cluster analysis aims to identify groups of similar customers whose variations among those in a group are not significant. While factor analysis groups variables, cluster analysis groups customers. Cluster analysis is used to separate respondents into specific groups that are not only mutually exclusive but also relatively homogeneous in opinions and behavior and attributes that make the market segments distinct.

Cluster analysis can be performed with SAS, SPSS, and even Excel.

Again, readers interested in a complete discussion on cluster analysis are referred to "Specialized Texts on Statistical Techniques for Market Research and Market Segmentation" section at the end of this chapter.

8.7.3. Techniques used in classification

Techniques used in this step of market segmentation, called multivariate techniques, aim to identify which of the several variables relating to customers (such as age or income levels) have greater effect on an independent variable (such as response to direct marketing).

Techniques commonly used here are discriminant analysis, multiple regression, and multidimensional scaling (MDS).

Discrimination analysis: This analysis computes a discriminant score on each variable (e.g., age, income level, or sex) indicating the relative importance of each variable on an independent variable (e.g., direct advertising). For instance, if age has a low discriminant weight, then it is less important than the other variables.

Multiple regression: This technique covered in basic statistics and business statistics courses is used to estimate the equation with the best fit for explaining how the value of a dependent variable changes as the values of a number of independent variables change. A simple market research example is the estimation of the best fit for advertising by looking at how sales revenue (the dependent variable) changes in relation to expenditures on advertising variables, such as medium, frequency, and target market (independent variables).

Multi-dimensional scaling: This category represents a constellation of techniques used to produce perceptual maps of competing brands or products. For instance, in multidimensional scaling, brands are shown in a space of attributes in which the distance between the brands represents dissimilarity. An example of multidimensional scaling in market research would show the manufacturers of single-serving coffee in the form of K-cups. The different K-cup brands would be arrayed in the multidimensional space by attributes such as the strength of roast, number of flavored and specialty versions, distribution channels, and packaging options.

Readers interested in comprehensive technical description of these techniques are referred to "Specialized Texts on Statistical Techniques for Market Research and Market Segmentation" at the end of this chapter.

8.8. Using Segmentation Results

In the preceding sections of this chapter, we saw the first set of steps in a typical market segmentation process. They are as follows:

- Setting objectives and goals for the segmentation exercise;
- Identifying segmentation variables;
- Research design;
- Data collection; and
- Analyzing data, identifying segments, and validating results/conclusions.

The next steps in the process are as follows:

- Developing marketing strategy for each segment and subsegment (niche);
- Implementing/launching the marketing plan for each segment or niche; and
- Monitoring effectiveness of marketing to each segment/niche.

Developing the marketing strategy starts with defining a marketing mix for each segment/niche of the health care market. This activity is discussed in Chapter 9.

Implementing and monitoring the marketing plan, based on the marketing mix, is discussed in the remaining chapters of the book.

References

Brinker, S. (2009). "Customer-Centric Segmentation", November 1, http://www.marketingprofs.com/articles/2009/3186/customer-centric-segmentation. Accessed August 23, 2018.

Butcher, L. (2016). "Consumer Segmentation Has Hit Health Care. Here's How It Works", *Hospital & Health Networks*, March 8, https://www.hhnmag.com/articles/6932-consumer-segmentation-just-hit-health-care-heres-how-it-works. Accessed November 17, 2018.

Chand, S. (2018). "Evolution of Market Segmentation Approaches Explained", http://www.yourarticlelibrary.com/marketing/evolution-of-market-segmentation-approaches-explained/22185. Accessed March 1, 2019.

Cox, N. C. and Dannehl, K. (2007). *Perceptions of Retailing in Early Modern England*, Aldershot, Hampshire: Ashgate, 155–159.

DeAsi, G. (2018). "10 Powerful Behavioral Segmentation Methods to Understand Your Customers", *Pointillist Blog*, https://www.pointillist.com/blog/behavioral-segmentation/. Accessed March 1, 2019.

Deloitte (2012). "Survey of US Health Care Consumers", www.deloitte.com/us/consumerstudies. Accessed March 1, 2019.

Dey, D. K. (2013). "Market Segmentation Techniques in the Health Care Industry: A Review for Applicability in India", *ZENITH International Journal of Multidisciplinary Research*, 3 (7), 253–257.

Dolinsky, A. and Stinerock, R. (1998). "Cultural Affiliation and the Importance of Health Care Attributes", *Marketing Health Services*, 18 (1), 28–37.

DSS Research (2016). "Market Segmentation", https://www.dssresearch.com/Solutions/StrategyResearchSolutionsGroup/MarketSegmentation/MarketSegmentationTechniques.aspx. Accessed November 8, 2018.

Elkind, J. (2014). "5 Steps to Becoming a Customer-Centric Marketing Organization", May 13, https://marketingland.com/5-steps-becoming-customer-centric-marketing-organization-83202. Accessed March 2, 2019.

Flnn, D. and Lamb, C. (1987). "Hospital Benefit Segmentation", *Journal of Health Care Marketing*, 6 (4), 26–33.

Fullerton, R. (2016). "Segmentation in Practice: An Overview of the Eighteenth and Nineteenth Centuries", in Jones, D. G. B. and Tadajewski, M. (Eds.), *The Routledge Companion to Marketing History*, Oxon, Routledge, 94.

Grenier, L. (2018). "An Expert's Advice on Successful Customer-Centric Marketing", *Hotjar*, July 18, https://www.hotjar.com/blog/customer-centric-marketing. Accessed March 2, 2019.

Jadczaková, V. (2013). "Review of Segmentation Process in Consumer Markets", *Acta Universitatis Agriculturae Et Silviculturae Mendelianae Brunensis*, LXI 135(4), https://acta.mendelu.cz/media/pdf/actaun_2013061041215.pdf.

Johnson, R., Saha, S., Arbelaez, J., Beach, C. and Cooper, L. (2004). "Racial and Ethnic Differences in Patient Perceptions of Bias and Cultural Competence in Health Care", *Journal of General Internal Medicine*, 19 (2), 101–110.

Jones, G. D. B. and Tadajewski, M. (Eds.) (2016). *The Routledge Companion to Marketing History*, Oxon, Routledge.

Kazbare, L., van Trijp, H. C. M. and Eskildsen, J. K. (2010). "A-Priori and Post-Hoc Segmentation in the Design of Healthy Eating Campaigns", *Journal of Marketing Communications*, 16 (1–2), 21–45.

Khanna, R. (2013). "Segmentation of the Healthcare Customer Base", March 7, http://www.pmlive.com/pharma_news/segmentation_of_the_healthcare_customer_base_466335. Accessed March 1, 2019.

Klein, M. (2013). "Driving Loyalty with Customer-Centric Marketing: The Building Blocks of Customer-Centric Marketing Methodology", October 25, https://www.dmnews.com/customer-experience/article/13037117/driving-loyalty-with-customercentric-marketing. Accessed March 1, 2019.

Kotler, P., Shalowitz, J. and Stevens, R. J. (2008). *Strategic Marketing for Health Care Organizations: Building a Customer-Driven Health System*, John Wiley & Sons.

Liu, S. and Chen, J. (2009). "Using Data Mining to Segment Healthcare Markets from Patients' Preference Perspectives", *International Journal of Health Care Quality Assurance*, 22 (2), 117–134.

Lockley, L. C. (1950). "Notes on the History of Marketing Research", *Journal of Marketing*, 14 (5), 733–736.

Lynn, J., Straube, B., Bell, K., Jencks, S. and Kambic, R. (2007). "Using Population Segmentation to Provide Better Health Care for All: The 'Bridges To Health' Model", *The Milbank Quarterly*, 85 (2), 185–208.

McKendrick, N., Brewer, J. and Plumb, J. H. (1982). *The Birth of a Consumer Society: The Commercialization of Eighteenth Century England*, Indiana University Press.

Moschis, G. and Friend, S. (2008). "Segmenting the Preferences & Usage Patterns of the Mature Consumer Health Care Market", *International Journal of Pharmaceutical and Healthcare Marketing*, 2 (1), 7–21.

Moschis, G. P., Curasi, C. and Bellenger, D. (2004). "Patronage Motives of Mature Consumers in the Selection of Food and Grocery Stores", *Journal of Consumer Marketing*, 21 (2), 123–133.

Navarro, F. H. and Wilkins, S. T. (2001). "A New Perspective on Consumer Health Use: 'Valuegraphic' Profiles of Health Information Seekers", *Managed Care Quarterly*, 9 (2), 35–43.

Pinnell, J. (2003). "Improving Healthcare Marketing through Market Segmentation and Targeting: The Benefit of Accounting for Individual Differences in Research and Analysis", *World Association of Research Professionals Publication*, https://www.warc.com/fulltext/ESOMAR/78785.htm. Accessed November 18, 2018.

Resnick, L. R. (2017). "Six Healthcare Marketing Trends for 2018", *Managed Healthcare Executive*, November 30, http://www.managedhealthcareexecutive.com/healthcare-executive/six-healthcare-marketing-trends-2018. Accessed July 1, 2018.

Robinson, R. (2011). "Customer Centric Segmentation", *PharmaVOICE*, September, https://www.pharmavoice.com/article/2011-09-customer-centric-segmentation/. Accessed March 2, 2019.

Smith, W. R. (1956). "Product Differentiation and Market Segmentation as Alternative Marketing Strategies", *Journal of Marketing*, 21(1), 3–8.

Suggested Additional Readings

Budeva, G., Desislava, R. and Mullen, M. (2014). "International Market Segmentation", *European Journal of Marketing*, 48 (7–8), 1209–1238.

Epstein, R. M. and Peters, E. (2009). "Beyond Information: Exploring Patients' Preferences", *Journal of the American Medical Association*, 302 (2), 195–197.

Govette, J. (2017). "9 Steps for Targeting Patient Niches with Your Medical Marketing", https://getreferralmd.com/2013/08/9-steps-targeting-patient-niches-medical-marketing/. Accessed January 12, 2019.

Greene, J. (2015). "Healthcare Marketers Reshape Ad Strategies", October 30, *Modern Healthcare*, http://www.modernhealthcare.com/article/20151030/MAGAZINE/310309995. Accessed January 15, 2019.

Hallums, A. (1994). "Developing A Promotion Plan for Health Care Marketing", *Journal of Nursing Management*, 2 (4), 167–174.

Institute for Healthcare Improvement (2016). "One Size Does Not Fit All: Think Segmentation", http://www.ihi.org/resources/Pages/ImprovementStories/OneSizeDoesNotFitAllThinkSegmentation.aspx. Accessed November 12, 2018.

Kroner, E. (2017). "The 7 Pillars of Customer Centricity", *AMA Marketing Insights E-newsletters*, https://www.ama.org/publications/eNewsletters/MarketingInsights Newsletter/Pages/7-pillars-of-customer-centricity.aspx. Accessed November 17, 2018.

Ravi, R. and Sun, B. (2016). *Customer Centric Marketing: A Pragmatic Approach*, MIT Press.

Stanton, M. W. (2002). "Expanding Patient-Centered Care to Empower Patients and Assist Providers", *Research in Action*, Issue 5, Agency for Healthcare Research and Quality, Rockville, MD, US Department of Health Services.

Specialized Texts on Statistical Techniques for Market Research and Market Segmentation

Jadczaková, V. (2014). *Lifestyle Segmentation: The Use of Multivariate Statistical Techniques to Target the Consumer*, Lambert Academic Publishing.

Malthouse, E. (2013). *Segmentation and Lifetime Value Models Using SAS*, SAS Institute.

McDonald, M. and Dunbar, I. (2012). *Market Segmentation*, John Wiley.

Moreira, J., et al. (2018). *A General Introduction to Data Analytics*, Wiley-Interscience.

Wedel, M. and Kamakura, W. A. (2000). *Market Segmentation: Conceptual and Methodological Foundations International Series in Quantitative Marketing*, 2nd edn., Kluwer Academic Publishers.

Chapter 9

Health Care Marketing Mix: Planning Health Care Marketing Strategy for Each Segment/Niche

9.1. The Concept of Marketing Mix

9.1.1. What is a marketing mix?

Marketing Mix is one of the fundamental concepts in marketing of any product or service. Therefore, it is a fundamental concept in health care marketing as well.

We will first review the meaning and evolution of this concept in marketing, in general. Thereafter, we will focus on the role of an effective marketing mix in health care marketing.

Marketing mix has been defined as (Kotler, 2000)

> "The set of marketing tools that the firm uses to pursue its marketing objectives in the target market."

This definition implies that the "set of tools" to be used depends on the "target market" and the marketing objectives.

Another definition of marketing mix is (*Economic Times*, 2019)

> "The marketing mix refers to the set of actions, or tactics, that a company uses to promote its brand or product in the market."

Implicit in this definition is the fact that marketing mix varies even within products or services of an organization. For example, in health care marketing, marketing a basic health insurance service such as Medicare is different from marketing a pharmaceutical product. The target customers in the two cases have different needs. The medium of communication in the two cases also may be different. One package of marketing tools cannot be used for both the cases.

> **An Example of the Marketing Mix Concept**
>
> A hospital with multiple sites/branches, wanting to market its services, does not commence advertising, promotion, and other marketing activities without a plan. It will start by identifying which of its services should be marketed: all services or a select set of services such as emergency services and outpatient surgery services. Is price important to consumers/patients/insurance payers for these services or are there other features, such as convenience, that consumers/patients look for? Which of the hospital's branches should be marketed: all campuses or only the city campus? Which channels are most effective for promoting the selected services? TV advertisements? Promotion to physicians in the area?
>
> Thus, the hospitals will make a list of these key aspects, such as service/s, price, and/or other features creating value to customers, patients, and referring physicians, locations (place), and promotion. Such a list is called "The marketing mix". The marketing mix provides direction to plan the total marketing effort.

The well-known marketing mix in the general marketing literature is the *4P marketing mix* which has become the dominant framework for marketing management decisions. It is believed to have been first published in 1960 (Grönroos, 1994). Some (Hunt and Goolsby, 2011) claim that the 4P marketing mix even dates back to the 1940s. The 4P marketing mix refers to four broad levels of marketing decisions, namely:

- Product,
- Price,
- Promotion, and
- Place.

For marketing managers, identifying the elements of the marketing mix for a particular product or service and the relevant market segment or niche is important in order to (1) successfully develop strengths and avoid weaknesses, (2) strengthen the competitiveness and adaptability of enterprises, and (3) make the internal departments of the enterprise work closely together (Mintz and Currim, 2013).

9.2. Traditional 4P Marketing Mix: Application in Health Care Marketing

As mentioned above, the traditional 4P marketing mix has four elements as follows:

- **Product**

Product refers to a physical product or service a consumer is ready to pay for. It includes tangible goods like furniture, garments, grocery items, etc. and intangible products like services that are purchased by consumers. The product is the key element of any marketing mix.

- **Price**

Price is the amount the consumer must exchange to receive the offering. The price of a product depends on different elements that may be changing over time. Therefore, pricing should be dynamic to meet changes over time. The important factor in pricing is the cost of the product, strategy for marketing, its expenses related to distribution and advertisement, and any kind of price variation in the market.

- **Promotion**

Promotion is one of the most powerful elements in the marketing mix. Sales promotion activities include publicity generation, public relations, exhibitions, demonstrations, samples, free gifts, price discounts, etc.

Promotional activities are mainly intended to supplement personal selling and advertising. Promotion helps the organization and sales force to represent the product or service to the consumers in an effective manner and induce them to purchase the goods or services.

Advertising is a key element of the promotion mix. Advertising is a marketing communication that uses a non-personal message to the mass market to promote or sell a product or service. Advertising is different from public relations and personal selling. Advertising uses mass media including traditional media such as newspapers, magazines, television, radio, billboard advertising, direct mail, and new media such as email, social media, blogs, websites, and text messages.

Some advertising activities are aimed at generating immediate sales. Others are aimed at developing a "brand image" of the product or service by repeatedly communicating the value of the product or service, and values of the organization.

- **Place**

This means the availability of the product or service. It is how and where the product or service is purchased. Decisions on place also involve intermediaries such as distributors, wholesalers, and retailers.

The four Ps are not independent, nor can decisions on each of them be made independently, from the other three. They are a "mix" where decisions on one element, say place, affects another, like price.

Included within these elements are the following management and marketing decisions (Singh, 2012):

- **Product:** Design, Technology, Usefulness, Value, Convenience, Quality, Packaging, Branding and Warranties
- **Price:** Retail, Wholesale, Internet, Direct sales, Peer to peer, and Multi-channel
- **Promotion:** Strategies, Skimming, Penetration, Psychological, Cost-plus, Loss leader
- **Place:** Distribution, Special offers, Endorsements, Advertising, User trials, Direct mailing, Leaflets/posters, Free gifts, Competitions, and Joint ventures.

9.2.1. Application of traditional 4P marketing mix in health care marketing

Many authors still apply the traditional 4P marketing mix to marketing health care products and services (Berkowitz, 2017; Hanks, 2019; Thomas, 2015).

Typical descriptions of application of the 4P marketing mix to health care marketing in the literature can be summarized as follows:

- **Product:** The patient's encounter with a physician or a hospital is, usually, the core health care service, but there are many other supporting services surrounding this core service. These include, appointment and scheduling systems, record keeping, information sought by patients, referral systems, and billing systems. The "product" in a health care service includes the core system and all these support systems. Health care providers must design quality core services as well as effective supportive services.

- **Price:** With health care costs in the US rising every year, price has become a key concern for many consumers/patients, especially those with no health care insurance or with restricted health insurance. Medicare has become quite selective in approving health care services and products, causing difficulties for many seniors.
- **Place:** Location and hours of services are very important in marketing health care services. Health plans usually require participating health care providers, such as physicians, to be available during normal office hours and on a 24-hour basis for emergency services. 24-hour emergency centers are increasingly being set up to provide access in non-life-threatening emergency situations. Some states, e.g., California, have set strict access standards in terms of distance and waiting times for providers participating in the state's Medicaid program.
- **Promotion:** Promotion of a healthcare provider's service is one of the most important aspects of the marketing mix, although health care providers, especially small health care practices, do not focus on this aspect. Larger providers such as hospitals and pharmaceutical manufacturers devote sizable budgets for mass media promotions. Hospitals also use much of their promotion efforts to convince physicians of the quality and efficiency of the hospital's services. A major innovation in modern health care marketing is promotions using digital means such as internet and social media.

9.3. Inadequacy of Traditional 4P Marketing Mix for Services Marketing (Including Health Care Marketing)

Over the years, marketing managers have come up with variations of the 4P marketing mix as they began to understand the need for variations in marketing different products and services.

These included a variety of approaches highlighting, from time to time, a 5P marketing mix, a 6P marketing mix, and most recently, a 7P marketing mix.

Kareh (2018) quotes Nick Nugent, a well-known marketing professor from Harvard University, as stating that the concept of marketing remains the same (even today), but the marketing mix, or combination of factors that influence the delivery of value, has evolved considerably.

Examples of these variations on marketing mix include the following:

- **A 5P marketing mix approach:** Product, Price, Place, Promotion, and People (Rick, 2013).

Rick makes the point that people who help the company spread the word about the business and its products and services are important. He identifies two groups of people who do this. First, satisfied customers who will introduce you to your new customers. 50% of advocates recommend a brand because they had a good experience with a product or service. He emphasizes that building strong and engaging relationships with customers is key to the successful communication of a product or service offering. Second, he recognizes the organization's staff. Engaged employees help satisfy customers.

We discuss employee engagement in health care marketing in Chapter 11.

- **A 6P marketing mix:** Product, Price, Place, Promotion, People, and Process (Mohammed, 2017).

Process is highly important in services. Customer satisfaction of a service depends on both the outcome and the process the customer goes through while receiving the service. For example, a patient expects a good outcome and to get well soon, but the various steps he or she goes through from consultation through diagnosis, treatment, and follow up care form the service process and this process also affects patient's satisfaction. Therefore, it is important to communicate to consumers and patients that the process at your organization, e.g., hospital or clinic, is more efficient than those of competitors.

- **A 7P marketing mix:** Product, Price, Promotion, Place, Packaging, Positioning, and People (Tracy, 2014).

Tracy emphasizes the need to focus on packaging the product or service to give an appealing external appearance. His sixth element, positioning, is equivalent to what is sometimes referred to as branding. He emphasizes focusing on the mindset of the customers: How do people think about you and talk about you when you are not present? How do people think and talk about your company? What positioning do you have in your market, in terms of the specific words that people use when they describe your products and services to others? His last element, People, refers to the same two kinds of people considered by Rick (2014) who would promote the company's product or service, namely customers and employees.

> What is important is not the count of elements (4, 5, 6, or 7) in a marketing mix. More elements do not mean a better marketing mix. These are all efforts by marketers to understand more deeply the factors their marketing strategy and practices should focus on. This is the objective of a marketing mix.

9.4. Modern 7P Health Care Marketing Mix

Several studies have highlighted the inadequacy of the 4P marketing mix for marketing modern services including health care marketing (Booms and Bitner, 1982; Grönroos and Helle, 2012).

The reasons advanced for this are as follows:

- **The Unique Features of the Services, including Health Care Services**

Services, including health care services, are intangible and non-standardized. Health care services are also highly regulated. Dimensions of quality, in the minds of the customer, for services are different from those for tangible products.

- **Information Revolution**

The advent of the internet has made it easier for customers to gather information about competing products online. This is true for health care services, too. Nowadays, patients do much internet-based online research about illnesses before going to see the physician.

- **Increased Reliance on Social Media**

Social media is hard to escape in the modern world, with millions of people sending texts and emails to friends when they see interesting items they want to share. They can also be an inexpensive way for smaller health care businesses with small advertising budgets to make an impact. A social media marketing strategy lets service providers take advantage of free tools such as Facebook and Twitter to educate consumers and get them to spread the word to their network of contacts.

- **Growth of Online Health Care Services**

For example, Telemedicine: appointment scheduling online. This has made the "place" somewhat less important for services including health care services.

- **Growth of B2B Services in Health Care Marketing**

For example, Hospital marketing is primarily directed at physicians who are the referring source of patients. Managed Care Organizations also focus on physicians for customer/patient referrals.

- **Growth of Global Opportunities for Exporting and Importing Health Care Services**

This subject will be discussed in Chapter 15.

- **Customer Focus on Solutions rather than Products or Services**

Both B2C and B2B customers of today know what they need. The owner of a building complex will not be shopping for a high capacity air conditioning unit. Rather, he will be looking for the most cost-efficient solution to maintain comfort in his building, perhaps by a combination of ventilation and air conditioning.

- **Customer Focus on Value instead of Price**

We may have some customers claiming that our service is too expensive, and that they can find a similar service for a lesser price. Actually, what the customer is saying is that total benefits they receive (outcome, convenience, information, and emotional responses), compared with the price, is lower with our service than the same cost benefit derived from the competitor's service. This ratio of benefits, both tangible and intangible, to price is what is called value.

- **Customer Focus on Education instead of Promotion**

Modern day service customers do not want us to present a service with a price and display a "take it or leave it" attitude. Many expect an education from us. For example, in shopping for a home or office security system and service, the individual or business customer wants to learn from us how security breaches occur and how they are prevented in the industry.

Summarizing, the modern view in services marketing, including health care marketing, is to focus on the following 7P marketing mix (White and Abrams, 2017; Zeithaml *et al.*, 2018):

- Product,
- Price,

Health Care Marketing Mix 235

- Place,
- Promotion,
- People,
- Process, and
- Physical Evidence.

> This 7P marketing mix is not superior to the traditional 4P marketing mix for service marketing/health care marketing because it has more elements. It is superior because it identifies more clearly the factors that service/health care service marketers should focus on to formulate their marketing strategy and plans.
>
> Later in the chapter, we will see that even the same terms from the 4P approach used in the 7P approach (Product, Price, Place, and Promotion) will have different meanings, and provide a deeper understanding, when applied to services/health care services marketing.

Before discussing this 7P marketing mix for health care services, it is worth considering the three basic guiding principles surrounding them. These are as follows:

- Health care marketers should understand that the traditional 4Ps (product, price, place, and promotion) are still included in the 7P health care marketing mix, but should not be interpreted and applied the traditional way. They must be revised to fit modern day customer needs for services. This will be explained in what follows.
- The three new Ps (people, process, and physical evidence) must be incorporated, again, to fit the special nature of services and services marketing. This too will be discussed in what follows.
- The marketing mix is a flexible platform for management and marketers to work on. Each element is not meant for marketers to take as a given. Instead, it requires planning of detailed marketing programs. They are there also for management to make improvements in policies and processes. For example, if process efficiency in a hospital is to be promoted as part of the product/service of the hospital, it mandates management to make improvements in the processes.

Now, we discuss the 7Ps in the modern health care marketing mix in detail.

9.5. "Product" in Health Care Marketing

In the case of tangible products such as pharmaceuticals, the product is easily identifiable. Garvin (1987) defines eight dimensions of quality for tangible products as follows:

- Performance,
- Features,
- Reliability,
- Conformance,
- Durability,
- Serviceability,
- Aesthetics, and
- Perceived quality.

We are familiar with pharmaceutical product promotions on mass media, such as television. Many of these focus on a specific drug and highlight its performance (citing clinical trials), reliability, and conformance. Conformance means suitability for the intended purpose. Pharma advertisements often use actual patients describing how the drug helped them.

Several studies find empirical support for Garvin's dimensions. Stone-Romero *et al.* (1997) show empirical evidence that support the multidimensional nature of product quality. Similarly, Paulson-Gjerde and Slotnick (1997) use a multidimensional approach to study the antecedents of manufacturing quality. Garvin's eight dimensions of product quality are well-established concepts that appear in most quality management books. See for example, Evans and Lindsay (2008).

In services, such as health care services, the "product" is usually the service itself. The customer faces two aspects in a service: an outcome and the process the customer goes through in receiving the services. Often, it is not easy to identify whether health care marketers should promote the outcome, the process, or both. Ivy (2008), applying this question to educational services, states that, "The dimensions of the service that needs to be promoted."

Usually, services have no, or a minor, product component. For example, consider a medical service or an educational service. In a medical service, the patient receives a diagnosis and treatment, both of which are intangible. In a classroom educational scenario, the students receive knowledge and interaction with other students and professors in a scholarly setting. In both these services, the "product" is really the outcome and the process.

> "The product of a service business is the process. Thus, process takes place of the traditional product."
>
> Grönroos (2000)

Another "product" customers seek in services is information. This is very relevant in the modern digital information era. Pistol and Tonis (2017) highlight the role of information in the digital marketing mix.

Therefore, in health care marketing,

- Our marketing effort should be focused on highlighting certain good characteristics of our service.
- We do not have a tangible product to show the customer to touch, feel, and test. What we provide the customer are the outcomes — functional outcome and emotional outcome.
- We should promote our good functional outcomes by showing performance statistics.
- We should promote happy emotional outcomes our services provide using testimonials from satisfied customers.
- Next, we have to show that our process is efficient (speedy) and error free. This also has to be done using objective statistics of low waiting times and low error rates.
- Customer/patient spends a significant time going through the process and at times contributing to it too. Services marketing should publicize the pleasant aspects of this customer journey.
- Organize health education and health care eligibility-related information programs for the community. Publicize these programs in your marketing. Many hospitals are now engaged in this practice.

   For example, Mayo Clinic (2019) in Minnesota announces that "Mayo Clinic patients, their family members and companions are welcome to use the resources of the Barbara Woodward Lips Patient Education Center to learn more about medical conditions and healthy living. The center has a health information library with medical models and exhibits, and offers classes taught by patient education specialists. Staff members are available to assist visitors."
- We should work with community-based organizations when organizing health education and wellness programs. These organizations are usually

interested in educating their ethnic and cultural groups on eligibility and health education issues.
- Health care customers not only seek a service, they seek solutions. Therefore, we should pay attention to providing useful information about health matters and services in the marketing mix.

9.6. "Place" in Health Care Marketing Mix Means "Access", i.e., Enhancing Access to Health Care Services

"Place" in the health care marketing mix is not merely identifying sites of the clinic, pharmacy, or hospital that provides services. It means focusing on ensuring access and enhancing access to services.

Access in health care services has several dimensions as follows:

- **Access to the health care services provided by the organization.** This usually means the type of insurance you accept and insurance systems you have contracted with. For example, many health plans and physicians make strategic choices not to participate in Medicaid or ACA health care exchanges.
- **Geographical access factors.** These include distance limitations to your health care service locations. Health plans are required by payers (such as Medicaid and Medicare programs) that provide access to primary care within 10 miles or 30 minutes from the beneficiary's residence.
- **Administrative limitations.** Cultural and language barriers are a prime example of access limitations that are to be handled by management policies and practices. Federal and state regulations requiring the provision of language assistance to Limited English Proficient (LEP) persons are discussed in Chapter 13. Another administrative type access requirement involves appointment times for patients. State of California requires appointments for non-emergency services for Medicaid patients within 10 business days.
- **Information-related access factors.** Sometimes, services available at your organization are not well known to potential beneficiaries. For example, Rudolph and Williams (2007) report that more than 60% of 16,000 Medicare beneficiaries they surveyed perceived that they knew nothing or almost nothing about drug cards among the drug card sample.

> **Misperceptions of Western Medicines (Cartaret, 2011)**
>
> A case study involving a Mexican immigrant child with diabetes mellitus type 2. During office visits with the physician, the girl's mother accepted the diabetes diagnosis and the use of insulin in treatment. However, the child was not responding to treatment as expected. As the physician was herself Latino and fluent in Spanish, the challenge in this case was not one of language, but there was miscommunication happening between cultures — the Mexican immigrant culture and the Western medical culture. Eventually, the mother admitted that she was not adhering to the recommended course of insulin injections at home because the grandmother believed that insulin was addictive and refused to allow the required insulin injections. She preferred instead to rely on the traditional remedies she herself trusted.

9.6.1. What is the role of health care marketing in "access"?

- Heath care managers should establish policies to enhance access to services for consumers/patients. These will be discussed in what follows.
- Health care marketing could communicate better access an organization provides to consumers, patients, and referring physicians. For example, availability of multiple clinics, pharmacies, or satellite hospital outpatient services units; availability of multilingual physicians and nursing staff; availability of interpreter services and multi-language information brochures; and shorter waiting times for appointments and services.

9.6.2. Guidelines for improving access to health care services

- Larger networks of providers (physicians, ancillary providers, pharmacies, and hospitals).
- Self-service technology.
- Online and mobile options to improve access.
- Opening limited service outlets (e.g., limited service urgent care centers) in distant locations.

- Setting access standards. For example, Health Maintenance Organizations (HMOs) assign subscribers to a primary care physician who is no further than 15 miles from the subscriber's home.
- Guaranteeing customers that they will be served (e.g., in a bank) within, say, 10 minutes.
- Regulations (that exist in many countries) that persons with an emergency medical condition must be treated immediately at hospitals and without insisting on the ability to pay (Emergency Medical Treatment and Active Labor Act (EMTALA)).
- Franchising and subcontracting services, e.g., subcontracting mobile services to be provided by independent small providers in places outside main cities.
- Flexible hours of operation.
- Increasing operators at call centers during peak period and high-volume calls days.
- Deploying additional reception staff when the waiting lines exceed a certain length, e.g., four customers.
- Call back options when customers call the organization and the waiting time to access a customer service representative is long.

The important management guidance again is to ensure that these access options, policies, and guarantees are "marketed", i.e., publicized. Be bold and place signs in your clinics, pharmacies, and hospitals announcing what consumers/patients can do if there are long delays. Include your innovative access policies in your advertisements.

9.7. "Price" in the Health Care Marketing Mix Means "Value"

In health care marketing, this means educating health care customers/patients of the total value of your offering rather than performance or need satisfaction only. Value is benefits less costs, including inconvenience and time spent waiting and travelling.

Traditional product and service pricing, usually based on cost plus marginal cost and competition-based cost, does not suit all health care services. For example,

- In Medicaid, most beneficiaries do not have any out-of-pocket expenses for medically necessary products and services. However, they have to pay

for elective services (such as cosmetic procedures) and the price becomes an important factor.
- In Medicare, the situation is almost the same, except that the consumer/patient is responsible for deductibles, co-pays, and services denied by Medicare as not medically necessary. They also have to pay for elective services and the price becomes an important factor.
- For persons with commercial insurance, the situation is very much similar to Medicare. Price is an important factor as co-pay is generally related to the charges billed by the health care provider, but for HMO and Preferred Provider Organizations (PPOs) plans, this cost is mediated by the health plan the consumer/patient belongs to.
- The persons directly exposed to high out-of-pocket costs, for non-emergency services, are the uninsured. The same is true for seniors seeking in-home health services and assisted living services.

A complex competition pricing situation arises between health plans and providers. Health plans contract with physicians and hospitals and the rates (price) the health plan has to pay to these providers are arrived at by negotiations. Although complex arrangements are usually negotiated and agreed upon, the basic pricing schemes between health plans and providers include:

- Capitation and fee-for-services (FFS) pricing between health plans and physicians and physician groups. Under the capitation schemes, the physician is paid a fixed dollar amount (e.g., US$20 per member assigned to the physician, per month). This is the pricing method typically used by health plans for primary care physicians. Under an FFS system, the physician is paid a pre-negotiated price for the type of service. This method is typically used with specialist physicians.
- Hospitals and health plans usually negotiate a per-diem rate for hospital stays of health plan members (beneficiaries). However, hospital reimbursements for in-patient services are now based on the new DRG (Diagnostic Related Groups) system under which payment categories are used to classify patients, especially Medicare and Medicaid patients, for the purpose of reimbursing hospitals with a fixed fee regardless of the actual costs incurred.

In modern health care management and marketing, a notable feature is the pricing mechanism adopted by a hospital. Evans (2015) reports several aspects of modern hospital pricing practices. He highlights the consumer/patient sticker shock when they pay for services out of pocket under high-deductible health plans. He also reports that hospitals are reviewing charge masters and prices of competitors. As an example, he cites the Memorial Hermann Healthcare System in Houston and the University of Utah Health Care in Salt Lake City as the few hospitals that have revised prices.

Availability of health care price information readily to consumers (referred to as price transparency) is a modern trend in health care policy and regulations. Kullgren (2015) reports that an April 2015 Kaiser Health tracking poll found that fewer than one in 10 Americans reported that in the past year they had seen information comparing prices of hospitals or doctors, and fewer than half of that subgroup said they actually used the information when making health care decisions. He also adds that a 2014 survey conducted by Public Agenda suggested broader engagement, finding that 56% of Americans had tried to determine the price they or their insurer would face for a service before getting care, not including any copayment. Yet, those searches were often limited: Fewer than half of price-seekers compared prices from multiple providers.

Educating consumers on how to find and evaluate health care pricing information, especially how pricing is done by your organization (e.g., hospital) is essential in health care marketing. This information must be a major part of the marketing mix and should be directed at the community, patients, and physicians.

9.7.1. Some guidelines for handling the "price" element in a health care marketing mix

- Pharmaceutical product marketing — Be aware of the current concern over pharmaceutical pricing. Discuss: Can value be demonstrated to market pharmaceutical products?
- Take advantage of current interest in price transparency. Use price transparency to market your health care services.

   Goozner (2014) states, "The future of meaningful healthcare competition lies in ensuring full transparency on pricing, quality and outcomes so that all participants in the healthcare marketplace have the information they need to make informed choices."

   Also refer to state pricing transparency laws such as the 2012 Massachusetts health care price transparency law; and reference pricing (Robinson et al., 2017).
- In publicizing your prices and competitor prices, do not use "billed charges", which is usually higher than the final payment expected by

providers. Kullgren (2015) reports a study conducted at University of Pennsylvania that found that 81% of the prices publicly reported on state websites were for billed charges. For services whose quality can vary substantially (such as outpatient surgeries), data on health care quality were reported alongside prices only 13% of the time.

- Hoffman and Bateson (2006) provide the following general guidelines for pricing services, which are applicable for health care marketing as well.
    o The demand for services is usually more inelastic than the demand for goods.
    o Price discrimination is a valid strategy in services to meet fluctuations in demand and supply.
    o In some health care services, e.g., professional services, a price cannot be fixed because of the uncertainly on how long the task would take.
    o Service customers usually equate higher price to higher quality.
    o Service customers find it harder to compare prices among competing services.
    o Service customers are able to do part of some services themselves.
    o Customers cannot buy services in greater quantity to get better prices and discounts (like one can sometimes do with goods).
    o The price should provide a perception of good customer relationships to the customer and provide an incentive for the customer to stay with the service provider.
    o The price should create and reinforce trust in the customer.

9.8. "Promotion" in Health Care Marketing is "Communication and Education" of Health Care Customers

Promotion in modern service marketing deviates from the old practices of eye and ear catching advertising in mass media (newspapers, radio, and television). Communication is the most visible and audible component of the health care marketing mix (Purcarea *et al.*, 2015). There is a great amount of interest in effective communication in health care marketing as seen by the recent *2nd Storytelling for Healthcare Marketing & Communications Conference*, in Boston, March 20–March 22, 2018. The theme of this conference was, "Strategies to uncover & deliver content that will engage, influence, and educate health care customers/patients and add value to your organization".

Health care marketing should communicate to consumers/patients positive features of the health care organization and its services. Planning to address this element of the marketing mix includes addressing the following issues:

- What are the objectives of the organization's marketing communication plans?
- Who constitutes the target for health care marketing communications?
- What should be communicated and publicized?
- What medium should be used? This is most important in the modern digital communication age.
- What communicating strategies should be used?

Objectives of health care marketing communications are often classified as follows:

- **Inform:** Introducing the services, creating awareness of the brand, and inducing to try out the service.
- **Persuade:** Communicating superior value of the organization's services compared to price and other factors of competing services.
- **Remind:** Encouraging repeat purchases, providing rewards for retention.
- **Relationship building with existing customers:** See discussion in Section 9.12.
- **Referrals:** Expanding the customer/patient base by referrals from existing satisfied customers is an objective of marketing communication. Effective communications with existing customers via direct mail, email, social media, and the company website can be used to encourage them to refer your organization to others. Rewarding customers for their referrals is also a common practice in service management.
- **Feedback:** Continuous collection of customer complaints, reviews, and comments.

The target for health care marketing communications should be wide and include the following:

- Current customers/patients;
- Potential customers/patients;
- Affiliates and partners such as physicians and suppliers;

- Groups that express opinions about your services (media and consumer advocacy groups);
- Politicians and political groups;
- Shareholders and employees; and
- General public.

9.8.1. What features of the organization's health care services should be communicated and publicized?

- Products and services, as discussed above under "product". This includes educational and information services offered by the organization.
- Competitive features such as quality, patient safety (especially for hospitals), convenience, exceptional customer experience, and flexibility.
- Availability of larger networks of providers.
- Availability of specialized services, if any. For example, cancer treatment at M.D. Cancer Institute at University of Texas.
- Value and cost-benefit of services compared to competition.
- Competence of physicians, excellence in nursing services, customer services; customer-oriented services.
- Customer/patient engagement efforts: meetings, educational events, committees.
- Pleasant features of the processes; customer journey; and high patient experience ratings.
- Outstanding features of technology, facilities, and servicescape.

Use the Following in Your Communications

Patient and consumer surveys (both independent surveys and company conducted surveys); Results of audits by independent organizations such as the National Committee of Quality Assurance (NCQA) and Joint Commission; Federal, state and local health authority audits and inspections; Health plan audits; Internal audits; Data from grievance and complaints systems; Aggregate data from quality and utilization management; Unsolicited commendations from physicians, patients, and community organizations.

The following media choices and strategies are suitable for communication in health care marketing:

- Conventional media such as print media and television.
- Newsletters and brochures.
- Sales force direct contacts with physicians.
- Promotional sessions at senior centers and restaurants for Medicare and other senior care products.
- Use of new information technology such as websites, social networking such as Facebook, Google, emails. These will be discussed in detail in Chapter 10.
- Communicating with Limited English Proficient (LEP) customers/patients using multi-language sources.

9.8.2. Communicating strategies in health care marketing

The importance of clear effective communication in health care settings is well established. However, much research and emphasis has been placed on communication between health care providers and patients. In this book, we adopt a health care marketing point of view and focus our attention on communication with consumers/patients at the organizational level.

The first and foremost principle in organizational level communications with the customers/patients is that it should be a two-way communication. That implies that the promotion or communication element of the marketing mix should focus on both:

- Outward communication from the health care organization and the customer/patient.
- Inbound communications from the customer/patient to the health care organization.

Inbound communications between customer/patient and the health care organization occurs via comments, inquiries, complaints, and grievances. Setting up effective inbound communication systems in health care organizations is discussed in Upgrowth (2018).

Content marketing is a form of marketing focused on creating, publishing, and distributing content for a targeted audience online (Pullizi and Barett, 2010). Content marketing does not involve a direct sales approach. Instead, it provides, typically using digital communication channels such as email, text messages, blogs, and websites, information consumers/patients are interested in receiving in order to answer their common health-related questions. Content marketing communications are not advertisements. They provide information that builds relationships and trust of the consumers and patients. Content marketing channels include news, video, white papers, e-books, email newsletters, case studies, podcasts, how-to guides, question and answer articles, photos, blogs, etc. (Steimle, 2014).

Content marketing, often using videos, is the latest trend in health care marketing. More consumers now favor mobile devices over desktops. They demand content in communications they can easily understand. This is the main reason for the popularity of videos in communications.

Examples of Content Marketing in Health Care

Rogers (2015) describes Mayo Clinic's Sharing Mayo Clinic campaign as an example of content marketing in health care. Rochester, Minn.-based Mayo Clinic used real patient stories to offer hope and inspiration on Sharing.MayoClinic.org. The organization shares the posts widely on social media, too. In addition, Mayo Clinic addresses specific health topics, such as living with cancer and managing diabetes, as well as specific medical videos on YouTube. Rogers also highlights The Cleveland Clinic Health Hub, which provides the opportunity for patients to get answers to a variety of questions via its HealthHub.com, which draws more than 1.5 million visits per month and is a leading channel for spreading the Cleveland Clinic brand. All of the editorial content is vetted by medical experts, and there is a complementary newsletter blasted to more than 500,000 subscribers. The blog focuses on health and wellness, but strives for a balance of topics, from medical innovation and breakthroughs to myth-busting and prevention topics.

Other important factors relating to health care marketing communication plans are:

- Ensuring that communications comply with legal requirements and ethical practices.

For example, Health Insurance Portability and Accountability Act of 1996 (HIPAA) has strict requirements affecting health care marketing. Most states also have regulations covering communications with Medicaid beneficiaries. These are discussed in Chapter 13.

- Establishing metrics to measure communication effectiveness.

A communication effort in health care marketing should always have metrics to measure the plan's effectiveness. Commonly used metrics for measuring effectiveness of health care communication are as follows:

- Website traffic — Reading of websites by existing customers/patients and potential consumers.
- Web interaction — With consumers and existing customers/patients that responded with comments and inquiries. This is sometimes referred to as the Click Through Rate (CTR), i.e., customers who moved beyond the home page of the website by performing some action.
- Email opening rates.
- Social media effectiveness measures.
- New leads and sales.
- Retention rates of existing customers/patients.
- Use of custom-built analytics for health care marketing campaigns using tools such as Google Analytics and Marketo (Cleverism, 2015).

9.9. "People" in Health Care Marketing are Health Care Service Staff, Employees, and Physicians

In Chapter 7, we discussed how customers'/patients' selection of health care providers and retention depends on their experience, i.e., customer/patient experience. Thus, customer/patient engagement is most important to health care marketing. The first line of contact for customers/patients is the contact employees, such as call center staff, reception staff, nursing staff, physicians, and ancillary services staff of the health care organization. Front-line employees in services play a critical role in how customers experience the organization because value is created when an employee interacts with a customer. The ability of an organization to provide value to customers and ensure their loyalty relies on how effectively this interaction between employees and customers works (Blount, 2011).

We will discuss employee engagement in health care fully in Chapter 11.

9.10. "Process" in Health Care Marketing is the Entire Customer/Patient Journey

In health care services, customer/patient satisfaction and experience depends on both the health outcome and the process the customer/patient goes through in interactions with the health care organization.

Health Care Marketing Mix 249

The process the customer/patient goes through was discussed in the previous chapter as the "customer journey". Mapping and understanding the "journey", which includes outcomes as well as emotions, and not just the "process" in a mechanical sense, was highlighted.

Following are key activities of the organization, with the participation of health care marketing, that fall under this element of the marketing mix:

- Health care marketing should be involved in the customer journey mapping process.
- The next step is a clear understanding of vital touch points and moments of truth. These must be solicited from customers/patients and contact staff (who are the first source of customer/patient complaints and concerns).
- Customer and staff input from vital touch points and moments of truth will reveal areas for process improvement.

    This is a function led by top management with the participation of all departments. The aim is to make processes more efficient, by ensuring shorter waiting times, handling emotional aspects of waiting, establishing fair policies in handling waiting lines, providing comfortable and accessible facilities, and eliminating waste (referred to in operations management literature as "lean operations"). Top management should ensure that health care marketing participates in process improvement.
- Communication of process improvements to customers/patients. Publicize improvements, comparisons of waiting times, satisfaction/experience from survey results.
- Health care marketing should publicize the pleasant aspects of the customer journey.

In summary, understand customer/patient expectations of the process, both outcome expectations and emotional expectations. Using customer journey mapping, improve the processes. Then publicize the improvements.

> Customers/Patients take part in the service process and bring in to the process their own needs, expectations, beliefs, and emotions. This is called co-creation, i.e., customers/patients are active participants in the process. Process mapping, in the traditional sense, does not identify values, expectations, beliefs, and emotions customers/patients bring in to the process. Only a good customer journey mapping will.

9.11. Physical Evidence/Servicescape

For consumers/patients visiting a health care clinic or facility, the service environment is the first aspect of the service that is perceived by the customer. At this stage, consumers/patients are likely to form impressions of the level of service they will receive (Hooper *et al.*, 2013). These non-human elements of the organization are called "servicescape" (Bitner, 1992).

Physical evidence plays a crucial role in shaping the customer's/patient's perceptions and expectations of the health care service. Physical and tangible things in health care services include buildings, landscaping, interior furnishing, equipment, staff members uniforms, signs, communication materials, forms customers/patients have to complete, and other visible cues that provide tangible evidence of a health care facility's service quality (Bitner, 1992; Lin, 2004; Sreejesh *et al.*, 2016).

Servicescape also influences the nature and quality of customer and employee interactions, especially in high contact services like medical encounters, most directly in interpersonal services.

Considering all these aspects that affect customer perceptions, expectations, and emotions, servicescapes definitely influence customer/patient experience.

Health care marketing has a role in servicescapes as much as it has in processes.

- Health care marketing should be involved in gathering customer evaluations relating to physical evidence of the health care service.
- Health care marketing should communicate superior aspects of the organization's servicescape. This is done by attractive photos and videos of facilities and staff in professional attire and friendly mood. Testimonials from satisfied customers/patients and commendable results from external inspections and audits are also used.

9.12. Relationship Marketing in Health Care

Relationship marketing is, in general, a direct marketing approach that targets a specific audience. It attempts to deliver a specific message and achieve a specific result. Avenues for reaching out to customers are a blend of old and new, including the internet, email communications, informational database applications, as well as print newsletters, surveys, and communication via postal mail (Lohrey, 2019).

Applying relationship marketing principles to the healthcare industry is a customer-driven approach to marketing, using marketing materials and educational programs, and in the modern world, digital communication methods such as emails, websites, and text messages to:

- Listen to customers/patients to understand their needs.
- Engage customers/patients by providing educational material and information,
- Create trust in the customers'/patients' minds with a health care provider such as a hospital, clinic, or individual doctor, and
- Through this trust and confidence in the provider, encourage retention and interest of potential new customers/patients.

Studies show that relationship marketing is particularly useful in professional services such as health care. "Simply stated, healthcare is a service industry that places great value in fostering relationships with its consumers" (Rooney, 2009).

Patients who have entered into a close relationship with their health care providers become brand ambassadors for the health care provider or organization. They will show the outside world their affection for the physician, hospital, or provider. Reviews by such engaged patients will be seen as credible by others.

This message is bound to reach associates of the health care provider such as other physicians, providers, and hospitals who will be encouraged to refer patients to this provider (Mikulski, 2013).

Manish Chauhan, a digital marketing manager and expert (Chauhan, 2016) emphasizes that relationship marketing is a smart approach for healthcare providers to market themselves well to attain their business objectives and a strategic lever for their marketing objectives that helps to manage and create lasting relationships with patients.

Following are some guidelines for effective relationship marketing in health care (Chauhan, 2016; Mikulski, 2013; Wagner et al., 1994):

- Communicate frequently with customers/patients.
- Proactively seek customer/patient feedback.
- Do not ignore customer/patient complaints and concerns. Use patient feedback for process improvements.
- Know your patients well and always follow the "patient first" policy.

- Differentiate your health organization from other organizations by excelling in customer satisfaction and experience.
- Build trust and strengthen relationships by touching human emotions of customers/patients.
- Show compassion in your gestures and actions, which helps them know you understand and empathize with their problems.
- Provide information that is scientifically correct, unbiased, and useful.
- Combine multiple communication methods such as email, social media, physician-review websites, and phones for connecting and communicating with your patients.

Mikulski (2013) emphasizes the requirements for successful health care relationship marketing as follows:

- Ethical conduct,
- Seamless patient relations,
- Responsive communication,
- Proactive communication, and
- Community outreach to community and society at large.

In a world where consumers increasingly adopt social media, it is a fitting idea to use social media for patient engagement. And be active on various social media platforms such as Facebook, LinkedIn, blogs, and Twitter. This allows the health care organization to stay well-informed about how patients perceive health care. Service staff must be motivated to establish relationships with key customers.

Almost all discussions on customer/patient relationship building emphasize that while health outcomes are important to customers/patients, it is their emotions that dominate their engagement with health care providers.

Trust and Communication have been found to have the strongest correlation with customer retention. These findings are consistent with findings of Grönroos (1997) that, "Integral elements of the relationship marketing approach are 'promise concept' and 'trust'."

Treating customers/patients as distinct and valuable human beings is an essential element in relationship marketing. This is called Consumer Personalization. In a Brightedge survey of 500 digital marketers, 29% of respondents said they think consumer personalization will be the next big marketing trend in 2018 (Nanji, 2018).

9.12.1. Customer centered marketing

A concept related to and similar to customer relationship marketing is Customer Centered Marketing, also called Customer-Centric Marketing (CCM).

CCM is based on the same premise that marketing strategy should put customers at the center (Ravi and Sun, 2016).

In CCM too, marketers assess the needs of each customer individually. Then the health care service organization communicates to these customers the educational information related to the customers' needs and the organization's capabilities in meeting them. Information made available should be tailored to patients' needs to permit meaningful deliberation and shared mind (Epstien and Peters, 2009). The aim of this type of marketing is to make the customer/patient understand the circumstances surrounding his or her health care situation or needs and build confidence and trust on this provider. This would, hopefully, encourage the customer/patient to seek services from this provider.

CCM is based on increase in negative customer attitudes towards intrusive marketing.

Customer resistance to intrusive marketing is increasing. They do not like the excessive advertisements and unsolicited mail that they get. Customers increasingly use "do not call options" or spam/pop up blockers (Ravi and Sun, 2016). They avoid meeting with sales persons because they do not like being sold products or services. They are generally tired of sales people who they think will say or do anything for a sale. Potential customers become defensive because they do not want to be "hustled" into purchasing unneeded or unwanted products/services (MyMarketingDept., Inc., 2018).

CCM avoids this situation by developing confidence and trust of customers who will themselves seek out information and services from this provider/organization.

Do not be concerned with overcoming objections, avoid any objections in the first place is the better approach. Trying to overcome objections often leads to arguments and lost sales opportunities.

Greene (2015) presents the following examples of CCM in health care marketing:

- Dignity Health in San Francisco, reorganized its marketing departments to establish a new consumer-centric, unified brand across its 39 hospitals and multispecialty medical groups.

- Meridian Health, a seven-hospital system in New Jersey, launched an advertising campaign that describes its continuum of care and encourages consumers to use it at the appropriate place for their specific needs.

Experts in health care marketing report witnessing an emergence of consumers who examine market offerings and create a customized consumption experience for themselves (Leone *et al.*, 2012 citing Etgar, 2008; Payne and Frow, 2005).

Health care marketing should focus on educational marketing that will engage patient populations.

In summary, steps in implementing CCM in health care are as follows:

- Learning about individual customers/patients from continuously gathering and analyzing information and data from them. Use internal data from customer interaction, conventional feedback via comments and complaints, and on-line collection of customer feedback. Seek customer input on communication channels, website quality and usability, marketing content, and customer support.
- Segmenting of customers into individual or small niche segments based on customer needs gathered from feedback.
- Improving clinical, non-clinical processes, and communication based on information gathered.
- Updating and developing insights about each customer or niche, with the aim of establishing long-term relationships.
- Publicizing improvements and successes in customer/patient satisfaction and experience.

References

Berkowitz, E. N. (2017). *Essentials of Health Care Marketing*, 4th edition, Burlington, MA: Jones & Bartlett.

Bitner, M. J. (1992). "Servicescapes: The Impact of Physical Surroundings on Customers and Employees", *Journal of Marketing*, 56, 57–71.

Blount, Y. (2011). "Employee Management and Service Provision: A Conceptual Framework", *Information Technology and People*, 24 (2), 134–157.

Booms, B. H. and Bitner, M. J. (1982) "Marketing Strategies and Organization Structures for Service Firms". In: Donnelly, J. H. and George, W. R. (Eds.), *Marketing Services*, Chicago, IL: American Marketing Association, 47–51.

Carteret, M. (2011). "Cultural Barriers to Treatment and Compliance", http://www.dimensionsofculture.com/2011/03/cultural-barriers-to-treatment-and-compliance/. Accessed January 11, 2019.

Chauhan, M. K. (2016). "A Roadmap to Relationship Marketing in Healthcare", Jan 29, 2016, http://www.physicianspractice.com/marketing/roadmap-relationship-marketing-healthcare. Accessed January 12, 2019.

Cleverism (2015). "How to Measure the Effectiveness of Marketing Campaigns", https://www.cleverism.com/how-to-measure-effectiveness-of-marketing-campaigns/. Accessed January 11, 2019.

Economic Times (2019). "Marketing Mix", https://economictimes.indiatimes.com/definition/marketing-mix. Accessed January 8, 2019.

Epstein, R. M. and Peters, E. (2009). "Beyond Information: Exploring Patients' Preferences", *JAMA*, 302 (2), 195–197.

Etgar, M. (2008). "A Descriptive Model of the Consumer Co-Production Process", *Journal of the Academy of Marketing Science*, 36 (1), 97–108.

Evans, J. R. and Lindsay, W. M. (2008). *The Management and Control of Quality*, 7th edition, Thomson/South Western Publishers.

Evans, M. (2015). "Repricing Healthcare: Hospitals Scrutinize Costs as Patients Grow More Price-Sensitive", *Modern Healthcare*, 45 (49), 16–18.

Garvin, D. A. (1987). "Competing on the Eight Dimensions of Quality", *Harvard Business Review*, 65 (6), 101–109.

Goozner, M. (2014). "Ensuring Competition Begins with Transparency", *Modern Healthcare*, 44 (22), 24.

Greene, J. (2015). "Healthcare Marketers Reshape Ad Strategies", *Modern Healthcare*, http://www.modernhealthcare.com/article/20151030/MAGAZINE/310309995. Accessed October 1, 2018.

Grönroos, C. (1994). "From Marketing Mix to Relationship Marketing: Towards a Paradigm Shift in Marketing", *Management Decision*, 32 (2), 4–20.

Grönroos, C. (1997). "Keynote Paper: From Marketing Mix to Relationship Marketing — Towards a Paradigm Shift in Marketing", *Management Decision*, 35 (4), 322–339.

Grönroos, C. (2000). *Service Management and Marketing*, 2nd edition, John Wiley & Sons.

Grönroos, C. and Helle, P. (2012). "Return on Relationships: Conceptual Understanding and Measurement of Mutual Gains from Relational Business Engagements", *Journal of Business & Industrial Marketing*, 27 (5), 344–359.

Hanks, G. (2019). "How to Implement the 4 P's of Marketing in Healthcare", https://smallbusiness.chron.com/implement-4-ps-marketing-healthcare-68980.html. Accessed January 3, 2019.

Hoffman, K. D. and Bateson, J. E. G. (2006). *Service Marketing, Concepts, Strategies & Cases*, 3rd edition, Thomson-South-Western.

Hooper, D., Coughlan, J. and Mullen, M. R. (2013). "The Servicescape as an Antecedent to Service Quality and Behavioral Intentions", *Journal of Services Marketing*, 27 (4), 271–280.

Hunt, S. F. and Goolsby, J. (2011). "The Rise and Fall of the Functional Approach to Marketing: A Paradigm Displacement Perspective", *Review of Marketing*

Research: Special Issue — Marketing Legends, Vol. 1, Naresh K. Malhotra, (ed), Bingley, UK, Emerald, 2011.

Ivy, J. (2008). "A New Higher Education Marketing Mix: The 7Ps for MBA Marketing", *International Journal of Educational Management*, 22 (4), 288–299.

Kareh, A. (2018). "Evolution of the Four Ps: Revisiting the Marketing Mix", January 3, 2018, https://www.forbes.com/sites/forbesagencycouncil/2018/01/03/evolution-of-the-four-ps-revisiting-the-marketing-mix/#51c8b4011200. Accessed January 9, 2019.

Kotler, P. (2000). *Marketing Management*, (Millennium Edition), Custom Edition for University of Phoenix, Prentice Hall, 9.

Kullgren, J. Y. (2015). "How to Teach People About Health Care Pricing", September 29, 2015, https://hbr.org/2015/09/how-to-teach-people-about-health-care-pricing. Accessed January 11, 2019.

Leone R. P., Walker C. A., Curry L. C. and Agee E. J. (2012). "Application of a Marketing Concept to Patient-Centered Care: Co-Producing Health with Heart Failure Patients", *OJIN: The Online Journal of Issues in Nursing*, 17 (2).

Lin, S.-M. (2011). "Marketing Mix (7P) and Performance Assessment of Western Fast Food Industry in Taiwan: An Application by Associating DEMATEL and ANP", *African Journal of Business Management*, 5 (26), 10634–10644.

Lohrey, J. (2019). "What is Relationship Marketing in Healthcare?", https://smallbusiness.chron.com/relationship-marketing-healthcare-68571.html. Accessed January 12, 2019.

Mayo Clinic (2019). "Patient Education in Minnesota", https://www.mayoclinic.org/patient-visitor-guide/education-centers/patient-education-minnesota. Accessed January 12, 2019.

Mikulski, L. (2013). "Healthcare Relationship Marketing: Tapping into Emotion", https://www.physicianreferralmarketing.com/healthcare-relationship-marketing/. Accessed January 12, 2019.

Mintz, O. and Currim, I. (2013). "What Drives Managerial Use of Marketing and Financial Metrics and Does Metric Use Affect Performance of Marketing-Mix Activities?", *Journal of Marketing*, 77 (2), 17–40.

Mohammed, R. U. (2017). "6 P's Marketing Mix: The Determinants of the Acceptance of Equity Financing Among SMEs", *Journal of Humanities, Language, Culture and Business* (JHLCB), 1 (6), (December 2017), 134–143.

MyMarketingDept., Inc. (2018). "Customer-Centric Marketing — No Selling Required", https://www.mymarketingdept.com/customer-centric-marketing/ Accessed March 3, 2019.

Nanji, A. (2018). "Online Marketers: The Next Big Trend in Marketing", https://www.marketingprofs.com/charts/2018/33819/online-marketers-the-next-big-trend-in-marketing. Accessed March 1, 2019.

Paulson-Gjerde, K. A. and Slotnick, S. A. (1997). "A Multidimensional Approach to Manufacturing Quality", *Computers and Industrial Engineering*, 22 (4), 879–889.

Payne, A. and Frow, P. (2005). "A Strategic Framework for Customer Relationship Management", *Journal of Marketing*, 69 (4), 167–176.

Pistol, L. and Tonis, R. (2017). "The '7Ps' & '1G' That Rule in the Digital World Marketing Mix", Proceedings of the International Conference on Business Excellence, 01 July 2017, 11 (1), 759–769. DOI: https://doi.org/10.1515/picbe-2017-0080. Accessed January 11, 2019.

Pulizzi, J. and Barrett, N. (2010). "Get Content Get Customers — Turn Prospects into Buyers with Content Marketing", *NSB Management Review*, 2 (2), 98–100.

Purcarea, V. L., Gheorghe, I.-R. and Gheorghe, C.-M. (2015). "Uncovering the Online Marketing Mix Communication for Health Care Services", *Procedia Economics and Finance*, 26, 1020–1025.

Ravi, R. and Sun, B. (2016). *Customer Centric Marketing: A Pragmatic Approach*, MIT Press.

Rick, T (2013). "Rewrite the Ps of Marketing — The Five Ps of Marketing". November 10, 2013 | Marketing Strategy, https://www.torbenrick.eu/blog/marketing/rewrite-the-ps-of-marketing/. Accessed January 2, 2019.

Robinson, J. C., Brown, T. T, and Whaley, C. (2017). "Reference Pricing Changes the 'Choice Architecture' of Health Care for Consumers", *Health Affairs*, 36 (3), 524–530.

Rogers, A. M. (2015). "The Best Health Care Content Marketing in 2014", *Marketing Health Services*, https://www.ama.org/publications/eNewsletters/MHSNewsletter/Pages/the-best-health-care-content-marketing-in-2014.aspx. Accessed January 11, 2019.

Rooney, C. (2009). "The Meaning of Mental Health Nurses Experience of Providing One-to-One Observations: A Phenomenological Study", *Journal of Psychiatric and Mental Health Nursing*, 16 (1), 76–86.

Rudolph, N. V. and Williams, S. S. (2007). "Medicare Beneficiary Knowledge of and Experience with Prescription Drug Cards", *Health Care Finance Review*, 2007 Fall; 29 (1), 87–101.

Singh, M. (2012). "Marketing Mix of 4P's for Competitive Advantage", *IOSR Journal of Business and Management* (IOSRJBM), 3 (6) (September/October 2012), 40–45.

Sreejesh, S., Sahoo, D. and Mitra, A. (2016). "Can Healthcare Servicescape Affect Customer's Attitude? A Study of the Mediating Role of Image Congruence and Moderating Role of Customer's Prior Experience", *Asia-Pacific Journal of Business Administration*, 8 (2), 106–126.

Steimle, J. (2014). "What Is Content Marketing?", https://www.forbes.com/sites/joshsteimle/2014/09/19/what-is-content-marketing/#25ae530110b9. Accessed January 11, 2019.

Stone-Remero, E., Stone, D. L. and Grewal, D. (1997). "Development of a Multi-Dimensional Measure of Perceived Product Quality", *Journal of Quality Management*, 2 (1), 87–111.

Thomas, R. K. (2015). *Marketing Health Services*, 3rd edition, Chicago, Ill. Health Administration Press.

Tracy, B. (2014). "The 7 Ps of Marketing", Healthcare Success blog, https://www.healthcaresuccess.com/blog/medical-advertising-agency/the-7-ps-of-marketing.html. Accessed January 2, 2019.

Upgrowth (2018). "Benefits of Inbound Marketing for Healthcare industry", https://blog.upgrowth.in/benefits-of-inbound-marketing-for-healthcare-industry/. Accessed October 20, 2018.

Valarie Zeithaml, Mary Jo Bitner and Dwayne Gremler (2018). *Services Marketing*. Seventh Edition, McGraw-Hill.

Wagner H. C., Fleming D., Mangold W. G. and LaForge R. W. (1994). "Relationship Marketing in Health Care", *Journal of Health Care Marketing*, Winter, 14 (4), 42–7.

White, K. and Abrams, M. (2017). "Leveraging the 7P's of Marketing in Healthcare", March 23, 2017 | Becker's Hospital Review, https://www.beckershospitalreview.com/hospital-transactions-and-valuation/leveraging-the-7p-s-of-marketing-in-healthcare.html. Accessed January 1, 2019.

Zeithaml, V., Bitner, M. J. and Gremler D. (2018). *Services Marketing*, 7th edition, McGraw-Hill.

Suggested Additional Readings

Ciotti, G. (2016). "Have the 4P's of Marketing Become Outdated?", June 23, 2016, https://www.helpscout.net/blog/new-4ps-of-marketing/. Accessed November 2, 2018.

Hill, R. C. (1988). "A New 'P' for Hospital Marketing?", *Journal of Hospital Marketing*, 2 (2), 5–18.

Leven, E. L. (1984). "Price — A Primer on the 2nd "P" for Hospital Marketers", *Health Marketing Quarterly*, 2 (Fall), 33–42.

McCarthy, J. E. (1964). *Basic Marketing. A Managerial Approach*, Homewood, IL: Irwin.

Nimer, D. A. (1985). "Is Pricing Health Care Services a Marketing Decision?", *Hospital Forum*, 29 (July–August), 57–58.

Sreejesh, S., Sahoo, D. and Mitra, A. (2016). "Can Healthcare Servicescape Affect Customer's Attitude? A Study of The Mediating Role of Image Congruence and Moderating Role of Customer's Prior Experience", *Asia-Pacific Journal of Business Administration*, 8 (2), 106–126.

Part 3

Health Care Marketing Program Implementation

Chapter 10

Integrating Digital Technology into Modern Health Care Marketing

10.1. Digital Technology in Health Care

10.1.1. Evolution of information age and digital technology

Almost all industries have had to cope with the modern-day digital technology revolution. The digital revolution, or the arrival of the information age, is considered by many as the next stage of societal change following the agrarian, the industrial, and the service economies. In terms of technology, the shift has been from mechanical and analogue electronic technology to digital electronics.

The Information Age, also called the Computer Age or the Digital Age, is associated with the advances in electronic computers in the 1950s culminating in smaller powerful personal computers. This, coupled with the development of the internet by the United States Department of Defense in the 1970s, further advanced technological changes, such as the development of fiber optic cables and faster microprocessors, accelerating the transmission and processing of information. The World Wide Web and Electronic mail (email), which enabled speedy exchange of information, soon became the primary mode of personal and business communications. All business sectors, in order to remain competitive, have had to advance their management information systems. For evolution of the information and digital revolution in businesses, see TechTarget (2018).

In the 2000s, the business–consumer interaction became highly digitalized due to the advent of cell phones, text messaging, smart phones, tablets, and internet-based personal computers.

Biesdorf and Niedermann (2014) in an article "Healthcare's Digital Future", claim that the adoption of information technology (IT) in health care systems has, in general, followed the same pattern as other industries. He explains how, in the 1950s, when other industries began using computers to automate highly standardized and repetitive tasks such as accounting and payroll, health care payors also began using IT to process vast amounts of statistical data.

Later, in the 1970s, manufacturing organizations used technology to integrate different parts of core processes such as manufacturing, accounting, and human resources (HR), and installed processes such as Materials Requirements Planning (MRP) to coordinate activities with suppliers, and the health care sector brought about electronic patient identity cards. It was also a catalyst for the Health Information Technology for Economic and Clinical Health Act in the United States and the National Programme for IT in the National Health Service in the United Kingdom.

All these technology adoptions were focused on process improvement and not on improving customer engagement. The third, or modern wave of technology adoption, includes the consumers/patients who have also adopted technology in their daily lives and are avid users of internet-based platforms like email, websites, and search engines. This has resulted in industrial organizations as well as health care organizations and providers realizing the importance of technology to connect with consumers/patients.

Today, digital technology is used in many facets of health care. These can be classified as follows:

- **Uses in Diagnosis and Treatment**

Technology has been able to develop many devices that improve treatment, especially surgeries. Examples include:

  o Robotic surgery, or robot-assisted surgery, that enables surgeons to perform many types of complex procedures with more precision, flexibility, and control than is possible with conventional techniques. These are sometimes referred to as minimally invasive surgeries as the procedures are performed through tiny incisions. Open heart surgeries are being reduced as a result of the availability of new technologies enabling less invasive methods (Mayo Clinic, 2019).
  o The Bionic Eye. A surgical team led by Dr. Thiran Jayasundera and Dr. David Zacks at University of Michigan has performed the first-ever surgeries that implanted artificial retinas into the eyes of patients with retinitis pigmentosa, a degenerative eye disease that

eventually causes blindness. The technology involved with the bionic eye includes a video camera on the patient's glasses which sends the information into a video processing unit that the patient wears on a belt. The image is converted into signals that are wirelessly transmitted to this device. The retinal prosthesis works wirelessly through a camera connected to electrodes. The electrodes stimulate remaining retinal nerve fibers, causing the perception of light in the brain (Michigan Daily, 2014).

o Prescription Management. The use of tablets for computerized physician order entry (CPOE) of prescription refills and Rx authorizations has helped to significantly improve turnaround times — some say up to 90% (Adil, 2012). The ability to send this information directly to pharmacies reduces errors usually created with handwritten prescriptions. These errors have been found to cause vital medical errors.

- **Medical Research**

Digital technology based on cloud computing has enabled medical researchers to access and analyze vast amounts of data (referred to as Big Data) (AIMS, 2018).

Forbes (2013), under the heading "Crunching Data to Offer a Better Diagnosis and Treatment" reports how researchers at IBM have been developing the supercomputer known as Watson to help physicians make better diagnoses and recommend treatments. Doctors could keep track of patient history, stay up-to-date on medical research, and analyze treatment options. Forbes continues, "Doctors at Memorial Sloan-Kettering Cancer Center in New York are expected to begin testing Dr. Watson."

- **Digitalizing Health Records**

Patient individual and aggregate health information is now collected, stored, and exchanged using digital technology such as computers, internet, and cloud computing. The number of hospitals with Electronic Health Records (EHRs) has quadrupled from 2010 to 2013 and physician adoption of the EHR has doubled from 2009 to 2013 (Klimpel, 2018).

The introduction of EHRs in replacing paper records has been a game changer for many allied health care professionals. Medical assistants, medical records and health information technicians (MRHITs), medical billing and coding professionals, and registered nurses are just some of the allied health care roles impacted by this implementation.

Nurses and technicians are now responsible for inputting patient data such as vital signs, weight, test results, etc. into a central, digitized system. On the administration side of things, medical billers and coders use EHRs for scheduling appointments, updating patient records with diagnostic codes, and submitting medical claims.

- **Uses in Improving and Coordinating Internal Processes**

Computer and specialized software programs are used in improving and coordinating internal processes of health care organizations, such as member eligibility data processing, provider information processing, utilization management, claims processing and payment, grievance handling, compliance monitoring, and reporting to regulatory agencies.

- **Uses to Facilitate Patients, Especially Seniors, to Stay Healthy**

These include digital devises to self-monitor their health, such as trackers, wearables, sensors, smart scales, multi-measure wellness tools and diet/weight loss/nutrition tools (Klimpel, 2018). There are also mobile apps and gadgets such as Fitbit, a pedometer that tracks daily sleep and activity, Lark, a silent alarm clock and sleep monitor that tracks and analyzes a person's quality of sleep over time, and other calorie-counting, food-monitoring, and menu-tracking apps to aid the diet-conscious (Forbes, 2013). Some of these digital equipments are capable of notifying an individual's health care provider if critical symptoms are detected.

- **Uses Enhancing Patient Education, Communication, and Patient Engagement**

Prominent among digital communication formats used for these purposes are smart phones and personal computer and internet-based communications such as emails.

Patient engagement is an ideal healthcare situation in which people are well-informed about — and motivated to be involved — in their own medical care.

> While all above modern uses of technology in health care relate to improved quality of care, coordination of care, and patient experience, it is the last of these, namely patient experience, including patient education, communication and engagement that impacts health care marketing most.

10.2. Impact of Modern Digital Technology on Health Care Marketing

In Chapter 1, we adopted the following definition of Health Care Marketing:

> "Health care marketing integrates multi-channel, highly-segmented, and targeted online and offline tactics that are designed to find and acquire the right patients, engage with them through strategic outreach, and nurture them to form lasting relationships throughout the entire patient journey."

We also established that modern health care marketing recognizes that the present health care consumer lives in a digital and experience economy that significantly affects his/her consumer behavior toward health and health care services.

We also recognized in Chapter 9 (Marketing Mix) that "promotion" in modern service marketing mix means communication and education of health care customers.

Combining these concepts, we can see that:

- Modern health care marketing is no longer dependent on mass advertising in billboards, newspapers, and television.
- It is focused on effective two-way communication between the consumer/patient and the health care organization.
- The focus is on smaller market segments, niches, and even patient-centered communications.
- Key objectives are long-term customer/patient relationships and engagement.
- As the modern health care consumer/patient lives in a digital and experience economy, the use of digital communications is imperative.

Industry surveys and expert views confirm the relationship between digital technology and health care marketing. For example, Conick (2017) claims that:

> "Technology (is) No. 1 Concern of Health Care Marketing in 2018."

He cites the Affect's Health Marketing Report 2018 (Affect 2017) that reports a survey of senior marketers from health care organizations. When asked, "What are your top marketing and public relations priorities this year and heading into 2018?" the main responses were as follows:

- Better segmentation and targeting key audiences (this was discussed in detail in Chapter 8);
- Creating more customized content for target audiences;
- Leveraging new/emerging technologies to better communicate with stakeholders; and
- Tie Public Relations (PR) or marketing more closely to business/financial metrics.

This report also listed five essential principles for health care marketing, including:

- **Advanced social media:** "the biggest opportunity for health care marketers in 2018."
- **Targeted content development and distribution.**
- **Creative media relations:** The majority of people affected who were spoken to had said PR has been more challenging in the last year due to the harsh political climate.
- **Emerging tech campaigns:** "It's time to seriously take a look at using emerging and immersive tech platforms in 2018," the report says. "Augmented reality, virtual reality, AI, voice applications — these technologies are being explored within health care delivery but have opportunities for health care marketing as well."
- **Business-oriented metrics:** Metrics and measurement have been discussed by PR and marketing execs for years, but they are often ignored. Health care marketers must stop ignoring them in 2018.

10.2.1. Health care consumer/patient dependence on digital technology

There are many surveys and reports that highlight the health care consumer/patient dependence on digital technology. A selected few of these studies and surveys are given below to establish why modern health care marketing should adopt digital technology.

- Health care consumers/patients use, and depend on, internet/social media for health and health care provider information.
- Anderson et al. (2018), in a Pew Research Center report, state that 89% of US adults use the internet currently compared to 52% in 2000.

- Caution must be exercised in using this figure in health care marketing because there are differences of use based on demographic variations. For example,
  o Seniors over 65 years of age (that is the Medicare population) — about a third do not use internet. Use has dropped by 7% since 2016.
  o Persons with annual income less than $30,000 (likely the Medicaid population) — 19% do not use the internet.
  o However, even these low internet use populations depend on their adult children for health care and provider selection decisions. This group, in age 18–50, are heavy users of the internet (97%).

10.2.2. Health care provider and organization dependence on digital technology

iPad usage is on the rise in health care environments (Englehardt, 2018). iPads are being used increasingly for:

- **Patient check-ins:**

Paperwork check-in processes are time-consuming and duplicative, especially for returning patients. The iPad lessens the time requirement on each end and allows for an easier way to update patient information.

- **Patient satisfaction surveys:**

iPads allow health care facilities to collect patient feedback speedily to improve processes and overall guest satisfaction. Hospitals qualify for Meaningful Use funding when they use tablets for patient satisfaction surveys.

"Meaningful Use" is a term used to define minimum US government standards for EHR to promote exchange of clinical patient data between health care providers, between providers and insurers, and between providers and patients. In 2018, the program was revised and renamed the Medicare and Medicaid Promoting Interoperability Programs by the Centers for Medicare and Medicaid Services (CMS). While the main objective of the program was improving exchange of health information, *increasing patient engagement was also an objective.*

- **Patient education, for example, during discharge planning:**

iPads allow physicians and nursing staff to supplement traditional verbal discharge and follow-up instructions with visual communications illustrating discharge information and follow-up care.

Out of hospitals around the country who have implemented iPads as a means of improving discharge communication, 63% saw an improvement in survey responses regarding patient satisfaction (Kang, 2013).

The ability to improve patient education ultimately leads to lower readmission rates and a higher return on investment (ROI) for hospitals and other medical facilities. This could save hospitals millions of dollars per year on patient reimbursement fees and Medicare penalties (Englehardt, 2018).

- **Prescription management:**

The use of tablets for computerized physician order entry (CPOE) of prescription refills and Rx authorizations has helped to significantly improve turnaround times — some say up to 90% (Adil, 2012). In serious medical situations, this turnaround time could mean the difference between life and death. The ability to send this information electronically also eliminates any errors in understanding handwriting — an issue that causes an estimated 7,000 deaths per year!

- **As an aid to physicians:**

Today doctors often carry a mobile device such as an iPhone or iPad. They often refer to medical apps. Doctors can now use these devices to conduct routine examinations and have access to advanced diagnostic tools for patients speeding up and improving diagnosis with larger amounts of information available speedily.

10.2.3. Patient engagement strategies (TechTarget, 2017)

There are a range of patient engagement strategies that use various technologies and their features, including the following:

- Patient portals, which are secure online sites that allow patients to access their health data, communicate with their health care provider, and more.
- Scheduling software, which lets patients request and book appointments on their own, often through portals.
- Appointment reminders, which can be sent via text, email, or as recorded messages.
- Secure messaging, which allows patients to communicate with their provider through the patient portal or using secure, HIPAA-compliant applications.

- Patient education that includes materials pertaining to a specific patient and his or her illnesses, such as continuing care information.

According to a survey done by the New England Journal of Medicine, the top patient engagement tools planned and implemented by health care organizations are as follows:

- Patient portals: 67%;
- Telemedicine: 58%;
- Secure communications such as email: 52%;
- Online and mobile scheduling and reminders: 46%;
- Remote patient monitoring: 35%; and
- Patient-generated data and social networks: 22% (TechTarget, 2017).

Smith (2015) cites the Pew Research Center report "US Smartphone Use in 2015", which reports that:

- Nearly two-thirds of Americans are now smartphone owners, and for many these devices are a key entry point to the online world.
- 10% of Americans own a smartphone, but do not have any other form of high-speed internet access at home beyond their phone's data plan.
- Using a broader measure of the access options available to them, 15% of Americans own a smartphone, but say that they have a limited number of ways to get online other than their cell phone.
- In all, one-in-five American adults (19%) indicate that at least one of those conditions apply to them, and 7% of the public say that both of these conditions apply — that is, they do not have broadband access at home, and also have relatively few options for getting online other than their cell phone. Throughout this report, we refer to this latter group as "smartphone-dependent" users.
- Certain groups of Americans rely on smartphones for online access at elevated levels, in particular:
  - Younger adults — 15% of Americans ages 18–29 are heavily dependent on a smartphone for online access.
  - Those with low household incomes and levels of educational attainment — Some 13% of Americans with an annual household income of less than US$30,000 per year are smartphone-dependent. Just 1% of Americans from households earning more than US$75,000

per year rely on their smartphones to a similar degree for online access.
- o Non-whites — 12% of African–Americans and 13% of Latinos are smartphone-dependent, compared with 4% of whites.
- Fully 97% of smartphone owners used text messaging at least once over the course of the study period, making it the most widely-used basic feature or app; it is also the feature that is used most frequently, as the smartphone owners in this study reported having used text messaging in the past hour in an average of seven surveys (out of a maximum total of 14 across the one-week study period). Younger smartphone owners are especially avid users of text messaging, but this group has by no means abandoned voice calls — 93% of smartphone owners ages 18–29 used voice or video calling on at least one occasion during the study period and reported doing so in an average of 3.9 surveys.
- Social networking, video consumption, and music/podcasts are especially popular with younger smartphone owners.

> 62% of smartphone owners have used their phone in the past year to look up information about a health condition.

McKinsey's 2017 Consumer Health Insights (CHI) Survey reports several findings with important implications for health insurers, providers, and other industry stakeholders. Four important emerging themes are reported (McKinsey, 2018; a summary appears in Walker, 2018) as follows:

- **Affordability:** The affordability of healthcare continues to be one of the most pressing consumer concerns and needs.
- **Continuity:** Many consumers lack continuity in their health care systems (e.g., in care delivery or health insurance).
- **Digital:** An increasing number of consumers are using digital health care tools, and interest in greater digital engagement continues to rise.
- **Engagement:** Consumers are willing to engage in solutions to reduce health care costs, but most believe that they cannot do so today.

Increasingly, consumers expect digital tools to be a core part of health care delivery. For example, most of this survey's respondents preferred digital solutions to phone/in-person solutions for many health care interactions.

Furthermore, 89% of the respondents said they were aware of digital appointment reminders; 55% said they had used them. As awareness of other digital tools increases, adoption is likely to rise. The respondents also selected many digitally advanced companies as the ones the health care industry should emulate.

Among the McKinsey survey respondents, digital tools were in high demand to:

- Shop for a health plan: 68%;
- Search for a doctor: 73%;
- Check my health information: 69%;
- Monitor health metrics: 77%;
- Pay my insurance bills: 79%; and
- Order prescription drugs or refills: 71%.

On the other hand, how is the health care industry responding to this rising demand by consumers/patients for digital engagement?

At present, the use of digital tools is lower in healthcare than in many other industries. For example, only 49% of the respondents in the McKinsey survey said they had used technologies offered by their health insurer. The primary ways the consumers have been using health insurers' technologies were to update personal information (17%), find out what benefits are included in their plan (15%), and identify the physicians and hospitals in their plan (13%) (Cordina *et al.*, 2018).

Some believe that this is due to health care organizations' concerns about health care privacy and security regulations. However, McKinsey reports that a previous consumer survey they conducted revealed that the comparatively low use of digital tools in health care was not due to data privacy concerns. It is possible that recent reports of massive data breaches in the health care industry are still holding up health care companies from further use of digital channels to communicate with consumers/patients.

The modern trend of patient-centered care and wellness promotion needs digital solutions that can manage information structures in a more content-specific and patient-oriented/centered way.

In summary,

- Modern health care marketing is about communication between the health care organization and stakeholders, especially customers/patients.

- Communication strategies must adopt modern modes of communication used by customers/patients.
  - *Outbound communications*: Modern health care customers/patients depend heavily on digital communications using internet-based technology (email, social media, and mobile platforms).
  - *Inbound communications*: Modern digital technology is also needed to gather useful information about industry and customers/patients efficiently, especially capturing, storing, and analyzing Big Data.
  - *Mutual communications*: Modern digital technology is also needed for meeting the emerging demands of data-driven medical care: video consults, telemarketing, patient portals, electronic medical records (EMR), healthcare communities, wellness tracking, and health apps.

10.3. Impact of Social Media on Health Care Industry and Marketing

The rise of social media globally has affected many different aspects of consumer life.

Social media has changed the way many consumers seek and exchange information with other people and with business organizations, including their health care providers, health plans, and pharmacies.

Mobile phones and applications have become an integral part of our lives. The internet allows people to research health information relating to symptoms, locate nearby doctors, research competence and cost of health care providers, and manage treatment and medications. Mostly via their portable or mobile electronic devices.

We will address the impact of social media on health care and how health care marketing should use social media in two steps.

> In this section, we will discuss the impact of social media in the health care industry affecting health care consumers, patients, health care management, and health care marketing.
>
> In Section 10.6, we will discuss opportunities and strategies for health care marketing to use social media.

10.3.1. What is social media?

A formal definition of social media given by Kietzmann and Hermkens (2011) is

> "Social media are interactive computer-mediated technologies that facilitate the creation and sharing of information, ideas, career interests, and other forms of expression via virtual communities and networks."

Social media is the collection of online communications channels dedicated to community-based input, interaction, content-sharing, and collaboration. Websites and applications dedicated to forums, microblogging, social networking, social bookmarking, social curation, and wikis are among the different types of social media.

Well known examples of social media platforms are Facebook, Twitter, Google+, Instagram, Wikipedia, and Linkedin.

Common features in social media platforms are as follows:

- They are interactive web and internet-based applications.
- They are generated by users who post texts, photos, videos, data, and information via online interactions with their digital equipment. "Users" here means individuals as well as organizations.
- Some users create websites or apps that form platforms or networks for interested users to create and exchange subject-specific material.

10.3.2. Mobile social media

Mobile devices such as smartphones and tablets have attracted consumers, especially younger people, to be engaged in social media creating the term "mobile social media".

Mobile social media provides great opportunities to health care marketing (as it has provided opportunities to mobile banking). It permits health care marketers to create and communicate customer/patient-centric messages with specific content. This offers opportunities for customer/patient engagement and customer relations development. As the customers/patients are almost constantly using, or have access to, their mobile devices, it allows marketers to incorporate the current location of the user (location-sensitivity) or the time delay between sending and receiving messages (time-sensitivity).

10.3.3. Social media use by consumers/patients has reached a very high level

Warden (2018) in an article, "30 Facts & Statistics on Social Media and Healthcare", presents the following key facts and statistics based on surveys by PricewaterhouseCoopers, Pew Research, and other leading health care marketing researchers. For sources used by the author, readers should refer to the original article.

Who uses social media for health care information and decision-making? Frequency and purpose of use:

- 74% of internet users engage in social media. 80% of those internet users are specifically looking for health information, and nearly half are searching for information about a specific doctor or health professional.
- 43% of baby boomers are starting to leverage social media for health care-related information. There are 27.4 million people over the age of 55 engaged in social networking, and 19 million of those use Facebook.
- 18–24-year-olds are more than twice as likely as 45 to 54-year-olds to use social media for health-related discussions.
- 42% of individuals viewing health information on social media look at health-related consumer reviews. This indicates that consumers are seeking others who have previous experience or knowledge on issues the consumer is interested in.
- 32% of US users post about their friends and family's health experiences on social media. For health care marketers, these persons are a source for collecting experiences of patients among their friends and families.
- 27% of patients comment or post status updates based on health-related experiences.
- 29% of patients viewing health information through social media are viewing other patients' experiences with their disease.
- Information on social media can have a direct influence on patients' decisions to seek a second opinion or choose a specific provider, particularly for people who are coping with a chronic condition or managing their diet, exercise, or stress.
- Some of the most engaged and active audiences on social media are individuals coping with a disability or chronic condition, including heart disease, cancer, diabetes, and people who have recently experienced a medical emergency.

Type of messages and content searched and used:

- Health care-related apps are a heavily used source. There are more than 65,000 health and medical apps now on the market. Nearly two-thirds are focused on general wellness issues like fitness, lifestyle and stress, and diet. The remainder is made up of apps focused on specific health conditions (9%), medication info and reminders (6%), and women's health and pregnancy (7%). Mental health apps led by disease-specific apps, followed by diabetes.
- 50% of health care apps available to consumers can be downloaded for free and are produced by a variety of developers.
- Of all the individuals viewing healthcare information on social media, 24% are viewing health-related videos/images posted by patients. Importance of videos is a frequently discussed topic in modern health care marketing.

  Prasad (2017) lists "Content marketing … health explanatory videos … mobile-friendly websites … health apps … social media presence …" as *Six Healthcare Marketing Trends in 2018.*

Physician activity on social media:

- 60% of consumers say they trust doctors' posts versus 36% who trust posts from a pharma firm.
- 88% of physicians use the internet and social media to research pharmaceutical, biotech, and medical devices.
- 53% of physician practices in the United States have a Facebook page.
- Mons (2016) reports that mobile is becoming the primary means of communication between providers within health care systems to diagnose health concerns, provide treatment recommendations, and offer specialist referrals.

Hospital activity on social media:

- Out of the 5,624 hospitals in the United States, only 1,501 are using a form of social media, which equates to approximately 26%.
- 81% of hospitals say service lines expressed an interest in participating in the hospital's social media strategy. California, New York, and Texas hospitals use social media the most of any other state.

- There are 695 hospitals on YouTube. There are at least 967 hospitals on Twitter, and around 3,000 hospitals have a company page on LinkedIn.
- YouTube traffic to hospital sites has increased by 119% year-over-year.

For another discussion, with statistics, on the impact of social media in health care, see Campanini (2016), "24 Outstanding Statistics and Figures on How Social Media Has Impacted the Health Care Industry". The statistics provided by Campanini conform the above statistics and trends. Two new statistics from Campanini worth noting are as follows:

- 19% of smartphone owners have at least one health app on their phone. Exercise, diet, and weight apps are the most popular.
- 41% of people say social media would affect their choice of a specific doctor, hospital, or medical facility.

These statistics and trends clearly indicate the importance of the use of social media by health care marketers to collect information and feedback, and communicate to enhance customer/patient experience.

10.3.4. B2B social media marketing in health care marketing

In health care, many organizations market their products and services to other business organizations. Examples are hospitals soliciting physicians for referrals, hospitals seeking managed care contracts from Medicare and Medicaid health plans, specialist physicians soliciting primary care physicians (and other specialists for referrals), ancillary providers such as physical therapists and audiologists depending on medical professionals for referrals, and pharmaceutical companies engaged in direct marketing to physicians.

Social media is a rich platform for such B2B marketing as well.

In general, it is reported that 93% of B2B marketers in all industries, and not specifically in health care, claim to be using social media as a marketing tactic (Vize and Sherrett, 2018).

Slayter (2017) cites HubSpot's 2015 Social Media Benchmarks Report, which found that health care companies were in the middle of the pack when it comes to using social media for marketing.

Slayter cites the experience of PreCheck, a health care background check and employment screening company that has successfully used social media marketing. The company shares interesting content on LinkedIn, Twitter, and Facebook to reach its audience and has grown followers exponentially (Slayter, 2017).

Hendricks (2016) in his article on "5 Strategies to Achieve Great B2B Healthcare Marketing" says, "Marketers have to realize that it's not simply selling to a business, it's selling to unique humans that are living in a world that's less responsive to traditional methods." In other words, in B2B marketing health care marketing should identify key persons in the other business (such as Chief Executive Officers (CEOs), Chief Financial Officers (CFOs), Chief Medical Officers (CMOs), and Physicians) and their behavior.

10.4. Online Sources for Health Care Marketing

With multiple social media sources and platforms available in modern times, which platforms are suitable for health care marketing to adopt?

Campanini (2016, citing Mashable, a well-known digital media website) presents the following as the most accessed online resources for health-related information by consumers and patients.

- 56% searched WebMD;
- 31% looked up Wikipedia;
- 29% browsed health magazine websites;
- 17% used Facebook;
- 15% looked through YouTube;
- 13% read up a blog or multiple blogs;
- 12% checked patient communities;
- 6% used Twitter; and
- 27% used none of the above.

Other notable statistics are as follows:

- Of parents who are likely to seek medical answers online:
    o 22% use Facebook;
    o 20% use YouTube; and
    o Of non-parents, 14% use Facebook and 12% use YouTube to search for health care-related topics (*Source*: Mashable).

Although Facebook keeps appearing as the source most used for health information, caution must be exercised in overdependence on it for health care marketing. For example, it is estimated that 52% of the adult population use Facebook every day. Although this is a large number, this also means that 48% of adult US citizens do not use it let alone depend on it. There are many views that even the users of Facebook do not believe everything placed by users on it.

Statista (2019) also provides the distribution of Facebook users by age as follows (in millions):

- 13–17 years of age   6.8
- 18–24 years of age   39.4
- 25–34 years of age   58.3
- 35–44 years of age   42.4
- 45–54 years of age   35.4
- 55–64 years of age   26.5
- 65+ years of age   21.1

This shows that use of Facebook as the primary social media platform.

As seen here, WebMD is by far the source consumers/patients turn to for health and health care services-related information. Therefore, an effective strategy for health care marketers would be to set up their health care organization or provider on Facebook, YouTube, and Twitter, and provide links to WebMD and other reliable health information sources.

> Although a health care provider or organization does not strictly need another website's permission to link, in good faith, that site to the organization's or provider's website, it is always a good idea to get permission. If you do link to another website without permission, be sure to link to its home page. Avoid picking selected portions from another website leaving doubts of ownership and authenticity in the minds of the consumer. Never use a linked site's trademark on your site without permission. You may be violating copyrights if you take graphics, photos, or videos from another site and publish in your site. Finally, be sure to place disclaimers regarding use of information from other sites you have directed the consumer to (Allbusiness Editors, 2018).

Note the following WebMD policy on linking:

"Linking Policy: For any article appearing on Medscape from WebMD, you may post the title, the author, and a brief summary of the article (or teaser), along with the URL linking to Medscape from WebMD on your site. Also, include a note after the link to the article notifying your readers that to view the entire article (and all other content on Medscape from WebMD), a one-time registration is needed, which is free of charge."

10.4.1. Multi-channel marketing

Consumers and patients interact with health systems on many platforms during their health care journey (information search, selecting providers, health care encounters, and recovery and follow-up). These include websites, social media, email, phone inquiries, and conventional sources like newspapers and TV.

The general consensus in the health care industry is that marketing should use multiple channels. This concept called "Multi-Channel Marketing" means the use of conventional and digital marketing channels in an optimal combination.

> Research shows that 72% of consumers want to be engaged with an integrated marketing approach, but only 39% are receiving that. Google found that consumers had 74% brand recall when the advertiser's integrated strategy carried across mobile, TV, and online (Mashable, 2012).

However, multi-channel marketing could lead to overload of information and inconsistent messages reaching consumers/patients.

Girardi (2018), in an article, "A Guide to Executing Impactful Multi-Channel Healthcare Campaigns", provides the following advice for successful implementation of multi-channel marketing in health care.

- **Integrate technology platforms to provide a seamless experience across channels**
Integrate electronic health record information, call center information, and other consumer/patient touch point data.

Also integrate customer/patient information collected from one channel to improve communication in another channel.

- **Personalize across channels**

Customers like to interact with organizations that personalize their communications. Efficient health care customer relationship management (HCRM) platforms that store and analyze customer/patient information derived from email, websites, social media, mail, and inquiries and complaints via call centers are able to provide information for this type of personalization.

- **Keep messaging consistent**

Messages via multiple channels should be consistent. Language and content can be varied depending on the channel, but the main message must be consistent.

Selecting the proper channel or multi-channels itself does not make a health care marketing effort successful. The choice must be backed up by other technologies that facilitate information collection, storage, and analysis to identify customer segments, niches and individual customers, the appropriate message, and timing. Some of these technologies are as follows:

- **Health Care Customer Relationship Management (HCRM) Platforms**

HCRM integrates inbound patient data from a variety of sources to build, launch, optimize, and measure multi-channel health care marketing campaigns. With an HCRM, it is possible to personalize marketing messages to improve patient engagement and relationships.

- **Content Management Systems (CMS)**

Content management systems (CMS) are software applications that are used to create and manage digital content on websites and other digital marketing channels. For example, if a consumer visited a search engine and searched for a health care product or service, a CMS will identify this customer for targeting other related health and product/service information.

WordPress is the most used CMS. It is reported to control nearly 60% of the CMS market! Nearly 30% of all websites are reported to be running on WordPress. Joomla and Drupal are the next most used CMS with 6.6% and 4.6% of the CMS market share, respectively. Magento is reported to have a 2.4% CMS market share (Mening, 2018).

10.5. Digital Health Care Marketing Tools

10.5.1. What is digital marketing?

- Digital marketing encompasses all marketing efforts that use an electronic device or the internet. Businesses leverage digital channels such as search engines, social media, email, and their websites to connect with current and prospective customers (Alexander, 2018).
- The marketing of products or services using digital channels to reach consumers. The key objective is to promote brands through various forms of digital media. Digital marketing extends beyond internet marketing to include channels that do not require the use of the internet. It includes mobile phones (both Short Message Service (SMS) and Multimedia Messaging Service (MMS)), social media marketing, display advertising, search engine marketing, and any other form of digital media (Financial Times, 2015).

> Experts are quick to point out that "digital" should not be interpreted as just another channel for marketing, and that it is a new approach to marketing based on a thorough understanding of customer behavior.

10.5.2. Motivation for adopting digital marketing in health care

Motivation for adopting digital marketing in health care stems from modern trends in health care consumer behavior. We saw in earlier discussions the modern health care consumer's/patient's use and dependence on digital technology for health and health care provider information. We also saw that as much as 80% of internet users are specifically looking for health information, and nearly half are searching for information about a specific doctor or health professional.

However, the health care industry is well known to lag behind other industries when it comes to innovative marketing approaches by about two years. This is applicable to digital marketing, too.

Some reasons advanced are that the health care industry is plagued by patient information privacy and security (HIPAA) compliance regulations and Food and Drug Administration (FDA) restrictions on how health care organizations can market their products and services. An example of the latter are restrictions on pharmaceutical marketing.

This trend seems to be changing. In a recent study, health care marketers reported a 35% increase in their digital advertising budgets; 31% reported spending more on social media; and 29% were increasing their website marketing budget (June 2013 MM&M/Ogilvy CommonHealth Healthcare Marketers Trends Report cited by Mood Media, 2018).

10.5.3. What is digital health care marketing (or digital marketing in health care)?

Industry experts and consultants have not generally tried to define the term "digital health care marketing". They seem to assume that it means adopting "digital marketing", as defined above, to the health care industry.

Their approach has been to describe strategies generally used to implement the concept. Some of these are discussed next.

Denton (2018), in an article, "3 Keys to Digital Marketing in Healthcare", outlines the following key features and strategies for digital health care marketing.

- **A responsive website:** Including websites that are mobile friendly.
- **Search engine optimization (SEO):** SEO is a technique used to increase the number of visitors to a website by obtaining a high-ranking placement in the search results page of a search engine. Usually, improved content, unique content, and skillful indexing improves SEO of a website.
- **Content marketing:** Blog posts, social media updates, e-books, webinars, videos. Content marketing will be discussed in Section 10.7.

Eddine (2018) presents the following key strategies for successful digital health care marketing:

- **An Easy-to-Navigate Website**

Eddine commends the Mayo Clinic's website on this feature in that it is user-friendly and has a robust offering right on the homepage. It is simple for visitors to make an appointment, contact Mayo Clinic, view resources, or log into the patient account.

- **An Informational Blog**

Eddine points out to 1% of all Google searches being related to medical symptoms, meaning 35 million online medical searches every day.

Consumers/Patients will build confidence and trust with the health care organization if it provides reliable and easy to comprehend information on health conditions, ideally, supported by contributions by patients with similar interests and conditions.

Blogs provide an ideal forum for patients to describe in their own way, often mixed with their own emotions, their patient experience.

Eddine commends The Harvard Medical School blog on this count as it has regularly updated content that covers a variety of health concerns, coupled with easy navigation to browse topics by health categories.

- **Resourceful Emails**

On top of good website design that makes access easy for consumers/patients who search for health information, outbound communications can still be done effectively by email.

Regular email information, videos, and short newsletters are a good strategy within a digital health care marketing plan. However, the message should be focused on narrow market segments, niches, or even individuals.

Eddine commends the newsletter email sent out by Akron Children's Hospital that focuses on health care issues of current interest. For example, during back to school times, it focuses on parents of young children.

- **Videos that Educate and Inspire**

Surveys show that digital media users increasingly prefer visual content and within that category, videos. A very effective approach in health care marketing is physicians and patients talking about health conditions and experiences in an eye-to-eye setting.

Eddine commends the video series used by Cleveland Clinic showing doctors speaking passionately about their areas of expertise and describing their views on caring for patients.

- Video Marketing Volume Statistics (Lister, 2019).
- 82% of Twitter users watch video content on Twitter; YouTube has over a billion users, almost one-third of total internet users; 45% of people watch more than an hour of Facebook or YouTube videos a week; more than 500 million hours of videos are watched on YouTube each day.

(*Continued*)

- o 87% of online marketers use video content.
- o One-third of online activity is spent watching video.
- o 85% of the US internet audience watch videos online.
- o The 25–34 (millennial) age group watches the most online videos and men spend 40% more time watching videos on the internet than women.
- o Over half of video content is viewed on mobile phones.
- o 92% of mobile video viewers share videos with others.

- **Strong SEO Attributes**

See the previous discussion on search engine optimization (SEO).

- **Engaging Social Media Strategy**

Engaging in social media marketing is essential for health care providers and organizations. Social media health care marketing is discussed in Sections 10.3 and 10.6.

Eddine refers the readers to Cedars-Sinai Medical Center, which she claims has the elements needed for a successful social media marketing strategy, which shares videos, and blog posts highlighting its staff caring for patients, upcoming events, and dozens of positive patient reviews. A feature highlighted by the author is a "Book Now" button that takes patients to the hospital's physician page where patients can find doctors in any specialty and even make appointments.

Hoag Medical center in Newport Beach, California, and Michigan Medicine at University of Michigan also have such features on their websites.

There are several other lists of tools suitable for digital marketing in general and in health care marketing. We list below two of these briefly only to save space and also because they partially overlap with tools we have already discussed above. For details, readers are advised to consult the sources which are listed under References at the end of the chapter.

- Digital Marketing Toolkit (Rowles, 2017):
    - o Data, insights, and blogs,
    - o Search,
    - o Social media,
    - o Email,
    - o Online advertising,

- o   Mobile, and
- o   Analytics.

- Red Crow Marketing (2015). Five Digital Tools Everyone in Healthcare Marketing Needs:
    - o   A mobile patient website;
    - o   Online rehabilitation and aftercare information;
    - o   Pre-registration to reduce patient wait time;
    - o   Online bill pay; and
    - o   Post-prescription refill request.

Summary of Techniques Commonly Used in Digital Health Care Marketing

- A website that is responsive (easy to negotiate) and interactive; a mobile friendly website.
- Strong Search Engine Optimization, so that the website pops up on top during consumer/patient searches.
- Engaging social media strategy. Multi-media channeling.
- Content Marketing using right platforms, that is focused on smaller target market niches, formatted with care, with catchy headlines, making target audience feel important.
- Informational blogs, resourceful emails, and inspiring videos, especially videos that have been found to be very popular among millennials and baby boomers.

10.6. Social Media Marketing in Health Care

In Section 10.3, we discussed, with statistics, the rise of social media globally affecting many different aspects of consumer life, and how social media has changed the way many consumers seek and exchange information with other people and with business organizations, including their health care providers, health plans, and pharmacies. We also saw how social media has changed the way consumers/patients interact with communities and health care providers; how mobile phones and applications have become an integral part of our lives; and how the internet now allows people to research health information relating to symptoms, locate nearby doctors, research competence and cost of health care providers, and manage treatment and medications, many of these actions via their portable or mobile electronic devices.

In this section we explore how health care marketing can adopt social media to market and communicate with consumers and patients.

"There is an increased focus on consumer engagement and content marketing through social channels" says Deborah Radcliffe, Former Director, Consumer Marketing, Digital Strategy and Innovation at Pfizer (cited in Affect Report, 2017).

In a Deloitte study previously mentioned by us, it was found that consumers' use of social media for health purposes rose from 18% to 21% between 2013 and 2015.

Objectives of social media marketing (SMM) are engaging customers, enhancing focus of marketing (by selecting proper target segments), and organizational improvements through consumer reviews and feedback (Mukesh and Rao, 2018).

10.6.1. Use of social media by health care marketers

Warden (2016) comments that health care marketers use social media less often than other marketers (*Source*: Content Marketing Institution). On average, health care marketers spend 23% of their total marketing budget on content marketing activities, compared to 31% for all marketers (*Source*: Content Marketing Institution).

Health care marketers appear to adopt a defensive posture for the fear of regulatory compliance mandates and potential financial and image consequences due to bad publicity.

Warden also reports that health care marketers tend to use print at higher rates than other marketers. With regards to print magazines, 47% of health care marketers use them versus 35% of other marketers, and as to print newsletters, 43% of health care marketers use them, versus 28% of other marketers (*Source*: Content Marketing Institution).

Popular social media sites in health care are reported as Facebook, Twitter, Linkedin, YouTube, and blogs.

Several authors have reported statistics on the impact of social media on health care marketing. For example, Campanini (2016) reports the following statistics using sources listed under each statistic.

- 31% of health care organizations have specific social media guidelines in writing (*Source*: Institute for Health).

- Two-thirds of doctors use social media for professional purposes, often preferring an open forum as opposed to a physician-only online community (*Source*: EMR Thoughts).
- YouTube traffic to hospital sites has increased 119% year-over-year (*Source*: Google's Think Insights).
- Global penetration of mobile devices has reached 87% as of 2011 (*Source*: International Telecommunications Union and mHealth Watch).
- 28% of health-related conversations on Facebook are supporting health-related causes, followed by 27% of people commenting about health experiences or updates (*Source*: Infographics Archive).
- 60% of social media users are most likely to trust social media posts and activity by doctors over any other group (*Source*: Infographics Archive).
- The Mayo Clinic's podcast listeners rose by 76,000 after the clinic started using social media (*Source*: Infographics Archive).
- 40% of people polled said information found on social media affects how someone coped with a chronic condition, their view of diet and exercise, and their selection of a physician (*Source*: HealthCare Finance News).

10.6.2. Principles of social media marketing in health care

Several industry experts and writers have developed principles on social marketing.

> As internet marketing, digital marketing, and social marketing are related and interwoven, we will always find in the literature overlapping principles and guidelines.

Given below are a set of general principles for health care marketers on social media marketing (adopted with suitable modifications from Aras (2011)).

- Social media marketing is a social behavior change strategy, not just advertising (in new media).
- Social media marketing is most effective when it activates people; it should not be limited to what appears to be clever slogans or messaging.
- Social media marketing should be targeted toward those who have a reason to care and who are ready for change. The aim should not be reaching everyone through a mass media blitz.

- Social media marketing is an organizational strategy requiring top management support, and efficient use of resources. It is not merely an image campaign.
- Social media marketing should be an integrated effort of all functions of the organization. It will not be a quick process undertaken by the marketing department.

Additional principles on internet and social media marketing include the following (Awl, 2011; Phillips, 2015; Sales and Marketing for You, 2015; Wood, 2012):

- Focus on value.
- Do not let offers run too long. Update with fresh new messages and offers.
- Provide for action by customer.
- Provide for interaction and expression by customer.
- Your posts, promotions, photos, and posturing should have a goal of sales, not branding.
- Engage the customer. Advertising alone is not enough.
- Do not write long description. Use testimonials, photos and videos.
- Good content marketing requires listening to customers' online discussions.
- Be patient. Social media and content marketing success does not happen overnight.
- Building relationships is important for social media marketing success. So, always acknowledge every person who reaches out to you.
- Consumers want to experience new things and influence.
- Avoid seeking commitments, contracts, memberships and personal information.

10.6.3. Consumer personalization

Consumer personalization has been discussed several times in this book. For example, content marketing is based on the premise that health care marketers can identify individual customers/patients and target them for the most appropriate communication.

In a BrightEdge survey of 500 search, content, and digital marketers in February 2018 (Nanji, *et al.*, 2018), 29% of respondents said they think consumer personalization would be the next big marketing trend in 2018.

Sterling (2015), in an article, "Consumers Want Personalization, but Retailers Just Can't Seem to Deliver", cites Retailer survey by Yes Lifecycle Marketing in September 2015 which reported that 52% retailers responded "identifying and engaging our most valued customers" as a key priority. Sterling also adds, "Many studies argue consumers are favorably disposed toward personalization. Some studies, addressing the privacy and 'big data' issues, are more nuanced than others. However, all seem to agree that consumers will share personal data to enable better experiences."

Sun (2017) in an article, "4 Consumer Trends Healthcare Marketers are Watching" reports from a survey by Accenture that 73% of consumers prefer to do business with retailers that create a personal, relevant shopping experience. Says Sun, "From a consumer standpoint, it feels like 1–1 communication, but it's actually fueled by marketing technology that allows this kind of communication on a mass scale by turning data retailers have on consumer behaviors into targeted advertising."

How does all this apply to health care marketing?

As for health care marketing, Sun (2017) cites health care industry digital marketing experts and says, "Marketers in healthcare are beginning to follow suit. On (name withheld) website, users can indicate if they are a patient, provider, donor, or one of four other personas. The site then serves up content and navigation that best suits their needs. Every page they visited and piece of content they downloaded fed an algorithm that automatically determined the next page or content asset to serve up. An expecting mother who starts clicking on information about a high-risk pregnancy might be served more content that educates her and puts her at ease about the risks."

> Sun (2017) concludes, again citing industry digital marketing experts, "It's only time before this type of hyper-personalization takes healthcare by storm."

It is true that the situation in health care is more constrained due to strict laws and regulations on privacy and security of individual health information. In other words, personalized messaging is more effective in health care marketing, but strict HIPAA regulations impose severe limitations on marketing using personal information. This subject is discussed in detail in Chapter 13.

10.6.4. Measuring effectiveness of social media marketing

As with all marketing efforts, measuring effectiveness of social media marketing strategies and specific programs is essential.

Mukesh and Rao (2018) present a framework for a social media audit. They suggest measurement of the following for each social media platform:

- Frequency of use;
- Engagement level;
- Number of followers; and
- Percentage change over time.

They also suggest the following key performance indicators (KPIs):

- **Increasing awareness:** Follower growth rate, content reach;
- **Generating leads and nurturing relations:** Sentiment indicator, share of conversation versus competitors, amplification rate, applause rate; and
- **Sale growth:** Social media ROI, sales from social media leads.

10.6.5. Case studies

An article, "5 Reasons Why Mayo Clinic Dominates Social Media in Healthcare", by Pennic (2014) provides a good description of Mayo Clinic's website, which almost undisputedly is recognized as the best website in the health care industry.

The 2013 Harris Poll EquiTrend survey named the Mayo Clinic website the top Health Information Website, ahead of WebMD.

The most popular searches are about a specific disease or medical problem; a particular medical treatment or procedure; diet, nutrition, and/or vitamins, and exercise or fitness information.

Apparently, Mayo Clinic deploys efficient SEO. When consumers research health care-related information, Mayo Clinic is one of the first websites to pop up.

Mayo clinic claims over 772,000 followers on Twitter and over 498,252 likes on Facebook. They are also active on YouTube with videos, podcasts, and blogs.

> All these programs at Mayo Clinic have come by conscious planning and organization. In 2010, the Mayo Clinic created the Mayo Clinic Center for Social Media which coordinates the Clinic's various social media initiatives and programs. Pennick (2014) reports, "Social media is at the forefront of missions/values" of Mayo Clinic, and, "Another good reason why the Mayo Clinic is on top of the social media game in healthcare, is because of support from executive leadership".

Mayo Clinic's philosophy of its social media is as follows: "Mayo Clinic believes individuals have the right and responsibility to advocate for their own health, and that it is our responsibility to help them use social media tools to get the best information, connect with providers and with each other, and inspire healthy choices."

Readers should visit Mayo Clinic's website using readily available links on the internet.

Other interesting and informative case studies on social media marketing in health care described by Gupta *et al.* (2013) include the following:

- Content Community — Centers for Disease Control and Prevention, and
- Collaborative Project/User Generated Content Internet Sexuality Information Services.

10.7 Content Marketing

10.7.1. Definition of content marketing

Content marketing is the marketing and business process for creating and distributing relevant and valuable content to attract, acquire, and engage a clearly defined and understood target audience — with the objective of driving profitable customer action (Content Marketing Institute, 2015).

The key words here are "a clearly defined and understood target market", "relevant and valuable content", and "to attract, acquire, and engagement".

Thus, content marketing, especially in a health care marketing context, is:

- Not directed at consumers at large. It is directed at smaller or even individual customers/patients.
- These smaller segments of customers/patients are derived from information from inbound information channels and from market research.
- The health care organization or provider has "understood" the outcome and emotional needs and expectations of this target segment or individuals.
- Content of message and communication should be relevant and valuable to each segment or individual defined.
- The ultimate objective is to immediately attract the attention of the target customer/patient/segment, and then long-term engagement through building customer/patient confidence and trust in the health care provider or organization.

"Content marketing is about delivering the content your audience is seeking in all the places they are searching for it. It is the effective combination of created, curated, and syndicated content" (Content Marketing Institute, 2015). This idea is related to multi-channel marketing we discussed previously.

Content marketing has become the key of a successful online marketing campaign and the most important tool of digital marketing (Baltes, 2015). In fact, Baltes calls content marketing "The Fundamental Tool of Digital Marketing", further adding, "Strong brands are based on a story that communicates who is the company; authenticity is to communicate what you really are". In other words, content marketing should be based on the company's values.

10.7.2. Principles and guidelines for effective content marketing

Content marketing specialists indicate several guidelines in creating a content marketing strategy. These include the following:

- Agrawal (2016)
    - Tying the message to current hot related news items. Health care organizations can attach their message to new discoveries in the field like new research findings and cures. Offer the organization's and experts' analysis.
    - Humanize your company.
    - Use of videos. "Video is king," says Agrawal.
    - Questions and answers focusing on common questions.
- Nite (2017)
    - Use data stories and infographics.
    - Include patient perspectives, genuine customer/patient images and voices.
    - Latest news (as suggested by Agrawal above).
    - Interactive content.
    - Influencer content.

Obviously, content of digital marketing communications appeals differently to various audiences. Content appealing to younger consumers may not be equally appealing to older consumers.

Clark (2019a) suggest the following for effective content marketing to this target group:

- Use the right formatting.
  Clark suggests larger more spacious formatting to this somewhat older group.

- Do not use too many abbreviations.
  Use full words and terms not abbreviations, especially with medical and digital technology discussions.

- Develop catchy headlines.
  In health care marketing, this would mean using headlines that immediately convey the topic and value to the consumer/patient. E.g., A Medical Group with All Specialists in One Building.

- Do not make boomers feel old.
  In health care marketing this would apply to many age and ethnic groups. Special groups must feel important that they belong to that group.

- Choose the right platforms.
  Though baby boomers are active on Twitter and Instagram, Clark suggests Facebook as a better platform for this age group.

- Focus on blogs and video content.
  A view that we keep seeing again and again — use videos.

In a companion article, "How to Connect with Millennials Through Content Marketing", this author (Clark, 2019b), sets out a set of similar guidelines:

- Remember the mantra.
  Clark highlights a special nature of millennials — they dislike hard sells with aggressive sales pitches. She suggests gentle but authoritative content.

- Do not underestimate their intelligence.
  They are most likely educated and not ill-informed. Studies show that millennials tend to do online research before they buy anything.

- Millennials are high on social justice.
  They would not like messages that sound like favoring one political spectrum or another.

- They like to make optimal looking decisions quickly.
  They are more likely to respond to limited-time or limited-quantity offers that make sense rather than postponing until they do time-consuming comparisons and research.

- They like visual content.
  Include graphics and videos in content aimed at millennials.

> Millenniums and baby boomers are just two groups in the health care market. The lesson we learn from the above discussion is that health care marketers should thoroughly understand behavior of key demographic, social, and ethnic segments, and then tailor the message content accordingly. One message does not fit all.

10.7.3. B2B content marketing (e.g., hospitals, pharma companies, and HMOs to physicians)

Infographics (2018) discusses content types that have been most effective in B2B environments. These are as follows:

- Research reports,
- Videos,
- Webinars,
- Case studies, and
- Articles and blogs.

This report also presents views of B2B buyers on what vendors can do to improve content quality. These include the following:

- Using more data and research to support content,
- Curbing the sales messaging,
- Providing more benchmarking data, and
- Including more thought-leader analyses/insights.

According to marketers, the most effective digital platforms/channels for B2B content promotions are Email, LinkedIn, YouTube, Twitter, SlideShare, and Facebook.

10.7.4. Case studies

NewsCred (2015) presents the following notable case studies of successful content marketing in health care.

- Johnson & Johnson's campaign to market its social responsibility. "Care Inspires Care" campaign where the company launched a Facebook page where people could share acts of care followed up by further campaigns providing scholarships to students who want to become nurses.
- GE Healthcare's campaign to attract technology competent employees. A series of innovative social media and content campaigns has boosted GE among millennial college graduates qualified to work in technology or health care. The videos showcase a creative and casual workplace culture highlighting GE Healthcare as a great employer for millennials.
- Arkansas Children's Hospital's campaign to raise awareness of, and reduce, teen deaths. The campaign featured a downloadable parent–teen driving agreement, infographics on topics like fireworks safety, and an Injury Prevention Center — a content hub — providing fact sheets about risks to child safety.
- Melanoma Patients Australia to reduce melanoma risks in young people. The campaign, which reached over 2 million people, targeted Australians at the exact moment they put themselves at risk for skin damage. It also drove a 1,371% increase to the Skincheck.com mobile site.
- United Health Care's social media campaign to promote women's health. As part of Source4Women, its digital and social media initiative promoting women's health, United Health Care created the #WeDareYou campaign. Every month, United Health Care posts a series of challenges, daring women to live healthier lifestyles.

Also see, Mayo Clinic's Blog: Sharing Mayo Clinic (https://sharing.mayoclinic.org/), which shares stories from patients, healthcare providers, and other Mayo Clinic employees.

10.8. Additional Implementation Issues

So far, we have discussed key issues relating to integrating digital technology with health care marketing. These included impact of modern digital technology and social media on health care marketing, digital and social media marketing tools and guidelines, and content marketing.

In this last section of the chapter, we discuss a few additional issues on implementing modern digital technology in health care marketing. These are as follows:

- Integrating key marketing activities.
- Factors influencing success of new technology in health care marketing.
- Mistakes to avoid in implementing digital marketing in health care marketing.

10.8.1. Integrating key marketing activities

As we have seen in earlier discussions, there are many tasks involved in organizing and implementing digital marketing in health care.

These include handling inbound information from, and about, customers/consumers/patients, customer data storage and analysis for segmentation, developing marketing campaigns, content management, managing marketing campaigns, integrating multiple marketing channels such as websites, blogs, email and social media, and marketing performance measurement and evaluation. While some of these activities are computerized, others are handled manually by managers. The modern trend is to integrate most of these activities via computer-based platforms. This concept is called *Marketing Automation*.

Marketing automation integrates computer platforms we have previously discussed, like CMS (Content Management Systems) and CRM/CXM (Customer Relations/Experience Management Systems).

In general, marketing automation is technology that manages marketing processes and multifunctional campaigns, across multiple channels, automatically (Salesforce, 2019). With marketing automation, businesses can target customers with automated messages across email, web, social, and text.

Salesforce (2019) states,

> "Marketing automation lets you implement a digital marketing strategy without having to manually press 'send' on each and every email, message, campaign, or post you create. Good automation tools help you identify your

audience, design the right content, and automatically trigger actions based on schedules and customer behavior."

Additionally, marketing automation provides tools to measure effectiveness of marketing efforts and campaigns. Salesforce (2019) reports that in surveys of marketing professionals, 63% have indicated that the ability to set measurable objectives, and perform measurements, for each of their campaigns is the biggest benefit of marketing automation. Marketo (2017) agrees highlighting that marketing automation enables measurement of results and ROI of digital marketing campaigns to know which programs are working.

10.8.2. Marketing automation in health care marketing

Druckenmiller (2017) strongly suggests integration of a marketing automation tool, CRM platform, and CMS system in health care marketing, which he calls a "healthcare marketing utopia".

In that sense, some consider Marketing Automation as a subset of CRM or CXM that focuses on the definition, segmentation, scheduling, and tracking of marketing campaigns (Salesforce, 2019).

Druckenmiller (2017) adds that the main goal of marketing automation using appropriate software in health care marketing is to automate the engagement process enabling the health care system or provider to continuously communicate with a wide range of consumers and patients.

With the data that health care CRM software can provide, marketing automation campaigns can be highly personalized. The CRM system is the data storage system that stores all consumer and patient information as well as helps to acquire and keep patients by making interactions personalized.

The marketing automation tool comes into play as a way for health care marketers to act upon this wealth of data. It streamlines, automates, and measures marketing tasks and workflow in addition to tracking and automating interactions with patients and consumers across channels like email.

The integration of marketing automation tools and CRM tools would allow health care marketers to personalize campaigns consistently. Patient engagement improves for both inactive customers/patients whose relationships should be kept alive and current patients who need to be retained.

The following is an example scenario of marketing automation integrated with CRM in a health care organization, adopted from Druckenmiller (2017).

"A CRM platform is set up to deliver an acquisition marketing campaign for a bariatrics service, with a lead goal of 800 people and a budget of $100,000. The target for this campaign is a middle-density population urban environment of consumers aged 25–55 years old.

"The health system is running display ads, social ads, and search, as well as a light remarketing campaign. Because bariatric services typically have significant lead times, a remarketing campaign is helpful to reinforce an individual's care decision over the long term. The health system wishes to ensure that the content that's reaching prospects is consistent with content on the primary website and across many other digital vehicles that reference bariatric services.

"Marketing Automation comes in to provide high-level nurturing for consumers that are lingering well past 6 or 7 months and have not yet sought clinical services. It also engages patients with cross-sell and up-sell content before and after their bariatric consultations or appointments. Marketing Automation also can reach recent patients who have had surgery for post-discharge and retention strategies, increasing chances of retention."

10.8.3. Factors influencing success of new technology in health care marketing

Implementation of new technology in organizations will be successful only if the organization is ready for and capable of adopting new technologies, and the customers who are expected to engage in these new technologies also accept and adopt them. This is true for health care organizations' implementation of digital technology and adoption of the same for health care marketing.

(a) *Factors for Success I: Organizational Readiness to Adopt New Technology (Gunawardane, 2017)*

There is a vast body of research and knowledge on organizational success in adopting change in general, and specifically new technology. It is generally accepted that success of implementing new technology depends on many high-level organizational factors such as leadership, organization's resources, organization structure, and organizational culture. We discussed these factors as an organization's "internal environment" in Chapter 3.

Top management commitment and support for adoption of new technology is well established in the literature. For example, Ramaseshan *et al.* (2015) in a survey of 257 service managers in USA reported in their paper, "Firm Self-Service Technology Readiness", find the need for what they called "Managerial Acquiescence", i.e., management understanding the need for new technology, management being proactive in the technological environment, management commitment to adopt new technologies, and management being open to new ideas on new technology. VMware (2006) points out the importance of "Top–down Sponsorship" meaning strong top management awareness and support. This study also highlights the importance of top management adopting the change as one affecting the whole organization and not affecting only one part of the organization, e.g., sales or customer service.

The next level of factors for successful adoption and implementation of new technologies has to do with organizational culture, which engages employees with the change. Weiner (2009) calls these elements, "Change Commitment" and "Change Efficacy". Change Efficacy, an important factor in process theories of motivation, is the employees' collective assessment of their ability to adopt and implement the new technology. This is related to employees' appraisal of task demands, resource availability, and other situational factors (Weiner, 2009). This coupled with the value assigned to the success, both the value to the organization and the benefits for them by way of improved processes and recognition (called "valence" in motivation theories), is what determines the total motivation or commitment to the change.

Finally, customer alignment with the change and channel integration (acceptance of, and ability to adopt, new technology by players in the supply chain such as network physicians) is also important for a successful outcome of the new technology.

These factors can be summarized as follows (Chan and Ngai, 2007; Gunawardane, 2017; Huron, 2018; Li *et al.*, 2012; Ramaseshan *et al.*, 2015; VMWare, 2006; Weiss, 2009).

- **Perceived Advantages:** The company performing sound cost–benefit analysis of gains from adopting IT (compared to the present system). These include direct advantages and indirect advantages.
- **Customer Alignment:** Customer/patient realization of benefits of new digital technology and accepting the same (this concept is discussed in the next section under "Factors for Success II: Health Care Customer Willingness to Adopt New Technology").
- **Organizational Consensus and Employee Buy in:** Employee involvement in system evaluation and implementation, training on integration of the new technology to existing processes, and handling implementation problems. Publicizing throughout the organization.

- **Designing for the Big Picture,** but deploying/implementing incrementally.
- **Channel Integration:** Acceptance of, and ability to adopt, new technology by players in the supply chain such as network physicians, suppliers, and contractors. It is vital that these partners are involved in the implementation; their needs are integrated; compatibility with their systems is ensured; and they are oriented and made knowledgeable of the new technology.
- **Organization for Implementation:** Forming a Core Implementation Team and a larger team represented by all departments of the organization.
- **System Quality:** Invest in proven technology, not in unknown technology that may be cheaper.
- **Information Quality:** System quality is useless if care is not taken to ensure quality, speed, and integrity of information that would flow through the system.
- **Simplified Management and Maintenance**

Li *et al.* (2012) report that "System Quality", "Information Quality", and "Simplified Management and Maintenance" accounted for 56.7% of the variance of the success of implementation in the company they studied.

(b) *Factors for Success II: Health Care Customer Willingness to Adopt New Technology*

Despite the ever-increasing use of the internet, social media, email, and similar digital technology by consumers, health care marketers should not assume that their target customers/patients will be receptive to the marketers' choice of channels and communication frequency and content.

We have previously seen that acceptance of digital technology varies among health care consumers by demographic variables like age (e.g., seniors, teens, millennials, and baby boomers), gender, social status and ethnicity.

Therefore, it will be prudent to look at concepts and applications relating to acceptance of new technology by consumers.

We start by a brief summary of factors affecting customer acceptance of new technology from a study in the hospitality industry (Rosenbaum and Wong, 2015).

- **Self-confidence**

Self-confidence with new technologies would be a positive factor for adoption.

- **Feeling of self-control**
Feeling of self-control by handling own matters without human assistance or interaction would also be a positive factor.

- **Discomfort with technology**
Feeling that the new technology would not be flexible enough for one's needs is a negative factor.

- **Insecurity**
Feelings of insecurity whether the transaction will go through and will get recorded properly, or uncertainty of safety of personal and health information, is a negative factor.

There are two well-known models on adoption of new technologies by customers. These are as follows:

- The Technology Adoption Model, and
- The Technology Readiness Index.

10.8.4. The Technology Acceptance Model (TAM) (Davis, 1989)

This is one of the most widely used models. The two primary predictors in TAM that affect technology usage are:

- Perceived usefulness and
- Perceived ease of use.

Perceived usefulness is the key determinant of intention to use. In fact, perceived ease of use is thought of as a determinant that enhances perceived usefulness. If so, what influences a person's perceived usefulness of a technology?

Venkatesh and Davis (2000) suggest, in a model they call TAM 2, that perceived usefulness is determined by

- **Subjective Norms:** Perception that most people who are important to the customer think he should or should not use the technology.
- **Voluntariness:** The extent to which the customer perceives the adoption to be non-mandatory.

- **Image:** The degree to which use of the technology is perceived to enhance one's status in his social system.
- **Job or Task Relevance:** Perception that the technology is applicable to one's job or task.
- **Output Quality:** How well the technology/system performs the tasks involved.
- **Tangibility:** Tangibility of the results of using the technology.

Empirical studies have found that TAM consistently explains about 40% of the variance in usage intentions and behavior toward technology acceptance by customers. TAM has become well-established as a powerful robust model for predicting customer/user acceptance (Venkatesh and Davis, 2000).

10.8.5. The Technology Acceptance Model (TAM) (Davis, 1989)

This approach is based on the concept that an individual's personality influences the potential acceptance of technology in general. Technology readiness is viewed as a composite of four personality dimensions:

- **Optimism:** It is defined as "a positive view of technology and a belief that it [technology] offers people increased control, flexibility, and efficiency in their lives". It generally captures positive feelings about technology.
- **Innovativeness:** It is defined as "a tendency to be a technology pioneer and thought leader". This dimension generally measures to what degree individuals perceive themselves as being at the forefront of technology adoption.
- **Discomfort:** It is defined as "a perceived lack of control over technology and a feeling of being overwhelmed by it". This dimension generally measures the fear and concerns people experience when confronted with technology.
- **Insecurity:** It is defined as a "distrust of technology and skepticism about its ability to work properly". This dimension focuses on concerns people may have in the face of technology-based transactions.

Optimism and innovativeness are drivers of technology readiness. A high score on these dimensions will increase overall technology readiness. Discomfort and insecurity, on the other hand, are inhibitors of technology readiness. Thus, a high score on these dimensions will reduce overall technology readiness. Results show that the four dimensions are fairly independent, each of them making a unique contribution to an individual's technology readiness.

> Above all, ensure that the technology-supported service encounter works. There is nothing worse than a new technology, e.g., a website or a link, that breaks down when customers use it.

10.8.6. Common mistakes to avoid in implementing digital marketing in health care marketing

We conclude this chapter by summarizing a few good guidelines on avoiding some common mistakes in digital health care marketing.

- Planning and implementing digital technologies in isolation. Marketing and IT (information technology) cannot work in isolation (Brinker, 2016).
- Failure to perform proper segmentation (FrescoData, 2015).

  As discussed in Chapter 8, segmenting the health care market using scientific and rational criteria, using valid data, is the first essential step in health care marketing. We also discussed the modern trend in health care marketing to divide the target market into smaller segments and niches, and in some circumstances, to customer-centric individual levels.

  Investing in expensive high technology to implement digital marketing is ineffective unless directed at the correct segment or niche of the market.
- Failure to focus digital marketing (actually, all marketing) strategies on customer/patient experience. CX/PX, based on the customer/patient entire journey, should be used as the primary catalyst for implementing digital technology initiatives.
- Short-term customer contact perspective. Digital marketing should aim to establish long-term relationships and engagement.
- Limiting focus of digital technology only to internal processes, e.g., EMRs, EHRs, clinical and quality management/utilization management processes in a hospital or health plan. Focus of digital technology must be substantially on customer's life when he or she is not a patient.
- Not establishing analytical goals of a campaign (Schiff, 2016).
- Insufficient attention to search engine optimization.
- Not focusing social media marketing at proper segments/niches. Social media marketing must focus beyond common demographic factors such

as age, gender, and education. It must be focused at narrower targets by customer/patient interest, by needs and topics searched, and life events.
- Lack of a customer-centric mindset (Schiff, 2016).
- Insufficient focus on mobile channels; lack of integration of multi-channel communication.
- Use of impersonal and non-authentic messages in digital marketing. Modern customers are quick to identify non-authentic messages. Such efforts do not help establishing customer/patient trust.
- Not measuring digital marketing success regularly (FrescoData, 2015). Not setting up metrics to measure digital marketing effort. For example, comparing different platforms used such as Facebook, Google, and LinkedIn, and hits, inquiries, and enrollments/purchases each platform has generated. Similarly, comparing alternative message content used.

References

Adil, R. (2012). "The Usage of Tablets in the Healthcare Industry", http://www.healthcareitnews.com/blog/usage-tablets-healthcare-industry?page=0. Accessed March 1, 2019.

Affect (2017). "Healthcare Marketing 2018: Guide to Meeting New Priorities in a Shifting Environment", http://www.affect.com/wp-content/uploads/2017/11/Affect_Healthcare_White_Paper.pdf. Accessed October 15, 2018.

Agrawal, A. J. (2016). "7 Content Marketing Tips for Healthcare Companies", *Forbes CMO Network*, https://www.forbes.com/sites/ajagrawal/2016/01/17/7-content-marketing-tips-for-healthcare-companies/#59bfcab63c44. Accessed November 5, 2018.

AIMS (American Institute of Medical Sciences and Education) (2018). "The Impact of Technology on Healthcare", https://www.aimseducation.edu/blog/the-impact-of-technology-on-healthcare/. Accessed January 11, 2019.

Alexander, L. (2018). "What is Digital Marketing?", https://blog.hubspot.com/marketing/what-is-digital-marketing. Accessed March 1, 2019.

Allbusiness Editors (2018). "Do You Need Another Web Site's Permission to Link Your Site to Theirs?", https://www.allbusiness.com/do-you-need-another-web-sites-permission-to-link-your-site-to-theirs-653-1.html. Accessed March 6, 2019.

Anderson, M., Perrin, A. and Jiang, J. (2018). "11% of Americans Don't Use the Internet. Who are They?", *Pew Research Center*, http://www.pewresearch.org/fact-tank/2018/03/05/some-americans-dont-use-the-internet-who-are-they/. Accessed November 22, 2018.

Aras, R. (2011). "Social Marketing in Healthcare", *Australasia Medical Journal*, 4 (8), 418–424. Published online, https://www.ncbi.nlm.nih.gov/pmc/articles/PMC3562881/. Accessed March 5, 2019.

Awl, D. (2011). *Facebook Me: A Guide to Society, Sharing and Promoting on Facebook*. Berkeley, California, Peachpit Press.

Baltes, L. P. (2015). "Content Marketing — The Fundamental Tool of Digital Marketing", *Bulletin of the Transylvania University of Brasov. Economic Sciences: Series V*, 8 (2), 111–118.

Biesdorf, S. and Niedermann, F. (2014). "Healthcare's Digital Future", https://www.mckinsey.com/industries/healthcare-systems-and-services/our-insights/healthcares-digital-future. Accessed January 10, 2019.

Brinker, S. (2016). "How Marketing Technology Could Transform Healthcare", *Chief Marketing Technologist Blog*, https://chiefmartec.com/2016/01/marketing-technology-transform-healthcare/. Accessed March 4, 2019.

Campanini, S. (2016). "24 Outstanding Statistics & Figures on How Social Media Has Impacted the Health Care Industry", May 12, 2016, https://www.linkedin.com/pulse/24-outstanding-statistics-figures-how-social-media-has-campanini. Accessed January 3, 2019.

Chan, S. C. H. and Ngai, E. W. T. (2007). "A Qualitative Study of Information Technology Adoption: How Ten Organizations Adopted Web-Based Training", *Information Systems Journal*, 17, 289–315.

Clark, A. (2019a). "How to Connect with Baby Boomers with Content Marketing", https://www.business2community.com/content-marketing/how-to-connect-with-baby-boomers-through-content-marketing-02176145. Accessed March 5, 2019.

Clark, A. (2019b). "How to Connect with Millennials Through Content Marketing", https://www.business2community.com/content-marketing/connecting-with-millennials-through-content-marketing-02173023. Accessed March 5, 2019.

Conick, H. (2017). "Technology No. 1 Concern of Health Care Marketing in 2018", *AMA*, https://www.ama.org/publications/eNewsletters/Marketing-News-Weekly/Pages/technology-top-concern-healthcare-marketing--2018.aspx. Accessed October 15, 2018.

Content Marketing Institute (2015). "What is Content Marketing?", https://contentmarketinginstitute.com/what-is-content-marketing/. Accessed October 15, 2018.

Cordina, J., Jones, E. P., Kumar, R. and Martin, C. P. (2018). "Healthcare Consumerism 2018: An Update on the Journey", McKinsey & Company, https://www.mckinsey.com/industries/healthcare-systems-and-services/our-insights/healthcare-consumerism-2018. Accessed October 23, 2018.

Davis, F. D. (1989). "Perceived Usefulness, Perceived Ease of Use, and User Acceptance of Information Technology", *MIS Quarterly*, 13, 319–339.

Denton, N. (2018). "3 Keys to Digital Marketing in Healthcare", https://blog.hubspot.com/insiders/digital-marketing-in-healthcare. Accessed January 12, 2019.

Druckenmiller, G. (2017). "How Does Marketing Automation Lead to a Proactive Healthcare Marketing Department?", Evariant, https://www.evariant.com/blog/marketing-automation-proactive-marketing. Accessed March 7, 2019.

Eddine, L. (2018). "6 Keys to a Strong Healthcare Digital Marketing Strategy", Kuno Creative, https://www.kunocreative.com/blog/strong-healthcare-digital-marketing-strategy. Accessed March 3, 2019.

Engelhardt, D. (2018). "7 Ways iPads are Being Used in Healthcare", ReadyDock, http://blog.readydock.net/bid/340500/7-Ways-iPads-are-Being-Used-in-Healthcare. Accessed January 11, 2019.

Financial Times (2015). "Definition of Digital Marketing", http://lexicon.ft.com/Term?term=digital-marketing. Accessed March 2, 2019.

Forbes (2013). "5 Ways Technology is Transforming Health Care", https://www.forbes.com/sites/bmoharrisbank/2013/01/24/5-ways-technology-is-transforming-health-care/#17f75ca826c5. Accessed December 4, 2018.

Forer, L. (2018). "The State of B2B Content Marketing: 6 Things Every Brand Needs to Know", Infographic, https://www.mdgadvertising.com/marketing-insights/infographics/the-state-of-b2b-content-marketing-6-things-every-brand-needs-to-know-infographic/. Accessed November 6, 2018.

FrescoData (2015). "4 Common Mistakes to Avoid in Healthcare Digital Marketing", https://frescodata.com/blog/4-common-mistakes-to-avoid-in-healthcare-digital-marketing/. Accessed March 4, 2019.

Girardi, C. (2018). "A Guide to Executing Impactful Multi-Channel Healthcare Campaigns", Evariant, https://www.evariant.com/blog/guide-impactful-multi-channel-healthcare-campaigns/. Accessed March 3, 2019.

Gunawardane, G. (2017). *Service Management: Concepts, Principles and Applications for Sri Lanka*, Colombo, Sri Lanka: Dayawansa Jayakody & Company.

Gupta, A., Tyagi, M. and Sharma, D. (2013). "Use of Social Media Marketing in Healthcare", *Journal of Health Management*, 15 (2), 293–302.

Hendricks, D. (2016). "5 Strategies to Achieve Great B2B Healthcare Marketing", Socialnomics, https://socialnomics.net/2016/06/10/5-strategies-to-achieve-great-b2b-healthcare-marketing/. Accessed March 5, 2019.

Huron (2018). "Ensure Successful Adoption of Your Technology Solutions", https://www.huronconsultinggroup.com/resources/enterprise-solutions/successful-adoption-technology-solutions. Accessed March 4, 2019.

Infographics (2018). "The State of B2B Content Marketing: 6 Things Every Brand Needs to Know", https://www.mdgadvertising.com/marketing-insights/infographics/the-state-of-b2b-content-marketing-6-things-every-brand-needs-to-know-infographic/. Accessed November 7, 2018.

Kang, C. (2013). "New Resources Help Lower Hospital Readmissions", http://westfaironline.com/57272/new-resources-help-lower-hospital-readmissions/. Accessed March 2, 2019.

Kietzmann, J. H. and Kristopher, H. (2011). "Social Media? Get Serious! Understanding the Functional Building Blocks of Social Media", *Business Horizons*, 54 (3), 241–251.

Klimpel, K. (2018). "How Digital Technology is Transforming Healthcare", https://www.rn.com/nursing-news/how-digital-technology-is-transforming-healthcare/. Accessed January 10, 2019.

Li, S.-H., Yen, D. C., Hu, C.-C., Lu, W.-H. and Chiu, Y.-H. (2012). "Identifying Critical Factors for Corporate Implementing Virtualization Technology", *Computers in Human Behavior*, 28 (6), 2244-2257.

Lister, M. (2019). "37 Staggering Video Marketing Statistics for 2018", WordStream, https://www.wordstream.com/blog/ws/2017/03/08/video-marketing-statistics. Accessed March 3, 2019.

Marketo (2017) "What is Digital Marketing?", https://www.marketo.com/digital-marketing/. Accessed March 7, 2019.

Mashable (2012). "5 Huge Digital Marketing Trends You Can't Afford to Ignore", https://mashable.com/2012/03/05/future-digital-marketing-trends/#UGhaQ98FamqU. Accessed March 3, 2019.

Mayo Clinic (2019). "Robotic Surgery", https://www.mayoclinic.org/tests-procedures/robotic-surgery/about/pac-20394974. Accessed January 12, 2019.

McKinsey (2018). "Healthcare Consumerism 2018: An Update on the Journey", https://www.mckinsey.com/industries/healthcare-systems-and-services/our-insights/healthcare-consumerism-2018. Accessed January 2, 2018.

Mening, R. (2018). "Popular CMS by Market Share", https://websitesetup.org/popular-cms/. Accessed March 3, 2019.

Michigan Daily (2014). "UMHS Doctors Implant First Bionic Eye", https://www.michigandaily.com/news/umhs-doctors-implant-first-bionic-eye. Accessed January 2, 2019.

Mons, J. (2016). "Mobile Technology's Impact on Healthcare Marketing", https://www.mediapost.com/publications/article/266756/mobile-technologys-impact-on-healthcare-marketing.html. Accessed January 4, 2019.

Mood Media (2018). "Developing Marketing Objectives in the Healthcare Industry", https://us.moodmedia.com/industry/developing-marketing-objectives-in-the-healthcare-industry/. Accessed March 5, 2019.

Mukesh, M. and Rao, A. (2018). "Social Media Measurement and Monitoring." In: Rishi, B. and Bandyopadhyay, S. (Eds.), *Contemporary Issues in Social Media Marketing*, Routledge.

Nanji, A. (2018). "Online Marketers: The Next Big Trend in Marketing", https://www.marketingprofs.com/charts/2018/33819/online-marketers-the-next-big-trend-in-marketing. Accessed March 6, 2019.

NewsCred (2015). "Health Care Content Marketing: 5 Awesome Case Studies", https://insights.newscred.com/health-care-content-marketing/. Accessed March 5, 2019.

Nite, J. (2017). "Don't Skip Leg Day: 7 Content Marketing Must-Haves for Healthcare Marketers", *Top Rank Marketing Blog*, http://www.toprankblog.com/2017/06/content-marketing-must-haves-healthcare/. Accessed November 8, 2018.

Parasuraman, A. (2000). "Technology Readiness Index: A Multiple Item Scale to Measure Readiness to Embrace New Technologies", *Service Research*, 2 (4), 307–320.

Parasuraman, A. and Colby, C. L. (2001). *Techno-Ready Marketing: How and Why Your Customers Adopt Technology*, New York: Free Press.

Pennic, J. (2014). "5 Reasons Why Mayo Clinic Dominates Social Media in Healthcare", https://hitconsultant.net/2014/02/17/5-reasons-mayo-clinic-dominates-social-media-in-healthcare/#.XILGvndFzIU. Accessed March 5, 2019.

Pennic, J. (2014). "5 Reasons Why Mayo Clinic Dominates Social Media in Healthcare", https://hitconsultant.net/2014/02/17/5-reasons-mayo-clinic-dominates-social-media-in-healthcare/#.XlstWUBFxlA. Accessed October 24, 2019.

Phillips, K. (2015). "6 Principles That Must Be Applied to Social Media Marketing", https://www.entrepreneur.com/article/251034. Accessed February 28, 2020.

Prasad, A. (2017). "6 Healthcare Marketing Trends in 2018: How to Leverage Them", https://blog.gmrwebteam.com/2018-healthcare-marketing-trends-how-to-leverage-them/. Accessed January 12, 2019.

Ramaseshan, B., Kingshott, R. P. J. and Stein, A. (2015). "Firm Self-Service Technology Readiness", *Journal of Service Management*, 26 (5), 751–776.

Red Crow Marketing (2015). "Five Digital Tools Everyone in Healthcare Marketing Needs", https://www.redcrowmarketing.com/2015/01/08/five-digital-tools-everyone-in-health-care-marketing-needs/. Accessed March 4, 2019.

Rogers, A. M. (2014). "The Best Health Care Content Marketing in 2014", *Marketing Health Services*, https://www.ama.org/publications/eNewsletters/MHSNewsletter/Pages/the-best-health-care-content-marketing-in-2014.aspx Accessed November 17, 2018.

Rosenbaum, M. S. and Wong, A. (2015). "If You Install It, Will They Use It? Understanding Why Hospitality Customers Take 'Technology Pauses' from SST", *Journal of Business Research*, 68, 1862–1868.

Rowles, D. (2017). "Digital Marketing Toolkit: Essential Tools Every Digital Marketer Needs", https://www.targetinternet.com/resources/DigitalMarketing Toolkit.pdf. Accessed January 12, 2019.

Rowley, J. (2008). "Understanding Digital Content Marketing", *Journal of Marketing Management*, 24 (5–6), 517–540.

Sales and Marketing for You (2015). "Social Media Marketing Principles", http://www.sales-and-marketing-for-you.com/social-media-marketing-principles.html. Accessed February 29, 2020.

Salesforce (2019). "Overview: What is Marketing Automation?", https://www.salesforce.com/products/marketing-cloud/what-is-marketing-automation/. Accessed March 7, 2019.

Schiff, J. (2016). "14 Digital Marketing Mistakes and How to Avoid Them", https://www.cio.com/article/3023553/14-digital-marketing-mistakes-and-how-to-avoid-them.html. Accessed March 5, 2019.

Slayter, M. E. (2017). "Social Media Marketing for B2B Health Care Marketing", Managing Editor, https://managingeditor.com/social-media-marketing-b2b-health-care/. Accessed March 4, 2019.

Smith, A. (2015). "U.S. Smartphone Use in 2015", Pew Research Center: Information and Technology, http://www.pewinternet.org/2015/04/01/us-smartphone-use-in-2015/. Accessed March 3, 2019.

Statista (2019). "Number of Facebook Users by Age in the U.S. as of January 2018 (in Millions)", https://www.statista.com/statistics/398136/us-facebook-user-age-groups/. Accessed March 2, 2019.

Sterling, G. (2015). "Consumers Want Personalization, but Retailers Just Can't Seem to Deliver", https://marketingland.com/consumers-want-personalization-but-retailers-just-cant-seem-to-deliver-144021. Accessed March 6, 2019.

Sun, T. (2017). "4 Consumer Trends Healthcare Marketers are Watching", *White Rhino blog*, http://blog.whiterhino.com/4-consumer-trends-healthcare-marketers-have-an-eye-on-in-2017. Accessed March 6, 2019.

TechTarget (2017). "Patient Engagement", https://searchhealthit.techtarget.com/definition/patient-engagement. Accessed January 10, 2019.

Tech Target (2018). "Information Age", https://searchcio.techtarget.com/definition/Information-Age. Accessed January 10, 2019.

Venkatesh, V. and Davis, F. D. (2000). "A Theoretical Extension of the Technology Acceptance Model: Four Longitudinal Field Studies", *Management Science*, 46 (2), 186–204.

Vize, R. and Sherrett, M. (2018). "Social Media Marketing for B2B" In: Rishi, B. and Bandyopadhyay, S. (Eds.), *Contemporary Issues in Social Media Marketing*, Routledge

VMware (2006). "The Roadmap to Virtual Infrastructure: Practical Implementation Strategies", White paper, www.vmware.com. Accessed October 4, 2018.

Walker, B. (2018). "Insights on Today's Healthcare Consumer", McKinsey, https://insights.c2bsolutions.com/blog/mckinseys-consumer-health-insights-survey-key-takeways-that-could-help-improve-outcomes. Accessed January 10, 2019.

Warden, C. (2018). "30 Facts & Statistics on Social Media and Healthcare", Referral md, https://getreferralmd.com/2017/01/30-facts-statistics-on-social-media-and-healthcare/. Accessed March 3, 2019.

Weiner, B. J. (2009). "A Theory of Organizational Readiness for Change", *Implementation Science*, 94, Article number 67.

Wood, M. (2012). "Marketing Social Marketing", *Journal of Social Marketing*, 2 (2), 94–102.

Suggested Additional Readings

Ackerman, C. (2017). "The Implications of Big-Data Marketing: Bigger than You Think", Our Perspective, https://blog.westmonroepartners.com/implications-big-data-marketing-bigger-think/. Accessed January 4, 2019.

Akesson, M., Edvardsson, B. and Tronvoll, B. (2014). "Customer Experience from a Self-Service System Perspective", *Journal of Service Management*, 25 (5), 677–698.

Barton-Jones, A. and Hubona, G. S. (2006). "The Mediation of External Variables in the Technology Acceptance Model", *Information & Management*, 43, 706–717.

Benetoliab, A., Chena, T. F. and Aslania, P. (2018). "How Patients' Use of Social Media Impacts Their Interactions with Healthcare Professionals", *Patient Education and Counseling*, 101 (3), 439–444.

Cabrita, M. and Cabrita, M. (2014). *Applying Social Marketing to Healthcare: Challenges and Opportunities*, IGI Global Editors: Avinash Kapoor, Chinmaya Kulshrestha.

Collier, J. E. and Barnes, D. C. (2015). "Self-Service Delight: Exploring the Hedonic Aspects of Self-Service", *Journal of Business Research*, 68, 986–993.

Considine, E. and Cormican, K. (2016). "Self-Service Technology Adoption: An Analysis of Customer to Technology Interactions", *Procedia Computer Science*, 100, 103–109.

Dias, J. (2014). "6 Big Benefits of Applying Automation to Healthcare", HIT Consultant Media.

Evariant (2016). "Why is Digital Marketing Important to Healthcare?", http://www.evariant.com/blog/digital-marketing-important-to-healthcare.

Hubspot (2018). "3 Keys to Digital Marketing in Healthcare", Written by Nicole Denton, https://blog.hubspot.com/insiders/digital-marketing-in-healthcare.

Kaur, G. and Gupta, S. (2012) "Consumer's Behavioral Intentions toward Self Service Technology in the Emerging Markets", *Journal of Global Marketing*, 25, 241–261.

Koumpouros, Y., Toulias, T. L. and Koumpouros, N. (2015). "The Importance of Patient Engagement and the Use of Social Media Marketing in Healthcare", *Technology & Health Care*, 23 (4), 495–507.

Radu, G., Solomon, M., Georghe, C. M., Hostiuc, M. Bulescu, I. A. and Purcarea, V. L. (2017). "The Adaptation of Health Care Marketing in the Digital Era", *Journal of Medicine and Life*, 10 (1), 44–46.

Rodriguez, A. (2014). "Why Digital Marketing Has Become the Health-Care Industry's Rx for Revenue", http://adage.com/article/digital/digital-health-care-industry-s-rx-revenue/294940/. Accessed March 4, 2019.

Rowles, D. (2017). "Digital Marketing Toolkit: Essential Tools Every Digital Marketer Needs", https://www.targetinternet.com/resources/DigitalMarketing Toolkit.pdf.

Stevens, A, (2013). "How Can Hospitals Use Social Media?", Evolve Digital Labs, http://evolvedigitallabs.com/how-can-hospitals-use-social-media/.

Top Ranking Marketing (2009) "Editorial: Social Media in Healthcare Marketing: Making the Case", http://www.toprankblog.com/2009/10/social-media-in-healthcare-marketing-5-tips-for-approval/.

Udell, M. (2017). "Health Care Marketing in the Era of Patient-Led Data." *Marketing Health Services*. AMA, https://www.ama.org/publications/eNewsletters/MHSNewsletter/Pages/health-care-marketing-in-the-era-of-patient-led-data.aspx.

Walker, R. H. and Johnson, L. W. (2006). "Why Consumers Use and Do Not Use Technology-Enabled Services", *Journal of Services Marketing*, 20 (2), 125–135.

Chapter 11

Employee Engagement and Internal Marketing in Health Care Marketing

11.1. What is Employee Engagement?

In Chapter 7, we saw that customers'/patients' selection of health care providers and retention depends on their experience, i.e., customer/patient experience. Paramount in improving customer/patient experience is customer/patient engagement discussed in Chapter 9.

The first line of contact in the health care organization (hospital, pharmacy, physician office or health plan) for customers/patients is the contact employees of the organization. Front-line employees in the service sector, including health care services, play a critical role in how customers experience the organization because value is created when an employee interacts with a customer. The ability of an organization to provide value to customers and engender their loyalty relies on how effectively this interaction between employees and customers works (Blount, 2011).

The concept of employee engagement (and engaged employees) was first introduced by Kahn (1990). Kahn disagreed with the management thinking at that time based on a top-down approach to get employees to be more motivated to work harder. The emphasis of this management approach was on changing the way employees thought about their work. Kahn believed that was the wrong approach. His research (presented in his 1990 paper entitled "Psychological Conditions of Personal Engagement and Disengagement at Work") demonstrated that the problem was less about employees being the right fit to the organization or lacking financial rewards, but fundamentally it was about the way they felt (Rheem, 2018).

11.1.1. Who is an engaged employee?

An "engaged employee" is defined as one who is fully absorbed by, and enthusiastic about, his/her work and, as a result of this, takes positive action to further the organization's reputation and interests. An engaged employee has a positive attitude toward the organization and its values (Paul, 2017).

Engaged employees (compared to the non-engaged employees who simply do their job and leave) believe in their organization's mission, vision, and values and will put in extra discretionary effort wherever they can (Dewar, 2015).

Engaged employees have an emotional commitment to their work and the organization. They actually care about their work and their company. They do not work just for a paycheck, or just for the next promotion, but work on behalf of the organization's goals. When employees care, i.e., when they are engaged, they use discretionary effort (Kruse, 2012). Note, however, that discretionary effort is not entirely in the hands of the employee; it is up to management to delegate essential discretionary authority.

The following are the findings of the 2014 Global Workforce Study by Willis Towers Watson (2012):

- Only four in 10 employees are highly engaged.
- Base pay is the reason most frequently cited by employees for joining or leaving an organization.
- 41% of employees cite job security as a key reason to join an organization.

This study, while advocating "Driving Engagement through a Consumer-Like Experience", emphasizes the following:

- Fundamentals should be addressed first. Base pay, job security, and career advancement opportunities matter most to employees when deciding to join or leave an organization. This finding is consistent with the well-known motivation theory by Maslow.
    - o In Maslow's motivation theory which presents a hierarchy of five levels of worker motivation, the first two levels are: (1) Physiological — the needs that must be met in order for a person to survive, such as food, water, and shelter and (2) Safety and security — personal and financial security and health and well-being (Maslow, 1943).

- The percentage of highly engaged workers is low — close to a quarter of employees are disengaged.
- Sustainable employee engagement requires strong leaders and managers. In companies where both leaders and managers are perceived by employees as effective, 72% of employees are highly engaged.

11.1.2. What is employee engagement?

Glint Inc., a leading consulting company in employee engagement, reports that over three-quarters of respondents in their 2018 survey agreed that employee engagement is both emotional commitment and a willingness to give your best at work (Glint, 2019).

Employee engagement is about having employees who are fully involved in their work and are also very happy about their work. Employee engagement can be measured by the degree of positive or negative emotional attachment the employee has to their job (Answers.com, 2019).

Stone (2017) explains employee engagement as follows: True employee engagement is the emotional commitment employees have to the company and its goals. When employees are truly engaged, they care, they give discretionary effort, and go the extra mile.

> The key word in both these definitions is "emotional attachment/commitment". Kruse (2012) confirms this and states, "Employee engagement is the emotional commitment the employee has to the organization and its goals."

Kruse also points out the following:

- Employee engagement does not mean employee happiness usually generated from having a socially satisfying work environment. In other words, making employees happy is different from making them engaged.
- Employee engagement also does not mean employee satisfaction. Companies spend a lot of effort and expenses on employee satisfaction surveys and related management actions. A satisfied employee is not the same as an engaged employee. Employee satisfaction does not ensure engagement and retention.

Employee engagement is a key management responsibility. It is up to the management to stimulate an employees' enthusiasm for work and redirect it toward organization's success (Chandani et al., 2016).

Glint Inc., which conducts surveys on employee engagement in US industries, reports the following in their study titled *The State of Employee Engagement in 2018* (Glint, 2019):

- Only 44% of companies that were surveyed strongly agree or agree that employees in their organization put discretionary effort.
- Most respondents believe that less than 70% of their employees are engaged, and about a third report that fewer than 39% of employees are engaged.
- However, over 90% believe there is solid evidence linking engagement to performance, and they believe it has the strongest impact on customer service and productivity.

More than anything else, leadership and culture drive employee engagement. About three-quarters link engagement to relationships, trust, and culture.

Respondents were most likely to view leaders as being responsible for engagement, and top leaders were viewed as nearly accountable as direct supervisors.

Yet, only two-fifths say their senior leaders prioritize employee engagement, and just 28% say their managers are highly skilled at fostering engaged individuals and teams. This suggests that many of the engagement problems organizations face can be boiled down to lack of leader skills and prioritization.

Respondents from more highly engaged organizations are much more likely to instill good leadership behaviors. While 57% of more highly engaged organizations instilled good leadership behaviors in managers to a high or very high degree, the same was true only for 34% of respondents from less-engaged organizations.

The ability to foster collaboration is a major differentiator between highly engaged and less engaged organizations. Being able to build trust by being fair is another differentiator. Leaders in more highly engaged organizations are also better at listening carefully to employee feedback and maintaining a positive work culture.

The remainder of this chapter will address the following key questions about employee engagement.

- Why is employee engagement important to health care organizations and their health care marketing? (Section 11.2)
- What are the management practices that would promote employee engagement?

In this discussion, we will address the following:

- Selection, development, and retention of customer-oriented service employees (Section 11.3);
- Effectively communicating and promoting company's objectives, products, and services to employees (called internal marketing, Section 11.4);
- Measuring employee engagement (Section 11.5); and
- The role to be played by the health care marketing function in employee engagement (Section 11.6).

11.2. Importance of Employee Engagement in Health Care Marketing

Our definition of health care marketing throughout this book is as follows:

> "Health care marketing integrates multi-channel, highly-segmented and targeted online and offline tactics that are designed to find and acquire the right patients, engage with them through strategic outreach, and nurture them to form lasting relationships throughout the entire patient journey."

Health care marketing depends on the organization's strategies to enhance customer/patient experience and engagement. As health care organizations continue to increase their efforts toward improving patient experience and engagement, one of the first places they should focus is employee engagement.

In fact, several studies have shown that employee engagement is one of the top variables correlating to mortality, complications, accidents on the job, patient safety, clinical outcomes, staff turnover, and absenteeism. In one study of 200 hospitals, researchers found that the engagement level of nurses was the number one variable correlating to mortality, even more significant than the number of nurses per patient day. Another study from National Health Service, UK (NHS) found that increasing engagement resulted in a strong correlation between engagement, absenteeism, and staff turnover but most importantly a significant reduction in mortality (Stone, 2017).

> Hospitals with the greatest gains and top 10% of engagement scores show the greatest increase in patient satisfaction (Decision-Wise, 2018).

Recalling from our discussion on employee engagement earlier in this chapter, true employee engagement is the emotional commitment employees have to the company and its goals. When employees are truly engaged, they care, they give discretionary effort, and go the extra mile. Stone (2017) provides the following examples of customer-oriented conduct of engaged employees of a health care organization:

- An engaged employee makes eye contact with patients, genuinely smiles, and welcomes them.
- An engaged employee escorts patients to their destination or helps family members find their loved ones.
- An engaged employee listens to a patient, unrushed, and answers every question regarding medications and discharge orders.
- An engaged employee checks on patients one last time before his/her shift is over.
- An engaged employee maintains cleanliness, e.g., never forgets to wash his/her hands.
- An engaged employee makes fewer mistakes.
- An engaged employee puts patients first.

Sherwood (2013) cites the Towers Watson global workforce study to highlight that less than half (44%) of the overall US hospital workforce was highly engaged. The study also shows a strong relationship between employees' level of engagement and their likelihood to remain with their employer, with just 17% of the highly engaged hospital workers interested in other employment options versus 43% of the disengaged group. Improving engagement, therefore, is another important advantage for the many hospitals already competing to find and keep a dwindling supply of people with critical skills, especially in clinical areas.

Research by Gallup and Loma Linda University Medical Center shows that employee engagement and employee safety work together to enhance patient safety (Burger and Sutton, 2014).

Additional evidence shows that employee engagement has a strong correlation with employee safety and enhances a safer environment for health care consumers. Likewise, employee engagement plays a significant role in reducing employee accidents on the job.

> **Case Study of a Hospital (Burger and Sutton, 2014)**
>
> A small hospital enlisted Gallup in 2010 to help boost employee engagement among its workforce. Hospital leaders wanted to ensure that all employees were devoted to their roles and deeply committed to their work. Leaders recognized that an engaged workforce would be more emotionally connected to the hospital's mission and willing to go the extra mile to meet and exceed expectations. To build and sustain an engaged workforce, this health care organization implemented three key interventions: (1) select employees based on talent; (2) invest in ongoing employee development; and (3) emphasize engagement from the top-down.
>
> The hospital's overall engagement score jumped from above the 20th percentile in 2010 to above the 70th percentile in 2013, when compared with results in Gallup's hospital-level database. Overall hospital turnover fell from 22% in 2010 to 15% in 2013. Registered Nurse (RN) turnover was reduced by about half, from 25% in 2010 to 13% in 2013. Workers' compensation claims decreased substantially. The number of workers' compensation claims went from 18 per year in 2010 to a mere 7 per year in 2013. From 2010 to 2013, the hospital's RN turnover costs had decreased by US$1.7 million, and the hospital had increased its operating margin.

While the significance of employee engagement is undeniable, what is of concern is that only 29% of the workforce are engaged, 45% are not engaged, and 26% are actively disengaged. This means nearly 71% of employees are not fully engaged. In addition, nearly 11 billion is lost annually due to employee turnover (Stone, 2017).

Management practices to foster employee engagement will be discussed in Sections 11.3, 11.4, and 11.5.

11.3. Management Practices to Promote Employee Engagement I: Selection, Development, and Retention of Customer-Oriented Service Employees

Studies link customer orientation of employees to customer/patient satisfaction.

318 *Modern Health Care Marketing*

Vredenburg and Bell (2014) in a survey of 114 customer contact employees of a radiology health care center in Australia, to ascertain employees' perception of patients' perceptions (as patients were not allowed to be contacted directly due to regulations), determined that service employee flexibility was positively associated with patient-perceived value of service and patient satisfaction. Flexibility of service employees is an important characteristic of customer-oriented staff because of the variability feature of health care services, i.e., the fact that different patients coming to a health care provider come with varying needs.

> **Characteristics of Customer-Oriented Employees**
>
> The following summary of characteristics of customer-oriented employees, from a large number of studies (citations omitted), is given by Gunawardane (2017):
> Professionalism, Civility, Friendliness, Competence, Providing individual attention to customers, Helpfulness, Courtesy, Promptness, Communication skills, Problem-solving attitude and skills, Engagement (with organization's mission and objectives), Confidence in ability (Self-efficacy), and Flexibility/Adaptability.

11.3.1. Organizational policies and management practices affecting customer orientation of service employees

A summary of findings from studies on management practices that affect customer orientation of employees, in general, is as follows (Conger and Kanungo, 1988; Dhar, 2015; Evans and Lindsay, 2005; Murphy, 2017; Rafiq and Ahmed, 1998; Scott and Bruce, 1994):

- Supportive organizational climate (including training, rewards for quality service, and empowerment);
- Job satisfaction;
- Customer-oriented culture of the service organization;
- Positive customer feedback ("customer delight");
- Internal service quality — quality of service within the organization with one department or group providing internal services to another;

- Management support — high levels of organizational support (provision of valued financial benefits along with employees' perception of support from supervisors and coworkers, and procedural fairness in decision-making);
- Proper organization structure — organization's structure has to be redesigned to achieve effective internal marketing (internal marketing is discussed in Section 11.4);
- Empowerment:
  o Giving service employees, especially contact staff, authority to make decisions based on what they feel is right, have control over their work, take risks and learn from their mistakes, and promote change (Evans and Lindsay, 2005).
  o Empowerment increases the self-efficacy of employees (Conger and Kanungo, 1988).
  o Empowerment leads to employees being more adaptive (Scott and Bruce, 1994).
  o Empowerment allows employees to respond faster to customer needs, especially during service failures, as they do not have to spend time referring matters to supervisors (Rafiq and Ahmed, 1998).
- Creating a service-oriented culture; and
- Providing training — availability of training and employees' perception of benefits from training, positively affect employees' organizational commitment and motivation to work toward service quality (Dhar, 2015).

11.3.2. Employee Engagement in Health Care Environments

In health care organizations, customer-oriented behavior by staff contributes to understanding the needs of patients and their families. By understanding their needs, nurses and other health care and administrative personnel are able to help the patients and provide solutions which meet patient needs (Chien *et al.*, 2008). Nurses who possess high customer-oriented behavior have been found to assist patients, provide better nursing care, and respond to patients' needs during their stay in the hospital (Ping and Ahmad, 2015).

Ping and Ahmad (2015) propose a model where health care staff's high-level of job satisfaction and strong affective commitment are the main contributors to their customer-oriented behavior. Affective commitment of an employee is based on an emotional attachment to the organization which makes the employee identify strongly with the company and its objectives, and remain with the organization even if the employee has financially other better opportunities.

The relationship between job satisfaction and customer orientation was also seen in a study of home health care agencies by Hoffman and Ingram (1991).

Lowe (2012) in a study of 10,702 employees from 16 health care facilities in Ontario, Canada, found the following engagement drivers among the top 10, ranked by their net influence on engagement scores:

1. I feel I can trust this organization;
2. I have an opportunity to make improvements in work;
3. The organization values my work;
4. Senior management is committed to high-quality care;
5. I have clear job goals/objectives;
6. I feel I belong to a team;
7. My organization promotes staff health/wellness;
8. I have a good balance of family/personal life with work;
9. My supervisor can be counted on to help with difficult tasks; and
10. I have adequate resources/equipment to do my work.

11.3.3. Selecting customer-oriented staff

Finally, we address techniques for selecting customer-oriented employees.

Thomson (1989) recommends asking open-ended questions from applicants to identify adaptability and customer orientation from past experience. Examples of questions suggested are as follows:

- From your past work experience, what type of customer was most difficult to deal with? Why?
- What was the customer's primary compliant or negative characteristic?
- How did you handle that customer?
- What would be the ideal way to deal with that type of customer?
- What is the most difficult aspect of your last/current job?
- What factors contribute to its difficulty?
- What have you done to cope with this difficulty?

Encouraging adaptive behavior in the workforce starts at the point of recruitment. Health care organizations should adopt recruiting techniques, such as the above techniques, to ensure recruitment of higher numbers of adaptive employees (Gwinner *et al.*, 2005).

11.4. Management Practices to Promote Employee Engagement II: Internal Marketing

11.4.1. Internal services encounter

In recent times, researchers and practitioners have also highlighted the existence and the importance of "internal customers" and the need to recognize the importance of "internal service encounters". More than one department in the health care organization contribute to the provision of a service to an external customer/patient. For example, during a patient interaction with a hospital, multiple departments/functions such as reception, clinical services, medical records, billing, member services, and quality and utilization management play a part during the patient's journey. Billing depends on medical records and utilizations management. Input from medical records is essential to billing. Here, billing is an "internal customer" and medical record is an "internal supplier" of services.

Each internal department of the health care organization (reception, records, call centers, nursing, billing, etc.) must perform efficiently and accurately. A well-known axiom in service management is "You cannot provide excellent service to your customers if your internal services are of low quality (meaning not efficient and coordinated)."

This concept is called the "Service Profit Chain" (Heskett *et al.*, 1994). It is one of the most well-known and accepted concepts in the field of management which highlights the vital significance of good internal services. The chain is described as follows:

- Good internal services lead to service employee satisfaction which in turn enables the service employee to provide better services to the external customer;
- This eventually leads to customer satisfaction, retention, and growth resulting in increased business and profits; and
- The firm will reinvest part of these gains in improving internal services. Thus, the service profit chain continues to perpetuate.

Berry and Parasuraman (1991) found that employees satisfied with internal service quality provide better service to external customers.

11.4.2. Internal marketing

Internal marketing is the promotion of a company's objectives, products, and services to the employees within the organization. The purpose is to increase employee engagement with the company's goals and fostering brand advocacy (TechTarget, 2017).

Employees who are enthusiastic about their company and its offerings are likely to share that enthusiasm with their social networks. As a result, internal marketing can be an effective part of external branding and marketing efforts. However, internal marketing can only go so far since an employee's attitude toward the organization is affected by every element of that individual's experience working for the business. Keeping employees happy and engaged is important to external marketing efforts as well.

"Internal Marketing is a planned effort using a marketing-like approach directed at motivating employees, for implementing and integrating organizational strategies towards customer orientation" (Ahmed and Rafiq, 1998).

Internal marketing is when an organization focuses on its employees as if they were customers. Basically, it is inward-facing marketing — marketing meant to influence your employees instead of trying to influence the public with your brand and message (HospitalPORTAL, 2018).

> Stewart Gandolf, Chief Executive Officer & Creative Director at Healthcare Success, summarizes internal marketing in health care by saying, "In short, it's about building your business from the inside" (Gandolf, 2019).

11.4.3. Internal marketing strategies and methods

According to a model for internal marketing proposed by Berry (1981), employees should be treated as customers, and jobs treated as products. This is consistent with the opinion we previously saw from HospitalPORTAL (2018).

Gronroos proposed another model (Grönroos, 1985) that is based on the empowerment of, and the delegation of control and discretion to, employees; the employee participation in marketing strategies; and the supportive top management.

Dimachkie et al. (2011) state, "The internal marketing plan describes how employees, and thus the organization, change and grow from an internal perspective. Ideally, internal marketing processes facilitate the interrelationships employees have with managers, other employees, patients, and key external stakeholders (e.g., payers, patient families, and partners."

Dimachkie *et al.* (2011) also report findings of a study conducted by University of Wisconsin and Northwestern University. This study found that patients had a higher level of satisfaction when their care was provided by highly satisfied employees.

When health care employees have a positive quality experience, they express positive behaviors toward their patients. In turn, the patients also encounter a positive quality service experience, which likely means patients leave the organization satisfied.

Therefore, customer satisfaction and customer/patient experience enhancement efforts should be first preceded by improvements in internal customer (i.e., employee) relationships.

Improvements in employee relationships come about via an organizational implementation of internal marketing. By focusing on internal marketing, health care managers will gain a motivated staff composed of knowledgeable and prepared employees.

Chang and Chang (2007): Study conducted at two medical centers in Southern Taiwan found that nurse perceptions of internal marketing had positive effects on job satisfaction and on organizational commitment.

The following internal marketing tactics for health care organizations are suggested by Gandolf (2019):

- Creating a reliable and effective system to convert phone inquiries to appointments;
- Consistently asking patients for referrals. The health club "24 Hour Fitness" regularly uses this tactic;
- Present a Theme of the Month message in one minute;
- Provide "Pass Along" invitation certificates;
- Using opt-in email for continued contact;
- Electronic phone communications for select messages, reminder calls, etc.;
- Office signs, posters, and video screens;
- Using active listening, open-ended questions, and tailored presentations;
- Identifying patient expectations in the office visit (and exceeding them); and
- Presenting educational classes, seminars, and events.

> Industry experts and writers believe that effective internal marketing programs create a feeling, among employees, of belonging to one team working toward a common objective.

Other internal marketing strategies presented in the literature include Dimachkie *et al.* (2011), Gunawardane (2009, 2012), Marketing-Schools.org (2012) and Thomas *et al.* (1990):

- Ensuring that all employees know that their contributions are essential to the company's success;
- Educating all employees about the company's products and services;
- Reinforcing the concept that customers are, when all is said and done, the source of employees' salaries;
- Providing adequate salaries and benefits, plus a pleasant work environment;
- Encouraging employee input on corporate policies, management, and operation — including criticism;
- Acting on employee suggestions that have merit and publicly acknowledging the value of the input;
- Confirming that the corporate mandate and objectives are clearly described and disseminated throughout the organization;
- Providing opportunities for advancement, professional development, and promotion;
- Ensuring that the corporate culture is consistent with work–life balance;
- Fostering communication and collaboration among employees through various methods from formalized settings to casual areas for gathering, such as lounges;
- Using newsletters or inhouse radio programs to spread information and reinforce organizational culture;
- Providing access to information as frequently as possible. Use technological tools like blogs, message boards, and wikis to spread information. Highlight success like new contracts awarded or sales targets met; and
- Creating performance-based incentives.

Internal marketing operates on the idea that customer opinions of a company are based on their experiences with the business, not just with the products. By treating employees as "internal customers", internal marketing helps employees align with the company's vision and operations. In turn, they provide their customers with a consistent and valuable experience. Internal marketing campaigns are often led by a company's human resources department, which is responsible for distributing information and providing training on the company's objectives and strategies.

> Effective internal marketing will lead to employee engagement. Engaged employees become ambassadors to external marketing.

11.5. Management Practices to Promote Employee Engagement III: Health Care Employee Engagement Measurement

Glint (2019) reports that only 53% of organizations measure employee engagement, of which 77% still use an annual formal survey. However, four-fifths of those that measure engagement use multiple methods for doing so.

Highly engaged organizations are much more likely to measure engagement continuously than less-engaged organization, and they are a little less likely to measure it once a year.

Following are methods of measuring employee engagement:

- Zoho survey: https://www.zoho.com/survey/templates/health-care/healthcare-employee-engagement-survey.html.
  - Key attributes measured: Civil duty, moral duty, salary, professionalism, and patient care.
  - Typical questions in employee survey:
    - Are you proud to work in your company?
    - Does your work give you a sense of accomplishment?
    - Do you feel that you are given opportunities to grow?
    - Do you feel respected in your workplace?
    - Do you feel your opinions matter?
    - How constructive is the feedback given to you at work?
    - Overall, how satisfied are you working there now?

- Gallup Employee Engagement Survey

This survey, reported to be used by health care organizations, asks employees to ask themselves the following questions (and respond):

- o Do I know what is expected of me at work?
- o Do I have the materials and equipment I need to do my work right?
- o At work, do I have the opportunity to do what I do best every day?
- o In the last seven days, have I received recognition or praise for doing good work?
- o Does my supervisor, or someone at work, seem to care about me as a person?
- o Is there someone at work who encourages my development?
- o At work, do my opinions seem to count?
- o Does the mission/purpose of my company make me feel my job is important?
- o Are my coworkers committed to doing quality work?
- o Do I have a best friend at work?
- o In the last six months, has someone at work talked to me about progress?
- o This last year, have I had opportunities at work to learn and grow?

Disclaimer: These surveys are proprietary information of the respective organizations. They should not be used without their permission. They are presented here only for illustrative educational purposes.

11.6. Role of Health Care Marketing in Employee Engagement and Internal Marketing

In the previous sections, we saw several actions that can be taken by the management in health care organizations to promote employee engagement. These included selection, development, and retention of customer-oriented employees, internal marketing, and employee engagement measurement. We also saw how high levels of employee engagement result in increasing quality of health care delivery and total customer/patient experience.

What is the role of, and relevance to, health care marketing in employee engagement and internal marketing? The answer is fairly simple from the following chain of concepts:

- Ultimate objective of health care marketing is to enhance current customer/patient/physician experience and satisfaction to retain them and

ensure the same for prospective customers/patients/physicians to attract them;
- Customer/physician/patient experience depends on how front-line employees are customer-oriented, and how internal organizational processes work;
- Employee engagement and internal marketing contribute to customer-orientation and process efficiency;
- The health care marketing function of the organization is one of functions of the health care organization closest to the "voice of the customer" and is heavily involved in in-bound customer/patient communications (of needs, expectations, concerns, and complaints); and
- Therefore, the health care marketing function should be involved in internal marketing and process improvement; in an integrated team effort with participation of top management, clinical management, health care operations, customer service/call centers, information technology, and human resource management.

> Haefner (2017) in his article ranks "Hospital marketers must enhance employee culture" as #2 among the eight trends.

Prasad (2017) agrees in his article:

"Physicians are tasking marketers to improve employee culture. Because patient satisfaction is now the biggest factor for hospital revenue, physicians and hospital executives are now looking towards marketers to device strategies and install processes that are focused on helping to improve patient experience".

Health care marketers should continuously provide interactive channels for customers and patients to bring up concerns, and also conduct surveys aimed on improving patient experience and care by addressing internal culture problems (Prasad, 2017).

Kennedy (2018) presents the following guidance to the health care marketing function to assist them in their task of enhancing internal culture in order to improve customer/patient experience:

- Get employees to amplify the brand as part of their day-to-day activities;
- Tap into the creativity of the workforce to create valuable content (see "Content Marketing" in Section 10.7);

- Energize employees, so they experience a deeper sense of belonging to a culture they care about;
- Encourage change in a highly regulated environment (see Chapter 13 for a discussion of the intensity of regulations in health care); and
- Engage people rather than having them sit in front of a computer all day.

To be consumer-centric, health care organizations should have an outward market orientation and a culture to support a customer-focused business model (Krivich, 2015).

In summary, the health care marketing function has the following key roles to play in employee engagement and internal marketing:

- Take the lead in organizing inbound customer's/patient's communications of needs, expectations, concerns, and complaints;
- Take the lead in inbound market intelligence information on competition, consumer trends, and supplier/physician behavior;
- Take part in team efforts, with top management, clinical management, health care operations, customer service/call centers, information technology, and human resource management to improve processes; and
- Take part in team efforts to develop an organizational culture aimed at enhancing customer/patient experience.

However, these objectives and activities of the health care marketing function will be effective only if the top management of the health care organization adopts market-oriented and customer-focused vision, mission, strategies, and programs. Some of these, discussed in the literature and adopted to suit health care organizations, are as follows:

- Externally focused business model development which focuses on meeting the needs of the customer and all touch points of the customer experience are identified by customer journey mapping and integrated into action programs.
- Marketing is a member of the senior team involved in all decisions affecting customer/patient experience.
- Interdepartmental cooperation at all staff levels; Interdepartmental barriers to meet the needs of the customer are identified and eliminated.
- Continuous evaluation and training on organization's customer-centered focus; Standards on customer service competency skills for all positions.

11.7. Concept of Employee Experience

11.7.1. What is employee experience (EX)?

This concept is based on the theory that, like customer experience, employee satisfaction is based on his/her long-term association, activities, satisfaction, and interactions with and in the organization.

According to Dukes (2017),

> "Focusing on employee satisfaction or employee engagement isn't enough. You need to think about the overall employee experience."

Wride (2017) compares the three concepts we have discussed in this chapter, namely: employee satisfaction, employee engagement, and employee experience.

(1) Employee satisfaction
Employee satisfaction measures whether an employee's needs are being met at work and how satisfied he/she is with the overall work experience.

The focal point in employee satisfaction is on the employee's individual feelings, positive or negative, about his/her employment relationship. Thus, employee satisfaction is subjective in nature and is internally focused on an employee's emotional state of happiness.

(2) Employee engagement
As we have seen previously in this chapter, employee engagement is about the employee's affective commitment to the organization. Emotions involved here are long lasting. As we noted earlier, Stone (2017) explains employee engagement as the emotional commitment employees have to the company and its goals. When employees are truly engaged, they care, give discretionary effort, and go the extra mile.

Engaged employees could be unhappy and dissatisfied at times but they might remain engaged. In other words, employee satisfaction is driven by short-term emotions while employee engagement is driven by long-lasting values and emotions. Of course, if employee satisfaction drops frequently in a long-time cycle, it will make the employee less engaged.

(3) Employee experience
We can equate employee experience (EX) with customer/patient experience (CX/PX) we studied in Chapter 7. CX arises out of the customer journey

which we measure with customer journey mapping. Here, we do not refer to a customer journey during one health care visit or encounter. We refer to the customer's lifetime interactions with the health care organization, a lifetime journey. We also saw how touch points in the journey create moments of truth, a combination of perceptions based on outcomes and emotions.

Employee experience similarly occurs during the employee's work life journey with the organization. Satisfaction/dissatisfaction arises at certain touch points (like a raise, reprimand, bonus, or promotion). Engagement occurs when the moments of truth are overwhelmingly satisfactions. Satisfaction, dissatisfaction, engagement, disengagement are all moments (or periods) during the employee experience.

Just like with CX, the organization must identify the touch points and moments of truth in the EX, and design policies and practices to ensure rewarding EX.

> The above discussion now enables us to define employee experience (EX) as, "The sum of the various perceptions employees have about their interactions with the organization where they work" (Dukes, 2017).
>
> Here, interactions are equivalent to touch points in CX and perceptions are equivalent to moments of truth in CX.
>
> Managerial strategies and action to improve EX should thus adopt an approach similar to those undertaken to improve CX.

Studies show that employee experience is influenced by the physical environment in which an employee works, the tools and technologies an employer provides, and how an employer demonstrates its commitment to the health and success of employees.

As we learnt in previous sections, employees of the health care organization are its first customers. In that sense, some experts and writers challenge the well-known axiom, "Customers come first" in favor of "Customers come second; employees come first". This is the reason we emphasized on employee engagement and internal marketing.

Wride (2016) presents some key concepts relating to EX to be understood by health care managers:

- EX is more than a human resources (HR) responsibility — EX is a fundamental concern of all business leaders;

- EX = design thinking;
- EX is based on the totality of perceptions, both good and bad; and
- When properly built, the right EX has the power to transform the organization.

Dukes (2017) highlights the importance of the employee's voice and input in organizational decision-making. She advises the management not to assume what the workforce wants or needs but to get their input. Employees know best how to enhance employee experience.

Including employees in the decision-making process by soliciting their views also helps create a sense of ownership and makes them care more deeply about their contributions to the business.

11.7.2. Enhancing employee experience

IBM Smarter Workforce Institute (2018) in its report on *Financial Impact of a Positive Employee Experience* states the following:

- Organizations that score in the top 25% on employee experience report nearly three times the return on assets compared to organizations in the bottom quartile; and
- Organizations that score in the top 25% on employee experience report double the return on sales compared to organizations in the bottom quartile.

Many industry experts and researchers have addressed strategies and practices to enhance employee experience in organizations.

Bersin *et al.* (2017) in an article present (shown here in summary form) the following five factors as those that contribute to a positive EX:

1. Meaningful work;
2. Supportive management;
3. Positive work environment;
4. Growth opportunity; and
5. Trust in leadership.

Globoforce (2019) in an article presents a summary of the report from IBM Smarter Workforce Institute and Workhuman Analytics & Research

Institute that explored data gathered from 23,000 health care workers in more than 20 job functions, across 45 countries and territories. The report presents dimensions in employee perceptions that influence their employee experience. These termed in the report as "The Employee Experience Index" contain the following five dimensions:

1. Belonging — feeling part of a team, group, or organization;
2. Purpose — understanding why one's work matters;
3. Achievement — a sense of accomplishment in the work that is done;
4. Happiness — the pleasant feeling arising in and around work; and
5. Vigor — the presence of energy, enthusiasm, and excitement at work.

The report highlights the importance of the following points in impacting the experience of health care workers:

- Trust;
- Coworker relationships;
- Meaningful work;
- Recognition;
- Voice; and
- Work–life balance.

It is leadership and management behavior and actions that influence the above six factors.

These six factors (trust, coworker relationships, meaningful work, recognition, voice, and work–life balance) then determine the level of employee experience (made up by the five dimensions in the Employee Experience Index).

A summary of recommendations from other authors found in the literature is listed below:

- EX is the journey. What should be enhanced are employee satisfaction and employee engagement. Therefore, all the guidelines presented previously in this chapter on ensuring employee engagement will contribute toward EX.
- Work design with modern digital technology. This makes employees benefit from improved and simplified processes. Technology connects workers with coworkers and across departments with whom they share tasks, workflows, and data. This makes the employee's job easier and rewarding.

- Workspace design (see discussion on Physical Evidence/Servicescape in Section 9.11).
- Recognition of engaged employees — regular one-on-one engagement with employees.
- Provision of personalized career development — a top priority. When new employees are continuously learning new methods using new technology, they feel more secure and engaged.
- Above all, creating a companywide customer- and employee-oriented culture.

11.7.3. A case study from an occupational health provider (Weiss *et al.*, 2009)

Weiss studies how occupational health nurses can be provided with an ideal employee experience. He suggests three steps in this endeavor:

- **Step 1.** Commit to the creation of an employee-centric culture;
- **Step 2.** Connect employees and employers to employee-centric care; and
- **Step 3.** Captivate, monitor, and measure attachment (differentiate).

For details of these steps, we refer readers to the original article listed in references.

References

Ahmed, P. K. and Rafiq, M. (1998). "A Customer-Oriented Framework for Empowering Service Employees", *The Journal of Services Marketing*, 12 (5), 379–396.

Answers.com (2019) "What Does Employee Engagement Really Mean?", http://www.answers.com/Q/What_does_employee_engagement_really_mean. Accessed January 15, 2019.

Berry, L. L. (1981). "The Employee as Customer", *Journal of Retail Banking*, 3, 25–28.

Berry, L. L. and Parasuraman, A. (1991). *Marketing Service, Competing through Quality*, The Free Press, New York.

Bersin, J., Flynn, J., Mazor, A. and Melian, V. (2017). "The Employee Experience: Culture, Engagement, and Beyond", *Deloitte Insights*, https://www2.deloitte.com/insights/us/en/focus/human-capital-trends/2017/improving-the-employee-experience-culture-engagement.html. Accessed March 11, 2019.

Blount, Y. (2011). "Employee Management and Service Provision: A Conceptual Framework", *Information Technology and People*, 24 (2), 134–157.

Burger, J. and Sutton, L. (2014). "How Employee Engagement Can Improve a Hospital's Health", *Business Journal*, April 3.

Chandani, A., Mehta, M., Mall, A. and Khokhar, V. (2016). "Employee Engagement: A Review Paper on Factors Affecting Employee Engagement", *Indian Journal of Science and Technology*, 9 (15).

Chang, C. and Chang, H. (2007). "Effects of Internal Marketing on Nurse Job Satisfaction and Organizational Commitment: Example of Medical Centers in Southern Taiwan", *Journal of Nursing Research*, 15 (4), 265–274.

Chien, C. C., Chou, H. K. and Hung, S. T. (2008). "A Conceptual Model of Nurses' Goal Orientation, Service Behavior and Service Performance", *Nursing Economics*, 26 (6), 374–383.

Conger, J. A. and Kanungo, R. N. (1988). "The Empowerment Process: Integrating Theory and Practice", *Academy of Management Review*, 13, 471–482.

Decision-Wise (2018). "Employee Engagement Survey Best Practices for Healthcare", https://www.decision-wise.com/wp-content/uploads/2016/03/DecisionWise-Employee-Engagement-Survey-Best-Practices-for-Healthcare.pdf. Accessed January 18, 2019.

Dewar, J. (2015). "4 Reasons Why Healthcare Must Invest in Employee Engagement", Published November 24, 2015, http://education.healthcaresource.com/why-healthcare-must-invest-in-employee-engagement/. Accessed November 15, 2018.

Dhar, R. L. (2015). "Service Quality and the Training of Employees: The Mediating Role of Organizational Commitment", *Tourism Management*, 46, 419–430.

Dimachkie, M. M., Oetjen, D. and Rotarius, T. (2011). "Internal Marketing: Creating Quality Employee Experiences in Health Care Organizations", *The Health Care Manager*, 30 (3), 196–204.

Dukes, E. (2017). "The Employee Experience: What It is and Why It Matters", https://www.inc.com/elizabeth-dukes/the-employee-experience-what-it-is-and-why-it-matt.html. Accessed October 30, 2018.

Evans, J. R. and Lindsay, W. M. (2005). *The Management and Control of Quality*, 6th edn., Thomson South-Western.

Gandolf, S. (2019). "The Power of Internal Marketing in Healthcare (and 10 Ways to Use)", https://www.healthcaresuccess.com/blog/physician-marketing/the-power-of-internal-marketing-in-healthcare-and-10-ways-to-use.html. Accessed March 7, 2019.

Glint (2019). "The State of Employee Engagement in 2018", https://info.glintinc.com/rs/586-OTD-288/images/The_State_of_Employee_Engagement_in_2018_Whitepaper_HRdotcom_Glint.pdf. Accessed January 18, 2019.

Globoforce (2019). "The Employee Experience of Healthcare Workers", https://resources.globoforce.com/papers/the-employee-experience-of-healthcare-workers. Accessed March 11, 2019.

Grönroos, C. (1985). "Internal Marketing: Theory and Practice", *American Marketing Association Services Conference Proceedings*, 41–47.

Gunawardane, G. (2009). "Relationship between Dimensions of Internal Service Quality and the Nature of the Internal Service Encounter", *California Journal of Operations Management*, 7 (1), 21–30.

Gunawardane, G. (2012). "Classifying Internal Service Encounters to Increase Their Effectiveness — An Empirical Study", *Journal of Supply Chain and Operations Management*, 10 (1), 131–141.

Gunawardane, G. (2017). *Service Management: Concepts, Principles and Applications for Sri Lanka*, Dayawansa Jayakody & Company, Colombo, Sri Lanka.

Gwinner, K. P., Bitner, M. J., Brown, S. W. and Kumar, A. (2005). "Service Customization Through Employee Adaptiveness", *Journal of Service Research*, 8 (2), 131–148.

Haefner, M. (2017). "8 Healthcare Marketing Trends for 2018", October 18, Becker's Hospital Review, https://www.beckershospitalreview.com/hospital-management-administration/8-healthcare-marketing-trends-for-2018.html. Accessed November 17, 2018.

Heskett, J. L., Jones, T. O., Loveman, G. W., Sasser, W. E. and Schlesinger, L. A. (1994). "Putting the Service Profit Chain to Work", *Harvard Business Review*, March–April, 164–170.

Hoffman, D. and Ingram, T. (1991). "Creating Customer-Oriented Employees: The Case in Home Health Care", *Journal of Health Care Marketing*, 11 (2), 24–32.

HospitalPORTAL (2018). "The Importance of Internal Marketing in the Healthcare Workplace", https://www.hospitalportal.net/blog/the-importance-of-internal-marketing-in-the-healthcare-workplace/. Accessed March 10, 2019.

IBM Smarter Workforce Institute (2018). "Financial Impact of a Positive Employee Experience", file:///C:/Users/Gamini/AppData/Local/Packages/Microsoft.MicrosoftEdge_8wekyb3d8bbwe/TempState/Downloads/the-financial-impact-of-a-positive-employee-experience%20(1).pdf. Accessed March 11, 2019.

Kahn, W. A. (1990). "Psychological Conditions of Personal Engagement and Disengagement at Work", *Academy of Management Journal*, 33 (4), 692–724.

Kennedy, H. (2018). "5 Healthcare Marketer Tips for Employee Engagement Programs", Blog Hugh Kennedy • 03.26.18, https://www.agencypja.com/insights/blogs/5-healthcare-marketer-tips-for-employee-engagement-programs/. Accessed November 23, 2018.

Kohli, A. K., Jaworski, B. J. and Kumar, A. (1993). "MARKOR: A Measure of Market Orientation", *Journal of Marketing Research*, 30 (4), 467–477.

Krivich, M. (2015). "What Does a Customer Focused Hospital or Healthcare Enterprise Look Like?", http://healthcaremarketingmatters.blogspot.com/2015/01/what-does-customer-focused-hospital-or.html. Accessed March 7, 2019.

Kruse, K. (2012). "What is Employee Engagement?", https://www.forbes.com/sites/kevinkruse/2012/06/22/employee-engagement-what-and-why/#7af49f977f37. Accessed January 11, 2019.

Lowe, G. (2012). "How Employee Engagement Matters for Hospital Performance", *Healthcare Quarterly*, 15 (2), 29–39, http://www.employeeengagementinstitute.com/wp-content/uploads/2013/06/EE-in-Healthcare.pdf. Accessed March 9, 2019.

Marketing-Schools.org (2012). "Internal Marketing", http://www.marketing-schools.org/types-of-marketing/internal-marketing.html. Accessed January 12, 2019.

Maslow, A. H. (1943). "A Theory of Human Motivation", *Psychological Review*, 50 (4), 370–396.

Murphy, R. (2017). "Built Brand Tough", *Marketing Health Services*, 27 (2), 29–31.

Paul, E. (2017). "Effective Ways to Improve Employee Engagement", http://www.emptrust.com/blog/employee-engagement-a-key-hr-strategy. Accessed January 12, 2019.

Ping, L. L. and Ahmad, U. N. U. (2015). "A Conceptual Analysis of Nurses' Customer-Oriented Behavior, Job Satisfaction and Affective Commitment in Malaysia", *International Journal of Caring Sciences*, 8 (3), 774–782.

Prasad, A. (2017). "6 Healthcare Marketing Trends in 2018: How to Leverage Them", https://blog.gmrwebteam.com/2018-healthcare-marketing-trends-how-to-leverage-them/. Accessed January 12, 2019.

Rafiq, M. and Ahmed, P. K. (1998). "A Customer-Oriented Framework for Empowering Service Employees", *The Journal of Services Marketing*, 12 (5), 379–396.

Rheem, D. (2018). "William Kahn: Father of Employee Engagement", https://donrheem.com/william-kahn-father-of-employee-engagement/. Accessed January 11, 2019.

Scott, S. G. and Bruce, R. A. (1994). "Determinants of Innovative Behavior: A Path Model of Individual Innovation in the Workplace", *Academy of Management Journal*, 37, 580–607.

Sherwood, R. (2013). "Employee Engagement Drives Health Care Quality and Financial Returns", October 30, 2013, *Harvard Business Review*, https://hbr.org/2013/10/employee-engagement-drives-health-care-quality-and-financial-returns. Accessed January 12, 2019.

Stone, J. (2017). "The Importance of Employee Engagement in Healthcare", http://blog.medicalgps.com/the-importance-of-employee-engagement-in-healthcare/. Accessed January 18, 2019.

TechTarget (2017). "Internal Marketing", https://whatis.techtarget.com/definition/internal-marketing. Accessed January 10, 2019.

Thomas, R., Farmer, E. and Wallace, B. (1990). "The Importance of Internal Marketing", *Journal of Health Care Marketing*, 11 (1), 55–58.

Thomson, A. (1989). "Customer Contact Personnel: Using Interview Techniques to Select for Adaptability in Service Employees", *The Journal of Services Marketing*, 3 (1), 57–65.

Vredenburg, J. and Bell, S. J. (2014). "Variability in Health Care Services: The Role of Service Employee Flexibility", *Australasian Marketing Journal* (AMJ), 22 (3), 168–178.

Weiss, M. D., Tyink, S. and Kubiak, C. (2009). "Delivering Ideal Employee Experiences", *AAOHN Journal*, 57 (5), 210–215.

Willis Towers Watson (2012). 2012 Global Workforce Study. Engagement at Risk: Driving Strong Performance in a Volatile Global Environment, https://www.towerswatson.com/en/Insights/IC-Types/Survey-Research-Results/2012/07/2012-Towers-Watson-Global-Workforce-Study. Accessed January 16, 2019.

Wride, M. (2017). "The Difference Between Employee Satisfaction, Employee Engagement, and The Employee Experience", https://www.decision-wise.com/the-difference-between-employee-satisfaction-employee-engagement-and-the-employee-experience/. Accessed March 6, 2019.

Suggested Additional Readings

Babakus, E., Yavas, U., Karatepe, O. M. and Avei, T. (2003), "The Effect of Management Commitment to Service Quality on Employees' Affective and Performance Outcomes", *Journal of the Academy of Marketing Science*, 31, 272–386.

Barajas, B. (2014). "Best Practices in Healthcare Employee Engagement", https://www.precheck.com/blog/best-practices-healthcare-employee-engagement. Accessed January 18, 2019.

Barcalow, N. (2016). "Why Does Employee Recognition Matter?" *Marketing Health Services*, Spring, 1.

Barnes, D. C., Ponder, N. and Hopkins, C. D. (2015). "The Impact of Perceived Customer Delight on the Frontline Employee", *Journal of Business Research*, 68, 433–441.

Brown, T. J., Mowen, J. C., Donavan, D. T. and Licata, J. W. (2002). "The Customer Orientation of Service Workers: Personality Trait Effects on Self and Supervisor Rating", *Journal of Marketing Research*, 39, 110–119.

Chen, S. Y., Wu, C., Chang, C. S. and Lin, C. T. (2015). "Job Rotation and Internal Marketing for Increased Job Satisfaction and Organizational Commitment in Hospital Nursing Staff", *Journal of Nursing Management*, 23, 297–306.

Cutler, J. (2016). "Employee Experience is Key to Productivity", *Management Services*, 60 (4).

Deshpande, R., Farley, J. U. and Webster, F. E. (1993). "Corporate Culture, Customer Orientation, and Innovativeness of Japanese Firms: A Quadrad Analysis", *Journal of Marketing*, 57, 23–37.

Dewar, J. (2018). "6 Healthcare Employee Engagement Trends for 2018", Published January 9, 2018, http://education.healthcaresource.com/healthcare-employee-engagement-2018/.

Frates, J. (2012). "Patient Experience Matters More Now Than Ever", http://patientexperience.com/pwcreport2/. Accessed January 12, 2019.

Gazzoli, G., Hancer, M. and Kim, B. (2013). "Explaining Why Employee Customer Orientation Influences Customers' Perception of the Service Encounter", *Journal of Service Management*, 24 (4), 382–400.

Goldstein, S. M. (2003). "Employee Development: An Examination of Service Strategy in a High Contact Service Environment", *Production and Operations Management*, 12 (2), 186–203.

Guenzi, P., De Luca, L. M. and Troilo, G. (2011). "Organizational Drivers of Salespeople's Customer Orientation and Selling Orientation", *Journal of Personal Selling & Sales Management*, 31 (3), 269–285.

Gunawardane, G. (2011). "Reliability of the Internal Service Encounter", *International Journal of Quality and Reliability Management*, 28 (9), 1003–1018.

Healthcare Success (2017). "The Power of Internal Marketing in Healthcare", https://www.healthcaresuccess.com/blog/physician-marketing/the-power-of-internal-marketing-in-healthcare-and-10-ways-to-use.html. Accessed November 13, 2018.

Keaveney, S. M. (1995). "Customer Switching Behavior in Service Industries", *Journal of Marketing*, 59 (2), 71–82.

Kim, H. J., Tavitiyaman, P. and Kim, W. G. (2009). "The Effect of Commitment to Service on Employee Service Behaviors: The mediating Role of Job Satisfaction", *Journal of Hospitality and Tourism Research*, 33 (3), 369–390.

Lee, Y., Nam, J., Park, D. and Lee, K. A. (2006). "What Factors Influence Customer-Oriented Prosocial Behavior of Customer-Contact Employees?", *Journal of Services Marketing*, 20 (4), 251–264.

Lin, W. (2008). "Factors Enhancing the Intentions of Employees Toward Customer-Oriented Behaviors", *International Journal of Commerce and Management*, 18 (3), 267–288.

Piercy, N. and Morgan, N. (1991). "Internal Marketing: The Missing Half of The Marketing Program", *Long Range Planning*, 24 (2), 82–93.

Sherwood, R. (2013). "Employee Engagement Drives Health Care Quality and Financial Returns", October 30, 2013, *Harvard Business Review*, https://hbr.org/2013/10/employee-engagement-drives-health-care-quality-and-financial-returns. Accessed January 12, 2019.

Yohn, D. L. (2016). "Design Your Employee Experience as Thoughtfully as You Design Your Customer Experience", *Harvard Business Review*, December 8.

Chapter 12

Marketing to Physicians: Physician Engagement and Physician Relations Management in Health Care Marketing

12.1. Relevance of Physician Engagement in Health Care Marketing

In earlier chapters, we recognized several important facets of the relationship between health care marketing and physicians. These included the following:

- While consumers, patients, and their families are the primary customers in health care marketing, important secondary customers include *physicians*, pharmacists, care coordinators, and community organizations.
- Heavy dependence of health care consumers/patients on family, friends, and *physicians* in selecting health care products/services. Therefore, in certain circumstances, there is a need to market health care services to intermediate parties rather than the end user, e.g., marketing to physicians to encourage referral of consumers/patients to a managed care health plan or hospital. Marketing hospital services and pharmaceutical products to physicians are discussed in Sections 12.3 and 12.4, respectively.
- Topics of interest among health marketing professionals, as shown by topics discussed at recent health care marketing conferences, and topics of interest in health care marketing-related journals (see Chapter 1) include "Exploring Techniques to Engage Physicians", "Using Emerging

Technologies to Grow Physician Referrals", and "Physician Engagement: Influencer (Physicians, Family and Community) Marketing".
- In general, modern emphasis on increased partnerships with physicians and other providers for referral of new enrollees/subscribers and hence, emphasis on "physician engagement" and "provider relations".

Physician relations management, sometimes called provider relations management, is an important function in health plans, hospitals, and pharmaceutical companies.

In an informal survey of 20 health plan marketers for health plans, Accountable Care Organizations (ACOs) and Independent Practice Associations (IPAs) in Southern California conducted by the author in September 2017 indicated that these health plan marketers spend 50% of their effort on physicians/relations.

> **A Sample Physician Relations Function Objective: Christiana Care Health System (Wilmington, Delaware)**
>
> The objective of the Physician Relations department is to be the primary liaison between Christiana Care and our medical dental staff community of over 1,400 physicians, dentists, and their office staff members. We are here to answer your questions, help you with issue resolution, keep you informed of important changes at Christiana Care, and finally to provide educational opportunities for you and your staff (Christiana Care, 2018).

It is important to note the key activities embedded in this objective, namely:

- Primary liaison between the health care organization and physicians;
- Answer physician questions and inquiries;
- Physician complaint handling and issue resolution;
- Dissemination of policy and practice information, and changes, in the health care organization; and
- Provision of educational opportunities.

In health plans (HMOs), the provider relations function typically comes under the Provider Contracting Department. Provider relations typically involve provider services and provider contracting. All these aspects of the relationship between the health care organization and the providers are important to keep physicians satisfied. A summary of these aspects of physician/provider relations from a large health plan is as follows (Kaiser Permanente, 2015):

- Provider Services
    - Provider orientation and education;
    - Resolve operational issues including payment issues;
    - Share best practices;
    - Promote mutual values and goals;
    - Understand unique health care communities;
    - Participate in the design of the community health care delivery system; and
    - Assistance with compliance with regulations.
- Provider Contracting
    - Contract negotiations;
    - Reimbursement;
    - Maintain current information about providers; and
    - Resolve contract-related disputes.

> Thus, we may say that the Provider Relations Department of a health plan or a hospital virtually performs the physician/provider marketing function.

12.1.1. What is physician engagement?

In Chapter 11, we discussed employee engagement, an essential factor for effective health care marketing. We observed that employee engagement is the emotional commitment employees have to the company and its goals. Similarly, physician engagement is the emotional commitment the physician has to the health care organization (hospital or health plan) and its goals, policies, and practices.

Burger and Giger (2014) identify engaged physicians as those "with emotional equity in the health system from those who did not buy in."

In summary, physician engagement serves several objectives of health care organizations such as hospitals, health plans, and pharmaceutical firms.

- Physicians being the most trusted source of consumers and patients, they are the best source of direct additional patient referrals.
- Physician engagement leads to improved patient experience resulting in patient retention.
- Health care systems need physician involvement and engagement for quality and cost improvements which in turn contribute to better patient experience (Kumar, 2013).
- Led by Medicare, Medicaid, and health plans, value-based payments (payments tied to quality and patient experience) to hospitals are becoming the standard. Physicians are highly responsible for both these elements.
- Engaged physicians contribute to productivity, efficiency, and quality improvement in hospitals.

Hospital strategies include waste reduction and operational efficiency. Physicians are a rich resource for ideas in these aspects. Oshiro (2015a) claims that physicians drive 75–85% of all quality and cost decisions.

A survey by Gallup highlights the importance of engaged physicians: for one hospital alone, there was a 26% increase in productivity for engaged physicians over disengaged physicians. One engaged physician adds an average of US$460,000 in patient revenue per year (Burger and Giger, 2014).

12.2. Physician Characteristics that Affect Marketing to Physicians

Physicians are well known to be very busy people. They have very little time beyond patient care and personal life. Physicians are business persons in addition to caring for patients. They have business needs to increase revenue for the practice, decrease costs of operations, and improve efficiency and staff efficiency (Pillow, 2010). Therefore, they are interested in the following:

- Short presentations — marketers should present unique opportunities their organization can offer into short presentations.
- Propositions to address their patient base and revenue increases, and cost savings, i.e., tangible benefits in addition to improving patient care.
- Present action and results rather than promises.

Physicians are highly educated and depend on clear data analysis. They like to see data to demonstrate propositions presented to them, e.g., data showing the following:

- Effect of hospital services or pharmaceutical products on specific patient types or in treating specific diagnoses.
- Studies showing health improvements in specific patient populations of the physician's specialty, e.g., children or patients with diabetes.
- Hospital data showing reduction in hospital stays or readmissions.

Pillow (2010) also suggests that health care marketers study the physician's background and practice data prior to meeting the physician if they are available on the physician's website, the website of hospitals, or professional networking websites (e.g., LinkedIn).

Office managers and administrators of physician's offices are the key people managing the physician's availability. They have substantial influence on the physician's calendar and decisions. Therefore, good public relations efforts with these office managers and administrators will be essential.

Physicians have difficulty understanding complex revenue-generating schemes and educating physicians on these schemes is a great way to win the physician's respect and trust. These schemes include the following:

- *Incentive payments from health plans and medical groups (IPAs)*: Most health plans have "Pay for Performance" (P4P) programs that pay incentive (bonus) payments at the end of the year for physicians who have met targets in patient access measures, quality improvement measures, patient visit (encounter) data, and other reports.
- *Revenue from risk-sharing arrangements with health plans entered into by medical groups/IPAs the physician is participating in*: Health plans and participating physician groups enter into arrangements called shared risk or full risk arrangements. These arrangements pay the medical groups a share of savings from reducing over utilization and often physicians participating in medical groups are entitled to a share of these payments.
- *Risk adjustment rates affecting payments from Medicare*: The Centers for Medicare and Medicaid Services (CMS) pays health plans participating in Medicare Part C (Medicare Advantage) and certain other programs according to the health status of enrollees. Health plans receive higher payments for high risk enrollees, i.e., those who have multiple health conditions. Health plans receive these additional payments only upon submitting data on services received by enrollees. Primary care physicians who manage these enrollees are the source of this data and health plans reward physicians with incentive payments for good record keeping and cooperation.

- *Role in patient satisfaction surveys that affect payments from Medicare to health plan in which physician is participating:* Beneficiary satisfaction is a component in CMS's Star Rating System of health plans and payments to Medicare Advantage health plans depend on these ratings. As physicians are the point of contact for plan patients whose satisfaction ratings depend on visits to physicians, physicians have a significant role in patient satisfaction. Health plans provide incentives for physicians who cooperate in improving patient satisfaction scores.
- *Care Plan Oversight (CPO) programs:* CPO includes certain services physicians provide but may not be getting reimbursed under direct billing programs. These are certain services for homecare or hospice patients such as reviewing charts, discussing drug treatments, reports and treatment plans, phone calls with health care professionals who are not employees of the practice and are involved in the patient's care, conducting team conferences, discussing drug treatment and interactions (not routine prescription renewals) with a pharmacist, and coordinating care if physician or non-physician practitioner time is required. If the physician is not billing for CPO, they will greatly appreciate information of this program.

It is also important to learn communication channels and modes preferred by physicians. Researchers and industry experts are of the opinion that:

- Modern physicians' use of internet and mobile devices has grown.

Around 80% of physicians use smartphones and medical apps (Information Week, 2011; Referralmd, 2015).

Wolters Kluwer Health's 2013 Physician Outlook Survey (Pennic, 2014) of more than 300 practicing primary care physicians found that 26–50% of these physicians use their mobile phone 46% of the day and use their tablets 37% of the day.

Additionally, 72% of these physicians use their smartphone to access drug information, 44% to communicate with nurses and other staff, 43% to access medical research, and 42% to access evidence-based clinical reference tools (Pennic, 2014).

- The following are the top physician information sources:
    - 84% professional medical journals;
    - 80% general web browsers such as Google;

- 80% colleagues; and
  - 76% online free services.
- Physicians have high professional ego. Physicians value ethical behavior and self-respect.
- Physicians have an aversion to use voice mail and email. One of the main reasons for this is their concern of Health Insurance Portability and Accountability Act of 1996 (HIPAA) privacy rules (or the lack of full knowledge of these rules).

Quarles (2018) in a series of articles, "Marketing to Doctors", makes several observations and suggestions on physician engagement and marketing to physicians:

- Market segmentation is vital. All physicians are not the same. The physician market should be segmented into very narrow niches and even down to the individual physician level (see Section 8.6 of Chapter 8).

> **Customer-Centric Market Segmentation of Physicians**
>
> In addition to the common demographic variable (age, gender, and income) used to segment average consumers, physicians can be segmented using certain other specific variables. These are specialty, medical school attended, residency programs attended, solo or group practice, income dependency on health plans, IPAs and direct patient payments, primary patient population (Medicare, Medicaid, commercial insurance, and cash patients), decision-making influencers (health plan formulary, peers, and health plan/group medical directors and pharmaceutical and therapeutic (P&T) committees), and geographical area of practice (which usually determines income and educational level of patients, e.g., Beverly Hills, California vs. a rural area).

- It is important to use multiple media such as direct mail, trade publications, fax, paid search, websites with search engine optimization, e-newsletters, email blasts (with opt-in/out options), affiliate marketing, publicity, telemarketing, and trade shows at physician conferences.
- Formulate value propositions to present to physicians. Value propositions are clear and concise statements that explain how your product would

meet physician's needs, have specific benefits (ideally shown with objective statistics), and show how your product is more suitable for physician's needs than competing products in the market. This, of course, means that health care marketers are supported by market research identifying the target physician's patient population and prescribing patterns.
- Formulate and present a unique selling proposition. Doctors are skeptical about similar presentations from multiple marketers.
- Content of presentations to physicians is important. This depends on media of presentation — personal one-to-one or digital media (see Section 10.7 of Chapter 10).

Several health care marketing consultants and writers emphasize the influence of a physician's office manager/administrator in managing the physician's availability to see marketers, his/her prescription patterns, physician's data management, and patient relations. Therefore, maintaining professional yet friendly relations with a physician's office manager/administrator is important in marketing to physicians.

12.3. Hospital Marketing to Physicians

From a hospital's perspective, the core market for referral of patients to the hospital consists of physicians who practice on its medical staff (Healthfutures, 2016).

Except for admission through emergency rooms, which do not require direct physician referral, hospitals must rely on their medical staff to bring in the vast majority of patients.

Physician engagement is vital to hospitals. Burger and Giger (2014), citing from Gallup's work with hospitals, highlight that physicians who were fully or partially engaged were 26% more productive (in hospital settings) than physicians who were not engaged or who were actively disengaged. They equate this increase to an average of nearly half a million US dollars in patient revenue per physician per year to the hospital.

In recent times, hospitals have increased hiring physicians and owning or supporting multispecialty medical groups. However, it is doubtful whether this has contributed to hospitals' revenue. Goldsmith *et al.* (2016) cite a recent report by Moody's Investors Service that found that physician employment was damaging hospital operating margins. They also report that in 2013, hospital-owned multispecialty practices are also making losses around $100,000 per physician.

These findings indicate that patient referral by physicians should continue to be the primary focus of hospital service marketing. In any case, the primary aim of owning or supporting medical groups is to increase patient referrals by physicians in those groups.

12.3.1. How hospitals can achieve physician engagement

Health care marketing consultants and experts suggest the following strategies for hospitals to enhance physician engagement (Burger and Giger, 2014):

- Proactively address and provide solutions for physician problems especially those related to changes brought about by Affordable Care Act (ACA), Medicare, and Medicaid. Hospitals should initiate provider relations departments in health plans that spend a significant portion of their time and effort in sending out representatives to meet physicians and bringing back physician concerns and complaints to the health plan for remedial actions.
- Promote effective communication between physicians and system administrators. Successful hospital–physician alignment. Removing conflicts between physicians and administrators.
- Encourage physician involvement with hospital administration. Ensure physicians' opinions are heard. Recognize the leadership roles physician can play. Physicians often complain about wanting more of a voice in hospital strategies and the hospital not listening to them enough.
- Efficient service operations (appointments, scheduling, discharge, and follow-up processes) that support physician's clinical activities.
- Accommodating patient's Primary Care Physician (PCP) involvement in patient care. Though not usually a part of the hospital staff, it is the PCP who initiates the referral via a specialist, facilitating involvement of hospitalists who carry on the work of PCPs and who do not wish to conduct hospital rounds.
- Provider education: Seminars, career-building, continuing professional development and continuing medical education events, and assistance with increasing efficiency of the practice, e.g., Electronic Medical Records (EMR).

Hospital support for physicians in exchange for increased referrals of patients has many potential legal ramifications and pitfalls. Hospitals should be aware of physician assistance strategies, joint ventures with physicians, and value-based care payments to physicians that might violate Stark Law which requires physicians to receive only fair-market prices for their services. For a complete discussion of these issues, see Chapter 13.

12.4. Marketing Pharmaceutical Products/Medical Devices to Physicians

Prescription medication sales are not made at the sole request of consumer/patient users. These medications are decided upon by a physician/other licensed provider who then issues a prescription to the pharmaceutical provider.

Therefore, the customer of pharmaceutical (pharma) companies, for prescription drugs, is the physician. Pharma companies engage in huge marketing efforts directed at physicians.

Bell (2018) presents figures, citing marketing analytics provider iSpot.tv, for just television advertising by pharma companies in 2018 which has accounted for 187 commercials for about 70 prescription medications at an expense of US$2.8 billion.

Swanson (2015) reports that nine out of 10 big pharmaceutical companies spent more on sales and marketing than on research in 2013. Pharma companies spent US$98 billion on sales and marketing, with Johnson & Johnson alone spending US$17.5 billion on sales and marketing in 2013.

> Swanson (2015) also reports that most of this marketing money is directed at the physicians who do the prescribing, rather than final user consumers. Drug companies spent more than US$3 billion a year marketing to consumers in the US in 2012, but an estimated US$24 billion was spent marketing directly to health care professionals.

Therefore, continuous study of prescribing behavior of physicians and physician-targeted marketing strategies, especially those using modern digital marketing techniques, is very important for pharma marketing.

Physicians claim that they depend on many factors while making decisions with regard to their prescriptions (Pharma.org, 2008).

This report presents some key information about physician prescription behavior.

- In a 2002 physician survey by the Boston Consulting Group, 54% of physicians reported that formularies have a major impact on prescribing decisions.

- Among the other factors identified as having a major impact were peers (50%) and clinical practice guidelines (47%), with pharmaceutical representatives at 14%.
- A 2007 physician survey by the Tufts Center for the Study of Drug Development yielded broadly similar results. Physicians named the following factors as influencing their prescription decisions: information gathered at continuing medical education (67%), information from peers (43%), and payers' decisions such as formularies and pre-approval requirements (37%). These outweighed information from pharmaceutical companies (13%).
- In a 2008 KRC Research survey, physicians reported giving more weight to their clinical knowledge and experience, the patient's particular situation, peer-reviewed journal articles, clinical practice guidelines, their colleagues and peers, and the patient's financial status than to information from pharmaceutical companies when prescribing medication.

Other research on physician behavior relating to prescribing drugs identify several key factors listed here which are consistent with these observations (Karyanni, 2010; Manchanda *et al.*, 2005).

- Key sources of information used are prescription experience and detailing (marketing material and techniques, and personal visits by drug company representatives to explain details of a new drug to physicians).
- Risk balancing: new drugs with insufficient data on efficacy vs. established drugs, for example, Trulicity injectable vs. oral Metformin for diabetes patients.
- Brand image.
- Efficacy and provision of scientific evidence from clinical studies.
- Opinion of colleagues.
- Information from scientific journals.
- Product price.
- Patients' compliance factors and ease of use.

Limited Authority of Physicians in Managed Care Environments

It is not surprising that, in the modern health care world of managed care, insurance payers (health plans and their pharmacy benefit managers (PBMs), Medicare, Medicaid, and commercial insurance)

(*Continued*)

> control physician prescribing patterns via formularies and tiered drug structures. Tiered drug structures incentivize patients to use generic and preferred non-generic drugs. Physicians almost have no choice in these situations.

Personal visits by drug company representatives to physicians to promote prescription drugs (called "detailing") are rare in modern times. Almost as a rule, academic health centers avoid having drug reps on their campuses, hospital, and clinics. Many medical institutions including the VA and Kaiser have also enacted similar policies banning drug reps. The number of doctors willing to see reps has declined about 20% since 2008. In 2010, about 11% of American physicians had "severe" or "no-see" restrictions on drug rep access, while 34% had "some" restrictions (Mintz, 2012).

Nevertheless, it may be worth looking at research findings on factors affecting detailing. Factors identified as affecting success at detailing are as follows:

- Detailer's scientific knowledge;
- Physician–detailer interpersonal relationship;
- Handouts and brochures with details about the medicine;
- Free samples of the medicine, a practice that has almost become ineffective with the advent of generics for many drugs;
- Educating the physicians on new medicines and opportunities to participate in conferences; and
- Value-adding incentives, i.e., office-practice items, patient record forms, etc.

Two practices relating to marketing drugs to physicians that come well within concepts and practices on modern health care management are discussed next. These are as follows:

- Adoption of digital technology in place of lengthy personal visits by drug company reps. We have already seen that modern physicians are quite tech savvy and are heavy users of mobile digital devices such as mobile phones and tablets. They are also very much open to digital communications via email and texts provided these messages meet guidelines we have presented throughout this book on content marketing.
- Alignment between physicians and pharmaceutical companies to improve care and access in their communities. Sponsoring wellness events that

introduce local doctors to large community patient pools. Supporting physician programs to help patients be compliant and adherent to their treatment.

12.4.1. Legal and ethical aspects of pharma marketing to physicians

As with hospital marketing to physicians, the area of pharma marketing to physicians is highly regulated by a variety of laws and ethical standards. As a result, attractive incentives such as ball game tickets and trips provided by pharma industry to physicians have almost vanished.

These issues are discussed in detail in Chapter 13.

12.5. Physician Relations Management

Physician Relations (PRM) Programs are established and operated usually by hospitals, pharmaceutical companies, and health plans.

Example: Physician Relations Program at MD Anderson Cancer Center

The strategic vision of MD Anderson's Physician Relations department is to integrate relationship building with operational excellence and engagement in order to develop an oncology referral network that will mostly benefit cancer patients. We strive to:

- Establish and sustain loyal physician relationships between MD Anderson and our physician colleagues who trust us with the care and treatment of their oncology patients,
- Use qualitative and quantitative analysis to facilitate patient referral processes that enhance the patient access experience and improve referring physician satisfaction, and
- Create opportunities to engage our faculty with their colleagues in their communities to foster communication and establish relationships.

Source: University of Texas, MD Anderson Cancer Center. https://www.mdanderson.org/for-physicians/physician-relations.html.

In health plans, this function is usually allocated to the Provider Relations Department. Nevertheless, PRM is not only the responsibility of one department of the health care organization. It is a key strategy to be initiated and supported by top management, and one that needs an integrated effort by all functions.

The aim of PRMs is very much similar to what we have previously seen under Customer Relationship Management programs (CRMs).

PRMs aim to engage physicians in long-term relationships rather than seeking satisfaction with a single interaction, product, incentive payment, or assistance/support project.

12.5.1. Implementing a successful physician relations program

Research studies and expert/consultancy views provide several guidelines for setting up successful physician relationship management programs (Barlow, 2011; Becker's Hospital Review, 2011a, 2011b, 2013; Gamble, 2011; Oshiro, 2013; Ruocco, 2015). These are listed as follows:

- The shift toward value-based care in the health care industry is affecting hospital–physician relationships. Hospital payments from Medicare, Medicaid, and private health plans are increasingly being based on quality and patient experience. Both these are heavily dependent on physicians employed and on the staff of the hospital. This makes it essential to change the approach to physician relationship management.
  These developments suggest the following:
    o Physicians should be included in the hospital's decision-making process.
    o Regular sharing of management information and financial data should be made mandatory.
    o Team-based structure that allows for group decision-making should be followed.
- An element in the physician–hospital (or health plan) relationship often discussed as missing is *trust*. Above actions by hospitals together with regular communications with physicians would contribute toward building trust between the parties.

- Physicians expect hospitals to continually assist them with legal financial assistance. These include:
  - Opportunities for physicians to participate in quality, cost, and process improvement activities with suitable compensation.
  - Partnerships opportunities and regional service expansions.
  - Support physician practice operations and management.
  - Assistance with office space needs and expansions.
  - Referring patients to physician group integrated care systems at the time of discharge.
- A key element in good physician relationship management is prompt attention by the hospital (or the health plan) to physician needs and concerns. These needs have been found to be:
  - Improved quality within hospital;
  - Improved operations that physicians have to interact with (patient scheduling, admissions, discharges, and turnaround times);
  - Hospitals to utilize well-documented, reliable, and consistent protocols and processes relating to emergency departments, inpatient admissions, and discharges;
  - Improved coordination with physicians at discharge that would result in reduced readmissions;
  - Improved coordination with physicians to reduce length of stay;
  - Coordinated electronic notification systems to alert physicians at admissions and discharges;
  - Many physician groups have a strong primary care physician base who have developed long-term relationships with patients. These PCPs should be more involved in patient care at the hospital especially in complex care situations involving patient family (e.g., hospice care and end of life decisions); and
  - Competitive, clear, good, and transparent price information to patients and physicians. Patients usually do not understand insurance coverage and prices. This affects their relationships not only with hospitals and health plans but with physicians as well.
- Do not assign responsibility of PRM programs to sales/marketing alone. Make physician relations an organization-wide team effort involving the Chief Executive Officer (CEO), medical director, Chief Financial Officer (CFO), physicians, clinicians, and administrative staff.

- Coordination of activities such as physician contracting, information technology (IT), and provider relations. Often these activities are assigned to different subdepartments without sufficient coordination.
- Use appropriate mobile and social marketing techniques. Modern physicians are active users of digital technology especially mobile devices for communication. They are reported to dislike print marketing materials. They do like useful educational material. Educational material, white papers, and e-newsletters with new and useful information delivered using digital media and effective content is part of good physician relations.
- Use of modern PRM software programs. These programs combine physician profiles with the capability to track physician referral patterns. They also monitor financial data relating to physician referrals and identify physicians for incentives and additional support. They also track physician concern and issues that need resolution and progress with resolution coordinating multiple departments involved. They have the mobile capability to send communications to physicians to keep them informed on progress with resolution of issues, Continuing Medical Education (CME) events, and hospital and community events. Ascend is a well-known PRM system.

> Romn (2011) summarizes "Five Things Physicians Want in Hospitals" as follows:
>
> (1) Responsiveness;
> (2) Agility;
> (3) Trust;
> (4) Ease of practice; and
> (5) Communication.

References

Barlow, K. (2011). *The Complete Guide to Physician Relationships*, HealthLeaders Media, HCPro, Inc.

Becker's Hospital Review (2011a). "4 Keys to Successful Physician Relationship Management", August 9, https://www.beckershospitalreview.com/hospital-physician-relationships/4-keys-to-successful-physician-relationship-management.html. Accessed October 4, 2018.

Becker's Hospital Review (2011b). "7 Critical Mistakes in Physician Relations Programs", July 7, https://www.beckershospitalreview.com/hospital-physician-relationships/7-critical-mistakes-in-physician-relations-programs.html. Accessed October 4, 2018.

Becker's Hospital Review (2013). "The Growing Value of Physician Relations in an Ever-Changing Health System", April 16, https://www.beckershospitalreview.com/hospital-physician-relationships/the-growing-value-of-physician-relations-in-an-ever-changing-health-system.html. Accessed November 6, 2018.

Bell, J. (2018). "Pharma Advertising in 2018: TV, Midterms and Specialty Drugs", https://www.biopharmadive.com/news/pharma-ad-dtc-marketing-2018-spend-TV-congress/533319/. Accessed March 11, 2019.

Burger, J. and Giger, A. (2014). "Want to Increase Hospital Revenues? Engage Your Physicians", *Business Journal*, June 5, https://news.gallup.com/businessjournal/170786/increase-hospital-revenues-engage-physicians.aspx. Accessed March 11, 2019.

Christiana Care (2018). "Physician Relations", https://christianacare.org/forphysicians/physicianrelations/. Accessed January 17, 2019.

Gamble, M. (2011). "6 Keys to a Successful Physician Relations Program", *Becker's Hospital Review*, January 5, https://www.beckershospitalreview.com/hospital-physician-relationships/6-keys-to-a-successful-physician-relations-program.html. Accessed January 18, 2019.

Goldsmith, J., Burnett, J. and Nelson, R. (2016). "Getting the Most Value from Your Physicians", October 11, *Hospital & Health Networks*, https://www.hhnmag.com/articles/7605-how-hospitals-can-get-the-most-value-from-their-physicians. Accessed March 4, 2019.

Healthfutures (2016). "Market for Health Care — An Overview", www.healthfutures.net/pdf/w-ch1.pdf. Accessed November 12, 2018.

Information Week (2011). "80% of Doctors Use Mobile Devices at Work", https://www.informationweek.com/mobile/80--of-doctors-use-mobile-devices-at-work/d/d-id/1100880. Accessed January 12, 2019.

Kaiser Permanente (2015). Provider webpage, https://provider.ghc.org/open/render.jhtml?item=/open/workingWithGroupHealth/providerrelations.xml. Accessed January 18, 2019.

Karyanni, D. (2010). "A Cluster Analysis of Physician's Values, Prescribing Behavior and Attitudes towards Firms' Marketing Communications", Working Paper, University of Patras, Greece.

Kumar, P. (2013). "Engaging Physicians to Transform Operational and Clinical Performance in the Post-Reform Health System: Meeting the Challenges Ahead", *McKinsey*, May, http://healthcare.mckinsey.com/sites/default/files/MCK_Hosp_MDSurvey.pdf. Accessed March 11, 2019.

Manchanda, P., *et al.* (2005). "Understanding Firm, Physician and Consumer Choice Behavior in the Pharmaceutical Industry", *Marketing Letters*, 16 (3–4), 293–308.

Mintz, M. (2012). "Is There a Harm to Not Seeing Drug Reps?", June 10, https://www.kevinmd.com/blog/2012/06/harm-drug-reps.html. Accessed March 7, 2019.

Oshiro, B. (2015a). "6 Proven Strategies for Engaging Physicians — and 4 Ways to Fail", *HealthCatalyst*, https://www.healthcatalyst.com/proven-physician-engagement-strategies. Accessed January 12, 2019.

Oshiro, B. (2015b). "The Best Way Hospitals Can Engage Physicians, Nurses, and Staff", Physician Engagement, *HealthCatalyst*, https://www.healthcatalyst.com/proven-physician-engagement-strategies. Accessed March 5, 2019.

Oshiro, B. (2016). "The Best Way Hospitals Can Engage Physicians, Nurses, and Staff", Posted in Physician Engagement, https://www.healthcatalyst.com/proven-physician-engagement-strategies. Accessed September 24, 2018.

Pennic, J. (2014). "Infographic: Top Physician Information Sources by Mobile Device", February 20, https://hitconsultant.net/2014/02/20/infographic-top-physician-information-sources-mobile-device/. Accessed November 13, 2018.

Pharma.org (2008). "Pharmaceutical Marketing in Perspective: Its Value and Role as One of Many Factors Informing Prescribing", http://phrma-docs.phrma.org/sites/default/files/pdf/phrma_marketing_brochure_influences_on_prescribing_final.pdf. Accessed March 3, 2019.

Pillow, M. (2010). "Home Health Referral Marketing to Physicians in 5 Easy Steps (Part 1 and 2)", February 22, https://kinnser.com/home-health-blog/post/home-health-referral-marketing-to-physicians-in-5-easy-steps-part-1/. Accessed November 12, 2018.

Quarles, R. (2018). "Marketing to Doctors, Part 1: Defining the Challenge", https://glasscanopy.com/marketing-to-doctors-part1/. Accessed January 12, 2019.

Referralmd (2015). "30 Amazing Mobile Health Technology Statistics for Today's Physician", https://getreferralmd.com/2015/08/mobile-healthcare-technology-statistics/. Accessed January 2, 2019.

Romn, C. (2011). "Simple Steps to Improve Relations with Physicians", *Hospital & Health Networks*, March 1, https://www.hhnmag.com/articles/4507-simple-steps-to-improve-relations-with-physicians. Accessed March 6, 2019.

Ruocco, E. (2015). "3 Strategies for Modern Physician Relationship Management", *Evaraint*, November 11, https://www.evariant.com/blog/physician-relationship-management. Accessed March 6, 2019.

Strongwater, S. (2016). "What Physician Practices Need from Hospitals", *NEJM Catalyst*, September 28, https://catalyst.nejm.org/physician-practices-need-hospital-partners/. Accessed March 12, 2019.

Swanson, A. (2015). "Big Pharmaceutical Companies are Spending Far More on Marketing than Research", *Washington Post*, February 11, https://www.washingtonpost.com/news/wonk/wp/2015/02/11/big-pharmaceutical-companies-are-spending-far-more-on-marketing-than-research/?noredirect=on&utm_term=.85afafbf94be. Accessed March 2, 2019.

Suggested Additional Readings

Hagland, M. (2004). "Physician Relations Programs: In Today's Operating Environment, a Whole New Ballgame", *Insight...not just news*, 5 (8), August, Cor Health LLC, http://www.corporatehealthgroup.com/ftpuser/CHG%20Library/Physicians%20Relations/Physician%20Relations%20Programs-a%20whole%20new%20ballgame-Insight%20Aug%2004.pdf. Accessed January 17, 2019.

Peltier, J. W., Boyt, T. and Westfall, J. E. (1997). "Building Relationships with Physicians: Internal Marketing Efforts Help Strengthen Organizational Bonds at a Rural Health Care Clinic", *Marketing Health Services*, 17 (3), 12–18.

Trilliant Health (2018). "Strategic Engagement with Physicians is Crucial to the Success and Strength of a Hospital", https://www.trillianthealth.com/our-solutions/physician-focused/. Accessed January 12, 2019.

Chapter 13

Legal and Ethical Issues Affecting Health Care Marketing

13.1. Evolution of Legal and Ethical Environment in Health Care Marketing

Health care is one of the most vigorously regulated industries in the United States, and health care marketing is an area within the health care industry that is also highly regulated and monitored.

There are many arguments supporting regulation of health care providers and delivery:

- Government regulations attempt to reduce or eliminate the effects of imbalances in the health insurance market.

Human behavior of insured persons would lead to overconsumption because they do not pay the full prices. Arrow (1963) termed this "moral hazard", which generally means that one party has an incentive to use more resources than otherwise would have been because another party bears the costs. The aggregate effect of moral hazard in any market is to restrict supply, raise prices, and encourage overconsumption (Ross, 2018). Also, insurance companies do not charge the same premium to all subscribers. They charge higher rates to riskier customers.

There is no evidence that government regulations directly reduce overconsumption. However, certain recent regulations do attempt to reduce or eliminate "moral hazard". An example is the recent trend to force price transparency in health care by regulations. For example, the Affordable

Care Act (Obama Care) contains several provisions to encourage greater price transparency in health care. The rationale for this is that better information to consumers/patients will help drive down high medical charges. Centers for Medicare and Medicaid Services (CMS) now requires hospitals to release a standard list of prices for their medical services.

- Regulations also attempt to prevent the concept called "adverse selection" presented by Arrow (1963).

This means that if insurance companies are unable to distinguish high-risk consumers from low-risk consumers, low-risk consumers will be left without insurance. Market outcome will be inefficient. Government regulations can improve this market outcome by requiring everyone to be insured or by providing insurance or medical care directly. This was an argument for enacting the Affordable Care Act (ACA or Obamacare). ACA prohibits health insurers from refusing to sell health insurance to people with pre-existing conditions and prohibits health plans from imposing annual or lifetime caps on benefits. It also requires health plans to cover a uniform set of essential health benefits (Davis, 2018).

- Government finances a large portion of health care in the US. Therefore, it should have a role in overseeing the delivery of health care.

More than 17.6% of US gross domestic product (GDP) is devoted to health care. Approximately US$1 trillion of that cost is borne by taxpayers. The six major government health care programs — Medicare, Medicaid, the State Children's Health Insurance Program (SCHIP), the Department of Defense TRICARE and TRICARE for Life programs (DOD TRICARE), the Veterans Health Administration (VHA) program, and the Indian Health Service (IHS) program — provide health care services to about one-third of Americans. The federal government has a responsibility to ensure that the more than US$500 billion invested annually in these programs is used wisely to reduce the burden of illness, injury, and disability and to improve the health and functioning of the population.

- Regulations are necessary to ensure quality of care and patient safety.

The health care delivery system is highly fragmented with a large number of providers, such as physicians, hospitals, senior living facilities, pharmaceutical companies, and ancillary providers, organized in multiple forms (Independent

Practice Associations (IPAs), health plans, Managed Care Organizations (MCOs), hospital chains, Pharmacy Benefit Managers (PBMs)), and the maintenance of quality becomes a challenge. Therefore, it is argued that regulation is necessary to ensure the safe and effective delivery of thorough and proper health care. "Regulations are legal restrictions aimed to produce outcomes that otherwise might not occur" (Nickitas et al., 2016, p. 23).

From hospitals, to clinics to pharmacies to long-term care facilities, health care is being delivered in almost every corner of the country. The regulations must be present in all these places as well. They must be clear, they must be firm, and they must be fair. They must always demonstrate that the care and the rights of the patient are always the priority (Nurses' Notes, 2016).

- Government has a responsibility to protect vulnerable populations in the health care market such as elderly (Medicare) and low-income persons (Medicaid).

Many government regulations are designed to prevent exploitation of low-income and elderly persons. This is highly applicable in health care marketing. Medicare closely monitors marketing of Medicare Advantage (MA) and Medicare Advantage Prescription Drug (MAPD) programs to senior citizens. State agencies monitor almost all communications, such as letters and newsletters sent to Medicaid beneficiaries. In the modern era, communications to Medicaid and Medicare beneficiaries by email is also governed by CMS and state regulations. We will discuss regulations affecting marketing to Medicare and Medicaid patients later in this chapter.

- Licensing and accreditation of health care providers and facilities will prevent unqualified persons from practicing medicine and related professions, and unsafe hospitals and similar facilities from providing inpatient services.

Health care providers of all forms are licensed by legislature and government agencies. Providers subject to such licensing and accreditation include medical education, physicians, hospital, outpatient surgical centers, assisted living and skilled nursing facilities, ancillary providers, and drugs and pharmaceuticals. Almost every aspect of the field is overseen by one regulatory body or another, and sometimes by several (Field, 2008).

Many health care providers and organizations are also surveyed and credentialed by independent bodies or Medical Boards such as the National

Committee on Quality Assurance (NCQA; Health Plans and large physician groups) and the Joint Commission (Hospitals).

- **NCQA:** The NCQA accredits many types of health care organizations. Among these, health plan accreditation is the most well-known. The objective of NCQA surveys and accreditation is to ensure that health plans support optimum levels of care for health plan members, control costs, and meet government requirements (NCQA, 2018). Significant in NCQA is that survey results are based on clinical performance and consumer experience (HEDIS® and CAHPS®). NCQA survey and accreditation framework is very comprehensive covering all aspects of operations of a health plan such as:
    o Quality management and improvement;
    o Network adequacy and contracting;
    o Utilization management;
    o Credentialing and recredentialing; and
    o Member rights and complaint/grievance handling.

- **Joint Commission:** The Joint Commission is an independent, not-for-profit group in the United States that administers voluntary accreditation programs for hospitals and other health care organizations. The commission develops performance standards that address crucial elements of operation, such as patient care, medication safety, infection control, and consumer rights (TechTarget, 2019). Joint commission accredits many types of organizations and most important of these being hospitals, nursing homes, and other long-term care facilities. Federal and state governments recognize Joint Commission accreditation in registering for Medicaid and Medicare reimbursements.

- It is important to safeguard consumers from providers who have been excluded for inferior quality of care or health care fraud.

The Office of Inspector General's (OIG) list of excluded individuals and entities exists to provide information regarding excluded providers to the health care industry and the general public. This list includes both individuals and entities currently excluded from participating in federal health care programs including Medicare and Medicaid (OIG, 2018). Health plans are prohibited from contracting with excluded providers which prevents such providers from providing services to Medicare and Medicaid beneficiaries enrolled in the health plan.

- Regulations are essential to ensure privacy and security of individual health information maintained and used by health care providers and organization.

Some of the most well-known regulations in health care relate to privacy and security of health information. These include the Health Insurance Portability and Accountability Act of 1996 (HIPAA) and its regulations, HITECH Act (2009), the Omnibus ("Mega") Rule of 2013, and state medical information privacy laws. Several of these regulations have a significant impact on health care marketing. These will be discussed in detail later in this chapter.

- Government must enact permissible regulations to ensure equal access to health care.

An example of such regulation is Executive Order 13166 signed by President Bill Clinton on August 11, 2000: "Improving Access to Services for Persons with Limited English Proficiency". This Executive Order requires federal agencies to examine the services they provide, identify any need for services to those with limited English proficiency (LEP), and develop and implement a system to provide those services so LEP persons can have meaningful access to them.

To follow up on this order, the US Department of Justice issued a policy guidance "Enforcement of Title VI of the Civil Rights Act of 1964 — National Origin Discrimination Against Persons with Limited English Proficiency" (2002 LEP Guidance). This LEP Guidance sets forth the compliance standards that recipients of federal financial assistance must follow to ensure that their programs and activities normally provided in English are accessible to LEP persons and thus do not discriminate on the basis of national origin in violation of Title VI's prohibition against national origin discrimination (LEP.gov, 2017).

This is a very broadly applicable regulation as "recipients of federal financial assistance", in the health care context, includes almost all health plans, hospitals, and other health providers active in the Medicare, Medicare, and CHIP programs. This resulted in Medicare and Medicaid programs, and state agencies, setting up stringent regulations upon health plans and hospitals that require provision of interpreter and sign language services, and translation of vital documents to persons with limited English proficiency.

For a comprehensive analysis of how government regulations attempt to ensure equal access to health care in the US, see Levesque *et al.* (2013), who present multiple dimensions and population capabilities associated with access to health care. There are several dimensions of access to health care services. These are recognized as follows (Levesque *et al.*, 2013):

- Approachability;
- Acceptability;
- Availability and accommodation;
- Affordability; and
- Appropriateness.

Also recognized are the following capabilities of populations that overlap with the above five dimensions:

- Ability to perceive;
- Ability to seek;
- Ability to reach;
- Ability to pay; and
- Ability to engage.

These are illustrated in Figure 13.1.

Access to health care by LEP populations and ACA (Obamacare) regulations and subsidies are clear examples of improving population capabilities in accessing health care. Setting up state and federal exchanges, formulating laws relating to essential benefits that insurance companies participating in ACA health care provide, and prohibiting lifetime caps and pre-existing condition provisions are examples of regulations set up to improve supply-side dimensions.

13.1.1. Health care regulation is not without criticism

Although everyone believes that there should be some form of regulation of health care delivery and quality, overregulation at time leads to inefficiency. As Field (2008) states, "The present regulatory structure is neither uniform nor consistent. A broad range of regulatory bodies and programs apply in different ways to various aspects of the industry. Health care regulations are

Legal and Ethical Issues Affecting Health Care Marketing 365

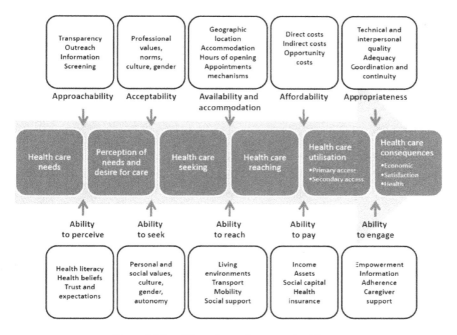

Figure 13.1. Dimensions of access to health care.

Source: Reproduced from Levesque *et al.* (2013). © Levesque *et al.*; licensee BioMed Central Ltd., 2013. This is an Open Access article distributed under the terms of the Creative Commons Attribution License (http://creativecommons.org/licenses/by/2.0), which permits unrestricted use, distribution, and reproduction in any medium, provided the original work is properly cited.

developed and enforced by all levels of government — federal, state, and local — and also by a large assortment of private organizations. At times, they operate without coordination." Many aspects of health care delivery are regulated by state and local agencies, and then again by federal agencies. Often, these multiple regulations subject health care providers to multiple inspections, audits, and reports. Sometimes these overlapping regulations are not consistent.

The path to marketing a new drug is similarly cumbersome. A pharmaceutical company must start by protecting its invention with a patent that is issued by the federal Patent and Trademark Office (PTO). It must then receive permission to conduct clinical testing from the federal Food and Drug Administration (FDA), which for many products culminates in review of the results by an advisory committee composed of private scientists. After approval for marketing is received in the form of a New Drug Approval (NDA), the manufacturer must adhere to marketing restrictions contained in the NDA. Next, in order to sell the drug widely, the manufacturer must obtain a place for it on the formularies of private pharmacy benefit management companies (PBMs) and health plans (Field, 2008).

Price and Norbeck (2013) in an article titled, "Healthcare is Turning into an Industry Focused on Compliance, Regulation rather than Patient Care" point out that many physicians are frustrated by the time and costs spent to comply with regulations on electronic medical records (EMR) and new diagnostic codes (ICD-10). Grimsley (2015) reports estimate by health care consulting forms that the new ICD-10 will not only decrease the time doctors have to spend with patients, but will also increase health care costs, for example increasing the cost to a large medical practice by as much as US$3 million per year. Usually, these increases in administrative costs are passed on to patients.

Regulations also impose a significant cost on health care delivery. Conover (2004) estimates that health services regulation imposes an annual cost of US$256 billion per year (with a range of US$28 billion to US$657 billion), suggesting that health services regulations could increase estimates of overall regulatory costs by more than 25% and that alternative computing approaches figure up to US$339.2 billion. He claims that regulation outweighs benefits by two-to-one and costs the average household over US$1,500 per year, and that high cost of health services regulation is responsible for more than 7 million Americans lacking health insurance, or one in six of the average daily uninsured. Moreover, 4,000 more Americans die every year from costs associated with health services regulation (22,000) than from lack of health insurance (18,000).

The multiplicity of government agencies regulating health care also merits an examination. It is virtually impossible to list all these agencies and their scope of regulation. Only the key agencies are listed in what follows:

- The Centers for Medicare and Medicaid Services (CMS) oversee most of the regulations related directly to the health care system.
- CMS and state agencies regulate Medicare programs for the elderly and disabled.
- CMS and state agencies regulate Medicaid for lower-income individuals and families.

- These same agencies regulate State Children's Health Insurance Program (SCHIP) for health insurance coverage for children under 19.
- CMS is also responsible for ensuring compliance to the Health Insurance Portability and Accountability Act (HIPAA).
- The Agency for Healthcare Research and Quality (AHRQ), another agency that falls under the US Department of Health & Human Services (HHS), conducts research aimed at improving the quality of health care, reducing costs and addressing patient safety and medical errors.
- The Centers for Disease Control and Prevention (CDC) in Atlanta examines public health and warns of possible health threats from infectious diseases. The CDC monitors birth defects, disabilities, diseases and conditions, emergency preparedness and response, environmental health, genetics and genomics, health promotion, injury and violence, travelers' health, vaccines and immunizations and workplace safety and health. The CDC is currently working closely with national, local, and international health organizations, including the World Health Organization, to control the transmission of the Ebola virus.
- The FDA is the federal regulatory agency responsible for controlling the safety and effectiveness of the country's drug supply for both humans and animals. The FDA regulates food safety, cosmetics, feed supply for animals, dietary supplements, and biologics as well as the national blood supply, medical devices, food additives, product recalls, and restaurant inspections.
- The United States Agency for Toxic Substances and Disease Registry (ATSDR) monitors and regulates the effects of hazardous materials on public health. The ATSDR responds to hazardous material threats, educates the public on hazardous materials (HAZMAT) risks and encourages participation from community members and organizations.
- The Environmental Protection Agency (EPA), another federal agency, was created to protect human health and the environment through the writing and enforcing of regulations based on laws passed by Congress.

Non-profit organizations that serve as watchdogs and accreditation institutions for health care in the US such as the Joint Commission (formerly JCAHO) and the National Committee for Quality Assurance (NCQA) were discussed previously.

13.1.2. Landmarks in regulations in the US affecting health care marketing

Finally, let us list landmarks in regulation in the US affecting health care marketing:

- Thirty-five years ago, professional advertising was illegal according to standards set by professional bodies in law and medicine.
- Health care providers and hospitals essentially did not advertise prior to 1977.
- Health care providers benefited from efforts by the legal profession. US Supreme Court decision (Bates v. State Bar of Arizona (1977)). State bar associations could no longer universally prohibit attorney advertising.
- In 1977, the Society for Healthcare Planning and Marketing was founded.
- In 1987, Medicare and Medicaid Patient Protection Act of 1987, referred to as the Anti-Kickback Statute (AKS), which affects marketing to, and via, physicians and provides criminal penalties for certain acts impacting Medicare and Medicaid reimbursable services was passed.
- In 1996, the Society for Healthcare Strategy and Market Development (SHSMD), a professional membership group of the American Hospital Association, was formed. It claims to serve more than 4,000 members — professionals who work in all sectors of health care, including hospitals and health systems, physician groups, consulting firms, advertising and public relations agencies, and service providers.

> Industry experts believe that physicians and dentists are still conservative about marketing; Younger physicians are reported to be more receptive to marketing than older physicians.

- In 1996, HIPAA and its regulations were passed.
- In 2009, HITECH Act, which imposes additional limitations on the three types of communications exempted under original HIPAA regulations, was passed. HITECH Act prohibits those communications without an authorization if

- o the covered entity receives direct or indirect payment in exchange for making the communications ("remuneration"); and
- o explicitly permits subsidized communications to be made without an authorization to provide refill reminders or otherwise communicate about a drug or biologic that is currently being prescribed for the individual, but only if the amount paid to the covered entity is reasonable in amount.
- In 2013, "Mega-Rule" (Omnibus Rule) came into effect (Ricoy, 2013).
  - o The Mega-Rule codified the additional HITECH Act limitations explained above and also addressed subsidized communications for treatment. In particular, the Mega-Rule determined that subsidized treatment communications also generally require authorization.
  - o The Mega-Rule did not make any changes to the existing exceptions for face-to-face communications or for promotional gifts of nominal value. Both are permitted regardless of whether they are subsidized communications.
  - o The Mega-Rule also codified the HITECH Act exception that permits covered entities to provide subsidized communications for refill reminders for a drug or biologic that is currently being prescribed for the individual, and determined that payments to covered entities for such reminders are reasonable only if they are reasonably related to the covered entity's cost of making the communications, such as postage.
  - o Mega-Rule provisions on marketing:
    - *Fundraising and marketing*: Requires fundraising communications to include a clear and conspicuous opportunity to opt out of receiving further communications. The Mega-Rule also makes clear that covered entities may also use the treating physician's name, department of service information, health insurance status, and outcome information in crafting their fundraising documents. While covered entities cannot sell patient information for fundraising and marketing purposes, they may continue to receive financial remuneration to provide refill reminders or to send out other communications about a drug or biologic currently prescribed for the patient as long as it is reasonably related to the covered entity's costs associated with making the communication.

- *Financial remuneration rules:* Because the Mega-Rule now imposes an authorization requirement in the situations described above where the covered entity receives "financial remuneration", understanding what constitutes financial remuneration is critical to any analysis of a marketing arrangement. The Mega-Rule defines "financial remuneration" as the "direct or indirect payment from or on behalf of a third party whose product or service is being described. Direct or indirect payment does not include any payment for treatment of an individual."
- In 2000s, marketing laws were created to protect vulnerable populations, i.e., low-income groups, seniors, and minorities.
- In the CMS, Medicare Marketing Regulations (CMS: Medicare Marketing Manual, 2016 version).
- CMS: Medicaid Managed Care Final Rule, 2016; State laws and regulations on Medicaid managed care marketing.
  - Non-discrimination;
  - Broker commission limits; and
  - Marketing material language requirements.
- In 2010, Affordable Care Act brought in several provisions affecting health care marketing practices.
  - Expanded the liability of the False Claims Act to definitively include Anti-Kickback claims as grounds for violation.
  - Exchanges are not federal health care programs. The federal Anti-Kickback law, 42 U.S.C. § 1320a-7b(b), does not apply to Exchanges.
  - Marketing material. Plain language requirement.
  - MLR affects expenditure on marketing.
  - Non-discrimination.
  - Broker commission limits.
  - Provide information in fair, accurate, impartial, and culturally and linguistically appropriate manner.

13.2. Medicare and Medicaid Marketing Regulations

The Centers for Medicare and Medicaid, the US federal government agency conducting and overseeing Medicare (for senior citizens) and Medicaid (for low-income populations) programs has strict regulations and guidelines on communications and marketing of these services. Medicare is funded by the US federal government and Medicaid is funded by both federal and state governments. As such, CMS and state agencies are concerned about marketing and other communications directed at these vulnerable populations by health insurers and health plans with whom CMS and state agencies contract for the provision of health care services. Mostly such services are provided in a managed care setting.

13.2.1. Medicare regulations affecting health care marketing

The CMS' Medicare Communications and Marketing Guidelines (MCMG) interpret and provide guidance on the marketing and communication rules for Medicare Advantage (MA) plans (referred to as "plans"), Medicare Prescription Drug Plans (PDP) (also referred to as "Part D sponsors"), and employer/union-sponsored group MA or Part D plans. These plans are governed under Title 42 of the Code of Federal Regulations (CFR), Parts 422, 423, and 417. These requirements also apply to Medicare–Medicaid Plans (MMPs), except as modified or clarified in state-specific marketing guidance.

According to these Medicare marketing regulations,

- Communication means activities and use of materials to provide information to current and prospective enrollees. This means that all activities and materials aimed at prospective and current enrollees, including their caregivers and other decision makers associated with a prospective or current enrollee, are considered "communications".
- Marketing is a subset of communications and includes activities and use of materials by health plans with the intent to draw a beneficiary's attention to a plan or plans and to influence a beneficiary's decision-making process when selecting a plan for enrollment or deciding to stay enrolled in a plan (retention-based marketing). Additionally, marketing contains information about the plan's benefit structure, premium and costs, or ranking.

Medicare marketing guidelines are very extensive. This can be seen by the scope of these regulations, some of which are given in summary form in what follows (a health plan here is the organization that hires health care marketers and brokers to market Medicare products to eligible beneficiaries).

- **Anti-discrimination in marketing**

No discrimination should be made based on race, ethnicity, national origin, religion, gender, sex, age, mental or physical disability, health status, receipt of health care, claims experience, medical history, genetic information, evidence of insurability, or geographic location.

May not target potential enrollees from higher income areas.

- **Communications to non-English-speaking populations**

Call centers must have interpreter services available to answer questions from non-English speaking or limited English proficient (LEP) beneficiaries.

Plans must make vital documents available in any language that is the primary language of at least 5% of the population in the area.

- **Electronic communications**

Health plans may initiate contact via email to prospective enrollees and to retain enrollment for current enrollees. Must include an opt-out process on each communication.

Text messaging and other forms of electronic direct messaging (e.g., social media platforms) would fall under unsolicited contact and is not permitted.

- **Inaccurate and misleading communications**

Plans are prohibited from distributing communications that are materially inaccurate, misleading, or otherwise make misrepresentations or could confuse beneficiaries.

Cannot claim that they are recommended or endorsed by CMS, Medicare, or the Department of Health & Human Services (DHHS).

Cannot use unsubstantiated absolute or qualified superlatives or pejoratives or use term "free" to describe reductions in premiums.

- **Product endorsements/testimonials**

The speaker must identify the plan, product or company by name; Medicare beneficiaries endorsing or promoting a plan must be genuine enrollees (not actors). If an individual is paid or has been paid to endorse or promote the plan or product, the advertisement must clearly state this (e.g., "paid endorsement"). If an individual, such as an actor, is paid to portray a real or fictitious situation, the advertisement must clearly state it is a "Paid Actor Portrayal".

The Plan must be able to substantiate any claims made in the endorsement/testimonial.

Reuse of individual users' content or comment from social media sites (e.g., Facebook, Twitter) that promotes a plan product is considered a product endorsement/testimonial and must adhere to these guidelines.

- **Comparisons with competing plans**

Health plans may compare their plan to another health plan, provided the health plan can support them (e.g., by studies or statistical data) and such comparisons are factually based and not misleading.

- **Marketing through unsolicited contacts**

Health plans may make unsolicited direct contact with potential enrollees using conventional mail, advertisements, or email (provided all emails contain an opt-out function.)

Cannot use door-to-door solicitation, including leaving information such as a leaflet or flyer at a residence; approach potential enrollees in common areas (e.g., parking lots, hallways, lobbies, sidewalks).

Cannot conduct telephonic solicitation, including text messages and leaving electronic voicemail messages.

- **Nominal gifts**

Health plans may offer nominal gifts (US$15 or less but even then not cash or monetary rebates) to beneficiaries for marketing purposes, provided the gift is given regardless of whether they enroll, and without discrimination.

Cannot provide or subsidize meals at sales/marketing events. Refreshments and light snacks may be provided.

- **Educational and marketing/sales events**

Must not include marketing or sales activities or distribution of marketing materials or enrollment forms at educational events. May not conduct a marketing/sales event immediately following an educational event in the same general location (e.g., same hotel).

- **Websites**

Health plans may include both communications and marketing information on their website.

Health plan websites must be clear and easy to navigate; maintain the current content.

Health plan websites may not provide links to foreign drug sales, including links from advertisements; require users to enter any information other than a zip code, county, and/or state for access to non-beneficiary specific website content.

- **Social media posts**

Health plans must submit social media posts (e.g., Facebook, Twitter, YouTube) that meet the definition of marketing into the CMS Health Plan Management System (HPMS) which is a web-enabled information system. This way, CMS can monitor these posts.

- **Mobile applications (apps)**

Health plans that use mobile applications (apps) must submit data that meet the definition of marketing into HPMS; provide CMS, upon request, access to the mobile app. If only limited information is provided in apps, instruct beneficiaries where to find complete information and provide equal prominence to all in-network providers/pharmacies if the app contains this data.

- **Customer service call center communications**

Informational scripts must make it clear when a beneficiary is going to be transferred to a sales/enrollment department (i.e., the conversation moving from a communication activity to a marketing activity). Before making any transfer to a sales/enrollment (i.e., marketing) department, CSRs must receive the beneficiary's consent, ideally with a yes/no question.

- **Marketing materials**

Health plans must submit all marketing material to CMS for review and approval.

- **Agents for marketing and their compensation**

Agents selling Medicare products must be licensed and appointed (if applicable) as per state law to sell Medicare products; trained and tested annually; and secure and document a Scope of Appointment prior to meeting with potential enrollees. Health plans should pay compensation to agents at or below the fair market value (FMV) as published annually by CMS.

Sources: Medicare Marketing Guidelines — MA, MAPD, PDP (42 C.F.R. §§ 422.2260–2276; 42 C.F.R. §§ 423.2260–2276; Medicare Managed Care Manual, Ch. 3; Medicare Prescription Drug Benefit Manual, Ch. 3); Medicaid Marketing Rules (42 U.S.C. 1396u–2(d)(2); 42 C.F.R. § 438.104).

The intent of such an array of regulations is to prevent health plans from directing false and misleading information at Medicare beneficiaries who are usually older and sometimes need extra assistance in comprehending complex benefit structures.

13.2.2. Medicaid marketing regulations

Federal agencies like CMS also have rules governing Medicaid marketing practices. These are in Federal Medicaid Managed Care Regulations for Marketing Activities (42 CFR § 438.104) and other federal Medicaid regulations (42 CFR § 438.10).

Each state also has additional requirements for Medicaid-managed care marketing.

Medicaid programs earmarked for low-income populations are managed by state departments of health services (DHS). These agencies hold a CMS-approved Medicaid Plan. These agencies in turn contract with health plans to provide health care service to eligible beneficiaries, and also provide certain limited benefits directly to beneficiaries.

Provisions regulating marketing to Medicaid beneficiaries are embedded in state Medicaid plans and contract between state DHS and health plans. Health plans are responsible for complying with these regulations when deploying marketers to enroll potential Medicaid beneficiaries into the health plan.

In what follows, we present key regulations governing marketing from California's state Medicaid Plan.

- Training and certification of marketing representatives.
    - Health plans must deploy only marketing representatives trained by health plan and certified by the state. Training program should be comprehensive and cover basics of the Medicaid Program (Fee for service and managed care capitation programs), eligibility,

covered services, excluded services, additional services, utilization review processes, grievance programs, beneficiary voluntary and mandatory disenrollment processes, and confidentiality of information requirements.

- Non-discrimination.
  - Marketing Representatives shall not engage in marketing practices that discriminate against an Eligible Beneficiary or Potential Enrollee because of race, color, national origin, creed, ancestry, religion, language, age, gender, marital status, sexual orientation, health status or disability.
- State Department of Health Care Services (DHCS) Approval of health plan's marketing plan.
- Marketing materials.
  - A Medicaid-managed care entity (such as health plans and Accountable Care Organizations (ACOs)) may not distribute directly or through any agent or independent contractor marketing materials within any state without the prior approval of the state, and that contain false or materially misleading information. A managed care entity shall distribute marketing materials to the entire service area of such entity covered under the health plan's contract with the State.
- No door-to-door or cold-call marketing for the purpose of enrolling members or potential enrollees, or for any other purpose, except at the request of a potential enrollee whose record must be documented.
- No marketing presentations at primary care sites.
- Cannot seek to influence an individual's enrollment with the entity in conjunction with the sale of any other insurance (like life insurance).

When there are overlapping federal (CMS) and state regulations on Medicaid marketing, stricter regulations providing greater safeguards for beneficiaries will prevail.

Regulations similar to above Medicare and Medicaid marketing regulations exist in every state to regulate marketing practices in private insurance products and ACA (Obamacare) exchange products.

> These Federal and State health care program regulations and guidelines on marketing are clear examples of the society, via its legislators, enforcing its moral and ethical standards such as protecting its older citizens being misled, misinformed, and defrauded by aggressive health care marketers.

13.3. Health Care Marketing and Anti-Kickback Statutes

There are two key statutes that can create controversies for health care marketing: the federal AKS, a criminal statute, and Stark Law, which can lead to severe civil penalties.

13.3.1. The Federal Anti-Kickback Statute (AKS)

The 42 USCS § 1320a-7b(b) states that a person may not knowingly or willfully solicit or receive any remuneration directly or indirectly, overtly or covertly, in cash or in kind, in return for referring an individual for the furnishing of a health care item or service that is payable in whole or in part by a federal health care program. Some exceptions called "safe harbors" are provided.

Health care marketing could be involved in the middle of such controversies. For example, hospital, laboratory or pharmacy marketing could agree with a physician to provide some gain to the physician for referrals to the laboratory or pharmacy.

The tendency is to be "creative" in such marketing practices to fall within safe harbors (which is legal) or interpret critical terms in the statute such as "referral". While creativity in health care marketing should be encouraged, thorough legal review of practices relating to physician referrals is essential.

There are many and frequent applications of this statute.

- Home health services provider, Amedisys, settled for US$150 million on a charge that Amedisys violated the AKS by engaging in improper financial relationships with referring physicians, including providing below market value patient care coordination services, among other false claims.

Of the full settlement amount, US$26 million was awarded to the whistle-blower who initiated this investigation (Dresvic, 2010).

- Walgreens was involved in a high-profile Anti-Kickback case back in 2012 in which it agreed to settle for US$7.9 million. Even though the company denied any fault, the drugstore chain allegedly offered gift cards and other promotions to Medicare and Medicaid beneficiaries in exchange for transferring their prescriptions to Walgreens pharmacies.
- Payments based on percentage of income generated by referrals.

In a case involving Medical Device Network (MDN) and Physical Respiratory Care (PRC), PRC agreed to pay MDN a percentage of all business developed by MDN's marketing to clients, which included physicians, nursing homes, retirement homes, and individual patients. The court found that this type of arrangement, whereby a third-party company is paid a percentage of the sales it generates for an HME provider, falls squarely within the AKS prohibitions.

- An Arkansas Federal Court found a similar arrangement in violation of the AKS, in which a third-party company entered an agreement with an HME provider to identify Medicare recipients in need of the equipment and put them in contact with the provider. The marketing company received a fee for each item sold by the provider to patients identified by the marketing company. The court found the arrangement an indisputable violation of the AKS.
- In United States v. Patel, 778 F.3d 607 (7th Cir. 2015), the United States Court of Appeals for the Seventh Circuit heard arguments in a case where Dr. Patel would authorize a referral and the Medicare patient would independently choose which home health provider to use. Dr. Patel never recommended a particular home health care provider. For each patient that chose to procure home health services from a provider, Dr. Patel would sign an authorization form. One such provider paid Dr. Patel $400 in cash for each such authorization. There was no dispute that all these patients needed home care. Dr. Patel argued that he did not "refer" patients to any home health provider. The Government argued that the term a doctor's authorization of care by a particular provider. The court accepted this expanded interpretation of the term "referral" (Bain, 2015).

13.3.2. Stark Law

The Stark Law is a health care fraud and abuse law that prohibits physicians from referring patients for certain designated health services paid for by Medicare to any entity in which they have a "financial relationship". Financial relationship includes any direct or indirect ownership or investment interest by the referring physician or any of the physician's immediate family members.

Unlike the federal AKS, the Stark Law is not a criminal statute. However, the Office of the Inspector General (OIG) for the Department of Health and Human Services (HHS) can pursue a civil action against Stark Law violators under the civil monetary penalties law. Stark Law violations can result in penalties of up to US$15,000 for each billed service that is based on a prohibited referral, plus three times the amount of the government overpayment.

Health care service marketers should be very cautious of Stark Law too as it does not require the physician's specific intent to violate the law. Physicians who make prohibited referrals even unknowingly can be subject to civil penalties. Those who are found to have knowingly and intentionally violated the law may face increased penalties and debarment or exclusion from participation in federal programs like Medicare and Medicaid.

13.3.3. Guidelines to health care marketers to avoid Kickback and Stark violations

- Health care providers should seek expert legal advice when contemplating any marketing involving physician referrals.
- Never assume or interpret safe harbors without legal advice.
- Enter into well-designed contracts with outside marketing agents and brokers.
- Train both internal and outside marketing staff on these laws.

13.4. Truth-in-Advertising Laws Applicable to Health Care Marketing

Marketing health care services of physicians, hospitals, health plans, and pharmaceutical companies are frequent targets of allegations of false or misleading advertising, and if proven could be subjected to penalties under federal laws.

> **Press Release by Department of Justice,
> US Attorney's Office, Southern District of Alabama —
> Friday June 8, 2018**
>
> United States District Judge Kristi K. DuBose sentenced Rassan M. Tarabein, 58, a former neurologist residing in Fairhope, Alabama, to 60 months, imprisonment in a health care fraud case. The judge ordered that Tarabein pay restitution totaling US$15,010,682 to six different health care benefit programs, including Medicare and the Alabama Medicaid Agency. Tarabein previously operated the Eastern Shore Neurology and Pain Center, a private clinic in Daphne, Alabama where he offered services relating to neurology and pain management, such as spinal injections. He had advertised himself as a "World Leading Physician" on his clinic's website. On June 28, 2017, a federal grand jury for the Southern District of Alabama returned a 22-count superseding indictment against Tarabein, charging him with health care fraud, making false statements relating to health care matters, lying to a federal agent, unlawfully distributing schedule II controlled substances, and money laundering.

The following are the key laws relating to truth-in-advertising:

- **The Federal Truth-in-Advertising Law**

This law is contained in the Federal Trade Commission Act that regulates most advertising content. It is administered and enforced by the US Federal Trade Commission and many states also have their versions of this law.

The purpose of this law is to deter deception, promote fairness and supporting evidence in advertising (Benge, 2019).

Deception. This law requires that all advertisements must be truthful, fair, and free of misleading representation. Federal truth-in-advertising laws also require that claims be substantiated with solid proof. The Federal Trade Commission has a Deception Policy Statement that describes an advertisement as deceptive if a misleading feature of the ad sways a consumer into purchasing or using the product or service. This definition also applies to information that is deliberately omitted or withheld from the consumer that affects purchase decisions.

Fairness. The FTC describes an unfair advertisement as one that causes injury to a consumer for no fault of the consumer. Unfairness in advertising is further described as harm that overrides any beneficial features that appeal to consumers.

Supporting Evidence. FTC's Bureau of Consumer Protection Business Center states that if a product or service is being advertised that deals with *health or safety*, documented scientific evidence must back the claims.

FTC, in its website, draws attention to allegations against health and fitness claims: https://www.ftc.gov/news-events/media-resources/truth-advertising/health-claims.

These are products advertised with claims that they can help people lose weight, combat disease, and improve their cognitive abilities. The Federal Trade Commission combats this type of deceptive advertising in coordination with the FDA. The FTC also seeks the expertise of other government authorities, including the National Institutes of Health.

FTC believes that rising health care costs are encouraging consumers to increase spending on these products, as consumers attempt to manage their own health care and avoid expensive doctor visits and prescription medications.

- **Federal Food, Drug, and Cosmetic Act (21 U.S.C. § 301–399a)**

This act bans false and misleading statements from the labeling of foods, drugs, and medical devices.

It defines the term "drug" to include, among other things, "articles intended for use in the diagnosis, cure, mitigation, treatment, or prevention of disease", as well as "articles (other than food) intended to affect the structure or any function of the body."

- **Prescription Drug Advertising Regulation (21 CFR § 202.1)**
  o Contains various rules that prescription drug advertisers need to follow. For example:
    - Ads must include information regarding the side effects, risks, and contraindications of the advertised drug, and must contain a fair balance between the benefits and risks; and
    - In most circumstances, a company may only advertise a drug for the specific use for which it was approved, i.e., no off-label marketing.

> **Off-Label Marketing Cases**
>
> September 2010. Off-label marketing of Trileptal. The Department of Justice (DOJ) claimed that Novartis created marketing materials that promoted Trileptal for the treatment of neuropathic pain and bipolar disease; neither of which is an approved use by FDA. While doctors can prescribe drugs to treat any ailment, it is illegal for drug companies to promote drugs for uses not federally approved. As part of the settlement, Novartis agreed to pay a forfeiture of funds and a criminal fine totaling US$185 million. It also agreed to settle four civil whistleblower lawsuits for US$237.5 million.
>
> May 2018. The city of Los Angeles accused top drug makers and distributors for engaging in deceptive marketing aimed at boosting sales of powerful, addictive painkillers such as OxyContin, methadone, and fentanyl.
>
> CBS/AP November 4, 2013: Health care giant Johnson & Johnson and its subsidiaries have agreed to pay over US$2.2 billion to resolve criminal and civil allegations of promoting three prescription drugs for off-label uses not approved by the Food and Drug Administration.

- **Nutrition Labeling and Education Act of 1990 (Public Law 101–535)**

Source: FDA: Guide to Nutrition Labeling and Education Act (NLEA) Requirements August 1994; Editorial Changes — February 1995. https://web.archive.org/web/20071014014547/http://www.fda.gov/ora/inspect_ref/igs/nleatxt.html.

This law authorizes the FDA authority to require nutrition labeling of most foods regulated by the Agency; and to require that all nutrient content claims (e.g., "low fat") and health claims meet FDA regulations.

The regulations became effective for health claims, ingredient declarations, and percent juice labeling on May 8, 1993 (effective from May 8, 1994).

Effective from January 1, 2006, the Nutrition Facts Labels on packaged food products are required by the FDA to list how many grams of trans-fatty acid (trans fat) are contained within one serving of the product.

- **Dietary Supplement Health and Education Act of 1994 (Public Law 103–417)**
Requires inclusion in any statements of nutritional support a prominent disclaimer that states: "This statement has not been evaluated by the Food and Drug Administration. This product is not intended to diagnose, treat, cure, or prevent any disease."

- **Lanham Act, 15 U.S.C. § 1125(a) Section 43(a)(1)(B)**
This law is often utilized when false or misleading statements are alleged to have hurt a business. A business claimant must satisfy three elements: there was a false or misleading statement made, the statement was used in commercial advertising or promotion, and the statement creates a likelihood of harm to the plaintiff.

- **State Business and Profession Code Restrictions on Physicians**
State laws have specific requirements for physicians who want to practice under a fictitious business name, e.g., Dr. Jones practicing as "Los Angeles Pediatric Clinic".

    Health plans are also prohibited from displaying larger Provider Directories claiming larger provider networks by listing physicians and other providers who are not contracted with the health plan.

    The following laws and regulations apply to direct marketing of health care products and services (for details, readers should visit websites of these agencies):

- Federal Trade Commission (FTC):
    - Mail or Telephone Order Merchandise Rule;
    - Telemarketing Sales Rule;
    - Children's Online Privacy Protection Rule;
    - Negative Option Rule; and
    - Guides against Deceptive Pricing.
- Federal Communications Commission (FCC):
    - Telephone Consumer Protection Act.

13.5. HIPAA Laws Affecting Health Care Marketing

The HIPAA of 1996, its regulations, and subsequent follow-up laws are generally known as laws and regulations to protect privacy and security of individual's health information. What is not that well known is that HIPAA also imposes several regulations on health care marketing.

13.5.1. HIPAA and health care marketing

(1) Basics

HIPAA defines marketing as any communication about a product or service that encourages recipients to purchase or use the product or service.

HIPAA Privacy Rule carves out the following health-related activities from this definition of marketing:

- Communications to describe health-related products or services, or payment for them, provided by or included in a benefit plan of the covered entity making the communication;
- Communications about participating providers in a provider or health plan network, replacement of or enhancements to a health plan, and health-related products or services available only to a health plan's enrollees that add value to, but are not part of, the benefits plan;
- Communications for treatment of the individual;
- Communications for case management or care coordination for the individual, or to direct or recommend alternative treatments, therapies, health care providers, or care settings to the individual;
- Communication is in the form of a face-to-face communication made by the supplier to the patient; and
- A promotional gift of nominal value provided by the supplier.

(2) Marketing activities prohibited by HIPAA

Arrangement between a covered entity (a health plan, a health care provider who submits transactions, like claims, electronically, and health care clearing houses) and any other entity whereby the covered entity discloses protected health information, in exchange for direct or indirect remuneration, for the other entity to communicate about its own products or services encouraging the use or purchase of those products or services.

A covered entity must obtain an authorization to use or disclose protected health information for marketing, except for face-to-face marketing communications between a covered entity and an individual, and for a covered entity's provision of promotional gifts of nominal value. No authorization is needed, however, to make a communication that falls within one of the exceptions to the marketing definition. An authorization for marketing that involves the covered entity's receipt of direct or indirect remuneration from a third party must reveal that fact.

(3) HIPAA and use of social media for health care marketing
- Covered entities should not create ads or posts using patient information or protected health information (PHI) of any kind (including names, photos, or treatment information) without obtaining explicit permission from the patients involved.
- Covered entities should not allow staff members to take photos within the practice if there is the potential that PHI such as documents, fax sheets, print-outs, or computer screens will be visible.
- Covered entities should establish policies and procedures for social media use by employees, capturing the necessary regulatory standards, with limitations on what they can and cannot post.

(4) HIPAA and email marketing
- Covered Entities should not create emails or email campaigns using patient information or PHI of any kind without obtaining explicit permission from the patients involved.
- If a covered entity uses a third-party email marketing firm, ensure that they are HIPAA compliant. Legal Business Associate Agreements (BAAs) must be executed with all vendors, including marketing firms.
- Encrypt email sent to patients containing any type of PHI (even including name or email address). Emails and any electronic transmissions must be end-to-end encrypted, which means that only the sender and recipient have access to the email's contents. Additionally, any servers that store emails or email data containing PHI must be encrypted with off-site back-up.
- Receive explicit authorization from patients before sending them emails. Even if a practice collects email as part of patient registration, they still need to gain explicit authorization before sending any emails.

(5) HIPAA-compliant websites and web hosting
- Any data gathered on a website must be encrypted. This includes web forms and appointment requests, in addition to any contact forms.
- Website data containing sensitive PHI should be stored on an encrypted server with off-site back-up.

- Implement a HIPAA privacy policy on the website to ensure patients are up-to-date with efforts to keep any collected data safe.

(6) Other related provisions
- HIPAA does not restrict marketing by physicians to current patients.
- HIPAA Privacy Rule excludes from the definition of "marketing" communications made to describe a covered entity's health-related product or services, i.e., information provided by, or included in, a plan of benefits of the covered entity making the communication.

(7) HITECH Act tightened marketing rules
Health Information Technology for Economic and Clinical Health (HITECH) Act, Title XIII of Division A and Title IV of Division B of the American Recovery and Reinvestment Act of 2009 (ARRA), Pub. L. No. 111-5, 123 Stat. 226 (February 17, 2009) codified at 42 U.S.C. §§ 300jj et seq.; §§ 17901 et seq. HITECH omnibus rule significantly tightened the HIPAA marketing restrictions.

It requires authorization for almost all treatment and health care operations communications where the covered entity receives, from a third party, financial remuneration for making the communication.

Prior to the HITECH Act, certain communications, including those related to treatment and care coordination, were excluded from the definition of marketing. Under the HITECH Act, if a covered entity or business associate receives direct or indirect payment in exchange for making certain communications (including those related to treatment and care coordination), the covered entity generally must obtain prior authorization — unless the communication qualifies for a limited exception for communications about currently prescribed drugs or biologics where the payment received is reasonable in amount.

13.6. Regulations Applicable to Digital Health Care Marketing

Digital health care marketing includes website marketing, mobile marketing, content marketing, search engine marketing, social media marketing, and email marketing.

There are several laws and regulations applicable to digital marketing in general and specifically to digital health care marketing.

We will present both these types of regulations here, but emphasis will be on those applicable to health care marketing.

13.6.1. The Controlling the Assault of Non-Solicited Pornography and Marketing (CAN-SPAM) Act of 2003

This law sets the rules for commercial email, establishes requirements for commercial messages, gives recipients the right to have organizations stop emailing them, and sets forth penalties for violations. It defines commercial messages as, "any electronic mail message the primary purpose of which is the commercial advertisement or promotion of a commercial product or service". Thus, it applies to electronic messages used in marketing health care plans, providers, pharmaceutical products, and hospitals. It also covers email that promotes content on commercial websites and makes no exception for business-to-business email.

Source: Federal Trade Commission: CAN-SPAM Act: A Compliance Guide for Business, https://www.ftc.gov/tips-advice/business-center/guidance/can-spam-act-compliance-guide-business.

13.6.2. Medicare marketing regulations

Sources: Medicare Marketing Guidelines, Medicare Managed Care Manual, Ch. 3; Medicare Prescription Drug Benefit Manual, Ch. 3.

Medicaid Marketing Rules (42 U.S.C. 1396u–2(d)(2); 42 C.F.R. § 438.104).

- **Electronic Communications**
  - Health plans that are included in Medicare Advantage and Prescription Drug programs may initiate contact via email to prospective enrollees and to retain enrollment for current enrollees. Must include an opt-out process on each communication.

- **Text Messaging**
  - Text messaging and other forms of electronic direct messaging (e.g., social media platforms) would fall under unsolicited contact and is not permitted.

- **Websites**
  - Health plans participating in Medicare Advantage and Prescription Drug programs are permitted to include both communications and marketing information on their websites subject to truth in advertising standards. Health plan websites must be clear and easy to navigate and maintain the content current.

- Health plan websites may not provide links to foreign drug sales, including links from advertisements; require users to enter any information other than a zip code, county, and/or state for access to non-beneficiary specific website content.

- **Social Media Posts**
  - Health plans participating in Medicare Advantage and Prescription Drug programs, must submit social media posts (e.g., Facebook, Twitter, YouTube) that meet the definition of marketing into the CMS Health Plan Management System (HPMS) which is a web-enabled information system for review by CMS.

- **Mobile Applications (Apps)**
  - Health plans participating in Medicare Advantage and Prescription Drug programs, that use mobile applications (apps) must submit data that meets the definition of marketing into HPMS; provide CMS, upon request, access to the mobile app; If limited information only is provided in apps, instruct beneficiaries where to find complete information; and provide equal prominence to all in-network providers/pharmacies if the app contains this data.

13.6.3. Health Insurance Portability and Accountability Act of 1996 (HIPAA)

Covered entities (health plans, most providers and health information clearing houses) should not create ads or posts using patient information or PHI of any kind (including names, photos, or treatment information) without obtaining explicit permission from the patients involved.

- **Social Media Use**

Covered entities should establish policies and procedures for social media use by employees, capturing the necessary regulatory standards, with limitations on what they can and cannot post.

- **Email Marketing**

Covered entities should not create emails or email campaigns using patient information or PHI of any kind without obtaining explicit permission from the patients involved. If a covered entity uses a third-party email marketing firm, ensure that they are HIPAA compliant.

Any email that contains PHI should be encrypted. Encrypt email sent to patients containing any type of PHI (even including name or email address). Emails and any electronic transmissions must be end-to-end encrypted, which means that only the sender and recipient have access to the email's contents. Additionally, any servers that store emails or email data containing PHI must be encrypted with off-site back-up.

Covered entities should obtain explicit authorization from patients before sending them emails. Even if a practice collects email as part of patient registration, they still need to gain explicit authorization before sending any emails.

- **Websites**

Any data gathered on a website must be encrypted. This includes web forms and appointment requests, in addition to any contact forms. Website data containing sensitive PHI should be stored on an encrypted server with off-site back-up. Privacy and Security Policies must be established that specify technical and administrative safeguards of PHI.

13.6.4. Truth-in-advertising laws applicable to health care marketing

These laws discussed in Section 13.4 and listed below also apply to the content of communications and advertisements made over digital media.

- The Federal Truth-In-Advertising Law (Federal Trade Commission Act of 1914).
- Federal Food, Drug, and Cosmetic Act (21 U.S.C. § 301–399a).
- Prescription Drug Advertising Regulation (21 CFR § 202.1).
- Nutrition Labeling and Education Act of 1990 (Public Law 101–535).
- Dietary Supplement Health and Education Act of 1994 (Public Law 103–417).
- Lanham Act, 15 U.S.C. § 1125(a) Section 43(a)(1)(B).

13.6.5. Other guidelines on digital marketing

- *Header information on emails*: It is not advisable to use false or misleading header information. Your "From", "To", "Reply-To", and routing information — including the originating domain name and email

address — must be accurate and identify the person or business who initiated the message.
- *Subject lines in emails*: Similarly, deceptive subject lines should be avoided. The subject line must accurately reflect the content of the message.
- *Disclosure that the communication is an advertisement*: It is always a good practice to identify the message as an advertisement. Disclose clearly and conspicuously that the message is an advertisement.
- *Sender information*: Provide information for easy identification of the health care provider or organization such as legal name, location/address, and phone numbers.
- *Opt-out opportunity*: It is extremely important in marketing emails to provide the opportunity to opt-out, and then honor opt-out requests promptly.

13.7. Health Care Marketing Ethics

The relationship between law and ethics in health care is somewhat unusual. Often, ethical dilemmas in health care are resolved by resorting to legal decisions. For example, many dilemmas relating to "right to die" end up in courts.

13.7.1. The four principles of health care ethics

The following principles are accepted as the key principles governing health care ethics and, when suitably tailored, health care marketing. They balance patient's rights, medical provider judgment of what is best for the patient, and social norms and values (Beauchamp and Childress, 1989; Saint Joseph's University, 2019).

(1) *Autonomy*: The right of the patient to retain control over his or her body. A competent patient has the final right to make decisions about his or her body and health irrespective of medical opinions.

In health care marketing, the final decision on selecting health care and provider options is with the customer/patient. As will be seen later, there are laws prohibiting health care marketers from coercing consumers, especially vulnerable persons like the elderly.

(2) *Beneficence*: Health care providers must do all they can to benefit the patient. This requires health care providers to be competent, trained, and practice within their competence, training, and licensure.

In health care marketing, state laws require health care marketers to undergo training and pass licensing/certification examinations. Health plans, hospitals, and pharmaceutical companies employing/contracting health care marketers are required to strictly supervise the health care providers. Regulators like CMS deploy several methods to verify integrity of health care marketing such as mystery shoppers.

(3) *Non-Maleficence*: This means "do no harm". Health care providers must ensure that the patient and others are not harmed by their decisions.

In health care marketing, this principle is valid and is monitored in conjunction with the principle of beneficence. False and misleading information causing consumers to suffer unfair financial burden in favor of health care provider's or marketer's financial gain fall within this category.

(4) *Justice*: There should be fairness in medical decisions for patient, family, providers, and society. Decisions must weigh benefits and burden to all parties and must be fair in allocating scarce resources.

In health care marketing, health care organization policies such as "cherry pocking" (health plans in managed care settings, focusing outreach on healthier consumers) and "patient dumping" (hospitals promoting their services to patients with health insurance and personal resources in favor of uninsured or low-income, e.g., Medicaid, populations) fall into this category.

13.7.2. Evolution of health care and health care marketing ethics

Following is a summary of the evolution of the ethical environment in health care with some of the developments affecting health care marketing as well (Scott, 2000).

- **1950s and 1960s:** Issues relating to patient care were some of the earliest issues creating ethical dilemmas.

- o The social consensus was that physicians should do what they thought was the best thing for the patient, what would benefit the patient and not harm the patient. On the other hand, patient's autonomy had to be respected. This dilemma gave rise to the ethical principle of "informed consent". Law then operationalized the society's view by requiring physicians to obtain patient's informed consent and allowing the patient to sue the physician if the physician treated her without prior consent. Such is the relationship between ethics and law in health care.
- **1960s:** Allocation of scare resources in health care based on society's ethical principles and values (Levine, 2009).
  - o The committee was formed in 1961 to choose which patients should be hooked up twice a week, 12 hours at a time, to an "artificial kidney" that could cleanse the blood of toxins that their failing kidneys could no longer filter a procedure now called hemodialysis. The committee was made up could be used only temporarily. Who should be chosen and on what basis? That task fell to a committee of seven citizens — lawyer, minister, banker, housewife, state government official, labor leader, and surgeon — selected by the King County Medical Society. The committee accepted kidney doctors' recommendations to reject anyone over 45 because older patients were likely to develop medical complications. Children were also excluded because, it was felt, they might be traumatized by the procedure. The committee drew up a list of all the factors they would weigh in making their decision, including age, sex, marital status and number of dependents, income, net worth, emotional stability, educational background, occupation, past performance and future potential, and references. This indicates how society applies ethical standards to health care decisions.
  - o Advances in technology made dialysis easier to access and by the end of the 1960s, the Seattle committee and similar hospital committees disbanded.
  - o In 1971, federal legislation made treatment of end-stage renal disease (ESRD) a supplement to Medicare.
- **1970s:** The right to die controversies, e.g., Quinlan case (In re Quinlan (70 N.J. 10, 355 A.2d 647 (NJ 1976))).
  - o The issue here was the doctors' ethical dilemma between keeping a patient alive by connecting the patient to a ventilator and removing

the ventilator and allowing patient to die. The hospital's ethics committee had a difficult decision to make in this case.

- **1980s:** Parents' right to withhold treatment for children.
  - Baby Doe and baby Jane Doe cases in 1982 and 1983 highlighted the ethical dilemma of physicians and hospitals between what they thought was appropriate medical care for these handicapped infants and the parents' refusal for such treatment. Federal authorities ruled that the Rehabilitation Act that governed treatment of people with disabilities applied to such handicapped children and that they should not be denied. However, the US Supreme Court decided in 1986 that the Rehabilitation Act is not applicable to such situations.
  - The ethical issue here was the belief by regulators and human rights advocates that life-saving medical services were provided or denied to these handicapped children based on their estimated economic worth to society.
  - After much debate, the prevailing consensus is that decisions to withhold or withdraw medical interventions are ethically and legally acceptable in many circumstances, and these decisions fall within the authority of parents or guardians in consultation with the child's physician (Diekema and Botkin, 2009).
- **1980s:** Patient dumping, practice by private hospitals of transferring poor or uninsured emergency patients to public hospitals.
  - Concern over this as a legal and ethical issue resulted in the enactment of the Emergency Medical Treatment and Active Labor Act. This issue and the Act will be discussed later in the chapter.
- **1990s:** Ethical issues arising out of managed care.
  - As managed care as a health care delivery and business model grew in the 1990s and early 2000s, health care providers and patients have expressed concerns about practices of health insurers and managed care companies who restrict care for their insured, and also prevent physicians from discussing with patients alternative but more expensive care ("gag orders").
  - Ethical issue dilemma here is between health plan/insurer position that health care treatment must be only for "medically necessary" services, usually interpreted strictly by their review processes, and

that this benefits society in reducing health care costs, and the claim by patients and health care advocates that this practice withholds even necessary treatments and interferes with physician autonomy and ethics.
  - Again, resolution has come via federal and state legislation in the form of "Patient Bill(s) of Rights" and "Provider Bill(s) of Rights".
- **1995:** Joint Commission (JC, formerly JCAHO) accreditation requirement of a Code of Organization Ethics.
  - Joint Commission created a new accreditation standard on organization ethics. The new standard required a hospital to implement a "code of ethical behavior" on the following activities: marketing; patient admission, transfer, and discharge; billing practices; and the relationship of the organization and its staff to other health care providers, educational institutions, and payers.
- **1997:** JCAHO added to this accreditation standard the requirement that a hospital "protects the integrity of clinical decision-making."
  - JCAHO was apparently concerned that, in the ever increasingly competitive health care environment, health care organizations might be tempted to compromise on patient care.
  - JCAHO also added a standard on ethics in marketing and advertising.
  - JCAHO added, "To support ethical operations, an organization must have in place a mechanism to ensure that ... marketing ... practices are conducted in an ethical manner." JCAHO "recommends that the hospital adopt a statement of marketing and public relations practices that addresses issues of truth, accuracy, fairness, and responsibility to patients, community and the larger public." Note the emphasis on ethical marketing practices (meaning socially responsible) and not just legal marketing practices (advertising is truthful, not false, deceptive, or misleading).

13.7.3. Ethical standards of American Marketing Association

The American Marketing Association has long emphasized on norms and values relating to marketing activities which apply to health care marketing as well. Their preamble explains their commitment to norms and values as follows (American Marketing Association, 2018):

> "The American Marketing Association commits itself to promoting the highest standard of professional ethical norms and values for its members (practitioners, academics and students). Norms are established standards of conduct that are expected and maintained by society and/or professional organizations. Values represent the collective conception of what communities find desirable, important and morally proper. Values also serve as the criteria for evaluating our own personal actions and the actions of others. As marketers, we recognize that we not only serve our organizations but also act as stewards of society in creating, facilitating and executing the transactions that are part of the greater economy. In this role, marketers are expected to embrace the highest professional ethical norms and the ethical values implied by our responsibility toward multiple stakeholders (e.g., customers, employees, investors, peers, channel members, regulators and the host community)."

Their code of ethics includes three ethical norms followed by six ethical values. These, in an easily readable summary form, are given in what follows.

- **Ethical norms**
  (1) Do no harm. Consciously avoiding harmful actions or omissions; adherence to all applicable laws and regulations;
  (2) Foster trust in the marketing system. Good faith and fair dealing in the exchange process; avoiding deception in product design, pricing, communication, and delivery of distribution; and
  (3) Embracing ethical values. Build consumer relationships and enhance consumer confidence in the integrity of marketing. Affirm core values described below.

- **Ethical values**
  (1) *Honesty*: Be forthright in dealings with customers and stakeholders. Be truthful in all situations and at all times. Offer products of value that do what we claim in our communications. Stand behind products if they fail to deliver their claimed benefits. Honor explicit and implicit commitments and promises.
  (2) *Responsibility*: Accept the consequences of marketing decisions and strategies. Strive to serve the needs of customers. Avoid using

coercion with all stakeholders. Acknowledge the social obligations to stakeholders that come with increased marketing and economic power. Recognize special commitments to vulnerable market segments such as children, seniors, the economically impoverished, market illiterates, and others who may be substantially disadvantaged. Environmental stewardship in our decision-making.

(3) *Fairness*: Balance needs of the buyer with the interests of the seller. Represent products in a clear way in selling, advertising, and other forms of communication. Avoid false, misleading and deceptive promotion, and manipulations and sales tactics that harm customer trust. Not engage in price fixing, predatory pricing, price gouging or "bait-and-switch" tactics. Avoid conflicts of interest. Protect the private information of customers, employees and partners.

(4) *Respect*: Acknowledge basic human dignity of all stakeholders. Value individual differences and avoid stereotyping customers or depicting demographic groups (e.g., gender, race, sexual orientation) in a negative or dehumanizing way. Listen to the needs of customers and make all reasonable efforts to monitor and improve their satisfaction on an ongoing basis. Understand and respectfully treat buyers, suppliers, intermediaries and distributors from all cultures. Acknowledge the contributions of others, such as consultants, employees and coworkers, to marketing endeavors. Treat everyone, including our competitors, as we would wish to be treated.

(5) *Transparency*: Create a spirit of openness in marketing operations. Communicate clearly with all constituencies. Accept constructive criticism from customers and other stakeholders. Explain and take appropriate action regarding significant product or service risks that could affect customers or their perception of the purchase decision. Disclose list prices and terms of financing as well as available price deals and adjustments.

(6) *Citizenship*: Fulfill the economic, legal, philanthropic, and societal responsibilities that serve stakeholders. Strive to protect the ecological environment in the execution of marketing campaigns. Give back to the community through volunteerism and charitable donations. Urge supply chain members to ensure that trade is fair for all participants, including producers in developing countries.

13.7.4. Ethical standards of the Direct Marketing Association

Direct marketing is a key area in health care marketing. Physicians, hospitals, retirement homes, nursing homes, and pharmaceutical companies market products and services directly to consumers/patients. Hospitals, health plans, and pharmaceutical companies do direct marketing to physicians.

Direct Marketing Association's (DMA's) ethical guidelines are summarized as follows:

- Clearly, honestly, and accurately represent products, services, terms, and conditions.
- Deliver products and services as represented.
- Communicate in a respectful and courteous manner.
- Respond to inquiries and complaints in a constructive, timely way.
- Maintain appropriate security policies and practices to safeguard information.
- Honor requests not to receive future solicitations.
- Guidelines for marketing to children:
  o Offers and the manner in which they are presented that are suitable for adults only should not be made to children.
  o Marketers should provide notice and an opportunity to opt-out of the marketing process to parents.
  o Marketers should not collect personally identifiable information online from a child under 13 without prior parental consent or direct parental notification of the nature and intended use of such information online and an opportunity for the parent to prevent such use and participation in the activity.
  o Marketers should take reasonable steps to prevent the online publication or posting of information that would allow a third party to contact a child offline unless the marketer has prior parental consent.
  o Marketers should not make a child's access to a website contingent on the collection of personally identifiable information.

For the sake of brevity, we omit here DMA standards on the following issues. Readers are referred to Direct Marketing Association (2007).

- Special offers and claims, use of the word "free," and other similar representations.
- Digital marketing online information standards.
- Social media and online referral marketing standards.
- Telephone marketing standards.
- Mobile marketing; obtaining consent to contact a mobile device.

> Despite these voluntary efforts by marketing organizations to establish impressive ethical standards, there is much criticism that some of the key standards are not followed in health care marketing.
>
> For example, Markgraf (2018) identifies how marketing orientation to maintain profit levels is forcing pharmaceutical, cosmetics, and infant formula industries to adopt marketing tactics that are ethically questionable. He highlights drug company continuing the practice of giving attractive gifts to physicians, the 2011 Walmart cosmetics campaign aimed at girls as young as nine years old emphasizing the "environmentally friendly" nature of the eye-liner, lip gloss and mascara, and Nestle marketing their baby formula products as a breast milk replacement in developing countries telling local mothers that formula was superior to breast milk.

13.8. Principles and Tools for Analyzing Ethical Dilemmas in Health Care Marketing

We discuss here certain principles and tools that can be used by health care managers and marketers to resolve ethical dilemmas in health care delivery and marketing.

13.8.1. Blanchard and Peale — 3 Step Model

Blanchard and Peale (1988) suggest an Ethics Check — answering three questions when faced with an ethical problem:

(1) Is the action or decision legal? Will I be violating law or company policy?
   If the answer to this question is "No," then do not proceed with the action or decision.

(2) Is it balanced? Is it fair to all stakeholders concerned in the short term as well as the long term?
(3) How will the action or decision make me, or the organization feel? Proud? What if gets publicity in media?

13.8.2. Other models in the literature

Other models include social media model, utility model, rights model, exceptions model, choices model, justice model, common good model, and virtue model (Florida Tech, 2018; Hammaker and Knadig, 2017):

- **Utilitarianism:** The most ethical action is the one that provides the greatest amount of good for the largest number of people.
- **The Rights Approach:** Best decision is the one that preserves and protects human dignity and moral rights.
- **The Fairness or Justice Approach:** Based on the principle that all humans should be treated equally.
- **The Common Good Approach:** Decision or action should promote public life.
- **The Virtue Approach:** Based on characteristics such as compassion and honesty. With this approach, decision makers should ask things like "What kind of person would I be if I take this action?"

Note that this is equivalent to Step (3) in the Blanchard and Peele Model.

13.8.3. Guidelines for ethical decision-making in health care marketing

The following are the guidelines for ethical decision-making:

- Physicians should avoid communications to patients that raise fears for business gains;
- Avoid being discriminatory in promotions;
- Do not employ actors to provide patient testimonials;
- Refrain from showing competitors in a bad light; and
- Refrain from using superlatives such as "the best", "top", "world-famous", and "most qualified".

> **Discussion**
>
> In public health marketing, is it ethical and justifiable to withhold full information for the purpose of changing people's health behaviors for the better?
> See, Musham and Trettin (2002) for an argument in the affirmative.
> Ethical dilemma here arises from one position that behavior can be changed by creating a link between the desired new behaviors and the target group's current value system, without imparting new information or instilling new values, and the other position that if behaviors are imposed on people without their full comprehension and consent, then aren't they being stripped of a basic right, freedom of choice.

Examples of other types of unethical health care marketing practices to avoid:

- Providing the same old service under a new name and suggesting that the service is somehow better or different.
- Making sales pitches for managed care that do not live up to or fail to mention the details contained in the fine print of the agreement with consumers.
- Using public services to gain referrals to the sponsoring organization.
- *Not disclosing material facts*: In managed care environments, health plans do not disclose many problems with services the consumers/patients face only when they start needing services, such as limiting providers patients can see to the HMO's network, excessive waiting time to get appointments with their primary care doctor or specialists, and utilization review procedures that restrict patients from seeing specialists.

13.9. Contracting in Health Care Marketing

Health care organizations such as health plans, hospitals, pharmaceutical companies, physicians and physician groups (including IPAs), ACOs, and other health care providers are normally related to each other by formal legal contracts.

For example, a typical health plan will enter into contracts with IPAs, hospitals, a Pharmacy Benefit Manager (PBM) representing a pharmacy chain, laboratory networks, ancillary providers, providers of durable medical equipment

(DME) and marketing agents, and/or a Field Marketing Organization (FMO). The typical health plan will have on its hand hundreds of active contracts.

Some of these contracting situations affect health care marketing. In this section, we will address those contracting issues.

Areas of contracting that will have an impact on health care marketing are:

- Contracts between a managed care health care plan or ACO and an independent marketing organization that enrolls members to that organization:
    - An example is a contract between a health plan and a "Producer" (an independent agent who enrolls, say, Medicare beneficiaries into a Medicare managed care health plan and gets paid a commission), or a "General Agent" (GA, who similarly contracts with the health plan and has a fleet Producers under the GA) or Field Marketing Organization (FMO), sometimes called an IMO or Independent Marketing Organization. An FMO basically does the same work as a GA. In this scenario, all these entities get paid by the health plan on enrollments of Medicare beneficiaries into the health plan.
- Physician compensation involved contracts negotiated by marketing:
    - Contracts of this type arise typically in hospital service marketing. As physicians are the main source of patient referrals to hospitals, hospitals seek arrangements with physicians whereby some form of benefit is conveyed to the physician (e.g., office space, consulting activities, or office support).

13.9.1. Contracts with marketing agents

The main concern of health care organizations, e.g., managed care health plans, is the marketing agent's compliance with enrollment regulations. These regulations vary by programs such as Medicare and Medicaid, and were discussed in detail in Sections 13.2, 13.5, and 13.6.

Without repeating these previous discussions in detail, it might suffice to recall that key requirements applicable to marketing agents include prohibition from making unsolicited contact with beneficiaries, including through door-to-door solicitation, leaving flyers, approaching beneficiaries in common areas such as shopping centers and parking lots, and telephonic or electronic solicitation including voicemail messages, text messaging, or sending unsolicited email messages.

The health care organization must ensure that it has written contracts with each marketing entity, producers, general agents, and FMOs and that contracts contain provisions on compliance with the above regulations.

The usual practice is to include all these regulatory requirements in an appendix to the contract which will be deemed as part of the contracts.

Health care organizations must also verify marketing agents' licenses and proof of professional insurance. It must see that marketing agents complete the health care organization's own training.

It must also ensure that information collected from potential enrollees are maintained securely and confidentially, and that this information is surrendered to the health care organization upon resignation or termination of the marketing agent.

Contracts with marketing agents must clearly specify their compensation structure. These structures usually contain a first-time enrollment commission and renewal commissions for a certain period (e.g., five years) provided the enrollee stays in the health plan's program.

Sample marketing agent contracts can be accessed via internet. For example, Aetna which is one of the largest health plans in USA has placed its marketing agent contract on the internet for read only (not to use without Aetna's permission). See, http://www.aetna.com/insurance-producer/document-library/aetna_producer_agreement.pdf.

CMS Sanctions for Marketing Violations

Sanctions were applied to Universal American Medicare Plan's Medicare Advantage–Prescription Drug plans because, according to CMS, "agents misled beneficiaries about network providers who were not actually part of the network or drugs that were not part of the plan's formulary."

CMS reported that Arcadian Health Plan was also imposed sanctions for similar marketing violations, saying "sales agents were misleading beneficiaries about network providers and/or drug plan formularies."

"It would be a mistake to dismiss these as cases of 'bad' agents who were intentionally misleading people to make a sale. Instead, look at yourself and ask, 'Am I doing everything I can to make sure my clients understand the plan they're buying and why they're buying it?'"

Source: Senior Market Sales (2018).

13.9.2. Physician compensation involved contracts negotiated by marketing

The main concern here is compliance with Stark laws and AKS we discussed in detail in Section 13.3. Violations of these laws appear in news quite frequently.

Swartley (2019) presents two 2018 cases that illustrate potential violations of these laws:

(1) One involved a Montana hospital along with six of its subsidiaries and related entities for allegedly overpaying more than 50 part-time employed specialists, including cardiologists, gastroenterologists, and surgeons. The hospital was accused of improper compensation agreements with the doctors based on referrals to its hospitals. The hospital and its related entities agreed to pay US$24 million to resolve allegations that they violated the False Claims Act by paying physicians more than the fair market value (FMV) and by conspiring to enter into arrangements that improperly induced referrals.
(2) A Michigan hospital reached an US$84.5 million settlement to resolve allegations claiming eight referring physicians received above FMV compensation and below-fair-market-value rent under the False Claims Act of improper relationships.

Commonly reported problematic compensation arrangements between hospitals and physicians involve renting of office space, providing computers and other equipment, employment in committees and review boards, incentive plans not based on bona fide quality improvements.

Hospital contracting processes with physicians should be closely scrutinized to ensure (Troxell, 2012):

- Having a signed, written contract. Stark and the AKS require signed, written agreements for independent contractor arrangements (Troxell, 2012).
- Specifying the services and compensation in the contract. Services must be commercially necessary. Do not pay or provide additional compensation, benefits or perks not specified in the contract (e.g., insurance, bonuses, side payments and free items or services) unless expressly permitted by a separate Stark or AKS exception.
- Use of actuarially computed FMVs as the basis for compensation in professional services agreements (PSAs) and management services agreements (MSAs) (Troxell, 2012).

- Legal review of physician contracts.
- Well-documented policies and procedures for physician contracting.
- That no payments based on referrals.

References

American Marketing Association (2008). Statement of Ethics, http://www.marketingpower.com/AboutAMA/Pages/Statement%20of%20Ethics.aspx. Accessed August 23, 2018.

Arrow, K. J. (1963). "Uncertainty and the Welfare Economics of Medical Care", *The American Economic Review*, LIII (5).

Bain, J. (2015). "The Anti-Kickback Statute: What Constitutes a 'Referral'?", https://www.floridahealthcarelawfirm.com/anti-kickback-statute-2/. Accessed March 12, 2019.

Beauchamp, T. L. and Childress, J. F. (1989). *Principles of Biomedical Ethics*, 3rd edn., Oxford University Press.

Benge, V. A. (2019). "The Federal Truth in Advertising Law", AzcEntral, https://yourbusiness.azcentral.com/federal-truth-advertising-law-7108.html. Accessed March 12, 2019.

Blanchard, K. and Peale, N. V. (1988). *The Power of Ethical Management*, William Morrow and Company, Inc., New York.

CMS: *Medicare Marketing Manual*, 2016.

Conover, C. (2004). "Health Care Regulation a $169 Billion Hidden Tax", *Policy Analysis*, https://object.cato.org/sites/cato.org/files/pubs/pdf/pa527.pdf. Accessed January 21, 2019.

Davis, E. (2018). "How Health Insurance Companies Prevent Adverse Selection", Updated May 03, 2018, *very well health*. https://www.verywellhealth.com/adverse-selection-what-it-is-how-health-plans-avoid-it-1738416. Accessed January 22, 2019.

Diekema, D. S. and Botkin, J. R. (2009). "Forgoing Medically Provided Nutrition and Hydration in Children", *Pediatrics*, 124 (2), 813.

Direct Marketing Association (2007). "Guidelines for Ethical Business Practice", http://ethics.iit.edu/codes/DMA2007.pdf. Accessed March 11, 2019.

Dresvic, A. (2010). "Key Regulations Impacting Healthcare Marketing: Entertainment and Gifts", https://www.thehealthlawpartners.com/files/rbma.january-february_2010.key_regulations_impacting_healthcare_marketing_-_entertainment_and_gifts.pdf. Accessed August 24, 2018.

Field, R. J. (2008). "Why is Health Care Regulation So Complex?", *Pharmacy and Therapeutics*, 33 (10), 607–608.

Florida Tech (2018). "3 Frameworks for Ethical Decision Making", https://www.floridatechonline.com/blog/business/3-frameworks-for-ethical-decision-making/. Accessed March 12, 2019.

Grimsley, J. (2015). "How This New Regulation Will Drive Up Your Health Care Costs", *The Daily Signal*, February 10, https://www.dailysignal.com/2015/02/10/how-this-new-regulation-will-drive-up-your-health-care-costs/. Accessed March 12, 2019.

Hammaker, D. K. and Knadig, T. M. (2017). *Health Care Ethics and the Law*, Jones & Bartlett Learning.

LEP.gov (2017). *Executive Order 13166*, https://www.lep.gov/13166/eo13166.html. Accessed January 2, 2019.

Levesque, J.-F., Harris, M. F. and Russell, G. (2013). "Patient-Centered Access to Health Care: Conceptualizing Access at the Interface of Health Systems and Populations", *International Journal for Equity in Health*, 12, 18.

Levine, C. (2009). "The Seattle 'God Committee': A Cautionary Tale", *Health Affairs* blog, https://www.healthaffairs.org/do/10.1377/hblog20091130.002998/full/. Accessed March 12, 2019.

Markgraf, B. (2018). "Examples of Questionable Marketing Ethics", *Chron*, https://smallbusiness.chron.com/examples-questionable-marketing-ethics-60520.html. Accessed March 12, 2019.

Musham, C. and Trettin, L. (2002). "Bringing Health Services to the Poor Through Social Marketing: Ethical Issues", *Journal of Health Care for the Poor and Underserved*, 13 (3), 280–287.

NCQA (2018). "Health Plan Accreditation", https://www.ncqa.org/programs/health-plans/health-plan-accreditation-hpa/. Accessed January 22, 2019.

Nickitas, M., Middaugh, D. and Aries, N. (2016). *Policy and Politics for Nurses and Other Health Professionals*, Jones & Bartlett Learning, Burlington.

Nurses' Notes (2016). "Why Regulate Healthcare", *Spring 2016 Nurses' Notes*, April 13, https://onlineedu.neit.edu/201630nur38495/2016/04/13/why-regulate-healthcare/. Accessed January 22, 2019.

OIG (Office of Inspector General, 2018). "What is an Exclusion and Why Do I Need to Search the OIG Exclusion List", http://www.oigexclusionlist.com/post/47574810437/what-is-an-exclusion-and-why-do-i-need-to-search. Accessed November 17, 2018.

Price, G. and Norbeck, T. (2013). "Healthcare is Turning into an Industry Focused on Compliance, Regulation rather than Patient Care", *Forbes*, 2013, https://www.forbes.com/sites/physiciansfoundation/2013/11/05/healthcare-is-turing-into-an-industry-focused-on-compliance-regulation-rather-than-patient-care/#7e5f7e752e3c. Accessed January 22, 2019.

Ricoy, P. D. (2013). "Marketing under the HIPAA Megarule: The Rules Become Tighter", *ABA Health eSource*, 9 (9).

Ross, S. (2018). "The Affordable Care Act Affects Moral Hazard in the Health Insurance Industry", Updated Nov 18, 2018, *Investopedia*, https://www.

investopedia.com/ask/answers/043015/how-does-affordable-care-act-affect-moral-hazard-health-insurance-industry.asp. Accessed January 23, 2019.

Saint Joseph's University (2019). "How the Four Principles of Health Care Ethics Improve Patient Care", https://online.sju.edu/graduate/masters-health-administration/resources/articles/four-principles-of-health-care-ethics-improve-patient-care. Accessed March 12, 2019.

Scott, C. (2000). "Why Law Pervades Medicine: An Essay on Ethics in Health Care", *Notre Dame Journal of Law in Ethics & Public Policy*, 14 (1), 245–303, http://scholarship.law.nd.edu/ndjlepp/vol14/iss1/9.

Senior Market Sales (2018). "CMS Marketing Violations: A Cautionary Tale", https://www.seniormarketsales.com/education/content-library/news-updates/cms-marketing-violations-a-cautionary-tale/. Accessed March 28, 2019.

Swartley, C. (2019). "Keep Physician Compensation Contracts in Compliance to Avoid Stark Law Violations", *Healthcare News*, https://www.healthcarenewssite.com/articles/01-2019/cswartley-0119.php. Accessed March 27, 2019.

TechTarget (2019). "Definition: Joint Commission", https://searchhealthit.techtarget.com/definition/The-Joint-Commission. Accessed January 23, 2019.

Troxell, H. (2012). "Audit Your Physician Contracts: Avoid Stark and Anti-Kickback Repayments", *Articles & Publications, Health Law*, January 19, https://hawleytroxell.com/2012/01/audit-your-physician-contracts-avoid-stark-and-anti-kickback-repayments-2/. Accessed March 28, 2019.

Suggested Additional Readings

Becker's Hospital Review (2014). "20 Things to Know about the Anti-Kickback Statute", https://www.beckershospitalreview.com/legal-regulatory-issues/20-things-to-know-about-the-anti-kickback-statute.html.

Bent, S., Pitts, R. E. and LaTour, M. (1993). "The Appropriateness of Fear Appeal Use for Health Care Marketing to the Elderly: Is It OK to Scare Granny?", *Journal of Business Ethics*, 12 (1), 45–55.

Continuous Care (2017). "Ethics of Healthcare Marketing for Physicians and Medical Practices", February 8, In Blog by Continuous Care, https://www.continuouscare.io/blog/healthcare-marketing-ethics-for-physicians-medical-practices/. Accessed October 4, 2018.

Goldman, R. L. (1993). "Practical Applications of Healthcare Marketing Ethics", *Healthcare Financial Management*, 47 (March), 46–48.

Gray, D. M. and Christianson, L. (2008), "Marketing to Patients: A Legal and Ethical Perspective", *Journal of Academic and Business Ethics*, 70, 69–78, http://www.aabri.com/manuscripts/08041.pdf. Accessed October 14, 2018.

Grimm, N. (2014). "Healthcare Regulations: Who Does What?", http://www.yourtrainingprovider.com/blog_main/bid/203291/Health-Care-Regulation-Who-Does-What. Accessed January 22, 2019.

Kalthoff, G. (2017). "How to Stay HIPAA Compliant When Using Social Media for Healthcare", https://www.medicalwebexperts.com/blog/how-to-stay-compliant-when-using-social-media-for-healthcare/. Accessed January 12, 2019.

Malhotra, N. K. and Miller, G. L. (1996). "Ethical Issues in Marketing Managed Care", *Journal of Health Care Marketing*, 16 (1), 60–65.

Moser, H. R., Stevens, R. and Loudon, D. (2016). "An Empirical Analysis of Ethical and Professional Issues in Physicians' Advertising: A Comparative Cross-Sectional Study", *Health Marketing Quarterly*, 33 (3), 255–273.

Nelson, L. (2016). "HIPAA and Digital Marketing: Can You Have Both?", https://www.clementinehealth.com/blog/hipaa-and-digital-marketing-can-you-have-both. Accessed March 12, 2019.

Terhune, C. (2018). "California Hospital Giant Sutter Health Faces Heavy Backlash on Prices", California Healthline, May 15.

Part 4

Health Care Marketing in Special Sectors

Chapter 14

Direct Health Care Marketing in Special Sectors: Physician Services, Hospital Services, Managed Care Products (HMOs and ACOs), Pharmaceuticals, and Public Health

14.1. What is Direct Marketing in Health Care?

Direct marketing is a promotional method that involves presenting information about a company, product, or service to the target customer without the use of an advertising middleman. It is a targeted form of marketing that presents information of potential interest to a consumer who has been determined to be a likely buyer (Shopify, 2018).

> Direct marketing is an interactive system of marketing; therefore, it is sometimes referred to as *Interactive Marketing*. It is expected to be a two-way communication with the customer or prospective customer. It always seeks a measurable response, e.g., an inquiry or order (Spiller and Baier, 2005).

In direct health care marketing, a health care organization such as a hospital, health plan, public health agency, pharmaceutical company, or physician group will communicate directly to consumers/patients through a variety of media including email, cell phone text messaging, websites, online advertisements, fliers, catalogues, promotional letters, and targeted television, newspaper, and magazine advertisements.

Results of direct marketing can be measured objectively. For example, if a marketer sends out 1,000 mailers to senior citizens inviting to explore a Medicare Advantage Plan, and 150 respond asking for more details or a presentation, the marketer can say that the direct marketing effort led to a 15% success (response rate). Measurement of results is a fundamental element in successful direct health care marketing.

One of the other benefits of direct health care marketing is that it enables promoting health care products or services that are either new or not well known, e.g., a new drug or a new high deductible health insurance plan.

In this era of digital communications, internet-based channels such as email and texts have made direct marketing easier and faster. Measuring response rates is also efficiently possible with internet-based direct marketing.

There are several modern trends that encourage direct marketing in health care.

- Modern health care consumers/patients are personally involved in searching for health information and managing their health care.
- They do so often using digital modes. Pew Research Center (2013) reports that Americans are turning to the internet frequently for health information. About six in 10 (59%) say they did so in the past year. Nearly eight in 10 (77%) of online health seekers say they began at a search engine such as Google, Bing, or Yahoo. Another 13% say they began at a site that specializes in health information, like WebMD. Just 2% say they started their research at a more general site like Wikipedia and an additional 1% say they started at a social network site like Facebook. When asked to think about the last time they went online for health or medical information, 39% of online health seekers say they looked for information related to their own situation. Another 39% say they looked for information related to someone else's health or medical situation. An additional 15% of these internet users say they were looking both on their own and someone else's behalf.
- Modern emphasis on patient-centered care. Patient-centered care replaces our current physician centered system with one that revolves around the patient. Effective care is generally defined by or in consultation with patients, rather than by physician-dependent tools or standards (Rickert, 2012).

    Patient-centered care has now made it to center stage in discussions of quality. Enshrined by the Institute of Medicine's "quality chasm" report as one of six key elements of high-quality care, health care institutions, health planners, congressional representatives, and hospital public relations departments now include the phrase in their lexicons. Insurance payments are increasingly linked to the provision of patient-centered care (Institute of Medicine, 2001).

Patient-centered care is a quality of personal, professional, and organizational relationships. Thus, efforts to promote patient-centered care should consider patient-centeredness of patients (and their families), clinicians, and health systems. Helping patients to be more active in consultations changes centuries of physician-dominated dialogues to those that engage patients as active participants (Epstein and Street, 2011).

- Rickert (2012) in an article on patient-centered care says that, what patients want from their physicians is:
    o A Personal Relationship,
    o Communication, and
    o Empathy.

Examples of direct marketing in health care include:

- Physicians communicating directly with their patients by mail, email, and texts about new developments in health care such as new methods of diagnosis and treatments.
- Hospital newsletters to their past cancer patients about developments in treating cancer and how the hospital has adopted new services and technology to provide these new services.
- Pharmaceutical companies advertising on TV targeting diabetes patients about new weekly self-administered drugs such as Trulicity.

> Direct-to-consumer pharmaceutical advertising (DTCPA) has grown rapidly during the past several decades and is now the most prominent type of health communication that the public encounters. The FDA regulates DTCPA, but critics say that the rules are too relaxed and inadequately enforced (Ventola, 2011).

- Health plans sending out newsletters to their beneficiaries identified as overweight during physician visits on health and wellness programs they offer on topics such as obesity.

14.2. Direct Marketing of Physician Services

There are many studies showing the increasing demand for physician services. See, for example,

- For 2015 through 2018, average growth in physician and clinical services is expected to be 5.5% per year, due to increased demand for services associated with the continuing coverage expansions and faster income growth (CMS, 2016).
- For 2019 through 2022, the aging of the baby-boom population is expected to be one factor that results in increasing use of physician and clinical services and projected spending growth of 6.6% per year, on average (CMS, 2016).
- For 2019 through 2022, the aging of the baby-boom population is expected to be one factor that results in increasing use of physician and clinical services and projected spending growth of 6.6% per year, on average (CMS, 2016).

However, the physician income and quality of professional and personal life seem to be stagnating, if not declining.

Dyrda (2017), in a recent article, "5 Trends in Physician Income and Compensation", cites The Medicus Firm's 2017 Physician Practice Preference & Relocation Survey to highlight some interesting facts relating to physician practices in the US. Among these are:

- Physicians are split on whether they are receiving fair compensation; 35.77% were satisfied, 32.46% were unsatisfied, and 31.77% were neutral on their 2016 income.
- Half of the physician respondents anticipated their income would remain around the same in 2017 as it was in 2016. However, 27.71% felt their compensation would increase in 2017 and 19.59% thought it would decrease.

Moawad (2017) in an article, "Are Physician Incomes Failing?", cites industry experts and states,

- There seems to be a downward trend, especially for specialties such as radiology that have traditionally been well-paying. While the high-paying specialties have not fared well, primary care physicians do not seem to be gaining ground either.

- In high cost of living areas like California, physicians in specialties as diverse as Obstetrics and Gynaecology (Ob/Gyn), emergency medicine, and pediatrics, are finding that income levels are not commensurate with home prices and cost of living.

The industry consensus is that the guaranteed high-income life of physicians has almost but vanished due to several trends. Among these are:

- Advent of health care reforms (like ACA, also called Obamacare) and managed care where health plans, employers, and Medicare and Medicaid agencies control the allocation of eligible beneficiaries and rates paid to physicians.
- Administrative requirements (paper work) relating to services provided to managed care patients are taking time away from seeing income generating patients.
- High cost of medical education including residency and fellowship programs.
- High cost of malpractice insurance.
- High cost of prescription drugs and deductibles that affects patients which in turn limits that authority physicians have on patient care and overall patient experience.
- High cost of, and frustration with, new requirements like electronic health records (EHR) which, despite all the claims of efficiency and quality at systems level, do not produce tangible gains to physicians at the practice level. Hixon (2015) in an article, "Why Doctors are Frustrated with Digital Healthcare", explains that doctors are frustrated because they do not see the digital health tools delivering value, and that EHRs are typically hard to use requiring extra time for data entry. Besides, EHRs are often local internal systems that are not linked to more useful clinical resources.
- Health care consumer activism. Health care consumers have access to online information to compare physicians, learn about illnesses (from sources like WebMD), and learn about alternative treatments such as natural remedies. These reduce their need to see physicians for routing health care needs.
- New Medicare utilization review policies that strictly review, and often deny, treatment and medication which for years have been approved as standard care.

These physician experiences, especially those relating to their practice level and income, suggest the need for physicians to engage in promotion and marketing of their services.

14.2.1. Who are the customers in marketing physicians services?

We should start by recalling the key portion applicable to physician services marketing from our definition and understanding of health care marketing from Chapter 1, which is

> " ... find and acquire the right patients, engage with them through strategic outreach, and nurture them to form lasting relationships throughout the entire patient journey."

In other words, marketing physician services is not just distributing pamphlets in the practice area or a few newspaper ads with photographs of the physician and his office.

Towards achieving these objectives, we should first understand the several segments in the market relating to physician services. These are:

- Primary payors such as health plans, CMS (for Medicare), and state departments of health services.

According to MCOL (2018), Managed Care Fact Sheets: National Managed Care Penetration 2017, Medicare managed care enrollment in 2017 was 32% of the total Medicare population; Medicaid managed care was 80% of total Medicaid population and commercial health insurance managed care was 99% of the total commercial insurance population. The total percentage of enrollees in managed care was 74.7% of the total health care enrollments in the US. In absolute figures, there are 243 million managed care enrollees in the US.

This enormous managed care population reaches primary care physicians (PCP) either by their own choice or by being assigned to a PCP by the primary payors (Medicare and Medicaid agencies, health plans contracted with these agencies, or commercial health insurers).

Every managed care enrollee must have a PCP. Thus, the importance of the PCPs in US health care is enormous. A survey research by the University of Missouri-Columbia (UMC) and the US Department of Health and Human Services predicts that by 2025 the United States will be short of 35,000 to 44,000 adult care primary care physicians (Colwill et al., 2008).

> These facts and figures highlight three important factors relating to marketing physician service.
>
> First, primary care physicians (PCPs) cannot ignore the importance of targeting the managed care enrollee population for growth;
>
> Next, PCPs need to focus on marketing to primary payors;
>
> PCPs should also focus on direct marketing to managed care enrollees because the managed care enrollees' choice of PCP always triumphs health plan assignment.

- Mid-level organizations such as Independent Practice Associations (IPAs) and Accountable Care Organizations (ACOs). Membership in these organizations brings recognition and new patients to physicians.

For a physician, membership in an IPA is a profitable and prestigious thing. Health plans prefer to contract with IPAs and not individual physicians. IPAs also want to have a larger and comprehensive network of PCPs and specialists to impress and secure health plans.

For physicians, criteria for admission into an IPA are the same that health plans consider important, that is licensure, geographic location, current level of patient activity, medical office and record keeping efficiency, quality of care, and patient satisfaction and experience. Additionally, IPAs might expect physicians to buy into the IPA with an initial investment.

- Consumers and patients: existing patients and potential patients in the community.

Marketing to consumers to gain new patients, and to current patients to ensure retention, is the primary marketing activity discussed in many chapters of this book. See below, the section on "Direct Marketing Challenges of Physicians".

- Quality accreditation organizations such as National Committee for Quality Assurance (NCQA).

Physicians do not, generally, seek direct accreditation from entities like NCQA. However, NCQA accreditation of health plans and large IPAs involve review of selected physicians in their network. Therefore, maintaining quality of care and patient satisfaction is highly important for physicians.

- Other physicians in the community.

Referrals from other physicians is an important factor in new business expansion for physicians. This is extremely important for health care providers in ancillary services such as physical therapists, speech therapists, and chiropractors who depend heavily on area physicians for referrals.

Practitioners recommend good personal relationships with area physicians and building trust, and regularly attending professional events and networking. Also effective are direct solicitation for referrals, leaving business cards in physician offices, emails educating one's specialty area and subspecialties, and relationships with physician's office staff.

14.2.2. Market segmentation

Primary care physicians (PCPs) usually select product lines to serve from among commercial insurance enrollees, Medicare beneficiaries, Medicaid beneficiaries, ACA exchange enrollees, and cash patients. Decision to participate in these programs is based on acceptance/accreditation by health plans, ACOs and hospitals, reimbursement rates, familiarity with managed care processes, tolerance of oversight by payers, and overall presence in community.

Each line of business brings in patients with different demographic characteristics, needs and expectations, compensation rates, and health behaviors.

Marketing strategy for physician services should, therefore, start by deciding which market segments to focus on. Should the primary focus be on attracting new patients via contracts with IPAs and health plans? Or should it be attracting new patients by direct marketing to area consumers? If so, which segment of consumers: Medicare? Medicaid? Commercial patients? etc.

For discussions on marketing strategies, once appropriate segments for marketing are selected, see the discussion above on marketing to primary managed care payors such as government agencies, IPAs, and health plans, and the section below on "Direct Marketing Challenges of Physicians".

14.2.3. Direct marketing challenges of physicians

PCPs get new/additional members from health plans and ACOs, either directly or via IPAS they participate in. Therefore, PCPs cannot market/influence managed care enrollees and beneficiaries directly.

Their key to increasing the patient base depends on relations with payers (IPAs and health plans). For this reason, physicians often engage office administrators or marketers to build relationships with IPAs and health plans.

Participation in managed care health plan networks depends on several factors:

- Geographic location. Health plans want to have their service area covered with sufficient primary care (and specialist) physicians. Therefore, strategic location of their practices and/or joining medical groups/IPAs in prime locations is a must for primary care physicians.
- Quality of care. In pre-contract reviews, health plans must be convinced that the physician has facilities that meet state standards, reliable medical records maintenance, adequate and competent nursing staff, quality of care, and acceptable utilization rates (no over- or underutilization of services by patients).
- Willingness to accept competitive discounted rates in negotiated contracts.
- In geographical areas with significant non-English speaking populations, ability of the physician to, or availability of staff who can, effectively communicate with patients in multiple languages.
- Level of coverage and risk physician or physician group is willing to accept. Accepting more services raises the financial risk of the physician and benefits the health plan.
- Overall patient satisfaction and experience, usually seen by years of practice in the area and patient retention rates.

> Improving the standing in above factors is the key to successful marketing of physician services to private health plans and government payers who control the managed care populations. Being accepted by reputable IPAs, health plans, hospitals, and Medicare/Medicaid agencies is essential.
>
> Recall from our earlier discussions that nearly 75% of health care consumers in the US are in managed care systems. The total number of managed care enrollees is around 250 million.

14.2.4. Direct marketing to consumers

From our earlier discussions, it should be clear that the average health care consumer/patient belongs to some form of managed care system — Medicare managed care, Medicaid managed care, commercial managed health care, or ACA exchange-based managed care.

Therefore, the purpose of marketing physician services is two-fold:

1. **Gain new patients:** Communicating the physician's education, competence, skills, experience, affiliations with highly regarded health plans and hospitals, and acknowledging excellent patient experience to influence this huge population of managed care enrollees to seek services from them.
2. **Retain current patients:** Communicating to current patients on matters important to them, including addressing their concerns, especially about office procedures and staff courtesy and efficiency; and educating them to build confidence and trust, and be engaged, all in an effort to retain them.

While marketing strategies to achieve these two different objectives are different, there are many common features in them. We discuss these next from multiple review articles such as Getweave (2019), Cloud-Moulds (2015), and Whitehurst (2014).

- Key to retention marketing is patient communication and engagement during the three stages of the physician–patient relationship, that is access to care, care delivery, and follow-up care.
- Address factors important to patients for selecting a physician, including competence, concern, staff behavior, assurance, empathy, physical access, courtesy, reliability, and communication (Gunawardane, 2010).
- For current patients, remember that expectations of physician's service changes over time and multiple visits (Gunawardane, 2010). Therefore, marketing/communication to longer standing patients has to be different from marketing/communications to new patients.
- Vital to patient experience during office visits are clean and comfortable office and clinic facilities, efficiency of processes, and competence and friendliness of staff.
- Specific processes important to patients have been found to be appointment scheduling, waiting times, parking, getting copies of records across to other providers, billing errors, timely prescription refills, office hours, physician absences, phone not being answered, long answering machine statements ("If this is an emergency call 911 ...."), and not returning phone class.
- Maintaining a patient feedback system (by emails, texts, and conventional means) and regular review of patient input.

- Efficient care coordination and sharing responsibility for post-service follow-up.
- Patient education via digital communications to show physician's currency in the field and to build confidence and trust in the physician.
- Engaging with other physicians via professional meetings, gatherings and hospital events. Participating in physician-only online communities (Dunlop, 2013). For example, Sermo now has more than 125,000 physician members representing 68 specialties. Doximity has now surpassed 100,000 physician members, which is over 15% of US physicians.
- Engaging with community by attending community events and sponsorships.
- Adopting modern digital technology: an efficient website, email, text messages with concern for patient preferences and usefulness to patients.
- Ensure that the physician's profiles are current in online search sources like Google, Healthgrades, and hospital, state, and health plan provider directories.
- While consumers in general are found to be increasingly using digital channels, and especially mobile devices, to research physician services and physicians, there are variations within market segments. For example, commercial insurance patients have higher educational levels and higher income. They use internet-based information sources more. Medicare and Medicaid patients' use of internet sources is low. Therefore, it is important to adopt a mixed marketing/communication strategy that uses direct mail, newsletters, websites, emails, and text messages.
- Nothing is more effective in physician marketing than word-of-mouth referrals and appreciations by patients who perceive receiving an excellent patient experience from the physician.

14.2.5. Specialist physician services marketing

As discussed earlier, referrals for specialist physicians come from PCPs. Therefore, the key marketing strategy for specialist physicians is relationship marketing with PCPs, strategies for most of which were discussed earlier in this chapter.

Lewis (1993) in an article, "Referral Physician Marketing" in the *Journal of Health Care Marketing*, presents the following views:

- Marketing of specialist services to referring physicians can be highly effective at influencing referral patterns if the referring physician's needs are taken into account.

- It is important to treat non-referring physicians as though they referred the patient, even when they did not. This practice allows the specialist to demonstrate communications service quality in a non-aggressive, non-sales context.
- Referrals from physicians can be increased by developing a relationship strategy that emphasizes legitimacy, notification, control, and patient experience.
- Communicating regularly with primary care physicians to convey specialist standing/competence, assurance of sending the patient back, providing good service to add to the patient's overall experience (with PCP and specialist).

14.3. Marketing Hospital Services

14.3.1. Current status of hospital marketing

> The discussion here is limited to marketing services of acute care hospitals. Discussing marketing of other hospitals, namely, specialty hospitals, tertiary hospitals, and teaching hospitals, is beyond the scope of this book.

A 2009 survey by the Society for Healthcare Strategy and Market Development found that the average marketing budget for an American hospital ranged from US$1.3 million for an independent hospital to about US$5.8 million for a big health system. Though that may seem like a lot of money, it makes up less than 1% of the typical hospital budget (Erickson, 2010).

A 2010 survey by the American Hospital Association showed that US hospitals spent an average of US$883,000 on advertising. However, this number varies significantly from hospital to hospital. Additionally, large institutions tend to spend disproportionately more on advertising. Hospitals with more than 400 beds spent an average of US$2.18 million on advertising in 2010.

More recent figures are consistent. Based on a BIA/Kelsey study reported by Ackley (2017), hospitals continue to be the largest sub-category of health care advertising spending with an estimated US$4.90 billion in local advertising in the US in 2017. There are approximately 5,564 hospitals in the United States. The average hospital will spend nearly US$830,500 on local advertising during 2017. Among all hospitals, larger marketing budgets are concentrated in research hospitals, where new technology and therapies are developed. How the money is spent: Hospitals are spending the bulk of their marketing budget on traditional television, newspaper, and billboard advertisements.

Hospitals are reported to be spending about 25% of their marketing budget on digital and social media advertising. The bulk of this money is spent on writing copy for a hospital's website and improving the hospital's ranking on online search engines. Other main items of hospitals' spending include hosting events like free health fair screenings or meet-and-greets between potential patients and doctors, and marketing to physicians to increase referrals.

14.3.2. Who are the "customers" in hospital services marketing?

What are the market segments for hospital marketing? The view that hospitals should focus on physicians because it is the physicians who refer patients to hospitals is correct, but as we will see here it has many more dimensions.

To arrive at a comprehensive answer to this question that would help in formulating hospital marketing strategy, we should look at the sources of income of hospitals (Becker's Hospital CFO Report, 2017; Cunningham et al., 2016; Steinberg, 2016; Tine Health, 2017), a summary of which is as follows:

1. Revenue from inpatient admissions/services from physician referrals and admissions.
2. Payments from insurance companies and health plans.
3. Revenue from emergency room follow-up admissions for inpatient services.
4. Patient-initiated outpatient services, including emergency room (ER) services.
5. Medicare and Medicaid payments from non-managed care patients.
6. Additional income sources such as Medicare Disproportionate Share Hospitals (DSHs) payments, Hospital Inpatient Quality Reporting, and use of Electronic Health Records (EHR).

From this analysis, we can infer that the customers for marketing hospital services are:

- Physicians who initiate revenue source 1 above.
- Insurance companies and health plans that initiate revenue source 2 above.
- Consumers/patients/community who initiate revenue sources 3 and 4 above.
- CMS and state departments of health agencies that govern revenue sources 5 and 6 above.
- Joint Commission and similar quality and patient satisfaction evaluators who influence almost all the above categories.
- Internal customers, that is hospital staff, who have a role to play in sources 5 and 6 above.

For example, Emergency Rooms (ERs, also called Emergency Departments or EDs), contrary to the popular belief as money losers, are reported to have an average profit margin of 7.8%. In 2009, ER/ED admissions were reported to have resulted in US$78.7 billion in revenue (Becker's Hospital CFO Report, 2014). Thus, focusing on educating ED staff on maximizing medically necessary admissions through ERs, and reviewing criteria (for extended treatment and hospital days) of health plans and insurers would be a useful internal marketing activity.

Additional Income Sources: These include Medicare Disproportionate Share Hospitals (DSHs) payments, hospital inpatient quality reporting, and use of electronic health records. Internal marketing strategy: Work with internal staff to improve record keeping and reporting to maximize these revenues. Also, with medical and nursing staff, to improve quality of service to minimize revenue lowering Hospital Value-Based Purchasing (VBP) Adjustments.

14.3.3. Marketing to physicians

Hospital marketing to physicians was discussed in Section 12.3, where we saw that the core market for referral of patients to the hospital is the physicians who practice on its medical staff, and that except for admissions through emergency rooms, which do not require direct physician referral, hospitals must rely on their medical staffs to bring in the vast majority of patients.

We also noted that physician engagement is thus vital to hospitals, and that physicians who were fully engaged or engaged in hospital settings were 26% more productive than physicians who were not engaged or who were actively disengaged. This is reported to be equivalent to an average of nearly half a million US dollars in patient revenue per physician per year to the hospital.

In recent times, hospitals have increased hiring physicians and owning or supporting multi-specialty medical groups. However, as we saw in Section 12.3, this practice has not significantly improved hospitals' financial positions. Hospital-owned multispecialty practices are also reported to be making losses (2013 figures), around US$100,000 per physician.

These findings indicate that patient referral by physicians should continue to be the primary focus of hospital service marketing. In any case, the primary aim of owning or supporting medical groups is to increase patient referrals by physicians in those groups.

Research and industry studies suggest the following strategies for marketing hospital service to physicians:

- Increasing physician engagement by proactively addressing and providing solutions for physician problems, especially those related to changes brought about by ACA, Medicare, and Medicaid.
- Encouraging physician involvement with hospital administration. Promoting effective communication between physicians and hospital administrators to remove conflicts between physicians and administrators. Ensuring that physicians' opinions are heard.
- Focusing on remedial actions to address physician concerns and complaints. Hospital concerns with hospitals are reported to be mainly on admission processes, discharge processes, and support for physician clinical activities.
- Hospital support for physicians, such as consulting assignments, office space support, and assistance with EMR/EHR systems, in exchange for increased referrals within boundaries of Stark Law.
- Focusing on physicians who refer patients for surgeries and complex procedures (which also require multiple tests and procedures within standards of care and ethical practices). Hospitals get paid well for surgeries, complex cases, tests, and procedures.
- Focusing on physicians who manage hospital days well. Longer stays are not necessarily more profitable.
- Focusing on physicians who have large Medicaid patient bases to increase Medicaid admissions.

Medicare payments to hospitals have been lesser due to application of diagnosis-related groups (DRG) systems, stricter utilization reviews, and policy changes imposing deductions for readmissions and deductions for hospital-acquired conditions. However, Medicaid payments have not been affected so much by these changes. In fact, Medicaid and CHIP Payment and Access Commission (MACPAC) report of April 2017 shows that Medicaid payments to hospitals were comparable or higher than Medicare, and that the average Medicaid payment for 18 selected conditions was 6% higher than Medicare (*Source*: MACPAC https://www.macpac.gov/wp-content/uploads/2017/04/Medicaid-Hospital-Payment-A-Comparison-across-States-and-to-Medicare.pdf).

- Educate referring physicians on higher professional fees for more complex treatments, achieving lesser readmissions, and hospital-acquired conditions, which have a negative effect on hospital revenue.
- Providing educational seminars on career-building, Continuing Professional Development and Continuing Medical Education, and assistance with increasing efficiency of the practice, e.g., EMR.

14.3.4. Marketing to health plans

All insurance and health plans are not the same. Some insurance plans are better than others. Insurance companies and health plans pay hospitals on a fee-for-service or per-diem basis. The modern tendency is to relate these payments to the Medicare DRG system, which pays according to diagnostic groups. Rates paid by insurance companies and health plans vary among hospitals depending on the bargaining powers of the parties. Large insurance companies with relatively more market power usually pay lower prices for given services than do smaller insurers with less market power.

Hospitals should focus on a healthy mixture of large and medium size insurers and health plans. The smaller the hospital, the better the rates, the lesser the demands on quality, and the better the relationships with smaller insurers and health plans.

Improved quality, patient safety, and patient experience are key elements health plans look for when contracting with hospitals.

14.3.5. Marketing to consumers/patients/community

While, physicians drive hospital revenues, consumers/patients seem to have an increasing say in the selection of a hospital for ER, outpatient, and even inpatient services.

In a study by Bertowitz and Flexner (1980), about 24% of the people that participated in the study said that they are highly involved in the process of choosing the hospital where they are to receive care. About 73% said their physician chooses the hospital for them.

This and other studies (e.g., Boscarino and Steiber, 1982) show that consumers/patients consider several factors in selecting a hospital. These include:

- Quality of care; patient safety.
- Cleanliness of the facility.
- Attitude of the staff.
- Hospital's reputation. As this book has repeatedly emphasized, a hospital's reputation (and brand image) comes from patient experience.
- Location of the hospital (a factor rated as important in many studies). The 2014 Healthgrades American Hospital Quality Report to the Nation states that consumers are more likely to choose a hospital based on location (58%) than based on what health outcomes it achieves for patients (30%). That means location is a bigger factor than the clinical quality of care (Infographics, 2014).
- Affiliation with reputed specialists.
- Customer/patient experience of trusted reference sources.

14.3.6. Importance of customer/patient experience: Internal marketing

Today's hospital patients are increasingly sophisticated customers who have come to expect the same level of consumer experience as they realize daily in the retail and service world outside of health care.

Johnston (2015) cites a study by Center for Studying Health System Change, reporting that Americans choose a new doctor or hospital based on word of mouth. 50% relied on input from friends and family. Even when seeking a specialist, almost 20% still turn to friends' advice. She also cites a study by PricewaterhouseCoopers (PWC) that found the rising importance of word of mouth on social media, reporting that more than two out of five individuals said social media affected their choice of a provider or organization.

On the other hand, the PWC study also found that only 54% of health care consumers tell friends and family about a positive experience. Research also show that if consumers have a bad experience, they tend to remember it longer.

According to National Research Corporation, once an individual gets treatment at a hospital, he or she is more likely to go to the same hospital for future needs.

Patient experience with hospitals is now available to consumers via government survey ratings. These ratings show whether patients would recommend the hospital, their overall assessment of it, and their experience with topics such as communication with doctors and nurses, pain control, and whether their rooms were kept clean and quiet.

Internal marketing is the key to improving customer experience with the hospital. Internal marketing promotes hospital staff to be engaged and become patient-oriented, and to coordinate internal processes that make them more efficient for the benefit of patients, families, and physicians.

Improving hospital patient experience is a key modern-day priority in US hospitals. Major hospitals are doing this, e.g. Cleveland Clinic and Mayo Clinic. This is in part due to the connection of reimbursement and Hospital Consumer Assessment of Healthcare Providers and Systems (HCAHPS) scores, as well as the influence of active involvement of consumers in their health and health care services (Healthcare Success, 2017).

The HCAHPS survey asks discharged patients 27 questions about their recent hospital stay. The survey contains 18 core questions about critical aspects of patients' hospital experiences (communication with nurses and doctors, the responsiveness of hospital staff, the cleanliness and quietness of the hospital environment, pain management, communication about medicines, discharge information, overall rating of hospital, and would they recommend the hospital).

Franklin Street (2015) boldly claims, "Hospital Marketing Trend #1: Patient Journey Mapping." And added, "Marketing will take the lead in creating better patient experiences."

Internal marketing also includes educating employees on maximizing hospital revenue and minimizing costs. For example:

Further Guidelines for Hospital Marketing

- **Develop a Clear Marketing Mix for the Hospital**

Babu and Rajalakshmi (2019) proposed formulating a clear marketing mix for hospitals following the 7P marketing mix we discussed in Chapter 9.

Their proposal, in summary form, included focus on:

- o **Product/Service:** Focus on different products and develop differentiation strategies for each: Regular inpatient services, Emergency services, Diagnostic services, Pharmacy services, and Health education and wellness programs.
- o **Price/Value:** Insurance acceptance policies; managed care negotiated per diem/DRG rates with health plans. Value propositions to patients and admitting physicians.

- **Promotion/Communication:** Use of digital marketing, content marketing, promotion via wellness programs, interpreter/translation arrangements. Use of brand ambassadors/influencers.
- **Place/Access:** Improving appointment scheduling process. Improving cleanliness. Capacity management. Satellite facilities. Urgent care centers.
- **People/Staff:** Extensive training on behavioral aspects and culturally and linguistically appropriate services. Improving emotional intelligence. Employee engagement to market services to patients.
- **Process:** Publicize use of modern technology. Improve discharge process. Content marketing using patients satisfied with the process.

- **Use Meaningful Metrics**

Healthcare Success (2017) calls "Meaningful Metrics" as Hospital Marketing Trend #2, adding, "We're seeing more and more hospital marketers getting away from "vanity metrics" — the number of Likes on Facebook posts, for example — and shifting focus to tracking activities that align with the ultimate goal of marketing: new patient acquisition. Also, conversions (from clicking on a digital marketing offer to taking a next step to becoming a patient); Email list growth; Calls for physician referral; Seminar and event registrations; Online appointment requests; Patient downstream revenue.

- Digital marketing (discussed in Chapter 10: Integrating Digital Technology into Modern Health Care Marketing) including Search Engine Optimization (SEO) optimized websites, and effective content marketing, including leveraging brand journalism — looking for ways to add the hospital's competencies to national and regional stories/trends.
- Customer Relationship Management/Use of CRM tools.

- **Targeting Niche Audiences**

For example, medical tourists, seniors, cardiac care for vulnerable ethnicities. For attracting medical tourists to US hospitals, see Chapter 15: Marketing Health Care Globally.

- **Location-Based Marketing and Advertising**

Use of digital tools such as Geoconquesting; Geofencing.

- **Creating Health-Related, Streaming, Live, and Real-Time Video Content**

Hospitals are generally recognized by consumers as an authoritative source of medical information. People are far more inclined to watch an informative video than to tackle a text explanation. Further, video is easily — and popularly — viewed on smartphones and other mobile devices.

Case study: Cleveland Clinic's Health Hub; An online center for health tips and news, physician blogs, and expert Q&As. The hospital's doctors and nurses have provided exclusive content, and consumers have come flocking. Since its launch in May 2012, the site has posted traffic numbers exceeding 100,000 visitors per month (*Source*: Cleveland Clinic MedHub: https://www.medhub.com/project/cleveland-clinic/).

- **Expanding Telemedicine**
- **Engage in Marketing to Community**

Invest in community health. Form partnerships with community stakeholders such as Community-Based Organizations (CBOs), schools, and elder care centers. Match advertising copy to culture and language of the region. Passively engage in sponsorships and community events. Market your presence and significance to the area.

14.4. Marketing Managed Care Plans/Services

Managed care accounts for the largest portion of the US health care services market.

Managed care is organized and provided by insurance companies and health plans. Although there are certain differences between these two types of entities, those minor differences do not affect concepts addressed in this book. Therefore, we will, in most discussions in the book, refer to them as "health plans". These entities are also called Managed Care Organizations (MCOs).

Based on data as of April 2017, the top five largest health insurance payers in the US were (*Source*: Healthpayer Intelligence, 2017):

1. United Health Group. 2016 Net Revenues: US$184.8B. Subscribers: 70 million. Network has over 1 million physicians and 6,000 hospitals.
2. Anthem (formerly Wellpoint–Anthem). 2016 Net Revenues: US$89.1 B. Subscribers: 39.9 million.
3. Aetna. 2016 Net Revenues: US$63.1B. Subscribers: 23.1 million.
4. Humana. 2016 Net Revenues: US$54.3B. Subscribers: 14.2 million.
5. Cigna. 2016 Net Revenues: US$39.7B. Subscribers: 15 million.

Health plans enter into contracts with, and receive payments from, CMS for Medicare managed care, with state departments of health for Medicaid managed care, and employers and individuals for private commercial health insurance. They then contract with a large number of physicians, physician groups, and independent practitioner associations (IPAs), hospitals, ancillary service providers, laboratories, and pharmacy chains. These entities called "providers" form the health plan's "provider network".

> For example, 11 health plans participate (meaning, they have entered into contracts with) the California ACA (Obamacare) exchange called "Covered California": Anthem Blue Cross of California, Kaiser Permanente, Sharp, Blue Shield, LA Care, Chinese Community Health Plan, Molina, Valley Health Plan, Health Net, Oscar Health Plan, and Western Health Advantage.
>
> These health plans have internal marketing and community outreach departments, and contracted marketing agents, who reach out to eligible individuals (and small businesses) to influence them to join their health plan. These marketing activities are regulated and monitored by Covered California.
>
> Enrollment in Covered California health plans grew 3.7% in the 12 months ending March 31, 2018, reaching 1,437,000 members.

14.4.1. Who are the Customers in Managed Health Care Marketing?

To expand their subscriber/member/enrollee base, health plan marketing efforts are directed at physicians, physician groups, IPAs, employers, individuals, and community organizations.

14.4.1.1. *Physicians*

Physicians have a great influence on patients' selection of a health plan. Therefore, a major portion of health plan marketing is directed at physicians.

In general, it is reported that physicians have a negative attitude towards managed care and managed care organizations (MCOs) due to low reimbursement rates and complex paper work requirements.

Health plans depend heavily on physician referrals of new members. Therefore, health plan marketers spend much of their effort (and budgets) in improving provider relations. An April 2013 survey of US healthcare marketers from Medical Marketing & Media and Ogilvy CommonHealth found that an average of 75% of health care marketing budgets were allocated to reaching health care professionals; only 25% were aimed at consumers. The same study found that 40% of respondents planned to increase marketing targeted at provider relations.

14.4.1.2. *Consumers*

Marketing managed care health products to consumers is controlled first and foremost by rules on individual eligibility for managed care.

Everyone is not eligible to enroll with a health plan for managed care. The individual has to be "eligible" first. For example, an individual must have reached 65 years of age and fulfilled other requirements for CMS to determine that individual as being eligible to join a Medicare managed care plan. Similar requirements exist for Medicaid and ACA (Obamacare) managed care enrollees. On the private health care side, the individual must be employed with an employer who provides health insurance as an employment benefit. Individuals not meeting any of these eligibility criteria can apply to join a private health plan (e.g. Blue Shield or Health Net). Examples of the last category are young married women whose husbands do not receive health care benefits from their employer. These women often purchase individual insurance policies from health plans (to cover the possibility they might become pregnant and need maternity related health services).

> In Chapter 6, Section 6.5, we discussed factors influencing health care, provider selection, and retention decisions of key consumer/patient groups. There we discussed how consumers/patients select physicians and hospitals. While the consumer/patient behavioral patterns discussed in Section 6.5 are generally applicable to selection of providers associated with health plans (health plan network providers), in this section we will discuss certain specific factors consumers consider in selecting a health plan.

Studies show that consumers' choice of health plans depends on several factors (Blumberg *et al.*, 2013; Grazier *et al.*, 1986; Moschis and Friend, 2008; Smith and Rogers, 1987).

- Demographic factors: Age, income, and health condition.
- Structural and system factors: Employer-provided insurance, eligibility for Medicare, Medicaid, or ACA benefits.
- Financial factors: Premiums, deductibles, co-payments, and total out-of-pocket costs, amounts payable for out-of-network care.
- Non-financial factors: Choice of physicians and other providers (network), availability of current providers, rules on accessing specialists in-network and out-of-network, range of services available, availability of help for managing a particular condition.

Competition and the health plan's own strengths (SWOT analysis discussed in Chapter 3) usually determine the market segments and niches it will enter in to.

For example, several health plans in California decided not to enter the ACA (Obamacare) exchange market because of low premiums. Similarly, certain health plans in the same area have not entered the commercial insurance market mainly because their experience and expertise are in the provision of managed health care to Medicaid populations, and the fact that Medicaid populations are generally younger and healthier and therefore easier to manage.

Once the health plan picks a segment or niche in the market, marketing strategies will depend on consumer behavior in that segment or niche.

14.4.2. Medicare managed care products marketing

The market for Medicare managed care is composed of consumers over 65 years of age (and a few other special eligibility categories). Therefore, health plan marketers should pay special attention to consumer behavior of older populations.

By 2029, when the last round of boomers reaches retirement age, the number of Americans 65 or older will climb to more than 71 million, up from about 41 million in 2011, a 73% increase, according to Census Bureau estimates. A huge proportion will switch from commercial plans to Medicare (Barr, 2014).

Studies show certain health care needs, and health care-related behavior of older population/senior consumers/patients (Moschis and Friend, 2008).

- 53.7% of mature Americans age 55 and over have a chronic condition for which they regularly take medication.
  This implies that this group prefers health plans that have better prescription drug benefits and formularies.
- 16.0% have self-diagnostic medical equipment at home.
  This implies that this group prefers health plans with better diagnostic equipment (e.g., free blood sugar and pressure monitoring equipment) and durable medical equipment benefits.
- 40.5% have exercise equipment at home.
- 58.0% use one or more hair-care or face-care products.
- They take a high personal interest in their own health.

This population is also known to be eager for education on complex managed care utilization review (approval and denial of benefits) and payment processes. They are also low in use of internet and digital modes of communication.

Health plans will face many challenges to meet health care needs of this growing population. Some of these are:

- As this population enters Medicare, CMS is likely to apply even more stringent utilization review policies that result in more denials of services and prescription drugs. Health plans with Medicare managed care plans that have more flexible benefit structures will be favored by this population.
- Health plans with larger networks that have specialist physician treating chronic conditions (e.g., geriatric specialists, and endocrinologists who treat diabetic patients) will be favored by this population.
- Also needed are providers of home health care and benefit structures that provide these services.
- Baby boomers have shown an inclination to adopt new technology. Health plans will have to adopt ehealth and mHealth technology to replace and enhance office visits, which are bound to become increasingly difficult for this older population.

> In 2017, Anthem (a health plan serving California) started offering a physical exercise program called "Silver Sneakers" for its senior enrollees. But this population, or some of them, are growing older and would find it difficult to go to a gym to participate in this program. Now Anthem has begun a program called "Spinzone Online" that engages seniors to self-manage back pains, which are common in this age group.

- The proportion of foreign-born persons in the baby boom Medicare population is also increasing. US Census Bureau estimate of the size of this group was 15 million in 2010. This implies the need for health plans to provide culturally and linguistically appropriate care and education models.

14.4.3. Marketing Medicaid managed care products

Populations that come under this category include beneficiaries of regular low-income Medicaid benefits, eligible children in the Children's Health Insurance Program (CHIP), and those who have Medicaid and another types of coverage, such as Medicare. This last category is called "Dual Eligibles".

According to CMS statistics (Medicaid.gov), 72.4 million individuals were enrolled in Medicaid in 2018. Of this, 65.8 million individuals were enrolled in Medicaid. 6.6 million individuals were enrolled in CHIP. In 2009, Medicaid enrollment was 50.9 million. Thus, Medicaid is a growing health care market in the US. This is more so with the Medicaid expansion brought about by ACA.

The total number of persons in Medicaid managed care programs is around 54 million.

14.4.3.1. *Marketing mix in Medicaid managed care marketing*

States set rates paid to managed care plans and adjust them annually based on actuarial studies on utilization of services. Therefore, price of basic health care services is not a significant factor in Medicaid marketing. However, additional needs such as cost of non-covered elective treatment, transportation, and over-the-counter drugs are a concern to low-income patients, and health plans that provide assistance on these items are preferred by this population.

Heath (2017) presents results of a recent survey conducted by Oliver Wyman and the Altarum Institute, funded by the Robert Wood Johnson Foundation, of nearly 4,000 low-income patients, including Medicaid beneficiaries.

Primary issues of concern to this population were lack of cost transparency (on non-covered items of care), finding information they needed, and insufficient language assistance.

The survey recommends that health care organizations should focus on their price transparency policies as well as their interpersonal relationships with low-income and vulnerable patients.

According to the survey, nearly half of Spanish-speaking patients consider language barriers their biggest challenges during physician visits and interaction with the Medicaid and health plan systems. Even when translators or bi-lingual material was available, cultural and language barriers prevented Hispanic patients from asking questions. This would be true with low-income populations in other ethnic groups as well.

Spanish-speaking patients were also found to rely on their friends and family to translate and offer health guidance. Spanish speakers were twice as likely to trust their friends' and families' viewpoints (40%) than information from English speakers (22%).

Perception of respect also presented barriers to patient-provider interactions, with 40% of low-income patients walking away from appointments feeling disrespected, adversely impacting their care. Patients who feel disrespected are three times less likely to trust their providers and two times less likely to adhere to treatments than those who do feel respected.

This implies the need for health plans to reduce cultural barriers by contracting with larger numbers of physicians and physician groups that have physicians and staff who are multi-lingual and respectful to minority ethnic groups and their values. Medicaid managed care health plans in California, which has large numbers of minority racial and ethnic Medicaid populations, are already doing this.

According to community outreach and Medicaid managed care marketing staff in health plans in California, elements in a marketing mix that would be important to low-income Medicaid populations are the product, place (access), promotion (communications and information), and process.

- **Product:** Low-income Medicaid beneficiaries favor health plans that provide additional benefits like transportation and assistance with non-covered benefits.
- **Place:** Medicaid populations prefer to be assigned to primary care physicians in their neighborhood. They also prefer to remain with their current providers.
- **Education and communication:** Medicaid health plans in California report large numbers of Medicaid member complaints about bills they have received from health care providers for services the patients were not aware would be their financial responsibility. Part of this may be due to lower educational levels of this population. Health plans should focus on providing clear information on covered services and rules for obtaining non-covered services.

> According to health plan managers handling complaints and grievances, Medicaid managed care enrollees often lack sufficient knowledge of the managed care process, the role of the primary care physician as gate keeper, need to receive services from health plan network of providers, pre-approval processes, non-covered services, and disenrollment (plan change) rights and processes. Retention of members in health plans requires disseminating clear information about these issues to members.

- **Process:** Medicaid member complaints analysis also show dissatisfactions with health plan call centers, and lack of respect and courtesy of physician office/clinic staff. Medicaid managed care marketing should be proactive in addressing these concerns.

14.4.4. Marketing ACA (Obamacare) exchange products

At the end of open enrollment 2017, more than 12.2 million people had signed up for plans using HealthCare.gov or a state-based exchange. Of those who enrolled, over 9.2 million used the federal site (*Source*: Obamacare. net. https://obamacare.net/obamacare-state-enrollment-results/).

Many enrollees in ACA products are young. For states that have Federally-Facilitated Marketplaces, 35% of those who signed up are under 35 years old and 28% are between 18 and 34 years old (2014 figures).

Younger adults are more familiar with digital information seeking, marketing, and enrollment. Health plans can use this behavior to engage in marketing ACA exchange products using digital channels and technology, such as email, websites, text messages, and mobile device-based communications.

Younger adults switch/disenroll from health plans more than mature older adults (Avalere Health, 2018). Across health plans and states, the Medicaid expansion population (which includes ACA enrollees) experience high disenrollment rates.

Across plans, states, and enrollment groups, about half of enrollees dropped coverage within 18 months. Voluntary plan switching rates among ACA exchange enrollees is around 40%. Therefore, a significant portion of health care marketing efforts in this line of business has to be focused on retention of current enrollees (Jacobson *et al.*, 2016).

For a discussion on retention of enrollees in managed care health plans, see the section below on "Retention of Enrollees in Managed Care Health Plans".

Health care marketing has another role in ACA exchange product business in health plans. That is, educating enrollees on preventive care. This is because studies show that ACA exchange enrollees cause health plans high claims costs in general as they remain in the plans, much of these claims coming from professional services (physician visits and physician portion of hospital services) and prescription drugs.

14.4.5. B2B marketing employee insurance plan to employers

Employer sponsored health plans typically marketed to employees via employers are regular group insurance plans (Health Maintenance Organization (HMO) plans and Preferred Provider Organization (PPO) plans) and Consumer Directed Health Care (CDHC) plans or Consumer Directed Health plans (CDHP), such as Health Reimbursement Arrangements (HRA), Health Savings Accounts (HSA), and Flexible Savings Accounts (FSA).

Group health insurance plans benefit employers as these are usually lower in cost because of the enrollment of a larger number of individuals. They provide tax benefits as well.

PPO plans are preferred by employers and employees (Dalzell, 1999). They are not subject to gatekeeper requirement as in HMOs, not subject to state HMO benefit mandates, have much lesser bureaucratic paper work, and better customer service at physician office or hospital.

As such, they are a better benefit for employers to attract good employees.

CDHC plans are also very popular now mainly due to the tax benefits they offer to employees. With some exceptions, these plans permit employees to contribute to plans on a before-tax basis, roll over funds from year to year, and have unused funds revert to the employee upon termination. HSAs provide all three of these advantages.

A marketing mix for CDHC plans should highlight the following advantages to prospective employers (Self Insured Plans, 2017):

- Stop loss limitations: Having increased control with a partially self-funded plan, the employer assumes a professionally calculated amount of risk (claims). Stop loss coverage is obtained to cover excess claims. Specific stop loss protects the plan against an individual catastrophic claim.
- Greater control: Self-funding gives employers greater control, since their funds may be contributed to an employer-established account and transferred when needed to pay claims. Excess funds remain in the account and collect investment earnings. With a $501(c)(9)$ trust account, these earnings may accrue tax-free.
- Lower costs: While most of the savings realized from self-funding is created by enhancements in plan design and claims administration functions, the following cost-saving features also apply: Premium taxes — usually 2% to 6%, do not apply to self-funded claim funds in most states; Operating costs generally are lower; Insurance carrier profits and risk charges often are reduced; Self-funded programs are regulated by ERISA, eliminating many costly state-mandated benefits.
- Flexibility: Self-funding adds flexibility.
- Access to information for employer and employees: Easy access to timely reports on claims experience, provider practices, and funding status. Also, benefits analysis reports, coverage analysis reports, and eligibility listing.

Marketing of CDHPs should be focused at younger employees (Beaton, 2017: "What are the Pros and Cons of Consumer Directed Health Plans?")

CDHPs are based on low cost-sharing, and higher deductibles, which require active engagement in purchasing decisions from the consumer. These plans are likely to attract younger individuals with higher health literacy and a desire to control more of their spending.

The Employee Benefit Research Institute (EBRI) found that Millennials tend to value their ability to interact with health plans and sponsors more than older generations.

EBRI determined that Millennials were more likely to be engaged when picking a health plan and making cost-conscious health care decisions. They also had a higher likelihood to engage in wellness and preventive health behaviors.

When considering or promoting CDHPs to potential enrollees, health plans should create flexible plans that meet the priorities of beneficiaries in different age groups and financial circumstances.

14.4.6. Community organizations

Greater involvement of community-based organizations (CBOs) and health care advocates who provide education and assistance on health care to Medicare, Medicaid, Children's Health, and ACA Exchange beneficiaries.

> Medicare and Medicaid managed care marketing is subject to many federal and state laws and regulations. These relate to non-discrimination, marketing material, certification of enrollers, electronic communications, telephonic contact, marketing at provider offices and health fairs, and use of social media. These were fully discussed in Chapter 13: Legal and Ethical Issues Affecting Health Care Marketing.

14.4.7. Retention of enrollees in managed care health plans

A major portion of marketing managed care plan products is focused on retention of current subscribers/enrollees. As with other industries, retention of current enrollees/members is less costly for health plans than enrolling new members.

There are several other reasons why managed care health plan enrollees leave plans. A major reason is losing eligibility due to changes in income or employment status. For example, a Medicaid beneficiary's income level may have exceeded the threshold level for Medicaid eligibility. Another reason for losing membership in a health plan is the enrollee not attending to certain enrollment renewal processes. Some of these processes are complex, requiring heavy paperwork, and not well understood by enrollees, especially enrollees in Medicaid, SCHIP, and Medicare managed care plans.

The New York State Coalition of Prepaid Health Services Plans, an association of 15 health plans sponsored by public and not-for-profit hospitals and community health centers, serving the majority of Medicaid and SCHIP families in New York City and a large proportion throughout the rest of the state, claims to have been losing half of their members each year. Since this realization, improving retention has been one of the organization's priorities for several years (Redmond, 2005).

The author describes a case study in which Keystone Health Plan East in Pennsylvania integrated renewal reminders into routine operations to meet the state's annual renewal requirement of SCHIP coverage. Keystone implemented a reminder process which even exceeded minimum state requirements to send renewal reminders to beneficiaries. Reminders about annual renewal requirement were also included in every issue of the quarterly health promotion newsletter sent to all families with children enrolled in SCHIP. Keystone reported a 85% response rate to the combination of letters and phone calls (Redmond, 2005).

Reasons for switching health plans by middle-class individuals and families in employer-sponsored commercial insurance plans appear to be: changes in relative cost to the subscriber, young age, shorter tenure in plan, individual subscriber rather than families, families with younger female subscribers, families with lower per capita incomes, and good health status (Buchmeller and Feldstein, 1997; Grazier *et al.*, 1986; Hennelly and Boxerman, 1983; Mechanic *et al.*, 1983; Schlesinger *et al.*, 1999; Sorenson and Wersinger, 1981; Travis *et al.*, 1989; Wrightson *et al.*, 1987. All cited by Brandon *et al.*, 2005).

Brandon *et al.* (2005) in an article, "Medicaid Enrollee Switching Among Managed Care Plans", report that the rate of switching for Medicaid enrollees is 5.3%. Medicaid enrollees virtually have no costs for basic health care needs. Therefore, the variable that showed a significant relationship to switching was more physician reimbursement claims for medical and surgical care prior to managed care enrollment. This implies that Medicaid enrollees in poorer health are shopping around in the hope of finding better physicians by switching. Thus, perceived quality of providers seems to be of concern to this population.

CMS reports that, on average, 10% Medicare managed care enrollees switch health plans annually.

However, the main reason for voluntary disenrollment or switching health plans is dissatisfaction with the health plan. Studies and industry expert opinion indicate that major reasons for switching health plans by managed care enrollees are (Avalere Health, 2018):

- Costs (in case of commercial health care plans)

In employer-sponsored commercial group health insurance plans, younger, healthier employees are between two and four times more sensitive to price than employees who are older and who have been recently hospitalized or diagnosed with cancer. Estimated premium elasticities are significantly higher for new hires than for incumbent employees.

Older employees and those who have recently experienced serious health events are less willing to switch health plans in response to a change in relative premiums than are younger, healthier employees.

- Poor quality often indicated by quality ratings.
- Limited access to services (geographical access, long wait times for appointments and services, language barriers, and communication problems with physician and staff).
- Access to a wide array of doctors.
- Consumer dissatisfaction, poor customer experience, and not being treated with dignity and respect.

14.4.8. Implications for health care managers and marketers

The following retention strategies are reported as successful in managed care health plans:

- Monitoring eligibility renewal times of enrollees and assistance with eligibility renewal processes.
- Contracting with providers in a wider geographic area to facilitate access to services.
- Assistance with non-covered needs such as transportation and over-the-counter medications.
- Health and wellness education, to educate enrollees on preventive care.
- Improving cultural and language barriers at physician clinics, which is the key touchpoint in the patient journey.
- Quick responses in finding alternative providers with the health plan network for dissatisfied enrollees.
- Informing enrollees regularly on the health plan's quality and access initiatives, and good star ratings and other quality ratings.
- Monitor patient satisfaction regularly and pro-actively with health plan processes and staff, and network provider processes (e.g. waiting times on calls, appointments, and during office visits) and staff.

- Assist network physicians with improving office systems (e.g., appointment scheduling and waiting times), procedures, and record keeping.
- Use digital technology (websites, emails, mobile channel-based communications) to engage patients especially the younger patients.
- Continuously measure patient experience and take corrective action. See Chapter 7.

14.5. Direct Marketing by Pharmaceutical Companies

Pharmaceutical products marketing dominates the health care marketing field.

Pharmaceutical companies currently spend one-third of revenue in marketing (Gagnon and Lexchin, 2008).

In total, the pharma industry spent US$6.4 billion on advertising in the United States in 2016. Among companies in the pharmaceutical sector, Johnson & Johnson invested most in advertising in 2015. Their US advertising spend amounted to US$30.12 million. Eli Lilly ranked second with a spend of US$22.5 million (*Source*: Statista: https://www.statista.com/statistics/275460/us-health-care-companies-distribution-of-marketing-budget-by-channel/).

More than half of this budget (56%) went for direct response advertisement. The remainder of 44% was spent on branding campaigns.

Currently, there is extreme pressure for cost containment. Governments will keep on applying drastic cost-containment measures on drugs because they are technically easy to implement and politically risk-free (Smart Pharma Consulting, 2015).

CMS (2016) in its National Health Expenditure Projections 2012–2022 reports that for 2015 through 2022, rising drug prices and expected increases in utilization drive faster overall projected average annual growth in prescription drug spending (6.5% per year). The generic dispensing rate is anticipated to level off, pushing average prescription drug prices up more rapidly. Faster projected income growth for 2014–2016 and the prescribing of drugs earlier in the treatment process as the population ages drive projected faster utilization.

Pharma marketing is directed mainly at physicians, and to consumers directly.

Brezis (2008) reports (based on 2005 figures) that pharmaceutical marketing spends 56% on free samples, 25% on pharmaceutical sales representative detailing (promoting drugs directly to) physicians, 12.5% on direct-to-user advertising, 4% on detailing to hospitals, and 2% on journal ads.

According to Emarketer (2016), US healthcare and pharma advertisers would spend US$2.02 billion on digital advertising in 2016, a 20.5% gain from 2015. The sector would account for 2.8% of total US digital ad spending for the year.

Industry experts are expressing their surprise and disappointment that only 26.5% of pharma digital marketing budget is focused on mobile formats. Wrzosiński (2014) says,

> "It is incredible if you look at this from the perspective the same crowd that claims 'we want more direct response and we spend more than half of our budget for it' in the same time neglects the channel that is the best to accomplish this objective. Healthcare and pharma marketing is the single industry that spends on mobile the smallest chunk of its budget. Even PC makers spend 33% of their budget on mobile, but we in pharma remain connected to the desktop. If we go mobile, pharma marketing focuses mostly on mobile search advertisement."

14.5.1. Marketing to physicians

See Section 12.4.

14.5.2. Marketing to consumers/patients

Modern pharmaceutical marketing is facing several new challenges which industry managers and marketers will have to overcome. These include (PricewaterhouseCoopers, 2017; Smart Pharma Consulting, 2015):

- Population increase and ageing;
- Strong development of generics market (though at the expense of R&D-based brands sales);
- Stronger demand for new and better medicines, including vaccines;
- Increasing demand for secondary care products, including biologicals;
- Increasing access to medicines by emerging markets;
- Increasing price pressure from payers (governments, HMOs, patients, etc.);
- Increasing price sensitivity of customers for over-the-counter (OTC) products;
- Increasing power of authorities, payers, patients, and patient advocacy groups, in the choice of the treatment, including the choice of the drug;

- Physician aversion to standard marketing calls and presentations; and
- Physician increased dependence on modern communication channels (e.g., digital marketing).

14.5.3. Implications for pharmaceutical marketing

Increase in patients playing a more active role in their health care management and asking their physician for a specific brand or type of product suggest implementing:

- Patient-focused programs.
- Social media activities. For example, organize projects with patient communities.
- Customer-centric marketing: Patient programs delivering superior value.
- Content marketing.

Influencer marketing to advocacy groups appears beneficial. These groups are eager to partner with pharma companies to get financial support, e.g., sponsorship of events and training programs.

The interdependence of the payer (insurance companies, health plans, and Medicare/Medicaid) providers/physicians, and pharmaceutical companies is increasing.

- Adopt flexible approaches to pricing.
- Offer prescription drug price supporting services.
- Programs to educate consumers.

Combined Media (2017) suggests the following marketing practices under the title Five Pharma Marketing Digital Trends to Watch in 2018:

- **Influencer Marketing:** Use of influencers and brand ambassadors. Deployment of real patients who suffer from a chronic disease or other medical condition. For example, TV advertisement promoting Trulicty, a diabetic self-administered injection, uses real life diabetes patients narrating their experiences.
- **Online Marketing:** Influencers can be induced to post positive experiences with a drug on Facebook.
- **Use of Messaging Apps:** Use of Apps like Facebook Messenger or WhatsApp to engage customers with relevant and valuable content.

Opportunity of one-to-one conversation with other willing customers, patients, and even doctors.
- **Use of Chatbots:** Use of chatbots to provide more personalized services and automate a number of time-consuming processes, in areas like customer support, marketing, or education.
- **Adopting Native Advertising:** Native advertising is advertising that takes the form of an article. The content is always marked with some kind of label, like "sponsored" or "advertisement", and it is displayed along with a publication's editorial content. It is usually more effective than traditional display ads in terms of interest and engagement.

For example, a native article about the importance of travel vaccinations can feature in the travel section of a national newspaper. Native content about getting help to quit smoking, or about the benefits of a new glucose meter synced with a mobile app, can be published in the health section of an online magazine.

www.healthtap.com is an example of a website and a downloadable app where patients can type health-related questions and get a list of answers provided by more than 108,000 doctors.

Medwhat.com is a virtual medical assistant that answers questions from both consumers and doctors: "The answers are provided by an intelligent super-computer that learns about medicine every day and over time about your health record and medical questions history."

14.5.4. Legal and ethical restrictions on pharma marketing

- Several states and the District of Columbia now require that pharmaceutical manufacturers report their marketing expenditures, including gifts to prescribers.
- Vermont and Massachusetts are acting to ban several types of gifts from pharmaceutical companies to health care providers.
- Several medical schools and hospitals have developed policies that limit the contact drug reps may have with providers, faculty, and students and that require disclosure of relationships that doctors, researchers, and faculty members have with pharmaceutical companies.

> **Pharmaceutical Marketing is Closely Monitored for Violations Under the Anti-Kickback Statutes**
>
> Los Angeles Times (May 14, 2018) "Did Drug Company Payments to Doctors Help Fuel the Opioid Epidemic?", a new research letter reports that doctors who received free meals and other kinds of payments from pharmaceutical companies tended to prescribe more opioid painkillers to their patients over the course of a year. Meanwhile, doctors who didn't get such freebies cut back on their opioid prescriptions (Kaplan, 5/14/2018).
>
> Walgreens was involved in a high-profile Anti-Kickback case back in 2012, in which it agreed to settle for $7.9 million. Even though the company denied any fault, the drugstore chain allegedly offered gift cards and other promotions to Medicare and Medicaid beneficiaries in exchange for transferring their prescriptions to Walgreens pharmacies.

14.6. Public Health Marketing

Public Health Marketing, also referred to as Health Marketing, is a multidisciplinary area of public health practice. It draws from traditional marketing theories and principles and adds science-based strategies to prevention, health promotion, and health protection.

14.6.1. Definitions

Health Marketing involves creating, communicating, and delivering health information and interventions using customer-centered and science-based strategies to protect and promote the health of diverse populations (CDC, 2015).

Center for Disease Control and Prevention (CDC) adds that Health Marketing is a multidisciplinary practice that promotes the use of marketing research to educate, motivate, and inform the public on health messages; an integration of the traditional marketing field with public health research, theory, and practice; a complex framework that provides guidance for designing health interventions, campaigns, communications, and research projects; and a broad range of strategies and techniques that can be used to create synergy among public health research, communication messages, and health behaviors.

An example of public health marketing is campaigns conducted by state agencies (e.g., California Department of Public Health) on smoking cessation.

Public health marketing is conducted by many entities. These include state agencies (state public health departments), health educators in health plans who regularly conduct sessions on health and wellness, university researchers and educators offering education in public health, nutritionists, social workers, and public health physicians and nurses.

In developing countries in Africa and Asia, public health programs are conducted by the government. Health workers and midwives play a key role in promoting good health practices of rural communities.

Master's degree in public health (MPH) is a very popular degree in US universities. Many physicians attend these programs and become holders of a MPH degree.

Maibach et al. (2007) trace some landmarks in modern day public health marketing back to Health Canada's Social Marketing Unit established in 1981, which continues to expand its social marketing. The U.S. Centers for Disease Control and Prevention (CDC) established the National Center for Health Marketing in 2004. A number of US states — Arizona, California, Ohio, and North Carolina, at a minimum — have recently established social marketing units. The National Health Service in the UK is currently considering a proposal to integrate social marketing as a core strategy in managing the health of the British population.

Just as understanding consumer behavior in health is important for health care marketing (see Chapter 6), it is important in public health marketing to understand factors influencing health behaviors of the public, and of various demographic and ethnic groups, on prevention and control of diseases.

Maibach et al. (2007) in a paper, "Communication and Marketing as Tools to Cultivate the Public's Health: A Proposed 'People and Places' Framework", summarizes these factors of influence as follows:

- Individual factors: knowledge, beliefs, demographic variables, motivations, and intentions.
- Social network-related factors: family, peers, mentors, and opinion and reference leaders.
- Population and Community factors: social norms, culture.
- Local level influences: home, school, neighborhood, work.
- Region: state, national, global level influences.

The first two factors are called "Attributes of People", and the rest are called "Attributes of Place".

These authors contend that,

"Communication and marketing each have potential to contribute to beneficial changes in all five fields of influence," and that, "Public health organizations should strive to enhance their competence in communication and marketing, because doing so can improve their impact even within current levels of funding."

Health Communication and Social Marketing are identified as the main strategies in public health marketing focused at "People" to influence their behavior.

14.6.2. Public health marketing focused at people. I: Health communication

This includes communication of important health information such as importance of immunizations and perils of smoking. A large number of theories in social and cognitive psychology have been used in formulating these communications. We omit details of these theories and refer the reader to Maibach *et al.* (2007) for full citations. Communication techniques used were conventional ones such as brochures, health education classes, DVDs, and newspaper and TV promotions of good health practices.

Having adopted the modern health care concepts and practices we have advocated throughout this book, we can now recommend the following strategies for public health communications/marketing:

- **Use of Digital Communications such as Email, Texts, and Communication Targeted at Mobile Technology**

These concepts and practices termed eHealth and mHealth interventions are being used more frequently now. Reports show success of eHealth and mHealth initiatives in communications with pregnant women in several African countries, which has significantly improved maternal health and live birth rates.

mHealth apps are very common today, sending out communications and guidance of diseases and preliminary self-diagnosis.

See Chapter 10.

- **Content Marketing**

Content Marketing, which we studied in Section 10.7, is highly relevant to communications in public health marketing.

We saw that content marketing is usually directed at smaller segments of the target market. In public health, children are a segment focused on to communicate perils of smoking. Language and presentation in communications to children need to be carefully chosen to fit their age and comprehension levels. This is a basic example of the applicability of content marketing in public health marketing.

Content marketing is aimed to immediately attract the attention of the target customer/patient/segment. Content marketing has become the key of successful online marketing campaigns and the most important tool in digital marketing.

For details on application of content marketing in health care marketing, see Section 10.7.

14.6.3. Public health marketing focused at people. II: Social marketing

The potential influence of other people (as opposed to potential influence of communications discussed in the previous sub-section) has been of interest among researchers and practitioners. Interest has been on activating existing relationships within social networks or developing new social networks in ways that enhance the provision of useful health information, positive sources of influence, and social support. Activating people within existing social networks to serve as agents of behavior change has proven to be a productive approach for cultivating health enhancement (Maibach et al., 2007).

Social marketing is defined as a program-planning process that applies commercial marketing concepts and techniques to promote voluntary behavior change (Grier and Bryant, 2005).

These authors give as an example, VERB, a national, multicultural, social marketing program coordinated by CDC. This program encourages "tweens" (young people ages 9–13) to be physically active every day.

Note that the first step in establishing this program has been the market segmentation, i.e., it is not a program for all, but one targeting a smaller segment of society.

Next, the program was based on extensive marketing research with tweens, their parents, and other influencers. Results were used to design an intervention that combines mass-media advertising, public relations, interpersonal marketing, and partnership efforts with professional sports leagues and athletes, well-known sporting-goods suppliers, and retailers and communities to improve access to outlets for physical activity.

After just one year, this program is reported to have resulted in a 34% increase in weekly free-time physical activity sessions among 8.5 million children ages 9–10 in the United States.

For details of this program, see Grier and Bryant (2015) and Wong et al. (2004).

14.6.4. Public health marketing to eliminate health disparities

The term "health disparities" is often defined as (Center for Medicare Advocacy, 2017)

> "A difference in which disadvantaged social groups such as the poor, racial/ethnic minorities, women and other groups who have persistently experienced social disadvantage or discrimination systematically experience worse health or greater health risks than more advantaged social groups."

There is a growing realization among health care researchers, clinicians, and advocates that a focus on health care disparities is an important aspect of improving health care outcomes and that activities toward improvement must bring together many elements of our health care delivery system. The populations that have customarily been underserved in the American health care system include African-Americans, Latinos, Native Americans, and Asian Americans.

Waidmann (2009) cites a report issued in September 2009 by the Urban Institute that shows the following estimated costs of health disparities:

- Medicare program would save US$15.6 billion per year if health disparities were eliminated.
- If the prevalence of a select set of preventable diseases among the Latino and African American communities, including diabetes, hypertension, and stroke, in the African American and Latino communities were reduced to the same prevalence as those diseases occur in the non-Latino white population, US$23.9 billion in health care costs would be saved in 2009 alone.

Causes for such health disparities among minorities is, to a great extent, due to language barriers, lower income levels, and their traditional cultural values and beliefs about human health, treatments, and western medicine and health care systems. Traditional and cultural values are among the prime areas of focus in health care marketing toward elimination/reduction of health disparities.

Many federal, state, and other non-profit organizations work hard to eliminate health disparities among racial, ethnic, geographic, socioeconomic, and other groups. CDC is in the lead in these efforts, so that barriers to health equity can be removed.

Public health marketing programs focus to a great extent on educating minorities. Some such programs (in addition to the VERB program we observed earlier) are:

- 100 Black Men Health Challenge program started in 2002 with the Atlanta chapter of 100 Black Men (Satcher and Higginbotham, 2008).

Concern here was that many African-American men were becoming ill and dying well before the age of 70 (given that the national average life expectancy was over age 77 years), even in higher socioeconomic groups. The program targeted 100 black men with three major personal health goals: regular physical activity and good nutrition; smoking cessation; and regular visits to a primary care provider. Quarterly screening proved the success of interventions in the program resulting in these men incorporating healthy lifestyle modeling and education for their mentees and increasingly being able to improve their community environments and support opportunities for healthy lifestyles.

- Diabetes Equity Project (DEP) at Baylor Health Care System (BHCS), Dallas, Texas (American Hospital Association et al., 2012).

The goal was reducing observed disparities in diabetes care and outcomes in the predominately Hispanic, medically underserved communities around BHCS. DEP was deployed in five community charity clinics and makes use of community health workers who receive extensive training in diabetes care and management. Patients are referred to the DEP from both community and private practice clinics, following emergency room visits and hospitalizations related to uncontrolled diabetes. The DEP seeks to be responsive to patient-reported needs like education, communication and respect, removal of financial constraints, and access to medication and transportation. Also implemented was an electronic diabetes registry that tracks patient metrics and facilitates disease management communication between community health workers and primary care clinicians. Within the first 18 months of the rolling enrollment, 806 patients were enrolled in the program. A preliminary analysis of the first year of results revealed a statistically significant drop in HgbA1c value from a baseline of 8.7% to 7.4%. Patient satisfaction surveys revealed that over 98% of participants indicated the highest level of satisfaction with the care they received.

14.6.5. Health marketing to reduce/eliminate health disparities due to cultural backgrounds

Another area of public health marketing aimed at eliminating health disparities targets racial, ethnic, and minority groups who are known to carry their own health beliefs.

> The concept of culture as distinct from race/ethnicity has been proposed as a better explanation for differences in health behavior and health outcomes.
>
> Egede (2006), citing Pasick, R J. Socioeconomic and cultural factors in the development and use of theory. In: Glanz K, Lewis FM, Rimer BK, editors. *Health Behavior and Health Education — Theory, Research, and Practice*. San Francisco, CA: Jossey-Bass Inc.

Of the many ethnic groups living in the US, we will study, as an example, the health beliefs of the Asians and public health marketing strategies focused on them.

Carteret (2010) presents a summary of the following cultural health beliefs among Asians:

- **Traditional Chinese Medicine:** These are linked to Chinese Cosmology, which believes that all of creation is born from the marriage of two polar principles, Yin and Yang. Examples are earth and heaven, winter and summer, night and day, cold and hot, wet and dry, inner and outer, body and mind. These pairs of opposites are connected via a circular harmony. The strategy of Chinese medicine is to restore harmony.
- **Chinese Herbal Medicine:** Herbal medicines are used to regulate the natural balance of the body and restore health. They come in the form of pills, powders, tinctures, and raw herbs taken internally or as balms for external use.

- **Japanese Herbal Medicine:** Kampo is Japanese herbal medicine, which has a long history of clinical application. Kampo uses precisely measured herbs to treat illness, based on the skillful use of well-known formulas. Diagnosis in Kampo is based on abdominal palpation.
- **Tibetan Medicine:** The basic principle is to balance the three principal energies of the body. The practitioner employs the ancient tools of pulse diagnosis and urine analysis, to find the root causes of disease. Treatment is carried out through diet, lifestyle adjustments, and herbal medicines grown naturally in Tibet and the Himalayas. Tibetan Medicine is based on Buddhist principles and the close relationship between mind and body.
- **Traditional Vietnamese Medicine:** Emphasis is on nourishing the blood and vital energy, rather than concentrating on specific symptoms. Building up the blood and energy is the key to good health. The main treatments employed are herbal medicine, acupuncture, and moxibustion (a traditional Chinese therapy, which consists of burning dried aromatic plants on particular points on the body).
- **Acupuncture:** Involves inserting tiny needles into specific points on the energy channels of the body, to promote healing and stimulate the free flow of energy in the body and mind. It is used to treat many conditions, including muscular pain, headaches, asthma, gynecological problems, digestive complaints, as well as anxiety and depression.
- **Coin Rubbing:** Coin Rubbing in Chinese is intended "to scrape away fever." Cambodians and Vietnamese in USA are known to use this technique.

14.6.6. Public health marketing addressing cultural beliefs

Studies show that health education programs for Asian populations are affected by several factors. These include language barriers, lack of cultural competency among educators, and general lack of trust in these populations of the western health care systems.

The strategy most often recommended to meet these challenges are culturally and linguistically competent health education programs.

An example of a program along these lines is the Community Outreach and Health Education program organized and conducted by AAHI, the Asian American Health Initiative (*Source*: http://aahiinfo.org/our-work/community-outreach-and-health-education/).

AAHI has implemented programs with culturally and linguistically-appropriate standards (CLAS) designed to improve community outreach and education among a diverse cohort, conducting health fairs, seminars, and community activities that raise awareness of specific issues of public health. Since 2008, AAHI has averaged more than 35 events per year, developing many longstanding, fruitful relationships.

AAHI's activities include:

- Dissemination of important health information.
- Provision of technical assistance and support to community members by trained, multilingual individuals with shared cultural background.
- Health seminars conducted by trusted community members, such as doctors and religious leaders, in partnership with low-cost medical care providers.
- Opportunities to consult with medical experts and health educators to learn more about the specific health issue and seek out screening and treatment opportunities.
- Provision of links to screening and referral services throughout the country.
- Developing and disseminating multilingual, culturally-relevant educational materials such as pamphlets, brochures, booklets, and posters regarding a variety of diseases and illnesses of concern to the Asian American community (with access by electronic means).

In general, effective CLAS public health marketing programs for minority ethnic populations should consist of (Brach and Fraserirector, 2000):

- Involvement of community organizations in developing culturally and linguistically-appropriate programs.
- Interpreter services (federal state laws have now mandated provision of interpreter services to Limited English Proficient populations).
- Recruitment and retention of minority employees in health care organizations (hospitals and clinics).
- Training cultural competency.
- Coordination with traditional healers.
- Use of community health workers.
- Culturally competent health workers.
- Inclusion of family and community members.
- Conscious immersion into other cultures.
- Administrative and organizational accommodations.

14.6.7. Additional cases on social marketing of public health

Readers are referred to Grier and Bryant (2005) for the following case studies of successful social marketing in public health marketing:

- Alcohol related driving accident prevention. The Road Crew project.
- Improving service delivery and enhancing program utilization. The Texas WIC Program.
- Healthy eating behaviors. The Food Trust.

References

Ackley, S. (2017). "Healthcare Advertising Spend to Reach $10.85 Billion in 2017", BIA/Kelsey, http://blog.biakelsey.com/index.php/2017/09/27/healthcare-advertising-spend-to-reach-10-85-billion-in-2017/. Accessed November 23, 2018.

American Hospital Association *et al.* (2012). "National Call to Action to Eliminate Health Care Disparities. Eliminating Health Care Disparities: Implementing the National Call to Action Using Lessons Learned", http://www.hpoe.org/Reports-HPOE/eliminating_health_care_disparities.pdf. Accessed March 17, 2019.

Avalere Health (2018). "Profile of the Medicaid Expansion Population: Demographics, Enrollment, and Utilization", https://antheminc.com/cs/groups/wellpoint/documents/wlp_assets/d19n/mzmw/~edisp/pw_g330411.pdf. Accessed November 14, 2018.

Babu, S. D. and Rajalakshmi, K. (2009). "Marketing Mix for Hospital Services in the Globalized Era", *Indian MBA*.

Barr, P. (2014). "Baby Boomers Will Transform Health Care as They Age. Hospitals and Health Networks", https://www.hhnmag.com/articles/5298-Boomers-Will-Transform-Health-Care-as-They-Age. Accessed March 16, 2019.

Beaton, T. (2017). "What are the Pros and Cons of Consumer Directed Health Plans?", Healthpayer Intelligence, https://healthpayerintelligence.com/news/what-are-the-pros-and-cons-of-consumer-directed-health-plans. Accessed March 18, 2019.

Becker's Hospital CFO Report (2014). "7 Things to Know About Emergency Department Profitability", https://www.beckershospitalreview.com/finance/7-things-to-know-about-emergency-department-profitability.html. Accessed March 19, 2019.

Becker's Hospital CFO Report (2017). "Fitch: Uncompensated Care Could Increase Next Year under ACA", March 27, 2017, https://www.beckershospitalreview.com/finance/fitch-uncompensated-care-could-increase-next-year-under-aca.html. Accessed October 14, 2018.

Bertowitz, E. N. and Flexner, W. A. (1980). "The Market for Health Services: Is There a Non-Traditional Consumer?", *Journal of Health Care Marketing*, 1 (1), 25–34.

Blumberg, L. J., Long, S. K., Kenney, G. M. and Goin, D. (2013). "Factors Influencing Health Plan Choice among the Marketplace Target Population on the Eve of Health Reform", *Health Reform Monitoring Survey*, http://hrms.urban.org/briefs/hrms_decision_factors.html. Accessed March 17, 2019.

Boscarino, J. and Steiber, S. R. (1982), "Hospital Shopping and Consumer Choice", *Journal of Health Care Marketing*, 2 (2), 15–23.

Brach, C. and Fraserirector, I. (2000). "Can Cultural Competency Reduce Racial and Ethnic Health Disparities? A Review and Conceptual Model", *Medical Care Research and Review*, 57 (Supplement 1), 181–217.

Brandon, W. P., Jennifer, L. T., Rajeshwari, S., Nancy, S., Yanqing, S. and Betsy, J. W. (2005). "Medicaid Enrollee Switching Among Managed Care Plans", *Journal of Health Care for the Poor and Underserved*, 16 (4).

Brezis, M. (2008). "Big Pharma and Health Care: Unsolvable Conflict of Interests Between Private Enterprise and Public Health", *Israel Journal of Psychiatry and Related Sciences*, 45 (2), 83–89.

Brooks, L. (2019). "Community Marketing: A Comprehensive Guide to Engaging Your Neighborhood", Healthcare Success blog, https://www.healthcaresuccess.com/blog/publicity/community-marketing-strategies.html. Accessed March 17, 2019.

Buchmeller, T. C. and Feldstein, P. J. (1997). "The Effect of Price on Switching Among Health Plans", *Journal of Health Economics*, 16 (2), 231–247.

Carteret, M. (2010). "Traditional Asian Health Beliefs & Healing Practices", http://www.dimensionsofculture.com/2010/10/traditional-asian-health-beliefs-healing-practices/. Accessed March 17, 2019.

CDC, Centers for Disease Control and Prevention (2015). "What is Health Marketing?", https://www.cdc.gov/healthcommunication/toolstemplates/whatishm.html. Accessed March 16, 2019.

Center for Medicare Advocacy (2017). "Racial and Ethnic Health Care Disparities", https://www.medicareadvocacy.org/medicare-info/health-care-disparities/. Accessed March 16, 2019.

Cloud-Moulds, P. J. (2015) "Eight Ways to Retain Old Patients and Attract New Ones", *Physicians Practice*, https://www.physicianspractice.com/marketing/eight-ways-retain-old-patients-and-attract-new-ones. Accessed March 14, 2019.

CMS (2016). "National Health Expenditure Projections 2012–2022", https://www.cms.gov/Research-Statistics-Data-and-Systems/Statistics-Trends-and-Reports/NationalHealthExpendData/Downloads/Proj2012.pdf. Accessed November 12, 2018.

Colwill, J. M., James, M. C. and Robin, L. K. (2008). "Will Generalist Physician Supply Meet Demands of an Increasing and Aging Population?", *Health Affairs*, 27 (3), 232–241.

Combined Media (2017). "Five Pharma Marketing Digital Trends to Watch in 2018", http://combinedmedia.ie/pharma-articles/five-pharma-marketing-digital-trends-watch-2018/. Accessed November 16, 2018.

Cunningham, P., Robin, R., Katherine, Y., Rachel, G. and Julia, F. (2016). "Understanding Medicaid Hospital Payments and the Impact of Recent Policy Changes", Kaiser Family Foundation, https://www.kff.org/report-section/understanding-medicaid-hospital-payments-and-the-impact-of-recent-policy-changes-issue-brief/. Accessed March 16, 2019.

Dalzell (1999). "PPOs: A Better Brand of Managed Care?", *Managed Care*, https://www.managedcaremag.com/archives/1999/6/ppos-better-brand-managed-care. Accessed November 12, 2018.

Dunlop, D. (2013). "A New Model for Physician Marketing", *Healthcare Marketing Advisor*, 14 (3), 21–22.

Dyrda, L. (2017). "5 Trends in Physician Income and Compensation", Becker's ASC Review, https://www.beckersasc.com/asc-turnarounds-ideas-to-improve-performance/5-trends-in-physician-income-and-compensation.html. Accessed March 12, 2019.

Egede, L. E. (2006). "Race, Ethnicity, Culture, and Disparities in Health Care", *J Gen Intern Med.*, 21 (6), 667–669.

Emarketer (2016). "The US Healthcare and Pharma Industry H2 2016", Update: Digital Ad Spending Forecast and Trends, https://www.emarketer.com/report.aspx?R=2001965&RewroteTitle=1. Accessed March 20, 2019.

Epstein, R. M. and Street, R. L. (2011). "The Values and Value of Patient-Centered Care", *Ann Fam Med.*, 9 (2), 100–103.

Erickson, A. (2010). "The Average Marketing Budget for a US Hospital", https://yourbusiness.azcentral.com/average-marketing-budget-hospital-17444.html. Accessed November 15, 2018.

Franklin Street (2015). "Hospital Brand Trends for 2016", http://www.franklin-street.com/hospital-brand-trends-for-2016. Accessed March 17, 2019.

Gagnon, M. A. and Lexchin, J. (2008). "The Cost of Pushing Pills: A New Estimate of Pharmaceutical Promotion Expenditures in the United States", *PLoS Medicine*, 5 (1).

Getweave (2019). "34 Ways to Increase Your Patient Retention", https://www.getweave.com/patient-retention/. Accessed March 15, 2019.

Grazier, K. L., Richardson, W. C., Martin, D. P. and Diehr, P. (1986). "Factors Affecting Choice of Health Care Plans", *Health Services Research*, 20 (6 Pt 1), 659–682.

Grier, S. and Bryant, A. (2005). "Social Marketing in Public Health", *Annual Review of Public Health*, 26 (1), 319–339.

Gunawardane, G. (2010). "An Assessment of the Dynamic Nature of Customer Expectations in Service Encounters", *California Journal of Operations Management*, 8 (1), 44–55.

Healthcare Success (2017). "5 Significant Hospital Marketing Trends to Watch in 2018", https://www.healthcaresuccess.com/blog/hospital-marketing/significant-hospital-marketing-trends.html. Accessed December 15, 2018.

Healthpayer Intelligence (2017). "Top 5 Largest Health Insurance Payers in the United States", https://healthpayerintelligence.com/news/top-5-largest-health-insurance-payers-in-the-united-states. Accessed March 17, 2019.

Heath, S. (2017). "Low-Income Patients Cite Financial, Cultural Barriers to Care", Patient Engagement Hit, https://patientengagementhit.com/news/low-income-patients-cite-financial-cultural-barriers-to-care. Accessed March 18, 2019.

Hennelly, V. D. and Boxerman, S. B. (1983). "Disenrollment from a Prepaid Group Plan: A Mulitvariate Analysis", *Medical Care*, 21 (12), 1154–1157.

Hixon, T. (2015). "Why Doctors are Frustrated with Digital Healthcare", *Forbes*, https://www.forbes.com/sites/toddhixon/2015/05/28/why-doctors-are-frustrated-with-digital-healthcare/#4498db827275. Accessed March 13, 2019.

Infographics (2014). "2014 Healthgrades American Hospital Quality Report to the Nation", https://www.infographicsarchive.com/health-beauty-safety/2014-healthgrades-american-hospital-quality-report-nation/. Accessed March 18, 2019.

Institute of Medicine (2001). "Committee on Quality of Health Care in America", *Crossing the Quality Chasm: A New Health System for the 21st Century*, Washington, D.C.: National Academy Press.

Jacobson, G., Neuman, T. and Damico, A. (2016). "Medicare Advantage Plan Switching: Exception or Norm?", Kaiser Family Foundation, https://www.kff.org/report-section/medicare-advantage-plan-switching-exception-or-norm-issue-brief/. Accessed March 19, 2019.

Johnston, S. (2015). "Three Factors Patients Use to Choose a Hospital", https://www.wearedh.com/blog/3-factors-patients-use-to-choose-a-hospital/. Accessed March 17, 2019.

Lewis, A. (1993). "Referral Physician Marketing", *Journal of Health Care Marketing*, 13 (4), 20–24.

Los Angeles Times (2018): "Did Drug Company Payments to Doctors Help Fuel the Opioid Epidemic?", (Kaplan 5/14/2018).

Maibach, E. W., Abroms, L. C. and Marosits, M. (2007). "Communication and Marketing as Tools to Cultivate the Public's Health: A Proposed 'People and Places' Framework", *BMC Public Health*, 7, 88.

MCOL (2018). "Managed Care Fact Sheets: National Managed Care Penetration 2017", http://www.mcol.com/managed_care_penetration. Accessed March 15, 2019.

Mechanic, D., Weiss, N. and Cleary, P. D. (1983). "The Growth of HMOs: Issues of Enrollment and Disenrollment", *Medical Care*, 21 (3), 338–347.

Moawad, H. (2017). "Are Physician Incomes Failing?", *Medical Economics*, http://medicaleconomics.modernmedicine.com/medical-economics/news/are-physician-incomes-falling. Accessed March 14, 2019.

Moschis, G. P. and Friend, S. B. (2008). "Segmenting the Preferences and Usage Patterns of the Mature Consumer Health-Care Market", *International Journal of Pharmaceutical and Healthcare Marketing*, 2 (1), 7–21.

Murphy, B. (2016). "Which Physicians Generate the Most Revenue for Hospitals?", *Becker's Hospital CFO Report*, https://www.beckershospitalreview.com/finance/which-physicians-generate-the-most-revenue-for-hospitals.html. Accessed March 15, 2019.

Pew Research Center (2013). "Majority of Adults Look Online for Health Information", http://www.pewresearch.org/fact-tank/2013/02/01/majority-of-adults-look-online-for-health-information/. Accessed January 23, 2019.

PricewaterhouseCoopers (2017). "Pharma 2020: Marketing the Future", https://www.pwc.com/gx/en/industries/pharmaceuticals-life-sciences/publications/pharma-2020/pharma-2020-marketing-the-future-which-path-will-you-take.html. Accessed October, 23, 2018.

Redmond, P. (2005). "Medicaid and SCHIP Retention in Challenging Times: Strategies from Managed Care Organizations", Center on Budget and Policy Priorities, https://www.cbpp.org/archiveSite/9-13-05health.pdf. Accessed March 17, 2019.

Rickert, J. (2012). "Patient-Centered Care: What It Means and How to Get There", *Health Affairs*, https://www.healthaffairs.org/do/10.1377/hblog20120124.016506/full/. Accessed January 24, 2019.

Robbins, R. (2016). "Drug Makers Now Spend $5 Billion A Year on Advertising. Here's What That Buys", https://www.statnews.com/2016/03/09/drug-industry-advertising/. Accessed October 23, 2018.

Satcher, D. and Higginbotham, E. J. (2008). "The Public Health Approach to Eliminating Disparities in Health", *American Journal of Public Health*, 98 (3), 400–403.

Schlesinger, M., Druss, B. and Thomas, T. (1999). "No Exit? The Effect of Health Status on Dissatisfaction and Disenrollment in Health Plans", *Health Service Research*, 34 (2), 547–576.

Self Insured Plans (2017). "Self-Funded Health Plan Benefits", https://www.selfinsured-plans.com/images/self-funded-health-plans-sip.pdf. Accessed march 18, 2019.

Shopify (2018). "Direct Marketing", https://www.shopify.com/encyclopedia/direct-marketing. Accessed January 24, 2019.

Smart Pharma Consulting (2015). "2020 Pharma Trends", http://www.smart-pharma.com/uploads/files/2020-Pharma-Market--trends--Marketing-challenges-SV.pdf. Accessed January 12, 2019.

Smith, H. L. and Rogers, R. D. (1987). "Factors Influencing Consumers' Selection of Health Insurance Carriers", *Journal of Health Care Marketing*, 6 (4), 6–14.

Sorenson, A. A. and Wersinger, R. P. (1981). "Factors Influencing Disenrollment from an HMO", *Medical Care*, 19 (7), 766–773.

Spiller, L. and Baier, M. (2005). *Contemporary Direct Marketing*. New Jersey: Pearson Prentice Hall.

Steinberg, S. H. (2016). "How Does a Hospital Make Money?", *Physicians News Digest*, https://physiciansnews.com/2006/11/16/how-does-a-hospital-make-money/. Accessed March 16, 2019.

Tine Health (2017)."Medicare Reimbursement Reduction due to Poor Hospital Quality and Patient Safety", http://tinehealth.com/2017/07/10/medicare-reimbursement-reduction-due-to-poor-hospital-quality-and-patient-safety/. Accessed March 15, 2019.

Travis, M., Russell, G. and Cronin, S. (1989). "Determinants of Voluntary HMO Disenrollment: An Examination of Consumer Behavior," *Journal of Health Care Marketing*, 9 (1), 75–76.

Ventola, C. L. (2011). "Direct-to-Consumer Pharmaceutical Advertising: Therapeutic or Toxic?", *Pharmacy and Therapeutics*, 36 (10), 669–674, 681–684, https://www.ncbi.nlm.nih.gov/pmc/articles/PMC3278148/. Accessed January 25, 2019.

Waidmann, T. A. (2009). "Estimating the Cost of Racial and Ethnic Health Disparities", http://www.urban.org/research/publication/estimating-cost-racial-and-ethnic-health-disparities. Accessed March 18, 2019.

Whitehurst, S. (2014). "Strategies to Maximize Patient Engagement and Retention", *Healthcare IT News*, https://www.healthcareitnews.com/blog/strategies-maximize-patient-engagement-retention. Accessed March 14, 2019.

Wong, F., Marian, H., Lori, A., Rosemary, B.-M., McCarthy, S., Londe, P. and Heitzler, C. (2004). "VERB — A Social Marketing Campaign to Increase Physical Activity Among Youth", *Preventing Chronic Disease*, 1 (3), A10.

Wrightson, W. Jr., Genuardi, J. and Stephens, S. (1987). "Demographic and Utilization Characteristics of HMO Disenrollees", *GHAA Journal*, 8 (1), 23–42.

Wrzosiński, P. (2014). "Pharma Digital Marketing in The U.S. Spending More and Wrong", *Pharma Marketing*, https://www.k-message.com/2014/06/01/pharma-digital-marketing-u-s-spending-wrong/. Accessed March 20, 2019.

Suggested Additional Readings

Anderson, M., Andrew, P. and Jingjing, J. (2018). "11% of Americans Don't Use the Internet. Who Are They?", *Pew Research Center*.

Bloom, P. and Novelli, W. (1981). "Problems and Challenges in Social Marketing", *Journal of Marketing*, 45, 79.

CMS, Center for Medicare and Medicaid Services (2018). "Reports on Medicare and Medicaid", CMS.gov.

Erickson, A. (2011). "Average Marketing Budgets for Hospitals. The Average Marketing Budget for a US Hospital", https://yourbusiness.azcentral.com/average-marketing-budget-hospital-17444.html

Frank, R. (2013). "Using Shared Savings to Foster Coordinated Care for Dual Eligibles", *New England Journal of Medicine*, 368: 404–405.

Goldsmith, M. and Leebov, W. (1986), "Strengthening the Hospital's Marketing Position Through Training", *Health Care Management Review*, 11 (Spring), 83–93.

Health Leaders (2016). "3 Hospital Marketing Trends to Watch in 2017", *Health Leaders Media News*, October 19, 2016, https://www.healthleadersmedia.com/welcome-ad?toURL=/strategy/3-hospital-marketing-trends-watch-2017. Accessed January 27, 2019.

Healthcare Business & Technology (2015). "4 New Rules for Effective Hospital Marketing", by a guest author December 15, 2015, http://www.healthcare-businesstech.com/effective-hospital-marketing/. Accessed January 25, 2019.

Healthcare Success (2018). "How to Market to Medicare Advantage Plan Patients", Healthcare Success blog, https://www.healthcaresuccess.com/blog/health-care-marketing/medicare-advantage-marketing.html. Accessed March 23, 2019.

Hill, R. C. (1988), "A New 'P' for Hospital Marketing?", *Journal of Hospital Marketing*, 2 (2), 5–18.

Medicarecode (2017). "Medicare Statistics US 2017", http://www.medicareccode.com/medicare-pdf/medicare-statistics-us-2017/.

Miller, K. (2002). "Doctors Beginning to See Benefit of Putting Their Practices Online", *Memphis Business Journal*, 23 (52), (Apr 19, 2002), 32.

Morgan & Co. (2018). "5 Hospital Marketing Trends to Look for in 2018", February 26, 2018, http://www.morganandco.com/hospital-marketing-trends/

Nanda, S., Telang, A. and Bhatt, G. (2012). "Hospital Advertising: A Literature Review", *International Journal of Healthcare Management*, 5 (1), 28–31.

Otani, K., Herrmann, P. A. and Kurz, R. S. 2011. "Improving Patient Satisfaction in Hospital Care Settings", *Health Services Management Research*, 24 (4), 163–169.

Robinson, L. M. and Cooper, D. (1980–1981). "Roadblocks to Hospital Marketing", *Journal of Health Care Marketing*, 1 (1), 18–24.

Spiller, L. and Baier, M. (2005). *Contemporary Direct Marketing*, New Jersey: Pearson Prentice Hall.

Strombom, B. A., Buchmueller, T. C. and Feldstein, P. J. (2002). "Switching Costs, Price Sensitivity and Health Plan Choice", *Journal of Health Economics*, 1 (1), (January 2002), 89–116.

Vaughan, C. (2011). "Physician Videos: A Marketing Gold Mine", *Healthcare Marketing Advisor*, 12 (8), (Aug 2011), 4–9.

Venkatesan, M. (1975). "Marketing of Health Maintenance Organizations: Consumer Behavior Perspectives", *Broadening the Concept of Consumer Behavior*, 45–69.

Winston, W. J. (1986). "The Evolution of Hospital Marketing", *Journal of Hospital Marketing*, 1 (1–2), 19–28.

Wright, R. A. and Stodghill, A. S. (1988), "Physician Marketing Comes of Age", *Journal of Health Care Marketing*, 8, (December), 3.

Chapter 15

Marketing Health Care Globally

15.1. The Modern Global Health Care Market

15.1.1. What is global health care marketing?

The term "global health market" usually refers to the health care systems across the world, health care organizing models, and measures on quality and access of health care in these countries. These important topics are typically addressed in books and courses on "Comparative Health Systems/Comparative Health Care Systems", e.g., Johnson *et al.* (2018) and Boslaugh (2013).

As this book focuses on marketing health care products and services, the aim of this chapter will be on marketing health care products and services across national borders and regions of the world. This is close to the concept of "internationalization" of health services introduced by McLean (1997) who describes it as (1) investing in foreign corporations; (2) managing foreign facilities; and (3) offering services to foreign patients (residents of other countries). Our main focus here is on this last mode of international health care business, i.e., offering health care services to foreign patients (residents of other countries).

15.1.2. Medical tourism

The act of residents of one country traveling to another country for medical treatment is referred to as "Medical Tourism". Seda (2014) reports that, according to Center for Disease Control (CDC) data, more than 750,000 US residents travel to another country for lower-cost medical or dental care each year and an Ipsos survey found that 38% of US residents are open the idea of to health care abroad. She continues that, "the rising cost of health care and thriving online communities of consumers present an optimal opportunity for the medical tourism industry."

Medical Tourism is not a new phenomenon (Lunt *et al.*, 2010; Smith and Puczkó, 2008). In terms of cross-border travel for health care, there is a long history including the use of spas and wellness tourism that gained a mass market throughout 18th- and 19th-century Europe. Traditionally, consumers from all continents and all forms of health systems have traveled abroad for their health care to avoid waiting lists or access state-of-the-art techniques and receive better aftercare services. What is new is that the easier and more affordable cross-border travel, rapid technological developments, and access to reliable medical information on the internet have made medical tourism an attractive option for treatment.

> Estimates of the global health care market open for marketing are impressive. Global medical tourism market was valued at US$61,172 million in 2016 and is estimated to reach US$165,345 million by 2023 (Sumant and Shaikh, 2017).

We organize our discussion by addressing the following key components of global health care marketing:

- **Outbound Medical Tourism Marketing**

For example, US residents traveling to Asia for the primary purpose of obtaining medical care usually inpatient hospitals care.

- **Inbound Medical Tourism Marketing**

For example, residents of European or Asian countries coming to USA for medical consultations, diagnostic services, and inpatient hospitals services.

- **Health Care Products and Services Marketing**

For example, medical devices and pharmaceuticals marketing across national borders and regions, and medical transcription, diagnostic, management and consulting services performed by US organizations for foreign countries.

The global market for pharmaceuticals reached US$1.2 trillion in 2018, up by US$100 billion from 2017, according to the Global Use of Medicines report from the IQVIA Institute for Human Data Science. The global market is expected to grow by 4–5%, reaching US$1.5 trillion by 2023.

15.1.3. Outbound medical tourism

Outbound medical tourism is the practice of patients traveling outside the established cross-border care arrangements to access medical services abroad, which are typically paid out-of-pocket (Crooks et al., 2010; Ramirez de Arellano, 2007). Some basic facts on outbound medical tourism (Accenture, 2013; Health Tourism, 2016; IMTJ, 2016; OECD, 2016; Patients Beyond Borders, 2017) are as follows:

- Thailand leads the Asian countries in the number of medical tourist arrivals every year from all over the world.
    Approximately 2.5 million foreign patients traveled to hospitals in Thailand in 2013. In Bangkok's prestigious Bumrungrad International Hospital, over 520,000 international patients received treatment.
- In 2015, medical tourism generated between US$60 and US$70 billion. Within five years, it is very likely that health tourism will generate at least twice these revenues (Health Tourism, 2016).
- The number of medical tourists from the United States has increased from about half a million in 2007 to an expected estimate of 1.25 million. The number of Americans who will travel abroad for medical treatment in 2014 beyond the US is estimated at up to 50 million (OECD, 2016).
- The industry is expected to grow approximately 20% per year. It is estimated that 1,400,000 Americans would travel outside the US for medical care during 2017 (Patients Beyond Borders, 2017).
- Singapore has been a growing medical tourism center in South East Asia, with 850,000 medical tourists arriving in 2012. Singapore, although slightly more expensive than its neighboring countries, has one of the best health systems in the world and is a favorite destination among Asians and Australians.
- Latin America, particularly Costa Rica and Panama, is fast becoming tourist spots for medical travelers with approximately 40,000 foreign patients seeking health care in Costa Rica in 2011.
- After more than doubling in the last five years, Malaysia is also becoming a famous destination with 770,134 medical travelers in 2013.
- India has become a medical tourism hot spot, with 166,000 international patients in 2012 coming to the country due to the selection of highly skilled doctors and improved medical infrastructure. With modern facilities being built and an abundance of highly trained medical personnel, India expects an increase of up to half a million medical tourist arrivals every year.

- There is a tremendous significance attached to positive perceptions and brand image for a niche product like health care where the human element is a crucial focal point throughout the service experience (Anvekar, 2012).
- Malaysia offers excellent facilities and competitive prices, and draws medical travelers mostly from neighboring countries such as Indonesia and Singapore.
- Other health tourism destinations in Asia include Israel, The Philippines, and China.
- Competitors in other parts of the world:
    o Turkey is an attractive choice for Europeans and Arab visitors, with the highest numbers of JCI-accredited hospitals and its proximity to Europe.
    o Europeans from the richer countries such as United Kingdom, Germany, Norway, Sweden, Austria, Ireland and Netherlands seek affordable private healthcare in Eastern Europe. Cheap flights, open borders and all-inclusive packages are attractions.
    o Spain, known for good quality health care system, attracts patients from UK and Ireland.
    o Germany has an excellent health care system and is considered a top destination for patients from the Middle East, UK, and the United States who are looking for high-quality medical care.
    o Hungary, Poland, France, and Austria are also popular European medical tourism destinations.
    o Latin America has the advantage of US-trained physicians and nurses. Proximity to United States and Canada is also an advantage. Popular destinations are Mexico, Costa Rica, Panama, Argentina, Colombia, and Brazil. These destinations have the tourist attractions appeal too. For some of the specialties these countries are known for, see Section 15.1.4.
    o South Africa is the leading medical tourism destination in Africa, having the best health care system south of the Sahara. It attracts patients from other African countries such as Zambia, Zimbabwe, Botswana, and Tanzania, as well as some American and European patients.

15.1.4. Inbound medical tourism

This refers to (a) patients from other parts of the world seeking medical care in, and drugs and equipment from, the United States, (b) US health care organizations (e.g., hospitals) expanding into other countries by opening branches/units in those countries and (c) health care professionals and institutions in other countries seeking expert knowledge, and technology from US sources.

Here are some basic facts related to the above-defined inbound medical tourism:

- Van Dusen (2008) cites a 2008 report of McKinsey & Co. that found that between 60,000 and 85,000 medical tourists traveled to the United States for the purpose of receiving inpatient medical care.

  Most of those patients headed to the United States in search of the best care included 38% from Latin America, 35% from the Middle East, 16% from Europe and 7% from Canada. Additionally, it is estimated that 32% of all medical travelers simply want better care than is available in their home countries, mostly those in the developing world, and 15% want quicker access to medically necessary procedures, i.e , compared to only 9% of medical travelers seeking medically necessary procedures at lower prices and 4% seeking low-cost discretionary procedures. The flow of foreigners heading to America's most prestigious academic medical centers, such as Cleveland Clinic, Mayo Clinic or John Hopkins appear to be seeking cutting edge cardiovascular, neurological or oncology treatments.

- US trade in health travel services (often called "medical tourism") has grown steadily in recent years; exports (i.e., travelers coming to the United States) have doubled. Despite rising costs, the US health system continues to attract foreigners because of its high-quality services and its proximity to large patient markets (Chambers, 2015).

  In 2013, US cross-border exports of health-related personal travel services were US$3.3 billion, up from US$1.6 billion in 2003, for a 7.7% compound annual growth rate (CAGR).

  About 0.5% of all air travelers entering the United States annually — between 100,000 and 200,000 people — list health treatment as a reason for visiting (this data exclude travelers from Canada and Mexico, the majority of whom travel to the United States overland).

  Foreign patients most often cite access to advanced medical care as their reason for traveling to this country for treatment. Some US health facilities, such as the Mayo Clinic, have long specialized in providing high-quality medical care to foreigners, particularly from the Middle East and Asia. These facilities actively market their services overseas, offering offices abroad and help in arranging travel. Several hospitals in

Florida specifically cater to health travelers from the Caribbean and Latin America, capitalizing on the availability of direct flights and bilingual staff.

The three largest source markets for foreign travelers visiting the United States for health treatment in 2011 were the Caribbean (with 44% of arrivals), Europe (24%), and Central America (10%). Restrictive visa requirements have reduced the number of patients who are able to enter the United States from certain countries and as a result many health travelers, for example from the Middle East, have opted to seek treatment in Southeast Asia instead.

- VoyagerMed, a medical tourism marketplace for international patients seeking high-quality medical care in the USA based in New York City, estimates that at least 500,000 overseas patients a year seek treatment in the USA (IMTJ, 2016).
- Stackpole Associates (2010) reports a March 2010 online survey of managers of international patient departments throughout the United States (87 representatives from 48 unique medical centers).

  Regarding total international patient volume, the highest percentages were Oncology (31.69%), Cardiovascular (14.17%) and Neurological (11.75%). "Other" at 23.26% was the second highest category, and this was further reported as a wide array of surgical and medical specialties.

  Regarding unique patient volume, international patients do not represent a high percentage, with the weighted average reported as 1.5%, although 75% of respondents reported this volume increased over the past 12 months, and the same proportion anticipates growth in this volume over the next 12-month period.

  The largest percentages of patients were derived from Mexico (21.18%), followed by Middle East (14.07%), South America (12.33%), Central America (excluding Mexico, 11.25%) and Europe (11.23%).
- Evans (2018) in an article in the Wall Street Journal entitled, "Expanding Health Care Operations to Other Countries" describes the case of ProMedica, a non-profit operating more than a dozen hospitals across Rust Belt communities in Ohio and Michigan, is looking to a new market to bolster its anemic growth: China. Executives and staff from the Toledo-based non-profit have been touring hospitals in Shanghai, Shenzhen and Chengdu, exploring possible deals in the world's second-largest economy that they hope will help offset weak revenue growth at home.

- In July 2018, Nashville-based Chinaco's new 500-bed CHC International Hospital in Cixi, a growing city of 2 million, 90 miles from Shanghai, admitted its first patients. The hospital is the first-ever joint venture between the company, which owns 70%, and the municipal government of Cixi, which holds a 30% stake (Johnson, 2014).
- Johnson (2014) also reports that health care investment firm Columbia Pacific Management announced plans to invest US$200 million in the construction of two 250-bed hospitals in China that would be wholly owned by the Seattle-based company under a Chinese government's pilot project to expand foreign investment in private hospital development.
- Boston-based Partners HealthCare, which operates Massachusetts General Hospital, has announced it was in preliminary talks with two Chinese partners to build a 500–1,000-bed facility.
- China's health care market is expected to boom over the next decade, driven by the country's giant economic expansion and its burgeoning senior population. China's health care sector continues to develop at an astonishing rate: spending is projected to grow from US$357 billion in 2011 to US$1 trillion in 2020. From pharmaceuticals to medical products to consumer health, China remains among the world's most attractive markets, and by far the fastest-growing of all the large emerging ones. It is not surprising that multinationals are flocking to take advantage of the opportunities (McKinsey & Company, 2012).

15.2. Outbound Medical Travel Customer/Patient Characteristics

It is important to understand special characteristics and factors influencing decision-making of US residents seeking medical care outside USA.

Understanding factors influencing decision-making of these customers/patients enables health care marketers to segment potential outbound customers/patients and appropriately formulate marketing strategies.

There are several factors motivating potential customers/patients to consider medical treatment outside their home country. These factors include:

- Cost savings
  - Treatment not covered by health insurance plan or cost savings due to high deductibles and copayments (Crooks *et al.*, 2010). Nearly 80% of the demand for medical travel is driven by cost savings (Medical Tourism Association, 2015).

> **Average Medical Care Cost Saving for Outbound US Residents by Destination**
>
> Asia: Singapore 33%; India 77%; and Malaysia 73%.
> Central and South America: Brazil 25%; Mexico 53%; and Costa Rica 55%. *Source*: Patients Beyond Borders (2017).

- Care not available in the home country.
  - For US patients, this is applicable for experimental drugs and treatments not approved by Federal Drug Administration (FDA) and holistic treatments (Burkett, 2007; Connell, 2006, 2011; Ramirez de Arellano, 2007; Unti, 2009).
- Long wait times in home country (especially for public-funded health systems, e.g., Canada and UK).
  - "Prompt medical treatment" was one of the top three factors indicated in a survey by Gill and Singh (2011).
- Tourism attractions in non-emergency care situations.
- Lack of health insurance.
  - Patient surveys indicate that 64% of patients who traveled abroad for care did not have health insurance (or health insurance with necessary coverage) (Medical Tourism Association, 2015).

Other significant characteristics of potential outbound medical care patients are summarized in what follows:

- Results from a survey of 194 respondents indicated that "competent doctors", "high-quality medical treatment facility", and "prompt medical treatment when needed" were the top three factors before deciding whether to take a trip abroad (Gill and Singh, 2011).
- Medical Tourism Association (2015) reports from their surveys that:
  - Almost 83% of patients traveled with a companion.
  - Almost 70% of patients rated their medical care as excellent.
  - Nearly 33% of patients traveled abroad for cosmetic surgery.
  - Almost 90% of patients or their companions engaged in tourism activities.

- Almost 85% of US patients found they received more personalized medical care than in the US.
- Almost 86% of US patients said they would travel again overseas for medical care.
- Nearly 27% of patients had previously traveled to a foreign country to receive medical care, most were female, all were between ages 45 and 64; the majority were White/Caucasian; all were American; all were college educated; half had household incomes between US$50,000 and US$100,000; and some had health insurance (50%), while others did not.
- Medical tourists spend between US$7,475 and US$15,833 per medical travel trip.
- Almost 48% of respondents would be interested in engaging in medical tourism again at some point in the future.
- The cost of medical treatment (85%) and state-of-the-art technology (83%) were the most important factors in their decision to travel abroad for treatment.

- Telephone interviews with 5,050 national adults aged 18 and older, split into samples of 2,524 and 2,572, were conducted on April 16–20, 2009, as part of Gallup Poll Daily tracking (95% confidence level margin of error: + or − 2%).
  - Almost 37% of respondents without health insurance would seek cancer care abroad as compared to 22% with health insurance.
  - Those without health insurance were on average 11 points more likely to say they would consider treatment abroad if the cost and quality provisions were included in the question than if they were not included.
  - By procedure, Americans would consider traveling abroad for medical procedures such as heart bypass surgery (14%), hip or knee replacement (15%), plastic surgery (10%), cancer diagnosis and treatment (24%), or alternative medical care (29%), even though all are routinely done in the United States.
  - By customer/patient region, respondents in the Midwest are consistently the least willing to consider obtaining treatments outside the country, whereas respondents in the West are consistently the most willing. Southerners are also below average in their willingness to obtain treatments outside the country, with the exception of hip or knee replacement.

- The US has begun to offer employer-sponsored outbound medical tourism programs within their employee health benefit programs.
    - Employers may offer incentives such as paying for air travel and waiving out-of-pocket expenses for care outside of the US.
    - Hannaford Bros. super market chain in Maine is considering saving up to 70% on medical costs by offering offshore medical treatments for its employees. Hannaford began paying the entire medical bill for employees to travel to Singapore for hip and knee replacements, including travel for the patient and companion.
    - BasicPlus Health Insurance at Roswell, one of the insurance companies, is collaborating with global health care companies to provide overseas options to members with maximum fixed benefits.
    - In 2000, Blue Shield of California began the United States' first cross-border health plan. Patients in California could travel to one of the three certified hospitals in Mexico for treatment under California Blue Shield.
    - In 2007, a subsidiary of BlueCross BlueShield of South Carolina, Companion Global Healthcare, teamed up with hospitals in Thailand, Singapore, Turkey, Ireland, Costa Rica, and India.

15.3. Medical Tourism Destinations and Treatment Sought

A wide choice of destinations across the world seems to be available for potential US customers/patients. The choice would depend on cost and specialties in which a given destination country has a reputation for good quality treatment. The following is a summary of destination countries and their specialized field(s) of care:

Latin America and Asia are the two leading regions for medical travel. Within these regions, Mexico and India, respectively, have the highest demand for medical tourism (Medical Tourism Association, 2013).

- According to Council for International Promotion of Costa Rica Medicine (PROMED), in 2012, Costa Rica attracted nearly 50,000 medical tourists (mostly from the US and Canada) and each one spent an average of US$7,000. Close to half of these medical travelers were

said to be seeking care in dental, followed by orthopedics, weight loss surgeries, gynecology, and plastic surgery. Medical tourism generated some US$338 million in revenue for the country that year (Medical Tourism.com, 2019).
- Tourism Research from the Australian Government reported that more than 10,000 medical tourism patients flew into the continent in 2013 pumping more than US$26 million into the national economy.
- According to the Indian High Commission in Nigeria, Indian hospitals received 18,000 Nigerians on medical visas in 2012, 47% of the Nigerians were in India to receive medical treatment and spent approximately US$260 million (Word Press, 2017).
- In 2012, the Ministry of Public Health, Thailand and the Kasikorn Research Center found that 2,530,000 international patients traveled to Thailand for treatment, the top five nations being Japan, US, UK, Gulf Cooperation Council (GCC) countries, and Australia. Revenues generated from medical tourism were approximately US$4 billion (Word Press, 2017).
- According to Mexico's Secretary of Tourism, out of almost 12 million international visitors who arrived in Mexico in 2013, 6.5 million of the visitors were from the US (Word Press, 2017).
- The Korea Health Industry Development Institute reported in 2012 that 159,464 patients from 188 countries visited Korea in 2012, and 32,503 of those patients were Chinese (Word Press, 2017).
- The 2010 Statistics on International Patients in Korea reports that 81,789 foreign patients traveled to Korea, of which 32.4% came from the US (4,829 were US Army patients), 19.4% from China, 16.8% from Japan, and 7.7% from Russia (Word Press, 2017).
- A 2012 report from the Taiwan Ministry of Health and Welfare found that more than 60,000 patients traveled to Taiwan for health care the previous year, with 50% of patients coming from mainland China. It was also noted in the report that the most popular procedure was a full health exam (Word Press, 2017).
- According to Alpen Capital Investment Banking, the United Arab Emirates' medical tourism sector is growing strongly and reached US$1.69 billion in 2013. Dubai Healthcare City (DHCC) is one of the largest health care tourist destinations in the region. According to DHCC, they handled approximately 500,000 patients in 2011, 20% of which were medical tourists (Word Press, 2017).

In summary,

> **Top Destinations for US Outbound Medical Tourism and Care Sought**
>
> Costa Rica, India, Israel, Malaysia, Mexico, Singapore, South Korea, Taiwan, Thailand, and Turkey.
>
> Top specialty care sought: Cosmetic surgery, Dentistry (general, restorative, cosmetic), Cardiovascular (angioplasty, CABG, transplants), Orthopedics (joint and spine; sports medicine), Cancer (often high-acuity or last resort), Reproductive (fertility, IVF, women's health), Weight loss (LAP-BAND, gastric bypass), and Scans, tests, health screenings and second opinions.
>
> *Sources*: Medical Tourism.com (2019); Medical Tourism Association (2015); and Patients Beyond Borders (2017).

15.3.1 Negative perceptions of medical tourists about certain destinations

- Risk of exposure to infectious diseases, e.g., Hepatitis A, amoebic dysentery, and paratyphoid.
- Risk of exposure to mosquito-bitten diseases. Dengue is prevalent in Sri Lanka despite major efforts to eradicate it.
- Risk of misdiagnosisusually attracted inbound. Having quality second opinions from India and the West could be helpful.
- The lower quality of post-operative care can also vary dramatically.
- Traveling long distances soon after surgery can increase the risk of complications. Long flights and decreased mobility associated with window seats can predispose one toward developing deep vein thrombosis and potentially a pulmonary embolism. Good tourist-class hotel-equivalent accommodation after surgery could be considered.
- Risk of exposure to tropical weather. For example, scars may become darker and more noticeable if they sunburn while healing.
- Lack of policies for fast acknowledgement and resolution of complaints.
- Qualifications and licensure of medical professionals which are hard to verify in developing countries.
- Patient safety. World Health Organization assists hospitals and governments around the world in setting patient safety policy and practices.

- Longer stays in case of complications. In such situations, the patient may need to stay in the foreign country for longer than planned. Arrangements and finances for this possibility should be planned.
- Language and culture barriers.
- Little or no legal recourse in case of poor quality of service or medical mistakes.

Suing Foreign Physicians and Hospitals

This is extremely difficult due to several reasons.

- Jurisdiction problems. US courts appear to be reluctant to assert jurisdiction over foreign health care providers, especially physicians, who have no practices in the US state where the suit is brought.
- Legal theories. It is difficult to equate US theories of legal liability to those in the foreign country.
- Delays in process. Foreign judicial systems and courts are known to be very slow with processing civil claims and are not known for providing timely resolution of civil cases (see Mirrer-Singer, 2007).

15.4. Sources of Information Used for Researching Outbound Medical Travel

What sources are used by potential customers/patients for information and research on outbound medical travel? Understanding this is very important for health care marketers to decide which sources and media to focus on promotion of outbound medical travel opportunities.

Gill and Singh (2011) report results of their survey of 154 respondents on their choice of sources for information on medical tourism. Of their sample,

- 73% preferred online research;
- 10% relied on family physician's opinion;
- 8% relied on family and friends;
- 6% relied on testimonial of hospitals abroad; and
- 1% each for printed brochures, videos providing tours, and television reports.

There is evidence from breast augmentation patients' use of the internet, with one survey suggesting that 68% of respondents utilized internet information, and of this subset of patients the information influenced decision-making around choice of procedures (in 53% of cases), choice of surgeon (36% of cases), and choice of hospital (25% of cases) (Losken *et al.*, 2005).

This high reliance of potential medical travel customers/patients on the internet for information is confirmed by other studies and industry experts. For example, Medical Tourism Review (2015) claims that perhaps the most popular use of technology within medical tourism is the use of the internet by patients to research destinations and treatments, and that opens gateway portals, such as the Treatment Abroad website, and compares providers and costs around the world.

Caution on using the internet for research on medical tourism has also been made. Studies have found problems with accuracy, completeness, readability, design, disclosure, and references on websites and warn that health information online should be used with caution (Medical Tourism Review, 2015).

Lunt *et al.* (2010) provide a list of internet-based channels of information typically used for information on medical tourism as follows:

- **Portals**

These allow potential patients to search for treatments, providers, and to compare costs. Examples are www.treatmentabroad.co.uk and www.placidway.com/.

Regional portals provide a gateway to treatments and countries for a particular region. An example is www.healthtourisminasia.com/.

There are also portals specializing on treatment types and others published by larger providers like hospitals and medical groups.

- **Media sites**

There are many trade and professional associations that publish information on medical travel. Some examples are Medical Tourism Review (https://medicaltourism.review), International Medical Tourism Journal (www.imtjonline.com), and Medical Travel Today (www.medicaltraveltoday.com).

- **Consumer-driven sites**

Examples are discussion boards and blogs produced by both consumers and professionals: www.medicaltourismblog.org/, www.healism.com/blogs/, and www.implant.uk.com/.

- **Commerce-related sites**

These are sites usually published by health care consulting and marketing companies. Information on health care markets and developments, usually based on secondary source surveys, are quite reliable although the bottom-line message is selling their own products and services.

15.5. Inbound Medical Travel Marketing

- Citing a study by McKinsey & Co., Van Dusen (2008) claims that between 60,000 and 85,000 medical tourists were traveling to the United States for the purpose of receiving inpatient medical care.
- Each year, some 300,000 international patients visit the United States seeking excellence in specialty care — especially in complex or "high-acuity" cases. Despite the cost, American specialists often are called upon to treat cases considered difficult or untreatable elsewhere (Patients Beyond Borders, 2017).
- US hospitals with reputed programs of tertiary care usually attract inbound medical customers/patients (Patients Without Borders, 2017).
- Academics, research, and clinical care come together to form a powerful combination in certain regions,
    o For example, Houston's Texas Medical Center (TMC) comprises 54 hospitals and specialty clinics, including luminaries such as MD Anderson (oncology); Methodist (orthopedics, transplants); Texas Children's Hospital and its recently opened Women's Pavilion.
    o Health care clusters in South Florida tend to attract the Latin American and Caribbean patients.
    o Boston and the greater New York region bring in affluent patients from all over, including Africa, the Middle East, Western Europe, and — increasingly — Russia and China.
    o Some leading US hospitals provide international patient packages that include airport pick-up and drop-off, hotel shuttle, translators, travel planning, and more.
    o An Intercontinental Hotel adjoins Cleveland Clinic, and the Marriott Texas Medical Center welcomes visitors from all walks, with special amenities for the TMC patient.
- Michigan hospitals — including Henry Ford Hospital, Detroit Medical Center, and Beaumont Hospital — draw patients from countries like India, Brazil, and Turkey who need procedures that are not widely

available at home or who have rare conditions that cannot be treated there. Patients come to Michigan from all over the world to receive robotic procedures and high-beam radiation treatments for cancer, as well as spinal cord rehabilitation and treatments for epilepsy and blinding eye conditions in babies (Terry, 2011).
- University of Chicago Medical Center and Rush University Medical Center in Chicago have both recruited well-heeled foreigners to pay full freight for procedures that are not as easy to obtain in their home countries. In some cases, these overseas patients are willing to pay as much as US$120,000 for heart surgery and US$40,000 for a prostate operation. That is good money for US hospitals that are often forced to give insurance companies big discounts (Terry, 2011).
- Focus of customers/patients is on medical care not tourism.
- Expanding US hospital operations abroad:
  o China's health care market is expected to boom over the next decade, driven by the country's giant economic expansion and its burgeoning senior population. The country is projected to reach US$1 trillion in total health care spending by 2020. Spending more than doubled from 2006 to 2011, from US$156 billion to US$357 billion, according to a 2012 report by McKinsey & Co.
  o Potentially speeding the growth, in 2009 the Chinese government launched a major health care reform initiative to expand health care access and improve quality of care for its population of 1.3 billion people. The initiative included the establishment of two new public insurance programs for low-income people.
  o The Chinese government has relaxed foreign ownership rules to attract private hospital operators who offer better quality care to consumers widely dissatisfied with the current public hospitals.

15.6. Inbound Medical Customer/Patient Characteristics

- Market is made up of the affluent citizens in the home country.
  o Affluent patients typically explore options beyond borders due to dissatisfaction with their domestic health system, such as the unavailability of appropriate treatments, relatively low quality of care, absence of modern technology, and/or shortage of health care providers.

- o Many well-funded patients travel to countries with a long tradition of receiving foreign patients, such as Switzerland or the USA; else to countries that have recently upgraded their health systems (e.g., India).
- o These customers/patients consider quality and competence of local health services, especially surgical procedures, poor.
    - For example, Chinese consumers currently view the quality of care at private hospitals, most of which are owned and operated by Chinese, unfavorably compared with their view of care at public hospitals, which provide the bulk of care.

- Stackpole & Associates (2010) report the following from their survey:
    - o Inbound medical tourists from every corner of the globe travel to the US for a wide variety of health care services with a focus on cardiology, oncology, and neurological services.
    - o International patient departments bring prestige to a hospital. On total international patient volume, the highest percentages within the international patient sector were oncology (32%), cardiovascular (14%), and neurological (12%).
    - o International patients on average represent 1.5% of total patient numbers, although numbers have increased over the past 12 months, and most expect further growth this year.
    - o Patients come from many countries, especially from Mexico (21%), the Middle East (14%), South America (12%), Central America excluding Mexico (11%), and Europe (11%).
    - o Most international patient departments offer additional services such as interpreter/translator, pre-arrival medical assessment, assistance with hotel reservations or housing options, special dietary needs, and coordination of aftercare services. Less than half provide assistance with transport and/or tourism-related services.
    - o Almost 62% reported that the staff of the international patient department had received specialized training on cultural issues.
    - o The emphasis is on medical treatment, not tourism.
    - o The price of US health care is rated as the greatest obstacle to international patients.
    - o Obtaining a visa was the second most difficult problem.
    - o Marketing is mostly word of mouth from patients and families, followed by referrals from doctors.

15.7. Guidelines for Global Health Care Marketing

Industry research and studies highlight the following guidelines in managing and marketing global medical care.

15.7.1. General

- Familiarizing with legal environment of health care travel:
  - Immigration and visa rules of destination country (outbound) and USA (inbound).
  - Privacy laws of destination country and USA governing medical records and transmission of medical data across borders.
- Familiarizing with banking, money transfer, and currency conversion regulations of destination countries.
- The key to both outbound and inbound health travel marketing is anchoring with a hospital in the destination country (outbound) or USA (inbound), with an international reputation (or even better, international accreditation) for excellent treatment of the care sought. For details, see the sections discussing outbound and inbound medical travel/tourism.
- For inbound medical travel, focus on cost, quality, and other factors directly related with health care sought. Focus minimally on tourism aspects.
- A local presence is a prerequisite for doing business in any foreign country, especially in emerging nations (Tuller, 2008). This is extremely important with outbound medical tourism.

  This is best achieved by forming a strategic alliance (agent or joint venture) with a local partner. The strategic partner will be able to facilitate getting necessary permits, linking with key suppliers and health care providers, handling banking and finance matters, and marketing inbound medical travel programs.

15.7.2. Outbound medical tourism

Segment the market by motivation of customer/patient, destination, niche specialty procedures, and cost.

Match customers/patients to destination by procedure sought and then supplement with tourism aspects.

Also, focus on proximity of the foreign destination, cost savings, and quality and reputation of medical care sought.

Other factors to be focused on are as follows (Patients Beyond Borders, 2017):

- Government and private sector investment in health care infrastructure.
- Demonstrable commitment to international accreditation, quality assurance, and transparency of outcomes; sustained reputation for clinical excellence; history of health care innovation and achievement; and successful adoption of best practices and state-of-the-art medical technology.
- Availability of internationally trained, experienced medical staff.
- International patient flow.
- Political transparency and social stability of the destination country.
- Tourism infrastructure.
- Deploy effective websites with Search Engine Optimization (SEO) and good content management.
  - Almost 87% of travelers use the internet for a bulk of their travel planning (Seda, 2014).
  - However, little is known about search strategies of potential medical tourism customers/patients, the use of the search terms, whether individuals seek out particular destinations and treatments, and how they judge and compare sites (Lunt and Carrera, 2010).
- Content marketing is a must.
  - Videos from medical professionals or previous patients.
  - Enticing photos and information about the destination.
  - Information they need for both their vacation and medical needs.
- Use social media effectively.
  The travel industry has harnessed the power of social media and medical tourism marketing should follow suit (Seda, 2014).

According to Nielsen's latest Global Trust in Advertising report (Neilson, 2012; Survey of more than 28,000 internet respondents in 56 countries), 92% of consumers around the world say they trust earned media, such as word-of-mouth or recommendations from friends and family, above all other forms of advertising — an increase of 18% since 2007. Online consumer reviews are the second most trusted source of brand information and messaging, with 70% of global consumers surveyed online indicating they trust messages on this platform, an increase of 15% in four years. Two-thirds (66%) say they trust consumer opinions posted online.

Engage on a personal level. Each medical tourism customer/patient is unique. Besides, medical treatment is a service that is highly personalized and emotional.

As in any typical international business venture, it is essential to have a partner in the destination country. Having a trustworthy local representative is a real advantage in building customer/patient trust.

Use accredited hospitals and, whenever possible, physicians trained in USA, Canada, and Europe. High quality/significant number of US-accredited hospitals and physicians are available in Southeast Asia and India (especially for orthopedic and cardiovascular cases), Canada, UK.

Explore employer-sponsored opportunities for medical care abroad for employees. Medical travel packages can integrate with all types of health insurance, including limited benefit plans, preferred provider organizations, and high deductible health plans.

Awareness of destination country's cultural and religious values is also very important.

15.7.3. Inbound medical tourism marketing

Again, the anchor should be a US hospital with international reputation for specific treatments.

A US hospital's ability to attract international patients depends on several factors (Al-Amin et al., 2011). These include the following:

- Hospital attributes: Hospital reputation (which also reflects the reputation and influence of hospital employees and physicians); Type of hospital (teaching, general, or specialty); teaching and specialty hospitals have better export performance than general hospitals; Hospital size (reflected in the number of beds the hospital has);
- The hospital's international competence and marketing success in multiple countries and regions;
- Hospital's network of accredited and contracted physicians and other hospitals; and
- Management commitment and clear strategic focus (cost leadership competencies; differentiation competencies).

Top US hospitals, such as Cleveland Clinic, Mayo Clinic, Johns Hopkins, MD Anderson Cancer Center or University of Michigan Hospitals, meet these criteria. Other smaller hospitals should focus on narrower niche markets fitting their special capabilities and differentiation factors such as lower cost, and travel and board support.

Generally, it is the affluent citizens in foreign countries who can afford medical treatment in USA. This fact is important in selecting promotional channels, language, and content.

References

Accenture (2013). "Global Consumer Pulse Survey — Global and US Key Findings", https://www.accenture.com/t20150523T052453__w__/us-en/_acnmedia/Accenture/Conversion-Assets/DotCom/Documents/Global/PDF/Strategy_3/Accenture-Global-Consumer-Pulse-Research-Study-2013-Key-Findings.pdf. Accessed October 1, 2018.

Al-Amin, M., Makarem, S. C. and Pradhan, R. (2011). "Hospital Ability to Attract International Patients: A Conceptual Framework", *International Journal of Pharmaceutical and Healthcare Marketing*, 5 (3), 205–221.

Anvekar, S. R. (2012). "Medical Tourism in India: A Strategic Approach Towards Effective Branding for Health Care Services Marketing", *American Journal of Management*, 12 (2/3), 108–116.

Boslaugh, S. E. (2013). *Health Care Systems around the World: A Comparative Guide*, Sage Reference.

Burkett, L. (2007). "Medical Tourism: Concerns, Benefits and the American Legal Perspective", *The Journal of Legal Medicine*, 28, 223–245.

Chambers, A. (2015). "Trends in U.S. Health Travel Services Trade", *United States International Trade Commission (USITC) Executive Briefing on Trade*, August 2015, https://www.usitc.gov/research_and_analysis/executive_briefings.htm. Accessed March 22, 2019.

Connell, J. (2006). "Medical Tourism: Sea, Sun, Sand and … Surgery", *Tourism Management*, 27 (6), 1093–1100.

Connell, J. (2011). *Medical Tourism*, CAB International, Oxford, U.K.

Crooks, V. A., Kingsbury, P., Snyder, J. and Johnston, R. (2010), "What is Known About the Patient's Experience of Medical Tourism? A Scoping Review", *BMC Health Services Research*, 10, 266.

Deloitte (2009). "Medical Tourism: Update and Implications", Deloitte Center for Health Solutions, see www.deloitte.com/centerforhealthsolutions. Accessed July 22, 2018.

Evans, M. (2018). "Expanding Health Care Operations to Other Countries", *Wall Street Journal*, April 22, 2018.

Gill, H. and Singh, N. (2011). "Exploring the Factors that Affect the Choice of Destination for Medical Tourism", *Journal of Service Science and Management*, 4 (3), 315–324.

Health Tourism (2016). "Medical Tourism Statistics and Facts", https://www.health-tourism.com/medical-tourism/statistics/. Accessed March 20, 2019.

IMTJ, International Medical Travel Journal (2016). "Bringing Medical Tourists to the USA", 1 December 2016, https://www.imtj.com/news/bringing-medical-tourists-usa/. Accessed January 30, 2019.

Johnson, J., Stoskopf, C. and Shi, L. (2018). *Comparative Health Systems*, 2nd edition, Jones & Bartlett Learning, LLC.

Johnson, S. R. (2014). "U.S. Hospital Operators See Opportunity, Risks in China", *Modern Healthcare*, 44 (50), 18–20. Also available at https://www.modernhealthcare.com/article/20141213/MAGAZINE/312139980. Accessed October 2, 2018.

Losken, A., Burke, R., Elliot, F. and Carlson, G. W. (2005). "Infonomics and Breast Reconstruction: Are Patients Using the Internet?", *Annals of Plastic Surgery*, 54, 247–250.

Lunt, N. and Carrera, P. (2010). "Medical Tourism: Assessing the Evidence on Treatment Abroad", *International Journal of Mid-life Health*, 66, 27–32.

Lunt, N., Hardey, M. and Mannion, R. (2010). "Nip, Tuck and Click: Medical Tourism and the Emergence of Web-Based Health Information", *The Open Medical Informatics Journal*, 4, 1–11. Published online February 12, 2010, doi: 10.2174/1874431101004010001, https://www.ncbi.nlm.nih.gov/pmc/articles/PMC2874214/. Accessed January 30, 2019.

McKinsey & Company (2012). "Health Care in China: Entering 'Uncharted Waters'" by Franck Le Deu, Rajesh Parekh, Fangning Zhang, and Gaobo Zhou, https://www.mckinsey.com/industries/healthcare-systems-and-services/our-insights/health-care-in-china-entering-uncharted-waters. Accessed January 29, 2019.

McLean, R. A. (1997), "Opportunities in The International Health Services Arena", *Healthcare Financial Management*, 51 (8), 60–64.

Medical Tourism Association (2015). "Facts and Statistics", http://medicaltourism.com/Forms/facts-statistics.aspx. Accessed July 2, 2018.

Medical Tourism.com (2019). "Facts and Statistics", https://medicaltourism.com/Forms/facts-statistics.aspx. Accessed July 3, 2018.

Mirrer-Singer, P. (2007). "Medical Malpractice Overseas: The Legal Uncertainty Surrounding Medical Tourism", *Law and Contemporary Problems*, 70 (2007), 211–232.

Neilson (2012). "Global Trust in Advertising and Brand Messages", https://retelur.files.wordpress.com/2007/10/global-trust-in-advertising-2012.pdf. Accessed March 25, 2019.

OECD (2016). "Medical Tourism: Treatments, Markets and Health System Implications: A Scoping Review", http://www.oecd.org/els/health-systems/48723982.pdf. Accessed October 2, 2018.

Patients Beyond Borders (2017). "Medical Tourism Statistics & Facts", https://patientsbeyondborders.com/medical-tourism-statistics-facts. Accessed July 4, 2018.

Pharmaceutical Commerce (2019). "Global Pharma Spending Will Hit $1.5 Trillion In 2023, Says IQVIA", January 29, 2019, https://pharmaceuticalcommerce.com/business-and-finance/global-pharma-spending-will-hit-1-5-trillion-in-2023-says-iqvia/. Accessed March 20, 2019.

Ramirez de Arellano, A. (2007). "Patients Without Borders: The Emergence of Medical Tourism", *International Journal of Health Services*, 37 (1), 193–198.

Seda, R. (2014). "5 Ways to Market Medical Tourism", posted: February 4, 2014, https://healthcarecommunication.com/Main/Articles/5_ways_to_market_medical_tourism__10052.aspx. Accessed October 22, 2018.

Smith, M. and Puczkó, L. (2008). (Eds.) *Health and Wellness Tourism*, Butterworth-Heinemann/Elsevier, Oxford.

Stackpole Associates Inc. (2010). "Inbound Medical Tourism: Survey of US International Patient Departments", http://www.stackpoleassociates.com/resources/articles/inbound-medical-tourism-executivesummary-10-06-15-2.pdf. Accessed January 30, 2019.

Sumant, O. and Shaikh, S. (2017). "Medical Tourism Market by Treatment Type (Cardiovascular Treatment, Orthopedic Treatment, Neurological Treatment, Cancer Treatment, Fertility Treatment, and Others): Global Opportunity Analysis and Industry Forecast", 2017–2023, https://www.alliedmarketresearch.com/medical-tourism-market. Accessed October 23, 2018.

Terry, K. (2011). "Reverse Medical Tourism Points Up Pluses and Minuses of U.S. Healthcare", CBS, updated on January 7, 2011, MoneyWatch, https://www.cbsnews.com/news/reverse-medical-tourism-points-up-pluses-and-minuses-of-us-healthcare/. Accessed January 31, 2019.

Tuller, L. W. (2008). *Doing Business beyond America's Borders*, Entrepreneur Press, Canada.

Unti, J. A. (2009). "Medical and Surgical Tourism: The New World of Health Care Globalization and What It Means for the Practicing Surgeon", *Bulletin of the American College of Surgeons*, 94 (4), 18–25.

Van Dusen, A. (2008). "U.S. Hospitals Worth the Trip", *Forbes*, May 29, 2008, https://www.forbes.com/2008/05/25/health-hospitals-care-forbeslife-cx_avd_outsourcing08_0529healthoutsourcing.html#1e131e9152e1. Accessed January 30, 2019.

Word Press (2017). "Medical Tourism in India", https://gaer2017.wordpress.com/2017/08/25/medical-tourism-in-india-statistics/. Accessed July 4, 2018.

Suggested Additional Readings

Azevedo, D. (1996). "America's Latest Export: Managed Care", *Medical Economics*, 73 (23), 71–79.

Badam, R. T. (2005). "Medical Tourists Go to India for Treatment", *The Toronto Star*, September 23, 2005.

Beerlin, A. and Martin, J. D. (2004). "Factors Influencing Destination Image", *Annals of Tourism Research*, 31 (3), 657–681, www.google.com; www.healthcare.com.

Bertowitz, E. N. and Flexner, W. A. (1980). "The Market for Health Services: Is There a Non-Traditional Consumer?", *Journal of Health Care Marketing*, 1 (1), 25–34.

Boscarino, J. and Steiber, S. R. (1982). "Hospital Shopping and Consumer Choice", *Journal of Health Care Marketing*, 2 (2), 15–23.

Chinai, R. and Goswami, R. (2007). "Medical Visas Mark Growth of Indian Medical Tourism", *Bulletin of the World Health Organization*, 85 (3), 164–165.

Connell, J. (2006). "Medical Tourism: Sea, Sun, Sand and ... Surgery", *Tourism Management*, 27 (6), 1093–1100.

Daniele, E. (1995). "Europe Wants American Managed Care", *Insurance & Technology*, 20 (7), 21–22.

Earnest & Young (1991). *Earnest & Young's Guide to Expanding in the Global Market*, John Wiley & Sons.

The Economist (2004). "Get Well Away; Medical Tourism to India", 372 (8396) (October 9), 60.

Eggerston, L. (2006). "Wait-List Weary Canadians Seek Treatment Abroad", *Canadian Medical Association Journal*, 174 (9), 1247.

Forgione, D. A. and Smith, P. C. (2007). "Medical Tourism and Its Impact on the US Health Care System", *Journal of Health Care Finance*, 34 (1), 27–35.

Gahlinger, P. M. (2008). *The Medical Tourism Travel Guide: Your Complete Reference to Top-Quality, Low-Cost Dental, Cosmetic, Medical Care & Surgery Overseas*, Sunrise River Press.

Garcia-Altes, A. (2005). "The Development of Health Tourism Services", *Annals of Tourism Research*, 32 (1), 262–266.

Glinos, I. A., Baeten, R., Helble, M. and Maarse, H. (2010). "A Typology of Cross-Border Patient Mobility", *Health & Place*, 16 (6), 1145–1155.

Hopkins, L. R., Labonté, V. and Runnels, C. P. (2010). "Medical Tourism Today: What is the State of Existing Knowledge?", *Journal of Public Health Policy*, 31, 185–198.

Howze, K. S. (2007). "Medical Tourism: Symptom or Cure?", *Georgia Law Review*, 41, 1013–1052.

Jenner, E. A. (2008). "Unsettled Borders of Care: Medical Tourism as A New Dimension in America's Health Care Crisis", *Research in the Sociology of Health Care*, 26 (2008), 235–249.

Klaus, M. (2005). "Outsourcing Vital Operations: What If US Health Care Costs Drive Patients Overseas for Surgery?", *Quinnipiac Health Law Journal*, 9, 219–247.

Marlowe, J. and Sullivan, P. (2007). "Medical Tourism: The Ultimate Outsourcing", *Human Resources Planning*, 30 (2), 8–10.

Mudur, G. (2004). "Hospitals in India Try and Woo Patients", *British Medical Journal*, 328, 1338.

Nassimbeni, G., Sartor, M. and Dus, D. (2012). "Security Risks in Service Offshoring and Outsourcing", *Industrial Management & Data Systems*, 112 (3), 405–440.

Olberhozer-Gee, F., Khanna, T. and Knoop, C. I. (2007). "Apollo Hospitals–First-World Health Care at Emerging-Market Prices", *Harvard Business Review*, No. 9-706-440.

Oliver Wyman (2013). *Globalization of Services*, Marsh & McLennan Companies.

Plock, E. (1996). "The Global Healthcare Services Market is Growing Fast as Foreign Consumers Look for Better Medical Care", *Business America*, 117 (7), 18–19.

Talbot, E. A., Chen, L. H., Sanford, C., McCarthy, A. and Leder, K. (2010). "Travel Medicine Research Priorities: Establishing an Evidence Base", *Journal of Travel Medicine*, 17 (6), 410–415.

Tritter, J., Koivusalo, M., Ollila, E. and Dorfman, P. (2010). *Globalization, Markets and Healthcare Policy: Redrawing the Patient as Consumer*, Routledge. New York.

Turner, L. G. (2007). "First World Health Care at Third World Prices: Globalization, Bioethics and Medical Tourism", *Bio Societies*, 2 (3), 303–325.

Turner, L. G. (2011). "Quality in Health Care and Globalization of Health Services: Accreditation and Regulatory Oversight of Medical Tourism Companies", *International Journal for Quality in Health Care*, 23 (1), 1–7.

Index

Access, 231, 238–240
    guidelines for improving, 239
Accountable Care Organizations (ACOs), 6, 8
Affordable Care Act, 359, 370
Agencies regulating health care, 366
Agents for marketing, 374
Anti-Kickback statutes, 368, 377
A priori segmentation, 206–208

B2C and B2B segmentation, 209
Behavioral segmentation, 207, 208
Big Data, 67, 77
Blanchard & Peale, 398, 399

CAHPS Health Plan Survey Measures (CAHPS), 156–158, 176, 179, 180
Call center communications, 374
Channel integration, 299, 300
CMS, 360, 361, 366, 367, 370–372, 374–376, 388, 391
Comparisons with competing plans, 373
Competition in the health care industry, 81, 82, 85
    among health plans, 87, 88
    among hospitals, 85–87
    among pharmaceutical companies, 88
    among physicians, 90
    in general, 91
Consumerism, 106, 125, 129, 130
Consumer/Patient analysis, 107, 110
Content marketing, 245, 247, 282, 286, 288, 291–296
Cost leadership, 47, 49, 56
Customer centered marketing, 253
Customer-centric segmentation, 215, 218
Customer delight, 318
Customer experience, 149–152, 155, 162, 163, 168–171, 173, 183, 185, 188, 189
    definition, 151, 153, 165, 181
Customer Experience Management, 170, 171
    guidelines, 179, 186
Customer feedback, 313
Customer orientation of employees, 317, 318
    factors affecting, 320
    management support, 319
Customer-oriented culture, 318
Customer-oriented employee, 318, 320, 326
    characteristics, 318
    selecting, 320

Customer/Patient Journey Mapping, 173
Customer Relations Management (CRM), 170–172
Customers, 9–16
  a patient's family, 10
  care coordinators, 11
  communities and consumers, 11
  end user customer: the patient, 9
  internal customers, 11
  pharmacists, 11
  the well person: the consumer, 10
Customer satisfaction, 150–153, 161, 176, 181–186, 188
Customers in health care, 104
  behavior, 103–109, 111, 112, 114, 116, 119–123, 129, 133, 134, 137, 138
  characteristics, 103–105, 108, 124, 129, 137
CX, 149, 151, 152, 154, 155, 161–163, 167, 169, 170, 175–177, 181, 183, 185, 187, 188
CXM, 170–172
CX/PX, 151, 154, 161, 162, 167, 170, 175–177, 183–185, 187
  and clinical outcomes, 159
  and employee satisfaction, 159
  and financial performance, 160
  and Medicare reimbursement, 160
  and retention, 159
  basic principles of, 161
  factors influencing, 165
  guiding principles of, 161
  improving, 150, 161, 167
  measuring, 175, 176
    CAHPS Survey to Measure Patient Experience, 176, 179, 180
    Customer Effort Score (CES), 176, 185
    HCAHPS (Hospital Consumer Assessment of Healthcare Providers and Systems) Survey, 176, 178
    Net Promotor Score (NPS), 176, 183
    Overall Patient Experience Score, 176, 184
    Patient Memorability Based Scores, 176, 185
    Patient Reported Experience Measures (PREM), 176, 177
    Traditional Customer Satisfaction (CS) Measurement Methods, 176, 181

Decision-making process, 108, 117, 120, 121
  millennials, 132, 133
  women's role in, 133
Definition of marketing, 23
Definition of services marketing, 25, 26
Demographics, 105, 107, 108
  importance, 105, 109, 111, 122, 123
  role of, 108
  variables, 109, 110, 114, 117, 120, 123
    age, 110
    cultural and religious differences, 111
    education level, 113
    family size, 116
    gender, 115
    income level, 112
    racial diversity, 110
    social relationships, 114
Demographic segmentation, 207, 209
Differentiation, 47, 49, 56

Digital health care marketing,
     281–283, 303
  common mistakes, 303
  techniques, 262, 285
  tools, 264, 269–271, 281, 284,
     285, 291, 296, 297
Digital technology, 261–263, 265–267,
     272, 281, 293, 296, 298–300, 303
  consumer dependence on, 266
  health care provider and
     organization dependence on, 267
  in health care, 261, 262, 267, 271,
     275, 276, 279, 281–287, 289,
     291, 293, 295–298, 303
    digitalizing health records,
       263
    enhancing patient education,
       264
    facilitate patients stay healthy,
       264
    facilitating communication,
       264
    in diagnosis and treatment,
       262
    in improving and coordinating
       internal processes, 264
    medical research, 263
    patient engagement, 264
Direct marketing, 383, 397, 411–414,
     417–419, 443
  examples in health care, 413
  health care products, 383
  health care services, 360, 364,
     371, 376, 379
  what is, 411
Direct marketing by pharmaceutical
     companies, 413, 443, 445, 446
  legal and ethical restrictions, 446
  to consumers, 411, 417, 419, 426,
     427, 432, 443, 444
  to physicians, 415, 417, 423–425,
     444

Direct marketing of physician services,
     414
  challenges, 417, 418, 434, 436,
     444, 454
  market segmentation, 418, 450

Electronic communications, 372, 387
Electronic Health Records (EHR), 263
Employee engagement, 311, 313–317,
     319, 321, 322, 325–330, 332
  in health care marketing, 311, 315
  management practices to promote,
     317, 321, 325
  measurement, 325, 326
Employee experience, 189, 329–333
  enhancing, 327, 328, 331
Empowerment, 318, 319, 322
Engaged employee, 311–313, 316,
     329, 333
  an engaged employee makes fewer
     mistakes, 316
  an engaged employee puts patients
     first, 316
  engaged employee maintains
     cleanliness, e.g., never forgets to
     wash their hands, 316
Ethical dilemmas, 390, 391, 398
  principles for analyzing, 390, 398
  tools for analyzing, 398
Ethical standards, 377, 392, 394, 397,
     398
  of American Marketing
     Association, 394
  of the Direct Marketing
     Association, 397
Ethical values, 395
Ethics in health care marketing, 390,
     394
  evolution, 359, 391
  principles, 390, 392, 398
Evolution, 359, 391
External environment, 53, 54, 58

Focus, 43, 47, 49, 50, 52, 54

Geographic segmentation, 209
Gerontographic segmentation, 200
Global health care marketing, 463, 464, 480
    guidelines, 480

HCAHPS, 157, 161, 176, 178, 179, 190
Health care marketing, 1, 3–6, 9, 11, 13–17, 19, 21, 26–36, 103–106, 108–110, 118–120, 123, 129–131, 134, 136
    definition, 26, 29
    evolution, 21, 25–27, 30
    modern trends and practices, 30
    need for integration with other functions, 15
    trends, 120, 129, 130, 134, 136, 138
Health care marketing strategy, 43, 46, 48, 58
    business level strategy, 44, 46–49, 56
    corporate level strategy, 44
    functional level strategy, 46, 48, 58
    health care marketing strategy, 44
    levels of strategy, 46
    marketing program, 43
    marketing strategy, 43, 46, 48, 58, 59
Health care products and services, 463, 464
Health care regulations, 364
    digital health care marketing, 386
    landmarks, 368
Health care services, 3–8, 11–16
    ancillary health services (e.g., audiology, speech therapy, and podiatry), 9
    dental care services, 9
    diagnostic services, 9
    hospital services, 8, 15, 17
    long-term care, 9
    long-term services and support (LTSS), 9
    Managed Care Organizations (MCOs), 6, 8
    mental health care, 9
    optometric services, 9
    outpatient surgery services, 9
    pharmaceuticals and medical devices, 9
    physical therapy and rehabilitative care, 9
    physician services, 8, 15, 17
    public health services, 5, 9
    special characteristics of, 11–13, 16
    urgent care services, 9
Health care services marketing, 3, 15, 26
Health disparities, 451–453
Health information, 107, 116, 120, 131, 133–135
    internet-based sources for, 107
    sources for, 107, 118
Health Insurance Portability and Accountability Act of 1996 (HIPAA), 363, 388
Health Maintenance Organizations (HMOs), 6, 8
Health marketing, 3, 5, 9, 11, 15
Health plan, 8, 10, 14, 16
Health status/Risk-based segmentation, 209
HIPAA laws, 383
    email marketing, 385, 386, 388
    marketing activities prohibited by, 384
    use of social media, 385
    website compliance, 374, 386, 389
HITECH Act, 363, 368, 369, 386
Hybrid/Nested segmentation, 207

Implementation, 41, 57–59
Inbound medical tourism, 464, 466, 467, 482
    customer/patient characteristics, 478
    focus of customers/patients, 478
Independent Practice Associations (IPAs), 8
Information age, 261
Institutional trust, 134
Internal customers, 104
Internal environment, 54
Internal marketing, 311, 315, 319, 321–328, 330
    techniques, 320, 321
Internal service quality, 318, 321
iPad usage, 267

Job satisfaction, 318–320, 323

Kotler, 22

Marketing, 21–40
Marketing ACA (Obamacare) Products, 437
Marketing Employee Insurance Plan to Employers, 438
Marketing hospital services, 422, 424
    guidelines for, 428
    to consumers/patients, 411, 426
    to health plans, 426
    to physicians, 415, 417, 423–425, 444
Marketing Managed Care Services, 411, 415, 416, 418–420, 428, 430, 433–438, 440–442
    to consumers, 426, 427, 432, 443
    to physicians, 415, 417, 423, 425, 444
Marketing materials, 373, 374, 376, 382

Marketing mix, 49, 59. 227–235, 237, 238, 240, 242, 243, 244, 246, 249
    4P, 228–230
    5P, 231, 232
    6P, 231, 232
    7P, 231–235
Marketing research, 63–72, 74, 76
    AMA definition of, 64
Marketing/Sales events, 373
Marketing to physicians (doctors), 339, 342, 345, 346, 351
    hospital, 339–343, 346, 347, 350–354
    legal and ethical issues, 351
    pharmaceutical companies, 340, 348–351
Market research, 63–67, 75–77
    data/information analysis, 70
    data/information collection, 68
        primary data, 67–69, 74, 75
        qualitative data, 68–71, 75
        quantitative data, 68–71, 75
        secondary data, 67–69, 71, 72
    developing the overall research plan, 66, 67
    overview of steps, 66
    typical steps in the process, 66
Market segmentation, 105, 107, 108, 134, 197–199, 201, 203, 205, 206, 208, 211, 212, 219–222, 345
    analytical techniques for, 219
    a priori, 206–208
    B2B, 209
    B2C, 209
    behavioral, 211, 212, 217
    benefits of, 203
    customer-centric, 215–219, 345
    definition, 197
    demographic, 197, 198, 200, 207–209, 214, 217
    generic methods, 206

geographic, 197, 209
gerontographic, 200, 201, 210
health status/risk-based, 209
hybrid/nested, 207
need for, 201, 217
product/payer, 208
psychographics, 210
Meaningful use, 267
Measuring competition, 91
sources of information for market research of, 95
Medicaid Managed Care Final Rule, 370
Medicaid marketing, 370, 375, 376, 387
Medical groups, 8
Medicare marketing regulations, 370, 371, 387
Mega-Rule (Omnibus Rule, 2013), 369, 370
Mission, 50, 51
mission statements, 50, 52
Mobile applications (apps), 374, 388
Modern 7P marketing mix, 233
people, 232, 233, 235, 248, 253
physical evidence, 250, 235, 250
place, 228, 230–232, 234, 235, 238, 240, 242, 246, 251, 253, 254
price, 228–230
process, 232, 235–237, 248, 249, 251
product, 227, 233–237, 240, 245, 253
promotion, 228, 230–232, 234–236, 243, 244, 246
reasons for using, 233
Moments of truth, 173–175, 185
Multi-channel marketing, 279, 292

NCQA, 157, 158
New technology, 296, 298–301
factors influencing success, 296, 298
Nominal gifts, 373

Online sources of information, 277
Outbound medical tourism, 464, 465, 472, 480
customer/patient characteristics, 469
destinations, 466, 472–474, 476, 481
negative perceptions, 474
treatment sought, 472

4P marketing mix, 228, 229, 231, 233, 235
application in health care marketing, 229
inadequacy of, 231, 233
5P marketing mix, 231, 232
6P marketing, 231, 232
7P marketing mix, 231, 232, 234, 235
PATH Institute, 211
Patient check-ins, 267
Patient education, 264, 267–269
Patient engagement, 267–269, 273, 280, 297
Patient experience, 152–156, 158–161, 164, 165, 168–170, 172, 173, 176–179, 183–187, 189
definition, 153, 165
Patient portals, 268, 269, 272
Patient satisfaction surveys, 267
Physician characteristics, 342
Physician engagement, 339–342, 345–347
by hospitals, 351, 352, 360
relevance to health care marketing, 339
what is, 341
Physician relations, 339, 340, 351–354, 360
Physician relations management, 339, 340
Physician relations programs, 343, 344, 351–354, 360

Plan of the book, 3, 15
Porter, 45, 47, 54, 56
Porter's five forces competition analysis, 93
    applied to health care organizations, 93, 95
    bargaining power of customers, 94
    bargaining power of suppliers, 94
    entry of new competitors, 94
    new thinking as applied to health care organizations, 95
    the rivalry among existing players in the market, 93
    threat of substitutes, 94
Prescription management, 263, 268
Price, 228–232, 234, 235, 240–244
    guidelines for setting, 242
Primary customers, 104
    end user, the patient, 104
Primary data, 108, 137
Primary data collection, 68, 69, 74, 75
Product differentiation, 198, 199, 205, 206, 225
    compared with market segmentation, 198
Product/Payer segmentation, 208
Promotion, 228–231, 235, 243, 246
    communication and education, 243
    communication strategies, 246
Provider contracting, 340, 341
Provider relations, 340, 341, 347, 352, 354
Provider relations management, 340
Provider selection, 103, 107, 123
    health plans, 124
    hospital, 126, 127
    physician, 123–126
Provider services, 340, 341
Psychographics segmentation, 210
Public health marketing, 447–456
PX, 149, 151–154, 161–163, 165, 167, 169, 170, 172, 173, 175–177, 179, 183–185, 187

Relationship marketing, 250–253
Retention, 103, 108, 117, 123, 129, 136, 419, 420, 438, 440–442, 455
    of enrollees in managed care health plans, 438, 440

Secondary customers, 104
    care coordinators, 104
    community of consumers, 104
    community organizations, 104
    health care advocates, 104
    pharmacists, 104
    physicians, 103, 104, 107–109, 125, 126, 129, 130, 132, 134
Secondary data, 108, 137, 138
Secondary data sources, 71, 72
Segment, 216–219, 222
    characteristics of, 204, 205, 207, 210
Segmentation, 105–108, 115, 134
    psychographic, 105, 108
Service concept, 56–59
Service Dominant Logic (SDL), 21, 22
    Vargo and Lusch, 21, 23
Services, 3–17
Services marketing, 21, 25, 26, 29, 36, 38
Smartphone, 269, 270, 273, 276
    use in looking up health information, 274
Social media, 266, 272–282, 284–291, 295, 296, 303
    hospital activity on, 275
    marketing, 276, 277
    physician activity on, 275
Social media posts, 374, 388
Sources of information, 475
    outbound medical travel, 469, 475
Stark law, 377, 379, 403
Strategic planning process, 49, 53
    information needed, 58
SWOT analysis, 54, 55, 58, 59

Technology adoption model, 301
Technology readiness index, 301
The American Marketing Association (AMA), 23
   definition of marketing, 23
Total experience, 135
Touchpoints, 152, 155, 161–163, 165, 171, 173–175, 177
Truth-in-advertising laws, 379, 380, 389

Unsolicited contacts, 373

Valuegraphic profiles, 211
Values, 49, 50, 52, 53
Vargo and Lusch, 21, 23
Video marketing, 283
Vision, 50, 52–54
   vision statements, 50, 52

Websites, 374, 383, 385, 387–389

CPSIA information can be obtained
at www.ICGtesting.com
Printed in the USA
BVHW040845140720
583467BV00007B/18